Educating
Republicans

**Recent Titles in
Contributions to the Study of Education**

Educating Republicans

THE COLLEGE IN THE ERA OF THE AMERICAN REVOLUTION, 1750-1800

DAVID W. ROBSON

CONTRIBUTIONS TO THE STUDY OF EDUCATION, NUMBER 15

Greenwood Press

WESTPORT, CONNECTICUT • LONDON, ENGLAND

Library of Congress Cataloging in Publication Data

Robson, David W.
  Educating republicans.

  (Contributions to the study of education, ISSN 0196-
707X ; no. 15)
  Bibliography: p.
  Includes index.
  1. Universities and colleges—United States—History—
18th century. I. Title. II. Series.
LA227.R56   1985   378.73   84-22436
ISBN 0-313-24606-8 (lib. bdg.)

Library of Congress Catalog Card Number: 84-22436
ISBN: 0-313-24606-8
ISSN: 0196-707X

First published in 1985

Greenwood Press
A division of Congressional Information Service, Inc.
88 Post Road West
Westport, Connecticut 06881

Printed in the United States of America

10 9 8 7 6 5 4 3 2 1

To the memory of
my mother and father

Contents

Tables

Abbreviations

AAP	William Sprague, ed., *Annals of the American Pulpit* (9 vols., New York: R. Carter and Brothers, 1857–69)
BUA	Brown University Archives (John Hay Library)
CAB	*The Cyclopaedia of American Biography* (12 vols., New York: The Press Association Compilers, Inc., 1915–31)
CSM	Colonial Society of Massachusetts
CWMA	College of William and Mary Archives (Earl Gregg Swem Library)
CUA	Columbia University Archives (Columbiana Collection, Low Library)
DAB	Allen Johnson et al., eds., *Dictionary of American Biography* (20 vols., New York: C. Scribner's Sons, 1928–36)
DaCA	Dartmouth College Archives (Baker Memorial Library)
DCA	Dickinson College Archives (Boyd Lee Spahr Library)
DHYU	Franklin B. Dexter, ed., *Documentary History of Yale University* (New Haven: Yale University Press, 1916)
Doc. Hist. Educ.	Edgar W. Knight, ed., *A Documentary History of Education in the South before 1860* (5 vols., Chapel Hill: University of North Carolina Press, 1950–53)
Doc. Hist. UNC	R.D.W. Connor, compiler, *A Documentary History of the University of North Carolina, 1776–1799* (2 vols., Chapel Hill: University of North Carolina Press, 1953)
F&MCA	Franklin & Marshall College Archives
H-SCA	Hampden-Sydney College Archives (Eggleston Library)
HUA	Harvard University Archives (Nathan Pusey Library)
Ind. Ref.	Milton M. Klein, ed., *The Independent Reflector* (Cambridge, Mass.: The Belknap Press of Harvard University Press, 1963)
Johnson Writings	Herbert and Carol Schneider, eds., *President Samuel Johnson of King's College: His Career and Writings* (4 vols., New York: Columbia University Press, 1929)

Mass. A&R	*Acts and Resolves, Public and Private, of the Province of the Massachusetts Bay [1692–1786]* (21 vols., Boston: Wright & Potter, 1869–1922)
Mass. Bay Rec.	Nathaniel Shurtleff, ed., *Records of the Governor and Company of Massachusetts Bay in New England* (5 vols., Boston: W. White, 1853–54)
MHS	Massachusetts Historical Society
NCAB	*National Cyclopaedia of American Biography* (49 vols., New York: J.T. White & Co., 1893–1966)
PRCC	James H. Trumbull and Charles Hoadly, eds., *The Public Records of the Colony of Connecticut* (15 vols., orig. 1850–90; reprint, New York: AMS Press, 1968)
PRSC	Charles Hoadly, Leonard Labaree et al., eds., *The Public Records of the State of Connecticut* (11 vols., Hartford: Lockwood & Brainerd Co., 1894–1967)
PUA	Princeton University Archives (Firestone and Seeley G. Mudd Libraries)
RUA	Rutgers University Archives
Rush Letters	Lyman H. Butterfield, ed., *The Letters of Benjamin Rush* (2 vols., Princeton: Princeton University Press, 1951)
St.JCA	St. John's College Archives (Woodward Hall Library)
Sibley's	John L. Sibley et al., eds., *Biographical Sketches of Those Who Attended Harvard College* (17 vols. thus far, Boston: Massachusetts Historical Society, 1873–)
Stiles Papers M	Harold E. Selesky, ed., *The Microfilm Edition of the Ezra Stiles Papers at Yale University* (New Haven: Yale University Press, 1976)
UCA	Union College Archives (Schaeffer Library)
UGA	University of Georgia Archives
UNCA	University of North Carolina Archives
UPA	University of Pennsylvania Archives
Va. Stat.	William W. Hening, ed., *The Statutes at Large of Virginia* (13 vols., Richmond: Samuel Pleasants, 1809–23)
UVtA	University of Vermont Archives (Bailey-Howe Memorial Library)
WaCA	Washington College Archives (Clifton M. Miller Library)
WCA	Williams College Archives
WLUA	Washington and Lee University Archives (Cyrus Hall McCormick Library)

WMCQ	*William and Mary College Quarterly*
WMQ	*William and Mary Quarterly*
Yale Sketches	Franklin B. Dexter, ed., *Biographical Sketches of the Graduates of Yale College with Annals of the College History* (6 vols., New York: H. Holt and Co., 1885–1912)
YUA	Yale University Archives (Beinecke and Sterling Memorial Libraries)

Preface

This study is the long-delayed result of a line of thought taken up while in graduate school at Yale University during the late 1960s and early 1970s. It was, of course, a tumultuous era for the nation and its colleges. At Yale, meaningful integration and the first phase of coeducation merged with national party politics, civil rights, and anti-war protest, the galvanic trauma of Kent State, and New Haven's own cause célèbre, the Bobby Seale trial and its accompanying demonstrations. Endless debate, teach-ins, strikes, and disorders of various kinds took place almost continually for the better part of three years, during which Yale tried (more or less successfully) to encourage open minds and the presentation of contrasting opinions. Clear resolution of issues seldom occurred; ambivalence and ambiguity were more common. Perhaps the most anomalous spectacle was provided by some post-graduate acquaintances who, during the Seale trial demonstrations, would go out to serve an eight-hour shift with the Connecticut National Guard and then change clothes to join the demonstrators. One thing was sure; few students could use the ivy-covered halls of academe to shield themselves from politicization.

My academic interests at the time centered on the American Revolution and especially the then-emerging argument that its leaders subscribed to and were motivated by a political ideology that provided them a world view and a language to use to explain events. My curricular and extra-curricular interests began to mesh; as a result this project became inevitable. I started to look at early American college communities, to study them in a time of turmoil, and to conclude that colleges, then as now, were excellent windows through which to view aspects of the larger culture. In this case, the political knowledge, values, and practices which an older generation sought to inculcate and the extent to which the younger generation absorbed its lessons go far to inform us about the political culture of the larger society. They give us an extra dimension of understanding about the Revolutionary era.

A word about format is in order. Paradoxically, the book is long even though there were so few colleges. For the most part, trends could not be demonstrated by sampling. To leave out an institution might slight a section of the colonies or states, obscure the relationships among educators of similar or different religious denominations, or fail to show the full range of an intellectual current, to cite a few possible problems. Consequently, full coverage was imperative. At the same time, I have injected humanity into the analysis by beginning each discussion with an account of a particular institution and its inhabitants, which I think illustrates especially well the theme to be developed thereafter. We must never forget that these college communities were not passively reflective of their environments, but actively sought to shape them. In such an atmosphere, individuals were often vitally important. Some of their stories are told here.

Over the years this book has been in the making I have incurred many debts. Some are financial. At various stages of the research support from the New Jersey State Historical Society, the American Philosophical Society, and the University of Wyoming have been indispensable. Some debts are the result of friendship and good will. Librarians and archivists at all the colleges and other research facilities mentioned herein have been unfailingly helpful in providing material and a good working atmosphere. Some have taken a personal interest in the project and its author. Diane Alexander, secretary to the History Department of the University of Wyoming, has been a gifted typist and good friend. Some of my former colleagues in the department have offered advice and encouragement during good times and bad—I value especially the help of Roger Williams, Bob Righter, and Peter Iverson.

Some of my debts are intellectual. At various times during the last decade helpful advice, criticism, and ideas have been offered by Rick Warch, Sydney Ahlstrom, and Robert R. Palmer of Yale, by Jim Axtell of William and Mary, by Colin Howell of St. Mary's University, Halifax, Nova Scotia, by Jurgen Herbst of the University of Wisconsin, and Fred Rudolph of Williams College. These gentlemen may not recognize their suggestions—there are probably too many I did not take—and they are absolved of responsibility for the errors that remain herein. Part of Chapter 6 has appeared previously in somewhat different form in *The History of Education Quarterly*, and I am grateful to the editors for permission to reprint it.

Finally, some special debts. Ed Morgan has nurtured me and this project for over ten years. He has been teacher, critic, and friend; the book would not have been written without his encouragement. Both it and I are better for his guidance. Mary Hart Robson has sustained me and my work in very different ways. She does not love history, but does love the historian, and that combination has been of incalculable value. The two people to whom this work is dedicated have never read it in any form, and did not quite understand why I wanted to write it or why I wanted to be a historian. Yet without their love, guidance, and support I would not have fulfilled any of my dreams. This is one small way of thanking them.

Educating
Republicans

1

The Political Heritage of the Colonial College

The Englishmen who formed the vast majority of the migrants to the American colonies before the mid-eighteenth century had little reason to ponder the characteristics of higher education as it had evolved in the home country at the time of their leaving. From their perspective collegiate education was but one part of an edifice including family, community, church, and school that had succeeded quite well in transmitting the dominant values of their culture from generation to generation. Consequently, the colonists unquestioningly accepted English forms and traditions regarding collegiate purposes, curriculum, and governance. Yet by the end of the colonial period, even though the forms would in large measure be retained, the inner meaning of those forms would be radically transformed to make higher education a crucial component of an emerging American culture. The first step in the process of transformation was awareness, a critical examination of the inherited forms and traditions. That awareness came as a result of a New York dispute known as the King's College controversy.

I

By 1750 New York was a boom town, its population explosion based on a burgeoning economy involving trade with Great Britain and with other colonial ports. Intensifying urban problems accompanied this growth—city services, public health, crime, and a more complex government affected by local and provincial political and economic interests all demanded attention. Addressing these problems was all the more difficult because ethnic differences divided the population. At mid-century there were many Germans, French Huguenots, and multiethnic Jews, and a substantial black population in the city, but the English, Dutch, and Scotch-Irish predominated.[1] Religious diversity compounded ethnicity. The Church of England, established in New York's lower four counties after 1693, retained the most influence in local affairs at mid-century even though its parishioners were outnumbered by both the Presbyterians and the Dutch Reformed. Minor sects included Moravians, German Reformed, some few Quakers, and Jews. Moreover, the major denominations were fragmented. New York's Presbyterians had split during the Great Awakening, the Dutch Reformed argued about Americanizing their sect, and even the Anglicans divided over how aggressively they should press for the privileges of their establishment.[2]

Ethnic and religious diversity coupled with the increasingly commercial, individualistic orientation of the urban economy to threaten community values. Yet many New Yorkers were anxious to improve the quality of the city they lived in. At mid-century, capitalizing on a high literacy rate, they paid special attention to developing its literary culture.[3] The institutionalization of culture, under way since 1730, had produced several newspapers, published by four active printers who together turned out over 120 publications a year. By 1754 booksellers were printing catalogs of their holdings and a public circulating library enjoyed a growing clientele.[4]

One institution that lagged behind was formal education. Some of the printers' titles were books for the instruction of adolescents, and there were more schoolmasters holding forth in 1750 than ever before, but there was no educational establishment.[5] In the late 1740s, some New Yorkers banded together to address that failing and, in a pattern not uncommon in colonial America, began at the top, with an effort to found a college. New York's increasing urbanization and its heterogeneity would play large roles in the evolution of the institution.

The New York Assembly sanctioned the campaign for a provincial college in December 1746, authorizing a public lottery to raise funds.[6] More than seven years passed before a college actually began instruction. Early on, the college proposal languished from lack of public concern, but there began in 1752 a vociferous public debate over the plans for the college. What became known as the King's College controversy tells us much about the political heritage of the colonial college.

The controversy began because Anglicans moved to take control of the proposed institution. In 1751, the Assembly appointed ten trustees to manage the lottery funds; seven were Anglicans, four of them vestrymen of Trinity Church, New York City. Early the next year the Trinity Church vestry donated several acres of its property for a campus. They attached no conditions but later claimed they "always expected that a gift so valuable... would be a means of obtaining some privileges to the Church."[7]

Whatever Trinity's vestrymen might have meant by privileges, the Anglican clergy around New York saw here a chance to develop a center of Church influence to rival the Congregationalism of New England and the Presbyterianism of New Jersey. These clerics, led by James Wetmore in New York and Samuel Johnson in Stratford, Connecticut, had concluded that the success of dissenting religion in the northern colonies endangered society and the well-being of church and state. To Johnson, dissenters, especially evangelicals, held "enthusiastical conceited notions" in religion and "republican mobbish principles and practices in policy." Every man thought "himself an able divine and statesman." The consequences were "perpetual feuds and factions" in religion and politics and "wild extremes" of "free thinking."[8]

Johnson had fought dissenters for years while battling to make some Anglican inroads into Harvard and Yale, with little success. With the founding of the College of New Jersey under the leadership of the New Side Presbyterians Jonathan Dickinson and Aaron Burr, whom he described as "bitter enemies of the Church," Johnson felt social order all the more threatened. New Jersey Anglicans also complained that the dissenters would "endeavor to warp [youth] from all other Principles, and Form them according to their own, and in the next Age, if not sooner, we shall have an Assembly entirely Independent [Presbyterian], and then what becomes of the Church?"[9]

But if dissenting views could be inculcated in colonial youth through the medium of higher education, so could those of the Church. And those principles, noted one Anglican minister, if "heartily embraced [,] do more thorowly dispose Men to the Love of Peace and Order, and a conscientious Submission to lawfull Authority" than any others.[10] Thus, to save society, and not incidentally to promote the Church, Johnson and other Anglican clergymen in and near New York set out to shape the province's college to their own purposes.

As early as 1747, James Wetmore had written an anonymous newspaper essay suggesting that the Rectors of the "Established Parishes" (read Anglican) and three political figures should manage collegiate affairs and select additional trustees. In the ensuing years, Samuel Johnson agitated behind the scenes.[11] The naming of the lottery trustees in 1751 and Trinity Church's gift of land in 1752 lent weight to the Anglican involvement. In November 1752, the Anglican private tutor William Smith published an anonymous essay in the New York *Mercury* calling for immediate incorporation, an Anglican majority on the board, and an invitation to Samuel Johnson to preside over the college and Trinity Church as well.[12] Against this background, the New York Assembly announced it would consider the matter of the college at its spring 1753 session.[13]

Not surprisingly, in a colony where Anglicans were significantly outnumbered, the Churchmen's plans aroused vigorous opposition. A young lawyer, William Livingston, newly turned Presbyterian, took the lead. For some years two of Livingston's principal concerns had been the enrichment of the cultural climate of New York and suspicion of the Anglican Church. He had been a booster of a New York college from 1749 and had served as a lottery trustee from 1751. But as Anglican plans for the college surfaced, Livingston joined fears about the control of the school to his other doubts about Anglicanism. He disliked both the doctrine of the Church and its campaign to strengthen its establishment; both too closely resembled Catholicism. He resented Anglican efforts to block a charter for the Presbyterians' church and was sure that the Society for the Propagation of the Gospel in Foreign Parts sought dissenter rather than Indian converts. To Livingston, all these Anglican activities aimed at domination of the religious atmosphere of New York and at full establishment, thereby fixing on the province "universal Priestcraft & Bigotry."[14]

To thwart the Anglicans in their larger design, Livingston and two like-minded associates, William Smith, Jr., and John Morin Scott, began to publish the *Independent Reflector* in late 1752.[15] It discussed many religious and political issues concerning the province, criticizing the Anglican attempts to influence their outcome.[16] In opposition to the Anglican desire for a royally-chartered, private, sectarian college under Church control, the *Reflector* proposed a legislatively incorporated, publicly controlled college of a non-denominational character, granting equal liberty to all Protestants. The *Reflector* maintained that a sectarian college would produce an intellectual atmosphere unduly influenced and narrowed by religious dogma, that in heterogeneous New York such a college would draw youths from only one religion and so be of little use, and that it would work only to advance its own polity, thus further unsettling New York's religious climate.[17] A sectarian college would also be political. It would be dangerous because it would fill government offices with the members of one religious sect, "and in consequence thereof affect the Politics of the Country." The students, after finishing their educations, "enter into the Ministry or some offices of the Government, and acting in them under the Influence of the Doctrines espoused in the Morning of Life, the Spirit of the College is transferred thro' the Colony, and tinctures the Genius and Policy of the public Administration, from the Governor down to the Constable." To prosecute a sectarian design for the college, then, would be to thwart the will of the people and provincial legislature which had supported the college but not the Anglican plans for it. A royal charter was dangerous because it was out of the control of the provincial assembly and might be perverted by present or future trustees or provincial governors.[18]

The *Reflector*'s alternative, non-denominational public control, would recognize the people's right to establish the form of education to be followed by their children. An Assembly charter would always be open to inspection and supervision, so the institution would be less likely to be used for partisan ends. The true design of the college was to improve public virtue, to cherish liberty, and to prevent tyranny and oppression. Those ends could not be perverted while an assembly elected by the people oversaw its operation.[19]

The challenge to the Churchmen offered by the *Independent Reflector* raised the consciousness of dissenters in New York and put the Anglicans on the defensive. Over the rest of 1753 and 1754, it stirred a heated debate in the public press not only about the college, but also about the whole character of colonial Anglicanism.[20] Meanwhile, the fate of the college rested in the hands of the politicians.

The political maneuvering was extremely complex and the details need not concern us. The Anglicans seemed to have the edge because Lieutenant Governor James DeLancey aided their campaign. Yet when the Anglican lottery trustees insisted that the college charter provide for an Anglican president and that daily religious exercises be based on Church of England liturgy, Livingston found the weapons he needed to alienate the Assembly from the charter. In the end, DeLancey bypassed the lower house and issued the King's College charter with only Council approval.[21]

The Reflectors were not finished. They switched tactics to try to stop King's from receiving the lottery money and also pushed for a separate, publicly-controlled college along the lines proposed in their newspaper. The alternatives spurred renewed discussion in the press, while in the Assembly each side courted the Dutch Reformed members to ensure victory. For well over a year the wooing went on, ending rather inconclusively. By November 1756, all the combatants were weary and the Seven Years' War was intruding on other Assembly business. In this atmosphere, the legislators divided the lottery proceeds between King's College and the City of New York, while the Anglicans gave up on efforts to have the Assembly confirm the charter. King's emerged better off financially, but its status, provincial or church, was still unclear.[22]

Several issues that would retain great significance in New York and elsewhere for many years to come emerged from the King's College controversy. There was Livingston's anti-clericalism and his suspicion of religious institutions and the Anglican defense of the priestly craft.[23] There were questions concerning church-state relations and the viability of religious establishments in America.[24] There were expositions of two fundamentally opposed conceptions of the origin of government and the relationship of rulers to ruled, with Livingston arguing for the Lockean notions of a state of nature, the social compact, and the limited nature of authority, while the Anglicans asserted that all governmental authority emanated from God, that it was paternal in nature, and that passive obedience to higher powers was necessary.[25] Debate on these matters would become increasingly frequent and contentious in the 1760s and 1770s—the last topic, especially, will command our attention when we consider the pre-Revolutionary atmosphere at King's.

But even more striking than the explicit arguments entered into by the Reflectors and the Anglican opponents were the implicit assumptions regarding higher education that allowed the King's College controversy to take place at all. Livingston blandly asserted, and his Anglican critics never denied, that the effects of higher education "will soon be visible throughout the whole Province. They will appear on the Bench, at the Bar, in the Pulpit, and in the Senate, and unavoidably affect our civil and religious Principles."[26] Each side thus assumed that possession of a college education was a passport to elite status in the civil and religious affairs of the colony, that control of the process of higher education was vital to its own interests and the colony's future. Each side also assumed that the content of the education was the key to shaping the future beliefs of civic and religious leaders. Livingston, arguing for a liberal, non-religious educational fare, asserted that

the true use of Education, is to qualify Men for the different Employments of Life...to infuse a Public Spirit and Love of their Country; to inspire them with the Principles of Honour and Probity, with a fervent Zeal for Liberty, and diffusive Benevolence for Mankind; and in a Word, to make them more extensively serviceable to the Commonwealth.[27]

The Anglicans were never quite so bold in their pronouncements, but linked their whole political ideology to submission to lawful authority, to hierarchy, to the idea that the assertion of natural rights was a socially dangerous phenomenon, for it led to radical individualism that undermined both church and state. Finally, each side believed it could best achieve the proper role for and content of education by allying itself and its proposed institution with the government. Here, too, there were differences in approach. Livingston, consistent with his Lockean ideology, extolled the public's right to determine the form of education for its youth and urged the public's arm of government, the legislature, to incorporate the college, select its governors on a non-sectarian basis, finance its programs, and ultimately supervise its operations. The Anglicans, rejecting Lockean notions of popular authority while linking closely church and state, sought sanction for the college from the Crown through its colonial representatives and proposed supervision by a self-perpetuating board of trustees dominated by Churchmen.[28]

These assumptions concerning higher education, the character of politics, and the role of the state together form the political heritage of the colonial college. To understand how colleges parlayed this heritage into significant involvement in the political activities of the Revolutionary era, we must explore the origins of the heritage and its effects on the colleges at mid-century.

II

The combatants in the King's College controversy could assume that the character of higher education would affect the political character of the state because such a belief had an ancient history. As the men of the Renaissance uncovered so much else of antiquity, so they found the concept of education for state service, perhaps best set forth in Plato's *Republic*. There Socrates identifies two classes of people, guardians and philosophers, who serve the state by protecting and ruling it, and describes the education appropriate to each.[29] The Platonic scheme served as a model for Renaissance political philosophers.

In the early sixteenth century Desiderius Erasmus provided the most direct link in the continuing tradition by describing the training of a reform-oriented monarch in *The Education of a Christian Prince* (1515). Sir Thomas Elyot's *The Book Named the Governor* (1531) enlarged the civility tradition by applying the concept of civic education to a larger group of people, the hereditary nobility, which would aid the monarch through qualification for service in a state bureaucracy. The elements of civic education emerging in Renaissance literature were, then, an ideal state, a recognition that proper education for rulers was necessary to achieve the ideal, and a curriculum designed to insure proper education.[30]

Elyot's *Governor* spawned a number of imitative works on civic education, probably the most important of which were Sir Humphrey Gilbert's *Queene Elizabethe's Achademy* (c. 1572) and Roger Ascham's *The Scholemaster* (1570), perhaps the archetype of Elizabethan manuals of private pedagogy. In the late sixteenth and early seventeenth centuries this material on civic education and the heroic poetry and didactic essays of Philip Sidney and Edmund Spenser merged the traits of the governor and the noble courtier, applying them to the English gentleman. Thus the entire gentry could avail itself of the tradition in such works as Henry Peacham's *The Compleat Gentleman* (1622) and Richard Braithwaite's *The English Gentleman* (1630).[31]

Abetting this diffusion of the ideal of civic education through England's upper classes was a call for restructuring education. The foremost pen belonged to Francis Bacon, who, in *The Advancement of Learning* (1605) and *The New Atlantis* (1627), insistently argued for a redefinition of learning to include the inculcation of virtue and the application of knowledge to practical ends, most importantly the good of the community.[32]

Both these strains of educational thought crossed the Atlantic with the colonists. Peacham, Braithwaite, Ascham, and Erasmus were well known. So were Bacon's works, and still others that advocated educational reform such as Erasmus' *Colloquies* (in frequent sixteenth-century editions) and Montaigne's *Essays* (1580, 1588, 1595).[33] Colonists were therefore knowledgeable about the theory of civic education and its attendant studies. Moreover, many of them, New Englanders especially, had experienced either directly or through friends and relatives the impact of this theory on the English universities.

Contemporaneous with the rediscovery of the ideal of education for state service by the Renaissance humanists were changes at Oxford and Cambridge that made humanism the primary educational philosophy there. Early in the sixteenth century, university humanists were largely overshadowed by the canon lawyers whose prestige and influence were paramount. But in the legal wrangle over the legitimacy of Henry VIII's divorce, canon law fell into disrepute while common law provided the effective kingly legal recourse. The loss of prestige suffered by canon lawyers and their field enabled the humanists to exert more influence and attract more students, and in 1535 the teaching of canon law at the universities was banned by Archbishop Thomas Cromwell. A little later, dissolution of the monasteries spelled the end of university faculty domination by monks and friars. From all this the humanists profited greatly.[34]

Because of the rise of humanism at the universities, an increasing number of laymen of the gentry class went up to Oxford and Cambridge. Not all went because they had imbibed the ideal of state service. Many were striving to attain or confirm gentlemanly status and thought university attendance (if not education) would help. Others were more traditionally motivated, seeking a Godly education or even a career in the Church, which was perhaps more appealing now that it was somewhat more secularly oriented. Whatever the interest of the students, the humanist philosophy of education made learning more attractive and it exposed them to education for state service.[35]

While humanism prevailed as the primary educational philosophy at the English universities, it never completely subsumed scholasticism. Indeed, the schoolmen's pedagogy made a comeback during the last decade of the sixteenth century and remained influential until the first decade of the eighteenth. The impetus for the resurgence of scholasticism was the need to buttress the status quo in a time of potential rebellion, to assert that the monarchy and social hierarchy were part of nature's plan, and that a government based on these social axioms was the best form.[36]

The curriculum at the English universities seemed always to reflect elements of both these philosophies. The temper of the education to be acquired at Oxford and Cambridge might best be assessed by taking note of the extra-statutory curriculum in the arts, the favorite preserve of the gentleman who did not seek a degree, but vital to degree seekers as well. The extra-statutory studies most quickly and thoroughly reflected changes in the university faculty and their intellectual concerns.[37] During the years when most of those who became emigrants to America were educated, scholasticism retained its hold on the formal curriculum while humanism made a much greater impact on the extra-statutory forms.[38]

Both modes paid increasing attention to politics and to other areas of knowledge held necessary to preparation for state service. The scholasticism of the required arts course brought Aristotelian ethics to the student. Gentlemanly virtues, valuable for the civic-minded, were the key to individual morality: justice, temperance, courage, liberality, magnificence, high-mindedness, mildness, truthfulness, urbanity, and friendliness in their Aristotelian connotations all contributed to the character of the statesman. The development of this ethical character allowed the statesman to participate properly as a member of civil society (it was this activity that Aristotle named politics). Because of the variety of its population, the state was the necessary agent for the solution of a number of ethical problems. The state was created for man's protection; to do so it had to promote what was morally right. The state's major task was to develop the moral capacity of its people—the willingness to sacrifice individual interest for the good of all. It was the statesman who could best promote the feeling of oneness among the people that allowed the state to perform its function; it was he who should exercise authority in the state. In the Oxford-Cambridge version of scholasticism, professors argued that the best form for the state was one that blended monarchy, aristocracy, and popular elements into a workable government.[39]

The extra-statutory studies also emphasized politics, as well as classical studies that served to illustrate moral and political maxims, logic that developed wit and reason, and history that cultivated taste and judgment while providing practical examples of political actions.[40] Humanist political thought appeared in More's *Utopia*, Erasmus' *The Education of a Christian Prince*, and Sir Thomas Smith's *De Republica Anglorum*. Political morality emerged through Machiavelli's *The Prince*, Bacon's *Essays*, and Erasmus' *Moriae Encomium* among the moderns, and from the works of Horace, Livy, Cicero, Sallust, and Demosthenes among the ancients. Modern history included not only commentary on the ancients such as Edward Leigh's *Twelve Caesars*, but also histories of England such as Camden's *Remains*, Speed's *History of Great Britain*, and Martin's *Historie and Lives of Twentie Kings of England*. Adding a final fillip to the studies aimed at producing a gentlemanly servant of the state were works in the modern languages, geography, manners and courtesy, and heraldry. Both the required curriculum and the extra-statutory studies thus contained sizable components of education designed to promote state service.[41]

The curricular changes occurring at Oxford and Cambridge in the Tudor and early Stuart eras were often the result of state intervention. Beginning with Henry VIII's attempt to pressure the universities into supporting his position on divorce in the mid-1530s, English monarchs were ever-conscious of the need for higher education to buttress both the form of English government and the public policy the government advocated. Consequently, the Crown did not hesitate to intrude upon the operations of the universities, sometimes to promote, sometimes to regulate, always to try to shape educational practice to serve its peculiar ends.

The record of state intervention is lengthy; it will suffice to highlight it here. During the reign of Henry VIII, Archbishop Cromwell became Chancellor of the two universities, linking in his person church, state, and education. He used visitations followed by injunctions to cement the universities to the Crown, to end the teaching of canon law, to dilute scholasticism with humanist-influenced liberal arts, and to impose reformed theology.[42] Also aimed at furthering humanism in the universities were the creation of Regius professorships in 1540 and the establishment of royal colleges (Trinity at Cambridge, Christ Church at Oxford) in 1546–1547.[43]

Edward VI used the same methods to advance the cause of the Reformation in the universities by ordering the arts course and increasing its humanist content. The Crown also sent a steady stream of visiting professors to the universities armed with new learning and new theology. In 1553 the Crown required the members of the universities to subscribe to the Forty-Two Articles when taking a master's or divinity degree or before teaching in the schools.[44]

Elizabethan and early Stuart methods of enforcing Crown policy relied more on royal appointment of lesser university and college officials and on royal edict, rather than on visitations. The object of state intervention, however, remained the same—university compliance with public policy, especially in matters of religion. Archbishop Whitgift, Chancellor of the universities, attempted to restrain the advance of Puritanism in 1570 by reorganizing the university bureaucracy along more authoritarian lines and increasing the rigor of the degree program. The same object was intended by the imposition of the Thirty-Nine Articles in 1575. James I imposed strict conformity upon the universities, reintroducing the wearing of surplices, demanding adherence to the Three Articles, and prescribing the oath of conformity.[45] Both Elizabethan and early Stuart intervention in university affairs aimed at reducing Puritan influence. One side effect was to lessen the humanist content of learning and reinvigorate scholasticism.[46] Constantly increasing interference in their internal affairs, coupled with the frequently changing theological emphases of the monarchs, prompted the universities to fight back. None of the reforms advanced by Elizabeth or James I were enforced unopposed, and a campaign began in 1589 that in 1604 succeeded in gaining Parliamentary representation for the universities.[47] They could finally present their positions to the public.

The English emigrants to the colonies who brought with them an acquaintance with higher education thus not only knew that education for state service was a legitimate and desirable object of college teaching and that there existed a recognized body of knowledge to foster that end, but they also knew that the state considered it a necessary exercise of its authority to intervene in the educational process to achieve its desired goals. Some were aware that the English universities had recently begun to counter Crown efforts to direct their internal affairs by acquiring Parliamentary seats from which to argue their own positions. All this formed the political legacy of higher education for the earliest colonists. It remains to be seen what they and their descendents made of it.

III

In assessing the way the colonists made use of the political heritage of higher education from their first migration to the mid-eighteenth century, three conditions of colonial culture must be kept in mind. First, colonial culture was derivative. England constantly served as a model for habits of mind and patterns of action, and the colonists sought to replicate in the new world what they had known in the old. To be sure, changes took place, sometimes forced by the American environment and sometimes by the coming together of settlers transplanted from regional subcultures in England or elsewhere. But where possible, and in the realm of high culture it generally was possible, colonists implemented new world versions of old world institutions.[48]

Secondly, although culture became increasingly secular as the years passed, the era was still one in which religious and political matters meshed. Religious predilections shaped the perceptions of most settlers to the point that their faith determined their civic conduct. The idea of separating civic activity from sectarian influence emerged only slowly, could be implemented only piecemeal, and occasioned much debate and protest.[49] Finally, throughout most of the period, the religiously dominant element in the respective colonies was the one concerned in college founding and nurture. Consequently, the adversary relationship that had often existed between the English universities and the monarchy did not characterize relations between colonial governments and colleges. Not until the end of the period under discussion did religious minorities or secular groups actively promote their own schools. When that happened, the harmony between religious ideals and educational goals, between governments and colleges, broke down—witness the King's College controversy.

Because of these conditions affecting colonial culture, the political legacy bequeathed by English to colonial higher education went largely unnoticed. The ideal of education for state service, a curriculum that prepared youths to serve the state in both religious and lay pursuits, and the benevolent intrusion of the colonial governments into collegiate affairs were accepted modes of thought and behavior, seldom articulated or analyzed. Unless and until a clash erupted between differing religious groups over the content of the state service ideal, or the curriculum to implement it, or over governmental favoritism shown one group, the political assumptions underlying collegiate education remained implicit. Rarely, before the 1740s and 1750s, did clashes occur.

The unthinking acceptance of the state service ideal usually found expression in charters or preambles to legislative acts affecting the colleges, or even in less formal documents. What is immediately striking in the language used is the value assumed to be present in higher education for the advancement of affairs in both church and state. A few examples illustrate this.

Writing of Massachusetts, the author of *New England's First Fruits* (1643) recalled that after establishing churches and civil government, "One of the next things we longed for, and looked after was to advance *Learning* and perpetuate it to posterity; dreading to leave an illiterate Ministry to the Churches." Thus the initial rationale for Harvard has often been held to have been clerical education, but the General Court, trying to promote a voluntary contribution for the fledgling college, observed in 1652:

If it should be granted that learning, namely, skill in the tongues and the liberal arts, is not absolutely necessary for the being of a common-wealth and churches, yet we conceive that, in the judgment of the godly wise, it is beyond all question not only laudable, but necessary for the well being of the same; and although New England...is completely furnished (for the present age) with men in place...to make a supply of magistrates, associates in court, physicians, and officers in the common wealth, and of training elders in the churches, yet for the better discharge of our trust for the next generation . . . [the college should be promoted].

The Charter of 1692 stated simply that Harvard should be incorporated because, among other reasons, "many Persons of unknown worth have by the blessing of Almighty God been better fitted for Publick Imployments both in the Church & in the Civil State."[50]

The acknowledgment that colleges served the state by producing competent candidates for offices both civil and ecclesiastical became almost formulaic. Sooner or later, no matter what the initial stated goals, college backers touted the dual contributions their institutions would make to the success of the colony. The charter of the College of William and Mary dedicated the school's founding to the end that "the Church of *Virginia* may be furnished with a seminary of Ministers of the Gospel, and that the youth may be piously educated in good letters and Manners, and that the Christian Faith may be propagated amongst the Western Indians." But civic education became a principal theme in 1699 when there took place a successful campaign to move the capital to Middle Plantation (Williamsburg) to join the college. With the blessing of the president and Overseers, one commencement orator firmly established the college-state connection:

I should say nothing else in praise of learning but only this; that no country can ever flourish, and be in repute and esteem, without it....Learning is of mighty force and efficacy both to secure states and cities from infinite evils and keep all good things upon them. For how can laws be made, justice be distributed, differences be composed, public speeches be begun or concluded, embassies be managed, and what is fittest and best to be done on all occasions be discerned, without the assistance of learning.[51]

Yale and the College of New Jersey, too, adhered to the formula. The charter for the Connecticut Collegiate School decreed in 1701 that it should be an institution "wherein Youth may be instructed in the Arts & Sciences who through the blessing of Almighty God may be fitted for Publick Employment both in Church & Civil State," and the General Assembly acknowledged, in granting a new charter for Yale College in 1745, that the college "under the blessing of Almighty God has trained up many worthy persons for the service of God in the State as well as in Church."[52] The seven founders of Princeton were all New Light Presbyterians who wanted the New Jersey college to be under religious control, but when they met with the Synod of New York in 1745, they discovered that so narrow a foundation would not be acceptable, for the tradition of state service was too deeply ingrained in the colonies. So they proposed a college with broad religious toleration and the by then almost commonplace dual goals: "Though our great intention was to erect a seminary for educating ministers of the Gospel, yet we hope it will be a means of raising up men that will be useful in other learned professions—ornaments of the State as well as the Church." The charters of 1746 and 1748 confirmed these purposes, making no mention of training up clerics, but rather stressing the "great Necessity of coming into some Method for encouraging and promoting a learned Education of our Youth in New Jersey."[53]

All the colonial colleges founded by the 1750s were subscribers to the civility tradition, recognizing that they must educate youth in the liberal arts and sciences in such a way that they might go on to serve both church and state. How did they attempt that latter task, training for state service? How was politics presented in the curricula of these colonial colleges?

These early American colleges trained their students for state service in the same way the English universities did; in fact, the colonial colleges, directly or indirectly, used the English universities as their curricular models. Harvard and William and Mary were at first staffed by English university graduates (William and Mary continued to be so until the Revolution). The other colleges founded before 1750, which we know as Yale and Princeton, were derivative: Yale was an offspring of Harvard, Princeton of Yale.[54] Colonial attempts to found colleges were high culture instances of the replication of old world institutions so evident in other facets of early American life.[55] This replication carried over to the curriculum, but two problems rendered exact duplication difficult. One was cultural lag; developments took place in England that did not affect the colonies for years and when they did they often appeared in somewhat altered form. Another difficulty was the relative poverty of colonial resources. There were too few of the latest books, too few well-qualified instructors, too few communities willing or able to afford high-calibre collegiate education, and too few young men to attend the colleges that did exist. What resulted was a growing qualitative gap between the American colleges and their English forbears, and as time passed the character of the educations available on opposite sides of the Atlantic came to differ somewhat. Yet the basic outlines remained similar. The colonial colleges fostered the study of the medieval arts and philosophies, the serious study of classical languages inspired by the Renaissance humanists, plus a smattering of belles lettres and other accomplishments deemed suitable for gentlemen. From the end of the seventeenth century and with more intensity during the eighteenth, science became popular. By mid-century there were even "practical" offshoots of science such as surveying and navigation.[56]

Throughout this evolutionary process the curriculum provided training for state service in the same unstructured way the English curriculum did. With few exceptions, politics did not appear as a subject, but there lurked within the regularly prescribed studies quite a bit of political material. The influence it might have had varied with the interests of teachers and students.

Politics, per se, and history appeared only in the earliest curriculum, that of Henry Dunster at Harvard in the 1640s and 1650s. The college program of 1642 indicates that Dunster lectured to second-year students once a week on the subject of ethics or politics. When treating politics, he probably used Aristotle's *Politics*, a wide-ranging study of the political culture of the Greek city-state. Among the topics examined are the nature of citizenship and slavery, the roles of the various classes in government, the various types of constitutions (which he calls monarchy, aristocracy, and polity), the perversions of those types, ways to preserve the various forms of government, the causes of revolution, and Artistotle's conception of the perfect state, which includes education for state service.[57] Dunster's history offering was likely Roman, served up from Thomas Godwyn's *Romanae Historiae Anthologia*, which attempts to explain obscure Latin phrases and to parallel certain Roman and English offices. The references make clear that Godwyn's book was an aid to reading Cicero and it provides cursory analyses of Roman governmental, military, and social organization, with a quite extensive explanation of the relationship between Roman social classes and governing bodies.[58]

The political knowledge that most students gained from their courses did not, then, come directly. Rather it appeared as a by-product of the student's constant immersion in the Greek and Roman classics and relatively brief exposure to ethics as a subdivision of moral philosophy.

The classics pervaded the curriculum. Since Latin and, to a lesser extent, Greek were the languages of learning and since they were necessary for true knowledge of the Bible, every student was supposed to know both languages upon entrance to college. Few did. They continued, therefore, to study the classics throughout their whole college careers. Rhetoric and oratory also drew substantially on classical authors, even if accompanied by modern guides. The great classical philosophers and statesmen also heavily influenced the presentations in metaphysics, moral philosophy, and natural philosophy, again even if updated or challenged by modern thinkers.[59]

The consequence was that many students read extensively in the Greek and Roman authors. Principal among them were Artistotle,[60] Catullus,[61] Cicero,[62] Florus,[63] Hesiod,[64] Homer,[65] Horace,[66] Isocrates,[67] Livy,[68] Sallust,[69] Sophocles,[70] Virgil,[71] and Xenophon.[72] What is striking about this group of authors is that almost all of them wrote at a time when their respective states were moving from democratic or republican forms of government to aristocratic or dictatorial forms, and that many of them included political commentary in their writings. Historians, poets, and orators all condemned tyranny, described just governments (especially republics) and explained their downfall, or provided insights into the characters of good and bad rulers.[73]

Since most of these classics descended to the colonial college curriculum from the handiwork of the English Renaissance humanists, perhaps we should not be surprised at the emphases on political commentary, political history, and proper education. These were elements of the civility tradition the humanists wanted to promote, and so they were received, however unconsciously, by the colonial colleges.

Exposure to politics and historical observations about government were common fare in classical studies, but rare in moral philosophy. Not until the second third of the eighteenth century was ethics treated as a secular rather than a religious matter. For example, Henry More's ethical treatise, used at Harvard until perhaps the 1730s and at Yale for even longer, concentrated on virtue alone, giving no consideration to the ethical relations of rulers and subjects, nor to the forms of government providing a context for those relations.[74] Of the volumes on moral philosophy in use by 1750, only David Fordyce, *The Elements of Moral Philosophy*, and Henry Grove, *A System of Moral Philosophy*, contained discussions of politics and government.

The bases of the political and governmental precepts found in the two works were Lockean theory and the model of balanced government available in contemporary Britain. Both discuss the state of nature, and governments derived from social compact for protection from the evil side of human nature and for the advancement of the common good. Rulers and ruled have mutual obligations; the former to provide leadership in defense and to execute faithfully laws embodying the popular will, the latter to obey just rulers. Rulers who violate their trust may be subject to the people's wrath; they are not protected by divine right.[75] Grove's model of a ruler is Ciceronian (the student reading this would recognize the precepts he had read in his classics). And both works argue that the ideal government is the English system, based on the balance of power, which includes the common people, the hereditary nobility, and the monarch, all performing necessary functions while insuring that no single element of society or government abuses power.[76]

This balanced system of government, functioning along Lockean lines, prompts both philosophers to extol in their readers a love of country. Grove urges citizens to

pursue therefore our private interests in *subordination* to the good of our country...to *chuse* such *representatives* as we apprehend to be the best friends to its constitution and liberties...and, if need be, to *die* for it; these are among the duties which every man, who has the happiness to be of our free and protestant constitution, owes to his country.[77]

The classical and philosophical elements of the curriculum, then, made available to the colonial college students varied knowledge useful in state service: analyses of political systems, narratives of political history showing the successes and failures of systems and rulers, skills and values necessary to be learned before becoming a civic actor. But this was just one part of a liberal curriculum designed to prepare the student for many different pursuits. Although at some times and in some places students did reflect their political knowledge in such activities as commencement theses, this industry did not indicate either special training or interest in politics or state service on the part of the college community.

At Harvard, for example, commencement theses included political topics from the late 1720s on: "Is unlimited obedience to rulers taught by Christ and His Apostles?" (1729); "Is the voice of the people the voice of God?" (1733); and "Is it lawful to resist the Supreme Magistrate, if the Commonwealth cannot be otherwise preserved?" (1743, 1747, 1751).[78] But before we infer substantial political interest and training, we need to look more closely at the context of these presentations.

While these topics no doubt reflected political interest on the part of the students who presented them, they were few in number. Generally, commencement topics were tied to career interests, so most of the politically oriented topics came from aspiring lawyers. Probably more important, the selection of a topic was an individual matter between the student and the college president, who usually reviewed the topic and occasionally the arguments as well. At Harvard in the years before 1770, this entailed use of a guide, for President Holyoke drew on Thomas Johnson's manual of collegiate debate topics after 1743.[79] In that year five of the nineteen questions virtually duplicated Johnson's wording and periodically thereafter the topics were those of Johnson's manual.

Proper use of Johnson's work mandated a short course in politics. Samuel Adams' 1743 argument concerning the ultimate limitation of the supreme magistrate's power should have led him, if he followed Johnson's suggestions, to treatises on law by Grotius and Pufendorf, and analyses of government by Locke, Algernon Sidney, and Benjamin Hoadly. Had he argued the negative or wanted to know the objections to his assertions, Johnson's suggestions included Thomas

Hobbes' *Leviathan*, Filmer's *Patriarcha* and *The Freeholder's Grand Inquest*, as well as lesser known works. Arguing a political topic for commencement or other debates enabled the interested student to become acquainted with many informed authors and to relate this new knowledge to his overall program of study, but the appearance of such topics did not mean that the curriculum was politically charged or that education for state service required a special body of knowledge distinct from the classical liberal arts tradition.

Politics, then, was included in the colonial curriculum incidentally, with no conscious effort to promote it as a field of knowledge or a specific vocation for students. Scholars had the opportunity to become acquainted with political theory and with political history, but this was a by-product of the standard liberal arts education designed to prepare students to serve the state in a variety of ways. Just as the colonial colleges adopted the idea of state service, so they also replicated the curriculum that implemented it. The final colonial reproduction of English high culture was the establishment of a tradition of guardianship of the college by the government.

Colonial governments, sometimes before the very foundation of the institutions, took an active interest in higher education. Unquestioningly, they accepted this English cultural pattern, just as the settlers had with regard to the civility tradition and a curriculum to foster it. And, just as in England, the relations between government and colleges were a function of the church-state relationship. Where that relationship was generally harmonious, as in New England, the governments were usually supportive, if somewhat paternal. Where those relations were uncertain, as in New Jersey in the 1740s, or quarrelsome, as in Virginia from the late seventeenth century on or in mid-eighteenth century New York, governmental attitudes might run the gamut from active support to hostile opposition. There was never any question about governmental involvement. Rather, the issues were which denomination, if any, should sponsor the college, and what degree of governmental supervision there should be.

The one responsibility requisite upon the governments was chartering the institutions. Both New England governments happily granted charters to their colleges and in Virginia, where it seemed proper to petition the Crown for a charter, the General Assembly dispatched the newly arrived Commissary of the Anglican Church, the Reverend James Blair, with a flood of instructions concerning the proper way to maneuver the charter through the royal bureaucracy.[80]

In New Jersey the legislature acted less enthusiastically. College supporters came to be identified with East Jersey New Light Presbyterian ministers Aaron Burr and Jonathan Dickinson. Their opponents were Anglicans prominent in the ranks of the royal colonial government and East Jersey proprietors who had been hoping for a non-denominational college. (They would have preferred an Anglican institution, but that was out of the question, given the weak position of the Church in New Jersey). The proprietors also connected Burr and Dickinson with the protest movement against the collection of proprietary quitrents. What developed was an alignment of pro-college, anti-proprietor, largely Presbyterian forces against Anglican, anti-college, pro-proprietor forces. A new governor, Jonathan Belcher, highly influenced by English dissenters, finessed the problem. By working for a new charter that moved the college to West Jersey and added various governmental officials to the board, including four Councillors and some proprietors, and by avoiding an appeal to the Assembly for financial aid, Belcher influenced the Council to approve his plan in 1748 at a session which six East Jersey proprietors boycotted. It was a masterpiece of short-term political games-manship, but it left a long-lasting bad taste in the mouths of Jersey politicians. Due to this religio-political strife, the college never became the beneficiary of a kindly disposed legislature.[81]

Princeton's lack of financial support from the government was the exception. All the other colleges benefited from legislative largesse. The New England governments appropriated annual subsidies for many years, Harvard generally receiving salary subsidies for its faculty, Yale obtaining either a flat sum of money or an amount to make up its annual deficit.[82] The Assemblies also rose to special occasions such as funding new construction or repairs, and reimbursing communities for ministers now become college presidents.[83] The Virginia Assembly preferred to establish sources of long-term revenue for William and Mary, granting a percentage of the duties on furs and skins and on imported liquor to college financing.[84]

The nurture that colonial governments gave to their colleges never came without a price, for parental authority was exercised when the institutions did not live up to the expected norms, secular and religious, at least in New England. In Massachusetts, for example, when Increase Mather became Harvard's pres-ident, and was involved in colonial politics centering in Boston, there took place a protracted campaign to get him to reside in Cambridge or, failing that, to replace him. This was but one part of a larger religio-cultural change that occurred in Massachusetts over the quarter century 1685–1710. Its most marked char-acteristic was the declining influence of orthodox Puritans over the affairs of church and state. Mather's eventual succession by the religiously liberal John Leverett and the reconfirmation of the Charter of 1650 were the culminating events in this shift as it affected the college.[85] The significance of the episode is that it kept up congruence between the religious and political stances of the college and the colonial government. In early eighteenth-century Massachusetts this could be done without pamphlet wars, excessive vituperation, or harm to the college. In mid-eighteenth-century New York that was not possible.

Connecticut's government proved just as willing to ensure that the benefits it derived from higher education were not sacrificed to collegiate unrest in any form. Starting in 1714, before the Collegiate School became Yale College, it was riven by faction, splitting into three different educational units at three locations. This may have been partly a personality clash among trustees, but mostly it was competition among three regional centers in Connecticut for the financial benefits a college would bring. This was just the sort of struggle to divide the legislature and it did, geographically and philosophically. Finally, when after three years of wrangling it appeared to reasonable people that the college's status as political and economic football was doing neither it nor the colony any good, the legislators hammered out a compromise to reunite the college in New Haven and placate the economic interests of the other towns. The college trustees remained divided; had the legislators not finally resolved the issue, meaningful higher education in Connecticut might have been delayed some years.[86]

A further revealing example of the Connecticut government's desire to protect the benefits derived from higher education occurred during the course of the Great Awakening in the 1740s. Yale's students were much taken by the message of the itinerant evangelists who made New Haven a regular stop on their tours. The college administration—Rector Thomas Clap and the trustees—were at first puzzled by and soon openly hostile to the Awakening, seeing it as a force disruptive of ecclesiastical harmony in the colony. Clap and the Reverend Joseph Noyes, pastor of New Haven's First Church and a trustee, initially enlisted General Assembly aid in approving a "General Consociation," or meeting, of ministers and lay representatives from all the colony's churches to discuss the Awakening and its effects. This meeting in November 1741 approved the Guilford Resolves, which generally endorsed traditional ways of selecting ministers and receiving converts. It also pronounced against itineracy and advised separates to give serious thought to what they had done. The May 1742 session of the General Assembly received the Resolves, translating those parts concerning the prevention of itineracy into an act providing high penalties for such activity.[87]

The college rector, having taken steps to protect the orthodoxy of the colony, then turned to internal matters, taking steps to quell student unrest and attraction to the Awakening. These included the expulsion of a pro-revival student in November 1741 and the closing of the college early in 1742. Such developments did not escape the General Assembly's notice. It demanded a report on conditions at Yale and digested it. Then, observing that "it is of great Importance, both to our Civil & Eclesiastical State that the true principles of Religion & good order be maintained at that Seminary of Learning," it recommended that true tenets of religion be carefully presented to the students, that those presenting false principles be kept from addressing the scholars, that recalcitrant students be expelled, and that suitable "Grave Divines" be called in to assist at colony expense. Under these injunctions Clap continued to suppress pro-revival spirit on the campus and the crisis gradually diminished in intensity. Its last flareup involved Clap's expulsion of two student brothers who had attended a separatist church meeting while on vacation, in violation of colony laws and (so Clap said) college laws. The brothers memorialized the General Assembly for redress but were turned down. Within a month the Assembly passed an act amending the college charter to give Clap a vote on the board of trustees, raise his status to that of president, and give him much greater control over the internal affairs of the college, which he proceeded to exercise by introducing a strict new disciplinary code. It appears that in Connecticut, as in Massachusetts, the government saw sufficient benefit to the state deriving from the college that it took pains to see that the two were philosophically in harmony and that the latter was powerful enough to protect itself from internal threats.

The College of William and Mary enjoyed no such benevolent paternalism as the governments of New England administered. Instead, the college almost always served as a divisive issue among the factional groups conducting Virginia politics. The root of the problem lay in the actions of one man, exercised in the context of the Crown's willingness to condone plural officeholding. In 1687 the Scot James Blair came to Virginia as an Anglican minister. He married into a prominent Virginia family, began to amass wealth, and joined the upper class. In 1690 he was appointed Commissary of Virginia, deputy to the Bishop of London. When he went to London to plead the cause of the proposed college, he was named its president. Returning to Virginia, he parlayed his status into an appointment to the governor's council, so by the mid-1690s he embodied the highest ranks of church, state, and education.[88]

The problem with this one-man triumvirate was that Blair was an independent thinker, politically astute, possessed of an iron will and an activist temper. He would and did meddle in affairs of church, state, and college, seldom keeping them separate, and in the process he created enemies for William and Mary. From 1690 to 1722 he was influential in the naming and replacing of three of the five Virginia governors. The basic theme running through the disputes was Blair's support of colonial autonomy in opposition to Governors Edmund Andros, Francis Nicholson, and Alexander Spotswood, who defended imperial policy. But they also disagreed over whether the governors or local vestries should appoint Anglican ministers to their parishes.

Blair entangled the college in these disputes in various ways. A number of his relations by marriage became college Visitors; they shared Blair's landed gentry independence from the governors, often were members of the council with him, and were known as the "college faction." One of Blair's favorite devices for bringing down a governor in disfavor was to accuse him of opposing the success of the college. Andros allegedly delayed construction of the buildings. Nicholson supposedly turned the college students against Blair, so that they "barred him out" in 1703. On the other hand, all three governors gained the support of the Anglican clergy, including the faculty of William and Mary, because Blair favored vestry appointments, which meant a certain degree of behavioral discipline and uncertain tenure. Gubernatorial appointment meant a permanent living and little oversight.

As a result of all this, the college had as many enemies as friends in Virginia. Many residents refused to support the college either with gifts or by sending their sons there. The General Assembly provided sufficient revenue but did not look after the college in the benevolent way her New England counterparts did. There were always critics of college administration and programs. Worst of all, while pre-occupied with political infighting, Blair neglected the college, which he allowed to remain no more than a grammar school until the late 1720s. In that decade, at last free of opponents in the governor's chair, Blair hired some collegiate level faculty, six of whom were in place by 1727, which allowed the transfer of day-to-day government to the president and masters and provided for the creation of a collegiate curriculum. But the faculty began to fall away almost as soon as it was assembled, the academic statutes went virtually unused, and the succession of British Anglican clerics of varying character and ability who filtered in and out of the college professorships did little to enlist Virginians' sympathies.

Even when Blair died in 1743, after a fifty-six-year presidency, his legacy so overwhelmed the college that matters did not improve during the tenure of his handpicked successor, William Dawson. The college remained caught in the middle of Virginia politics, receiving only half-hearted Assembly support and experiencing little academic growth.[89]

Although the circumstances differed depending upon whether their colleges or their governments were or were not on the same side of religious and political issues, there is no question that the colonists everywhere accepted their English heritage, implicitly assuming that the state had a vested interest in supervising the affairs of higher educational institutions. They made this assumption in the same way they had assumed that one of the functions of colleges was to educate for state service, and that colleges should offer a curriculum with that end in mind. Colonists assumed all these things because they were part of the English culture to which Anglo-Americans subscribed, had been part of that culture for many years, and no one in the colonies saw any reason to examine them.

Until the King's College controversy arose. The controversy stands like a Janus face, looking backward and forward across colonial American history. Neither the Reflectors nor their Anglican opponents questioned the assumptions about higher education and politics that had guided their fellow colonists for 120 years, but they did examine the implications of those assumptions. While coming to different conclusions, the combatants in the controversy asked how one should serve the state, what kind of state one should serve, what was the best curriculum to promote that end, and what was the best relationship between college and state to achieve their desired ends?

These questions, appearing here for the first time, raised the connection between politics and higher education from an implicit to an explicit level. They sought to link higher education not just to politics generally but to a politics. Increasingly from the mid-1750s to the mid-1770s, college communities would consider these questions. In the process they would become politicized.

NOTES

1. Carl Bridenbaugh, *Cities in Revolt: Urban Life in America, 1743–1776* (New York: Oxford University Press, 1955), 4–5, 16–17, 28–31, 98–133; Gary B. Nash, *The Urban Crucible: Social Change, Political Consciousness, and the Origins of the American Revolution* (Cambridge, Mass.: Harvard University Press, 1979), 176–80, 409, for a

chart showing New York City's eighteenth-century population growth; Michael Kammen, *Colonial New York: A History* (New York: Charles Scribner's Sons, 1975), 280–83, 288–89; Douglas Greenburg, *Crime and Law Enforcement in the Colony of New York, 1691–1776* (Ithaca, N.Y.: Cornell University Press, 1976), 134–53; Patricia U. Bonomi, *A Factious People: Politics and Society in Colonial New York* (New York: Columbia University Press, 1971), 140–78.

2. Kammen, *Colonial New York*, 216, 220–22, 232–38.

3. Ibid., 244. Kenneth Lockridge, in his study of colonial literacy, concludes that the ability to sign wills is an accurate reflector of society's true literacy. New York's 80 percent literacy rate was quite similar to New England's estimated 85 percent rate in 1760. *Literacy in Colonial New England: An Enquiry into the Social Context of Literacy in the Early Modern West* (New York: Oxford University Press, 1974), 7–13.

4. Kammen, *Colonial New York*, 244–47.

5. Ibid., 247–50.

6. David C. Humphrey, *From King's College to Columbia, 1746–1800* (New York: Columbia University Press, 1976), 4. While there are other treatments of the King's College controversy, Humphrey's is the most clearly focused on the college. The account that follows relies heavily on it.

7. Trinity Church Vestry and Episcopal Clergy of New York to S[ociety for the] P[ropagation of the] G[ospel in Foreign Parts], November 3, 1755, *Johnson Writings,* IV, 39.

8. S. Johnson to William Samuel Johnson, January 20, 1755 and S. Johnson to the Archbishop of Canterbury, July 12, 1760, ibid., I, 209, 295.

9. S. Johnson to the Bishop of London, April 28, 1747, and Samuel Seabury et al. to the Bishop of London, enclosed in a letter of S. Johnson to the Bishop of London, June 25, 1753, quoted in Humphrey, *King's College*, 25, 27.

10. Isaac Browne to [SPG], March 25, 1748, quoted in ibid., 28.

11. New York *Evening Post*, May 18, 1747; Joseph J. Ellis, *The New England Mind in Transition: Samuel Johnson of Connecticut, 1696–1722* (New Haven: Yale University Press, 1973), 180–85.

12. New York *Mercury*, November 6, 1752.

13. *Journal of the Votes and Proceedings of the General Assembly of the Colony of New York, Began the 9th Day of April, 1691; and Ended the [23rd of December, 1765]*, (2 vols., New York, 1764–1766), II, 336.

14. [William Livingston], *Some Serious Thoughts on the Design of Erecting a College in the Province of New York, Shewing the eminent Advantages of a liberal education, more especially with Regard to Education and Politics...* (New York, 1749); *Ind. Ref.*, 24–37; Humphrey, *King's College*, 35–40, quotation 35; Kammen, *Colonial New York*, 250–52.

15. *Ind. Ref.*, 32. Beverly McAnear argues that Livingston, while concerned with Anglican activities, saw the King's College controversy as a political issue, one likely to unseat the DeLanceys and bring the Livingstons and their allies into power. Thus the episode resembles many others in New York's factional-familial political climate. See McAnear, "American Imprints Concerning King's College," *Papers of the Bibliographical Society of America*, 44 (1950): 301–2.

16. There is no published biography of Livingston, but see Milton M. Klein, "William Livingston: The American Whig" (Ph.D. diss., Columbia University, 1954); on Livingston, Smith, and Scott, see Dorothy Dillon, *The New York Triumvirate: A Study of*

the Legal and Political Careers of William Livingston, John Morin Scott, and William Smith, Jr. (New York: Columbia University Press, 1949).

17. *Ind. Ref.*, 32, XVII (March 22, 1753), XVIII (March 29, 1753).

18. Ibid., XVIII, XVII, XIX (April 1, 1753).

19. Ibid., XX (April 12, 1753).

20. The argument appears in a few pamphlets and some newspapers. See especially: William Smith, *A General Idea of the College of Mirania* (New York, 1753); Benjamin Nicholl, *A Brief Vindication of the Proceedings of the Trustees* (New York, 1754); William Livingston, *The Querist* (New York, 1754) and *The Watchtower* (New York, 1754); *John Englishman in Defense of the English Constitution* (New York, 1755); New York *Mercury* (1753–1755).

21. The best account of the events highlighted here is Humphrey, *King's College*, Chapter 3; S. Johnson to the Bishop of London, July 6, 1754, S. Johnson to William Samuel Johnson, May 6, 1754, Henry Barclay to S. Johnson, November 4, 1754, S. Johnson to Dr. Bearcroft, Secretary of the Society, December 3, 1754, *Johnson Writings*, IV, 20, I, 184, IV, 24, 28–29.

22. Humphrey, *King's College*, 52–53, 63–65; Kammen, *Colonial New York*, 233–37; Henry Barclay to S. Johnson, November 4, 1754, Journal of the New York General Assembly, November 1, 1754 (extract), S.Johnson to William Samuel Johnson, November 25, 1754, S. Johnson to William Samuel Johnson and William Johnson, December 2, 1754, S. Johnson to William Samuel Johnson, May 14, 1755, November 8, 1756, *Johnson Writings*, IV, 24, 189, 26, 27, 35, I, 268.

23. *Ind. Ref.*, XLI (Sept. 6, 1753), XLVII (Oct. 18, 1753), XLVI (Oct. 11, 1753).

24. Ibid., XXXVI (Aug. 2, 1753), XXXVII (Aug. 9, 1753); New York *Mercury*, July 9, 1753. For a discussion of the King's College Controversy in this context, see Milton M. Klein, "Church, State, and Education: Testing the Issue in Colonial New York," *New York History*, 45 (1964): 291–303, and Donald F. Gerardi, "The King's College Controversy, 1753–1756, and the Ideological Roots of Toryism in New York," *Perspectives in American History*, 11 (1977–78): 179–81.

25. *Ind. Ref.*, IV (December 21, 1752), XXXIII (July 12, 1753), XXXVI–XXXIX (Aug. 2, 9, 16 and 23, 1753); New York *Mercury*, Aug. 27, Sept. 10, 17, and 24, 1753.

26. *Ind. Ref.*, XVII.

27. Ibid., XVIII.

28. Ibid., XX, XXI (Apr. 19, 1753); Humphrey, *King's College*, Chs. 2, 3.

29. *The Republic of Plato*, Francis M. Cornford, trans. (orig. 1941; reprint, New York: Oxford University Press, 1967), 63–102, 175–79, 235–63.

30. The discussion in this and the following paragraphs draws on Lawrence A. Cremin, *American Education: The Colonial Experience, 1607–1783* (New York: Harper & Row, 1970), 58–79; William H. Woodward, *Studies in Education During the Age of the Renaissance, 1400–1600* (Cambridge: Cambridge University Press, 1906); Kenneth Charlton, *Education in Renaissance England* (London: Routledge and Kegan Paul, Ltd., 1965); Jack H. Hexter, "The Education of the Aristocracy in the Renaissance," Hexter, ed., *Reappraisals in History* (Evanston, Ill.: Northwestern University Press, 1961), 45–70. For works considered, see Desiderius Erasmus, *The Education of a Christian Prince*, Lester K. Born, trans. (New York: Columbia University Press, 1936), and Thomas Elyot, *The Book Named the Governor*, ed. S.E. Lemberg (London: J.M. Dent & Sons, 1963).

31. Cremin, *American Education*, 72–79. For works considered, see Humphrey Gilbert, *Queene Elizabethe's Achademy*, ed. Frederick J. Furnivall (London: N. Trubner &

Co., 1869); Roger Ascham, *The Scholemaster*, ed. Richard J. Schoeck (Don Mills, Ontario: J.M. Dent & Sons, 1966); Philip Sidney, *Arcadia*, ed. Jean Robertson (Oxford: Oxford University Press, 1973); Edmund Spenser, *The Faerie Queene*, ed. A.C. Hamilton (London: Longman's Group, 1977); Philip Sidney, *The Defense of Poesie* (orig. 1595; reprint, London: N. Douglas, 1928); Henry Peacham, *The Compleat Gentleman*, ed. Virgil B. Heltzell (Ithaca: Cornell University Press, 1962); Richard Braithwaite, *The English Gentleman* (London, 1630).

32. Cremin, *American Education*, 83–95. For works considered, see Francis Bacon, *The Advancement of Learning and the New Atlantis*, ed. Arthur Johnston (Oxford: Oxford University Press, 1974).

33. Cremin, *American Education*, 68, 86–88. For works considered, see Francis Bacon, *Essays* (orig. 1625; reprint, Manston, Eng.: Scolar Press, 1971); Desiderius Erasmus, *Colloquies*, trans. Craig R. Thompson (Chicago: University of Chicago Press, 1965); Michel Eyquem de Montaigne, *Essays*, trans. John Florio (orig. 1603; reprint, New York: AMS Press, 1967).

34. On the divorce and the attendant confrontation between canon and common law, see A.G. Dickens, *The English Reformation* (New York: Schocken Books, 1964), 104–13, and J. J. Scarisbrick, *Henry VIII* (Berkeley: University of California Press, 1968), 163–240. For the effects of this dispute on Oxford and Cambridge, see Hugh Kearney, *Scholars and Gentlemen: Universities and Society in Pre-Industrial Britain, 1500–1700* (Ithaca: Cornell University Press, 1970), 15–20, and Mark H. Curtis, *Oxford and Cambridge in Transition, 1558–1642: An Essay on Changing Relations Between English Universities and the English Society* (Oxford: Oxford University Press, 1959), 63–70.

35. Kearney, *Scholars and Gentlemen*, 23, 26–28; Curtis, *Oxford and Cambridge*, 63–64, 71–72, 75–76; Joan Simon, *Education and Society in Tudor England* (Cambridge: Cambridge University Press, 1966), 138, 149, 245–46.

36. Kearney, *Scholars and Gentlemen*, 78–82; William T. Costello, *The Scholastic Curriculum at Early Seventeenth Century Cambridge* (Cambridge, Mass.: Harvard University Press, 1958), 4, 67–68; Simon, *Education and Society*, 394–95.

37. Curtis, *Oxford and Cambridge*, 83–84, 127.

38. Ibid., 105, 130–36.

39. Costello, *Scholastic Curriculum*, 67–68.

40. Curtis, *Oxford and Cambridge*, 110–13; Samuel Eliot Morison, *The Founding of Harvard College* (Cambridge, Mass.: Harvard University Press, 1935), 51–53. The evidence for these generalizations and the particular illustrations that follow consists largely of interpretations of the plan for required and extra-curricular studies of Cambridge tutor Richard Holdsworth, virtually the only surviving record of the studies actually pursued at early seventeenth-century English universities. Both Curtis and Morison contend that Holdsworth's plan is a guide to the curriculum of the 1620s and 1630s, and Morison argues that Holdsworth was a moderate Puritan, so his plan represents the studies of many Harvard founders (*Founding of Harvard*, 62). But Kearney questions that the plan is Holdsworth's, argues that it represents studies in the 1640s or later, and contends that the plan is, in fact, conservative, uninfluenced by the new learning or Baconian criticism of higher education (*Scholars and Gentlemen*, 103–5). On this point, I follow the judgment of Curtis and Morison.

41. Curtis, *Oxford and Cambridge*, 136–37, 132–33; Morison, *Founding of Harvard*, 66–67, presents a class-by-class breakdown of the curriculum.

42. James Bass Mullinger, *The University of Cambridge* (3 vols., Cambridge: Cam-

bridge University Press, 1874–1911), I, 630, II, 9–10; Kearney, *Scholars and Gentlemen*, 19; Simon, *Education and Society*, 198–201.

43. Mullinger, *Cambridge*, II, 76–81; Simon, *Education and Society*, 211–13.

44. Mullinger, *Cambridge*, II, 109–13, 145–47; Kearney, *Scholars and Gentlemen*, 21–22; Simon, *Education and Society*, 252–67.

45. Mullinger, *Cambridge*, II, 222, 230–31, 249–50, 455–56, 461–62.

46. Kearney, *Scholars and Gentlemen*, 78–79, 81–82; Simon, *Education and Society*, 394–95.

47. Mullinger, *Cambridge*, II, 306, 459–60.

48. For commentary on this, see Bernard Bailyn et al., *The Great Republic* (lst ed., Lexington, Mass.: D.C. Heath, 1977), 34–122; Louis B. Wright, *The Cultural Life of the American Colonies, 1607–1763* (New York: Harper & Row, 1957), 126–54, 176–95; David Grayson Allen, *In English Ways: The Movement of Societies and the Transferal of English Local Law and Custom to Massachusetts Bay in the Seventeenth Century* (Chapel Hill: University of North Carolina Press, 1981).

49. Such episodes as the founding of Massachusetts Bay and Pennsylvania, the struggle for religious toleration in New England (outside Rhode Island) and Maryland, the Glorious Revolution in New York, Maryland, and Massachusetts Bay, and, of course, the Great Awakening illustrate the pervasiveness of the influence of religious belief on civic activity.

50. "New England's First Fruits," reprinted in Morison, *Founding of Harvard*, 432–33; *Mass. Bay Rec.*, IV, part 1, 100–101; *Harvard College Records*, "Charter of 1692," CSM *Publications*, 15 (1925): 335–36.

51. "The Charter of the College of William and Mary in Virginia," *Doc. Hist. Educ.*, I, 401; "Speeches of Students of the College of William and Mary Delivered May 1, 1699," *WMQ*, New Series, 10 (1930): 324.

52. "Charter of the Collegiate School, October 1701," *DHYU*, 21; "An Act for the more full and compleat Establishment of Yale College in New Haven, and for enlarging the Power and Privilieges thereof, May 7, 1745," *PRCC*, IX, 113.

53. Thomas J. Wertenbaker, *Princeton, 1746–1896* (Princeton: Princeton University Press, 1946), 19, 396.

54. Morison, *Founding of Harvard*, 193–94; Jack E. Morpurgo, *Their Majesties' Royall Colledge: William and Mary in the Seventeenth and Eighteenth Centuries* (Williamsburg: The College of William and Mary, 1976), 17, 61, 85–87, 109–10; Richard Warch, *School of the Prophets: Yale College, 1701–1740* (New Haven: Yale University Press, 1973), 39–40; Wertenbaker, *Princeton*, 16–30; Francis L. Broderick, "Pulpit, Physics, and Politics: The Curriculum of the College of New Jersey, 1746–1794," *WMQ*, 11 (1949): 46–47.

55. One aspect of collegiate affairs that seemed not to follow English patterns was institutional government. Although the faculty did have some voice in the operation of some colleges, generally the colonial schools acquired non-faculty boards of governors made up of prominent community members. The origins and significance of their form of government are matters of dispute. For a recent exploration of these issues, as well as a review of stances previously taken, see Jurgen Herbst, "The First Three American Colleges: Schools of the Reformation," *Perspectives in American History*, 8 (1974): 7–52.

56. For an overview of the evolution of the colonial college curriculum, see Louis F. Snow, *The College Curriculum in the United States* (New York: Teacher's College Press of Columbia University Press, 1907), 20–96, 102–112n; Frederick Rudolph, *Curriculum:*

A History of the Undergraduate Course of Study Since 1636 (San Francisco: Josey-Bass, 1977), 25–53; Joe W. Kraus, "The Development of a Curriculum in the Early American College," *History of Education Quarterly*, 1 (1961): 64–76. Some sense of the increasing gap between English and colonial higher education may be obtained by reading Morison's accounts of the English curriculum (*Founding of Harvard*, chapter 4) and Harvard's seventeenth-century curriculum (Samuel Eliot Morison, *Harvard College in the Seventeenth Century* [2 vols., Cambridge, Mass.: Harvard University Press, 1935], chapters 7–13) and then Warch's commentary on the Yale program of 1740 (*School of the Prophets*, chapters 8–9).

57. Morison, *Harvard in the 17th Century*, 144–45, 259; Aristotle, *Politics and Poetics*, trans. Benjamin Jowett and S.H. Butcher (New York: Oxford University Press, 1964).

58. Morison, *Harvard in the 17th Century*, 142–43, 264; Thomas Godwyn, *Romanae Historie Anthologia, Recognita et Aucta: An English Exposition of the Roman Antiquities, Wherein Many Roman and English Offices are parallel'd, and divers obscure Phrases explain'd* (Newly revised and enlarged, London, 1764).

59. The influence of the learned languages on sixteenth- and seventeenth-century higher education is well accepted. For some idea of their importance in these colleges, see Morison, *Harvard in the 17th Century*, chapters 7, 8, 12; Warch, *School of the Prophets*, 188, 193–95, 198, 226–29; Broderick, "Pulpit, Physics, and Politics," 46–51; Morpurgo, *Royall Colledge*, 77–83; Lyon G. Tyler, "Some Early Courses and Professors at William and Mary College," *WMCQ*, 14 (1905–1906): 72–73.

60. *Politics* in use at Harvard, 1642; title unknown in use at William and Mary before 1750.

61. Poetry in use at William and Mary before 1750.

62. *Orations* almost universally required for entrance; *De Oratore* in use at Princeton in 1750s; *De Officiis* in use at Harvard, 1690s–1740s.

63. History in use at Harvard, 1690s–1740s.

64. Poetry in use at Harvard, 1690s–1740s.

65. The *Iliad* in use at Harvard, 1690s–1740s, at Yale early 1750s.

66. *Odes and Epodes* in use at Princeton in 1750s.

67. Oratorical works in use at Harvard, 1690s–1740s.

68. History in use at William and Mary before 1750.

69. History in use at Harvard, 1690s–1740s.

70. Plays in use at Harvard, 1690s–1740s.

71. The *Aeneid* in use at Yale from 1714–1750s, at William and Mary before 1750.

72. The *Cyropaedia* in use at Princeton in the 1750s.

73. A more thorough discussion of the political content of these works follows in Chapter 3, which focuses on their use in the pre-Revolutionary curriculum.

74. Henry More, *Enchiridion Ethicum, praecipia moralis philosophiae rudimenta complectus* (London, 1669) was available in English translation as *An Account of Virtue* after 1690. For its use at Harvard, see Morison, *Harvard in the Seventeenth Century*, 146–47, and Benjamin Rand, "Philosophical Instruction in Harvard University from 1636 to 1900," *Harvard Graduates' Magazine*, 37 (1928): 32. For its use at Yale, see John C. Schwab, "The Yale College Curriculum, 1701–1901," *Educational Review*, 22 (1901): 4, and Warch, *School of the Prophets*, 231–34.

75. Henry Grove, *A System of Moral Philosophy* (2 vols., London, 1749), II, 516–

20; David Fordyce, *The Elements of Moral Philosophy* (orig. 2 vols., 1753; London, 1754), 190–202.

76. Grove, *System of Moral Philosophy*, II, 521, 527–29; Fordyce, *Elements of Moral Philosophy*, 202–4.

77. Grove, *System of Moral Philosophy*, II, 529, 532; Fordyce, *Elements of Moral Philosophy*, 198–201.

78. Samuel Eliot Morison, *Three Centuries of Harvard, 1636–1936* (Cambridge, Mass.: Harvard University Press, 1936), 90–91; David Potter, *Debating in the Colonial Chartered Colleges* (New York: Teacher's College Press of Columbia University Press, 1944), 23.

79. Thomas Johnson, *Quaestiones Philosophicae in Justi Systematis Ordinem Dispositiae...* (2d ed., Cambridge, 1735). This discussion derives from Minor Myers, Jr., "A Source for Eighteenth Century Harvard Master's Questions," *WMQ*, 38 (1981): 261–67; there is no reason to believe that a similar process did not take place for undergraduates.

80. Morison, *Harvard in the 17th Century*, chapter 1; *Mass. Bay Rec.*, IV, pt. 1, 12–14; *PRCC*, IV, 63; Park Rouse, Jr., *James Blair of Virginia* (Chapel Hill: University of North Carolina Press, 1971), 37, 43–44; *Doc. Hist. Educ.*, I, 377–80.

81. This account derives from two articles that separate the causes of the conflict over the Princeton charter. See Alison R. Olson, "The Founding of Princeton University: Religion and Politics in Eighteenth Century New Jersey," and David C. Humphrey, "The Struggle for Sectarian Control at Princeton, 1745–1760," *New Jersey History*, 87 (1969): 133–50, and 91 (1973): 77–90.

82. See, for example, *Mass. Bay Rec.*, I, 183, II, 86, IV, pt. 1, 314, 535–37, V, 51; *Mass. A & R*, VI, 452, VIII, 257, XIII, 674, XIV, 482; *PRCC*, VII, 133, 178, VIII, 24, 203, IX, 256, 535–36.

83. See, for example, *Mass. Bay Rec.*, II, 84, IV, pt. 1, 216, V, 32; *Mass. A & R*, IV, 834, IX, 105, X, 639; *PRCC*, V, 529, VI, 256, 283, 569–70, VII, 24, VIII, 206, IX, 113–18.

84. *Va. Stat.*, III, 123–24, 356–57, IV, 248, V, 237, 317–18, VI, 91–94.

85. Morison, *Harvard in the 17th Century*, chapters 22–24; *Mass. A & R*, I, 38–39, 288–90, VI, 452, 609–10, VII, 228, 230, 245, 250–53, 255, 257–60, 265, 271–72, 308, 312, VIII, 257.

86. Warch, *School of the Prophets*, 70–90; *PRCC*, VI, 30, 30n, 83–84. The contest can be easily followed in documentary form in *DHYU*, 65–66, 95–180.

87. This and the following paragraphs are based on Stephen Nissenbaum, *The Great Awakening at Yale College* (Belmont, Calif.: Wadsworth Publishing Co., 1972). For the text of the 1745 charter amendment, see *PRCC*, IX, 113–18.

88. This and the following paragraphs derive largely from Rouse, *Blair of Virginia*, esp. chapters 3–7, and Morpurgo, *Royall Colledge*, chapters 4–7. For an account of these events emphasizing their political and institutional character, see Richard L. Morton, *Colonial Virginia* (2 vols., Chapel Hill: University of North Carolina Press, 1960), I, chapters 22–24, II, chapters 1–8.

89. Rouse, *Blair of Virginia*, 209; Morpurgo, *Royall Colledge*, 80–81, 88–90, 98, 116–18; Morton, *Colonial Virginia*, II, chapter 18.

2

Politicizing the Faculty

During the two decades between the King's College controversy and the separation of the American colonies from Great Britain, the college communities altered their relationship to the politics of the day. They went from vague proclamations and superficial implementations of an education for state service to a consciously shaped and vigorously advocated inculcation of republican political principles. The first step in the transformation of pre-Revolutionary higher education was the embracing of a politically active role by the collegiate faculty. The politicization of the faculty did not take place overnight, nor did it produce uniform results, but by the eve of the Revolution no college was exempt from its effects. To see the process at work, we examine the career of Provost William Smith of the College of Philadelphia.

I

In early February 1758 the trustees of the College of Philadelphia bravely sanctioned a rather unorthodox pedagogical procedure:

The Assembly of the Province having taken Mr. Smith into Custody the Trustees considered how the Inconvenience from thence arising to the College might best be remedied. Mr. Smith having expressed a Desire to continue his Lectures to the Classes, which formerly had attended them, the Students also inclining rather to proceed in their Studies under his care they ordered that the said Classes should attend him for that purpose at the usual Hours at the Place of his present Confinement.[1]

The trustees having agreed, the Reverend William Smith, Provost of the College, lectured to his moral philosophy class in the Philadelphia jail, and continued to do so until the first week in April.

Smith was in jail because the Pennsylvania Assembly had declared him guilty of libelling them by sanctioning the publication, in a magazine which he edited, of a memorial to the governor from a disgruntled Pennsylvania judge, a memorial the Assembly branded virulent and slanderous.[2] This was actually a trumped-up charge. Smith's real crime was that he had become politically active and a thorn in the side of the Pennsylvania Assembly, for he was outspoken in his opposition to its policies during the Seven Years' War.

Smith's politicization, extreme in its activities, peculiar in its objects, nonetheless typifies a process that many college faculty engaged in between the outbreak of the Seven Years' War and the beginning of the Revolution. Many of these men, usually clerics as well as educators, had apparently absorbed some of the civility tradition they had been teaching. They, who were already active in college and church, became to some degree ornaments of the civil state. Even though William Smith's political opinions did not represent these educators as a group, the ways in which the Seven Years' War and the alienation from Great Britain affected his politicization bear closer scrutiny as an example of the process.

Smith had been born, raised, and educated in Scotland where he attended (but may not have graduated from) the University of Aberdeen. He spent a few years as a schoolmaster in Scotland, then went to London to work for a mission society. Offered a chance to tutor in New York, Smith jumped at it. In 1751 the ambitious 23-year-old Scot began his tempestuous career in America.[3]

Always interested in education, Smith soon joined the group promoting a college for the rapidly growing colony. In October 1752 he published "Some Thoughts on Education" advocating the college, suggesting New York City for the site, and urging that money be spent on quality faculty rather than buildings. This pamphlet brought him to the attention of Samuel Johnson, and the two developed a close working relationship. Smith penned a blueprint for the proposed New York College. A General Idea of the College of Mirania appeared early in 1753, presenting several notable innovations, the most striking being different systems of education for those intent on the mechanic trades and the learned professions.[4]

Just how embroiled in the King's College controversy Smith might have become is hard to say, but he soon turned his attention elsewhere. Benjamin Franklin and Richard Peters, looking for someone to superintend the academy they had helped to found in Philadelphia, had made futile overtures to Samuel Johnson, and were then attracted by the educational ideas of his young protege. A complimentary correspondence concerning the College of Mirania led to Smith's visit to Philadelphia and the offer of a position. After spending the winter of 1753–1754 in England receiving Anglican orders, Smith took up his post in May 1754.[5]

William Smith established himself in Philadelphia just as the Seven Years' War began on the Pennsylvania frontier. It was the danger posed to the colony by the early fighting, the Assembly's response to that danger, and the larger context in which Smith viewed events in the colonies that prompted his politicization.

George Washington's defeat in an attempt to oust the French from their posts at the forks of the Ohio (now Pittsburgh) opened the way for French-allied Indian raids on white settlers and friendly Indians in western Pennsylvania. The English response, a military expedition under Major General Edward Braddock, produced not only a catastrophic defeat, but also a major political crisis for Pennsylvania. The Quaker-dominated Assembly had somehow to provide for colonial defense and it had to do it while accommodating both Quaker pacifism and proprietary restrictions on the ways the colonial government could raise money. The ensuing political machinations were complex, involving a split between pacifist and non-pacifist Quakers, confrontations between the Assembly and the proprietary governor over taxing proprietary lands to raise defense funds, compromises on this issue, and the drafting of a militia law that would both furnish a defense force and yet be acceptable to Quakers. Working all this out kept two sessions of the Assembly engaged for about a year, made permanent a rift between Assembly and governor, and involved a precedent-setting official breach of Quaker pacifism.[6]

Into this political maelstrom ventured William Smith. He began tentatively in a June 1755 sermon that was an oblique, disjointed critique of the Assembly.[7] But no such hesitation characterized *A Brief State of the Province of Pennsylvania*, published in the summer after Braddock's defeat. It was a direct and thoroughgoing attack on Quaker influence in Pennsylvania politics. Smith asserted that the Quakers had subverted the mixed form proper to governments, with dire results. Because the Assembly had gained complete control over the governmental purse, all officials in the province were Assembly dependents. This made the Assembly proud, factious, and contentious; it disregarded proprietors and their governors and was now separating itself from imperial policy by refusing to defend Pennsylvania or America. The French, well aware of the divisions within the province, had chosen it to begin their colonial invasion and would probably seize the whole colony once war was formally declared.[8]

Not only were the Quakers contentious, argued Smith, they were hypocritical as well. Pacifism based on religious scruple was a sham; self-interest lay at the heart of Quaker conduct. Politically, they feared a militia law would create, by extension, a whole new series of relationships in the colony that would result in future electoral losses. Rather than suffer this, the Quakers were willing to let Pennsylvania's defenses lag, trusting other colonies to rescue her. Out of avarice they turned down Parliamentary defense appropriations because they wanted their own paper currency, thinking it better for their business interests. Since the governor was prohibited from allowing this, no money was available for defense.[9]

Smith accused Quakers of taking special pains to dupe the ignorant Germans into thinking that proprietary government was tantamount to slavery, thus gaining valuable allies. This political union made reform within Pennsylvania hopeless. To save the colony and protect the empire Smith proposed that all Assemblymen be made to swear an oath of allegiance to the King and to declare that they would defend the colony against its enemies, and that Germans be prohibited from voting until they were well enough educated to understand the issues.[10] Since swearing oaths and military activity would violate cardinal Quaker religious tenets, adoption of these proposals would have debarred devout Quakers from politics. There can be little wonder that Smith's *Brief State* roused the ire of Quakers and their associates both within and without the Assembly.

Stung by criticism of his political commentary, Smith responded by arguing that it was part of God's commission to ministers to "explain to others their great interests, not only as they are creatures of God, but also as they are members of a particular community." He went on to hint that there was a cosmic dimension to Pennsylvania's struggle, describing the French and Indian invaders as parts of a "popish menace."[11] The war therefore, involved more than local issues.

In a May 1756 fast day sermon, Smith articulated the cosmic theme he had embraced. The address was a jeremiad, comparing Pennsylvanians to the ancient Jews and indicting them for having taken God's bounty in the form of the plenty of a new land and then turning their backs on Him. After enduring this for over a century, God ran out of patience and visited His wrath on the colonists through the invading French papists and their Indian allies. Yet even in the midst of this tribulation there was no turning to God: "Strifes, discords, hatred, uncharitableness, licentiousness, civil broils, calumnies, and contention about trifles have been uppermost in your thoughts." In the tradition of the jeremiad Smith proclaimed that there was only one way to lessen God's wrath—repent, reform, become good Christians and good citizens.[12]

The popish menace played an increasingly important part in Smith's thinking after mid-1756, almost balancing his critique of the Assembly. He preached encouragingly to British troops in early 1757, sure they would succeed, for God would not abandon His Protestant cause, not even when challenged by "Popish Perfidy, French Tyranny, and Savage Barbarity, leagued in triple combination."[13]

In the *American Magazine and Monthly Chronicle for the British Colonies*, which he served both as editor and contributor in 1757 and 1758, Smith carried forward his two themes. The November 1757 issue printed articles on the feasibility of a militia for Pennsylvania. In February 1758 there appeared Judge Moore's memorial to the governor regarding the conduct of the Assembly which would provoke it against Smith, as well as other articles critical of its actions. Intermittently through the issues, "Antigallican" castigated French customs, policy, and its system of "slavery," while warning Pennsylvanians at some length about the dangers of succumbing to luxury, vice, and corruption, for these paved the way for submission to French tyranny. Smith's own contribution was a series of essays under the pseudonym, "The Hermit." In July 1758 he explicitly linked the current warfare to a long-time Catholic conspiracy. This anti-Christian attack on English religious and civil liberty had begun with the Spanish Armada and continued with internal rebellions and several devious plots. Finally, "thus defeated everywhere in the parent land of Protestantism and liberty, our inveterate foes are making their last desperate push against our holy establishment, civil and religious, in these remote parts of the globe."[14] At the time of the "Hermit" essays, Smith was already in trouble with the Assembly. Shortly thereafter he went to jail.

Smith's jailing and a subsequent trip to England during which he persuaded the Privy Council to reverse his conviction[15] removed him from the ranks of Pennsylvania political commentators. By the time he returned in mid-1759, the war had turned in favor of the British and the question of Pennsylvania's defense was moot. Smith chose to keep silent thereafter.

Within five years William Smith had progressed from an unknown Scottish immigrant with some ideas on educational reform to a man widely known on both sides of the Atlantic as a churchman, educator, and political analyst. Most striking was his development in the last area. After having himself absorbed and subsequently advocated the civility tradition, Smith in these years began to apply his educational precepts. He not only became a participant in politics, but he also chose to embrace a specific politics: he supported the British empire against its French Canadian and Indian adversaries and so defended the proprietary prerogative against Assembly encroachments. In this process Smith was symptomatic of a group of clerical educators who were politicized during the Seven Years' War.

Another wave of faculty politicization took place during the dispute-filled years between the passage of the Stamp Act and the outbreak of the Revolutionary War. For the most part it was a new generation of college educators who became involved. There were even new colleges to serve as centers of agitation: Queen's College (now Rutgers) in New Jersey, The College of Rhode Island (now Brown), and Dartmouth College in New Hampshire. At these and other places, faculty participation in the political disputes that plagued Anglo-American relations seemed more natural due to the precedent set some years before. There was also some continuity from the earlier era, for William Smith and a few others had retained their positions and their inclinations to speak out. Again, Smith's attitudes differed from those held by most of his peers, but the type and degree of his involvement in the pre-Revolutionary debates were typical, so a continued look at his career is instructive.

Smith never withdrew completely from political commentary. He rejoiced along with other colonists at the success of British-American arms in the contest with the French. He mourned the passing of an old king and celebrated the succession of a new. He roused himself to defend the proprietary government from the Franklin-led attempts to replace it with the royal standard. And in the early 1770s he sharply criticized Connecticut's government and citizenry for trying to exploit the Wyoming Valley of Pennsylvania through the Susquehanna Company. None of these efforts, however, engaged his mind in quite the same way as the growing estrangement between Great Britain and her colonies.[16]

During the course of the Anglo-American debate Provost Smith suffered the agonies of one torn between conflicting loyalties. His nationality, religious affiliation, and even a sense of gratitude toward the British for backing his college all drew him toward support of Parliament and Crown. Yet Smith loved his adopted land and its people, and often felt that right and equity were on their side. As a result, he sought compromise and reconciliation long after most Philadelphians had decided upon revolution. It was Smith's tragedy to be a conservative patriot in an environment where that stance was often interpreted as Toryism.

Smith first spoke out publicly on the issues dividing the colonies from the mother country at the College of Philadelphia commencement in May 1766. He presented an exercise which praised the repeal of the Stamp Act, proclaiming that the repeal allowed liberty to return to America. The king was due homage for taking no vengeance on the colonists, and the members of Parliament who led the repeal movement were legislators comparable to Roman senators at their best. Smith then took the opportunity to suggest the best future course for British-American relations. Because of the repeal of the Stamp Act, Americans once more should recognize that "the cause of Liberty, Civil and Religious, is the cause of Britain herself" and that she had transplanted that liberty to the colonies. Union was therefore vital to advance the cause. "This sentiment, it is hoped, will more and more gain ground among good men both here and in the mother country; convincing them that to check the spirit of Freedom. . .here in *America* would, on the part of Great Britain, be to wound her own members."[17]

The cautious assertion of American rights blended with a profound hope that colonies and mother country would reconcile their differences was the attitude that underlay all Smith's pronouncements. Completely convinced that speaking out was appropriate, he tried to assume the role of mediator, striving to mute differences, glossing over hostile pronouncements. In the process he often seemed to argue that America owed subservience to Great Britain. That tone, which Smith would have said was merely an expression of gratitude to the propagator of the colonies, fellow Philadelphians interpreted as Toryism.

For a while Smith gained the respect of at least the conservative element of the community. He was selected to the Philadelphia Committee of Correspondence in 1774, attending a meeting that resolved to support Boston in her suffering under the Coercive Acts. Smith probably backed the resolution for he was the likely drafter of a letter to Boston that urged her not to pay for the tea destroyed in the famous party, arguing that such action would not settle the question of Parliament's right to tax the colonies. The letter also offered Philadelphia's support for a general congress to discuss common concerns. Shortly thereafter Smith wrote to the Bishop of London to argue the correctness of America's position on taxation.[18]

But these actions, strong as they were for Smith, did not keep him in the forefront of Philadelphia's anti-British agitation. Many fellow townsmen passed him by, not taking kindly to the ambivalence expressed in presentations such as his "Sermon on the Present State of American Affairs," preached before the Continental Congress over two months after Lexington and Concord. Manifestly, Smith was deeply torn by conflicting loyalties that prompted contradictory statements. He asserted that the colonists' ties to the British were their "greatest felicity," and that they were always "ready to maintain, at the risque of everything that is dear to us, the most unshaken fidelity to a common sovereign." But he then attacked "forced Devotion" to the mother country and taxation without consent. He implied that a people when deprived of liberty and freedom had the right to resume government themselves, but went on to state that Americans were contending for a final settlement "of the terms upon which this country may be perpetually united to the parent state." No matter how much legitimacy he granted to American rights, no matter how boldly he drew the picture of British tyranny, Smith could not bring himself to advocate separation, in the end praying for "the salvation of a great empire, and reuniting all its members in one sacred bond of harmony and public happiness."[19]

As Smith saw himself falling farther out of the mainstream of public sentiment, he actually turned more toward his religious faith, perhaps as a refuge from a stituation he was increasingly powerless to alter. In July 1775 he preached on the first public fast day proclaimed by the Continental Congress. He urged "the maintenance of Religion as the true way of restoring our lost peace, preventing the further effusion of kindred-blood, and healing our country's wounds, upon a true plan of Constitutional Liberty, which can only stand upon that just subordination to the parent state, which is for the mutual interest of both parent and children."[20] To many of his auditors, this was Toryism in the guise of faith, and they would not accept it. No longer would Smith be a powerful influence in Pennsylvania's Revolutionary councils.

William Smith's political sentiments placed him among the minority of American ministers on the eve of the Revolution, but once more his outspokenness typified a process that engaged large numbers of them. Politicization turned the bulk of colonial clerics into a "black regiment"[21] that greatly aided the American cause. Cleric-educators formed no small part of that influential band.

II

Smith's politicization resulted from his embroilment in colonial issues, his perceptions of the cosmic religious overtones of the Seven Years' War, and his immersion in the British-American crisis of the 1760s and 1770s. These developments caught the attention of other colonial faculty, who likewise chose to act upon the political precepts they set forth in their classrooms. The consequence was the creation of an atmosphere on college campuses wherein educators increasingly understood prevailing political discourse and contributed to it, having formed definite political loyalties of their own. Four collegiate faculties, at the College of Philadelphia, King's College, the College of William and Mary, and Princeton, remained thoroughly enmeshed in politics throughout the period. Americans came to perceive the first three as Tory groups, and Princeton's as the leading Patriot faculty. Others came late to politicization, but all had been affected by the outbreak of the Revolution.

At the College of Philadelphia, the most politically active faculty aside from Provost Smith were Vice-Provost Francis Alison and medical professors John Morgan and Benjamin Rush.[22] All were Patriots, but they could not overcome the impression created by Smith's seeming Toryism. Francis Alison, an Irish-born, Old Side Presbyterian minister who became Vice-Provost in 1755, provided a constant counterpoint to Smith throughout the pre-Revolutionary period, working with him to promote the college, often opposing him in provincial and American politics.

Alison shared with Smith a sympathy for the victims of French and Indian depredations on the frontier at the outset of the Seven Years' War. Protest against the Quaker-dominated Assembly's inaction on the defense issue brought Alison into politics. He criticized the Assembly throughout the war, and returned to public prominence in 1763 when he met with the Paxton Boys after the Assembly refused to hear their grievances. He worked behind the scenes to mobilize a coalition of unhappy Pennsylvanians so as to defeat the Assembly Quakers in the 1764 elections.[23] Even more significant than his actions was Alison's developing conviction that the war was a Godly test of America's virtue, with the Indians and the Papist French Canadians serving as agents. America passed the test, Alison concluded, and the future appeared bright.[24]

Yet Alison's now strongly developed political consciousness would not let him withdraw from civic affairs. He remained concerned about the problem of the responsiveness of Pennsylvania's government, an issue soon complicated by the efforts of a number of Pennsylvanians, led by Franklin and Joseph Galloway, to have the colony taken away from the proprietor and made a royal province. More important, as events unfolded Alison realized this contest had implications for all America. Through these years God was still testing the colonists' capacity to demonstrate religious and civic virtues. But now the testing agent was not the Papist French but the British, themselves now tyrants in the twin guises of Parliamentary laws and Anglican bishops. Alison's concerns thus grew to encompass imperial as well as provincial affairs. In this analysis, Alison did not stand alone. Other collegiate educators shared his views as they became politicized by the growing alienation of the colonies from the mother country.[25]

As Alison became convinced in the early 1760s that the movement to create Anglican bishops in America was serious, and that it might be successful, his fear of the Assembly Party's efforts to have Pennsylvania made a royal colony grew, for he was sure Crown control would further the Anglican scheme. Given these beliefs, he opposed the royalization of Pennsylvania. He worried that the Episcopal Party, concerned over its lack of power, would use royal government to try to tighten control over civil affairs, perhaps requiring a test oath. During the later 1760s William Smith pushed unceasingly for American bishops and the campaign for royal government went on. In 1767 Alison formally abandoned all political ties with Smith (the two continued to run the college, albeit in uneasy connection) and the Presbyterians once more tried to collect new allies who would oppose royal government. By this time so many Pennsylvanians were alienated by British policies that the Presbyterians succeeded.[26]

The passage of the Stamp Act forced Alison to analyze the imperial relationship. He thought the act unconstitutional and argued that the concept of virtual representation by which it was defended defied common sense. But it was the

Townshend Duties of 1768 that really angered and frightened Alison. He saw the twin engines of civil and ecclesiastical tyranny at work in his colony. The Episcopalian element had already subverted the values of the college, corrupting the students through promises of an opulent lifestyle and Church preferment. Now, he thought, the bishops would have ecclesiastical courts at their command to take away colonial liberties. It was a clever campaign to betray a people. The revenue to finance it would be raised by the illegal taxes that Parliament was imposing upon the colonists. Political and religious slavery loomed.[27]

In a series of essays under the pseudonym "Centinel," Alison made his concerns public in 1768. He outlined his fears, then analyzed the imperial relationship as he understood it. His arguments were simple. All citizens of the empire had equal rights and privileges, but because British and American society differed fundamentally there could not be one legal system, and governmental sovereignty had to be divided. Thus Parliament and King legislated for Great Britain, the colonial assemblies and governors for the respective colonies, and all were united by allegiance to the Crown and reverence for the rights of Englishmen. Virtual representation of the colonists in the British Parliament was unworkable, Parliamentary legislation on matters of internal colonial concern was illegal, and Parliament's authority over the external concerns of the colonies was historically established but not conceded as a matter of constitutional right. By the same token, the Anglican Church had no right to meddle in the internal ecclesiastical affairs of the colonies: there should be no bishops. If the British accepted this analysis and behaved accordingly, the colonies would remain content within the empire. But if colonists had to choose between equality and loyalty to Great Britain, American nationalism would prove triumphant.[28]

After 1768, Alison rarely commented publicly on events, but in 1775 he announced his sympathy for the Revolutionaries. In the course of a decade of political involvement Alison had become convinced that the true enemy to God's plan for His American Eden was not the Catholic French agents of Antichrist who would attack it from without, but the English high Churchmen and their governmental allies who would undermine it from within. As was the case for so many Americans, Alison had gone from patriotic Englishman to potential Revolutionary:

To take any man's money, without his consent, is unjust and contrary to reason and the law of God, and the Gospel of Christ; it is contrary to Magna Charta, or the Great Charter and Constitution of England: And to complain and even to resist such a lawless power, is just and reasonable, and no rebellion.[29]

The medical school faculty, assembled first in the mid-1760s, taught fewer students than did the college's professors but they were equally prominent in the community. John Morgan and Benjamin Rush were the faculty members most active in politics. Morgan was a graduate of the College of Philadelphia who, shortly after joining the medical school faculty, published an address on the reciprocal advantages of colonial union with Great Britain. Written in response to the Stamp Act, the address urged the British not to try to extort money from the colonies or to control them, and urged the colonists to avoid violence in response, so as to preserve mutually beneficial commerce. Morgan's essay was a counsel of conservative patriotism. He kept that posture until the military crisis of 1775 when he cast his lot with the colonies and the Continental Congress selected him to be director general of the military hospitals and physician-in-chief of the Continental Army.[30]

Benjamin Rush was a Princetonian and a native of Philadelphia who, like Morgan, returned to practice medicine after a British education. Even before Rush left for Edinburgh, he had been politicized by the Stamp Act. He rejoiced at Boston and New York resistance, hoped that the same would happen in Philadelphia, and deplored both Franklin's and the Quakers' actions in furthering implementation of the act.[31] Rush never thereafter lost his interest in politics. He claimed to have been converted to republicanism by a classmate at Edinburgh. Later, he joined a pro-American political discussion group in London where he conversed with people like Richard Price, Catherine Macaulay, and John Wilkes about American affairs.[32] After returning to Philadelphia, he began commenting about politics, working out his concepts of inalienable natural rights. A late 1773 pamphlet on patriotism called for resistance to the landing of tea in Philadelphia. It brought him to the notice of Pennsylvania resistance leaders Thomas Mifflin, Charles Thomson, John Dickinson, and George Clymer, which gave him an excuse to become a hanger-on at the First Continental Congress and to gain acquaintance with delegates such as George Washington and John Adams. When news of Lexington and Concord arrived in Philadelphia, Rush was heading a local effort to develop American manufactures and he moved easily to become one of Pennsylvania's first advocates of independence. He tried to impress his ideas on his acquaintances at the Second Continental Congress and also befriended a recently arrived Englishman named Thomas Paine. He urged him to write a pamphlet on the subject of independence and when it was finished, Rush suggested a title and engaged a publisher.[33] Rush always thought he and Paine together gave birth to the child independence.

Whether the agent of involvement was the Quaker activities during the Seven Years' War, the campaign for royal government in the 1760s, or the growing British-American alienation, the faculty of Philadelphia's college could not resist politicization. Some faculty were outspoken on current political issues at every point during the twenty years from 1755–1775. An association resulted in the public mind between the college and political activity. As we have seen, the faculty was not united on political questions; most opposed royal government in the 1760s and British policy after 1765, but Provost Smith's support for royal government and American bishops coupled with his conservative patriotism convinced many that the college was a tool of the Anglicans and the Tories.

The two other Anglican affiliated colleges, King's and the College of William and Mary, also seemed to American colonists to be bastions of Loyalism, with much better cause. King's College's Samuel Johnson embraced politics some years before taking over the presidency, due to the difficulty of promoting the Church of England in a colony with a Congregational establishment. As early as 1737 he complained to the Archbishop of Canterbury that Americans were both anti-monarchical and anti-episcopal. To remedy that, the Crown should "send us wise and good bishops. . .as well as governors (and I could wish a Viceroy) to represent his most sacred majesty in the affairs of civil government."[34]

A dozen more years' experience with the Connecticut fathers did not soften his views. Sometime around 1750 he catalogued his grievances regarding the colonial government. The basic failing of the Assembly was its independence, which resulted in legislation contrary to English policy and assertions that Parliamentary legislation did not apply to Connecticut unless it was specifically named in the act. The Assembly behaved this way because it was too dependent on the people. The only remedy for such perverse notions of the functions of government was to remove the conduct of it from the populace. The Crown should introduce a new constitution. At the very least it should establish common law, give the governor a veto, and make the Council less dependent on the people.[35]

The desire to have the Church operate under and play a part in forming a proper mode of government was a prime consideration in Johnson's association with King's College. And, when the colonists took up a course of resistance to British policies after 1760, he renewed his criticism of their governments, calling again for their reform by increasing British spiritual and temporal authority. He once more urged the establishment of American bishops and asked "whether it is for the best public good, that the Charter Governments should continue in their present republican form, which is indeed pernicious to them, as the people are nearly rampant in their high notions of liberty."[36]

Interestingly, when Parliament did assert greater authority over the colonies through such actions as the Stamp Act, Johnson became persuaded that ignorance of America, wrong-headedness, and corruption characterized the mother country's policy. No true reform would result from it and it threatened dissolution of the empire. By this time, Johnson was no longer associated with King's College and had seen others become more influential in the counsels of the Anglican Church than he.[37]

Myles Cooper succeeded Johnson as president of King's College in 1763 and in 1765 was selected president of the convention of episcopal clergymen for the Atlantic colonies (New York, New Jersey, Pennsylvania, and Delaware), thus assuming the mantle of Anglican leadership. A native Englishman, educated at Oxford, and personally selected for his role by Archbishop Thomas Secker, Cooper quickly became a controversialist for both the Anglican and Loyalist causes, the one tied to the other as the colonists resisted the establishment of Anglican bishops as part of the British plot to take away their liberties.[38]

Cooper worked hard for the cause of Anglican bishops all over the colonies[39] and as the opposition to them and to the rest of British colonial policy grew, he and other New York Loyalists formed a pact in 1772 to familiarize themselves with "all that should be published, whether in Pamphlets or News-Papers, and for suffering no thing to pass unanswered, that had a tendency to lessen the respect or affection that was due to the Mother Country." Cooper probably wrote none of the Loyalist attacks on American opposition that appeared in New York before the Revolution, but his close association with those who did linked him with them in the public mind.[40] His only known public statement on this controversy, a sermon preached at Oxford University in 1776, was harshly anti-American, arguing that the colonists had no reason to protest British policies, but did so because hereditary republicanism on the part of the people at large made them willing dupes for the self-interested few who, for motives of economic and political gain, were engaged in a conspiracy to foment rebellion and secure independence.[41]

Whether or not New Yorkers correctly perceived Cooper as a Loyalist pamphleteer, there was no mistaking what he wanted to do with the college. Smith and Alison used the College of Philadelphia as a base from which to work, only incidentally embroiling the institution itself in controversy, but Cooper strove to turn King's into an engine of Loyalism. Starting in 1771, he and the college governors tried to obtain a royal charter for a university to encompass King's College. To be sure, part of the project was curricular and administrative reform, but the larger purpose the governors voiced to Crown and Church. King's was to become a vehicle for "cementing the Union between Great Britain and the Colonies." A successful university would "diffuse a Spirit of Loyalty...thro' his Majesty's American Dominions."[42] No other college was so overtly involved in political affairs.

Cooper's Loyalism was matched by most of his colleagues. None of the others developed quite so great a reputation in New York politics, but four of his five arts curriculum cohorts and two of the three medical school faculty were also Tories. For example, John Vardill, a King's graduate whom Cooper hired to teach classical languages and history and who went to England in 1773 to promote the university charter, became one of the Loyalist pamphleteers. When war broke out, he became a British spy.[43] Samuel Bard, a medical school professor, sympathized with the American position regarding British policy even after Lexington and Concord, but he drew the line at independence and retired to New Jersey until British forces occupied New York.[44] Conversely, Robert Harpur, who taught mathematics and natural philosophy, and John Jones of the medical school became Patriots. Harpur inspired such a regard among Revolutionary New Yorkers that they elected him to the Third Provincial Congress in 1776, while Jones left New York for Philadelphia at the outbreak of the war, there helping to organize the medical branch of the Continental Army.[45] Despite the activities of these two men, King's was an overwhelmingly Tory campus, with its faculty eager participants in the political broils of the British-American dispute.

Similar Tory sentiments affected most of the faculty at the College of William and Mary in Virginia, but if King's College Loyalists could proclaim their sentiments in a relatively friendly environment, such was not the case in Williamsburg. The political activities of the faculty went back a long time and so did the animosity that existed between them and the surrounding community.

The one exception to this prevailing hostility was William Stith, who succeeded to the presidency in 1752. A native Virginian who married a Randolph and became chaplain to the House of Burgesses, Stith was markedly anti-royalist.[46] He made his stance public when he wrote *The History of the First Discovery and Settlement of Virginia* (1747). The most striking theme to emerge from the work was a pronounced antipathy to the Crown. Stith blamed James I for subverting the colony's ends from the first settlement out of a desire to preserve despotic power and a fear of Puritanism. James always acted toward Virginia "with mean Arts and Fraud," but that comported with his character which was "simple and injudicious, without any steady Principle of Justice and Honour."[47]

Stith applied his anti-imperial perspective to Governor Robert Dinwiddie in the early 1750s during the Pistole Fee controversy, which rose from an attempt by the governor to collect a fee for affixing his seal to land patents. Stith, still concerned about governmental corruption, branded Dinwiddie's action tyrannical and accused him of trying to line his own pockets at the expense of the people. He criticized the governor freely, calling his actions illegal and subversive of the people's rights. A majority of the House of Burgesses agreed with Stith, branding the fee unconstitutional. They appealed the action to England, where after the usual lengthy delays the Privy Council upheld Dinwiddie. The governor, in turn, called Stith an enemy to public order in Virginia, a person who sought to "sow sedition." Just how much of an antagonist Stith might have become for the royal government in Virginia cannot be known, for he died prematurely in 1755.[48]

Stith followed James Blair's tradition of championing the people and the Burgesses against the Crown. His colleague John Camm, Professor of Divinity after 1749, took a very different tack. Camm was an Oxford-educated Englishman who became a consistent and ardent supporter of the Crown's prerogative, especially when royal edict coincided with his personal interests. Such a coincidence occurred when the expenses of the Seven Years' War greatly strained Virginia's finances. The Burgesses responded initially with an issue of paper money. When in 1755 the tobacco crop failed they passed an act that allowed debts due in tobacco to be paid at the rate of two pence per pound of tobacco until the next crop came in. The hope was to prevent inflation, but the clergy, whose salaries were generally fixed in tobacco, were outraged at the loss of prospective income. That some college incomes were fixed in tobacco provided a gloss of altruism for the clergy's petition to the Bishop of London which claimed the Assembly's act was a purposeful attack on themselves and the college. The author, almost certainly Camm, asked for equity and an assertion of the royal prerogative, claiming that the college was necessary to maintain Virginia's dependence on England.[49]

This clerical protest angered both Burgesses and the Board of Visitors of the college. The issue simmered through two years wherein tobacco crops were sufficient to avoid fixing their value in currency. Then in 1758 disaster struck again and the Burgesses passed another Two Penny Act. Camm, already dismissed from William and Mary's faculty in a struggle with the Visitors over internal discipline, again led the protest, this time traveling in person to London to present the clergy's case to the Bishop and the Privy Council. The Council disallowed the Two Penny Act and ordered Camm restored to the faculty. The disallowance led directly to the famous suit by the Anglican priest James Maury to recover lost salary, a suit which Patrick Henry defended against by proclaiming that disallowance of a law passed for the general good of the people violated the original compact between the king and his subjects. Thus Camm's protest over the Two Penny Act helped propel Virginia into a posture of resistance to the Crown.[50]

The immersion of William and Mary's faculty in provincial politics continued throughout the pre-Revolutionary period. Tempers were kept aflame by the ever-present dispute between the faculty and the Visitors over who had control of the internal affairs of the college.[51] Since many of the Visitors were either members of the House of Burgesses or the Council, and since almost all the clerics who served on the college faculty were English born and educated, even these internal disputes took on political connotations.[52] But more important were the faculty's reactions to unfolding British policy for the colonies. The Stamp Act protests elicited criticism from Camm and James Horrocks, the college's president, who had warned about upsetting civil order and the necessity of obedience to constitutional authority as early as 1763. Yet, for the most part, the faculty kept its attention rivetted on the old power struggle, acting as if nothing had changed in the larger community.[53]

In the early 1770s the college faculty divided over the propriety of an American bishop for the Anglican church and went public with their dispute. A 1771 convention of Virginia's Anglican clergy voted in favor of the bishopric and commissioned Camm to draw up a petition to the king. President Horrocks left for England shortly thereafter (possibly to seek the office for himself), while Samuel Henley and Thomas Gwatkin, both first-year professors, voted against the measure. A pamphlet and newspaper war ensued, with proponents and opponents quickly making the connections between the religious and secular sides of British imperial policy.[54]

Compared to the enthusiasm they showed in the dispute over the bishopric, the faculty's immediate pre-Revolutionary activities were tame. Camm, as a member of the Council, was an intimate of Governor Lord Dunmore. Gwatkin was Dunmore's chaplain. The faculty as a whole publicly greeted the governor on his return from a successful Indian campaign in 1774, not long after his dismissal of the Assembly had led it to vote extra-legally to participate in a continental congress. They compounded this error by dismissing usher James Innes for joining the local militia company. These actions angered the public sufficiently that Henley and Gwatkin decided life in England presented a more pleasant prospect than remaining in Virginia, but Camm grimly hung on to his post and survived, unmolested, into the Revolution.[55] The resolution of twenty years of disputes between the English-oriented faculty and an increasingly American community, disputes in which the faculty mastered the techniques of political activism, awaited calmer days.

Princeton was the fourth colonial college with a lengthy pre-Revolutionary tradition of faculty political activism, but there the politicizing process produced Patriots, not Tories. Three of the men who led Princeton before the Revolution—Aaron Burr (1748–1757), Samuel Davies (1759–1761), and Samuel Finley (1761–1766)—came to understand politics through church-state confrontations. Burr had been active in the movement to found the College of New Jersey, which involved him in repeated contests with prominent New Jersey Anglicans, the East Jersey Proprietors, and various royal governors, all in an effort to obtain a satisfactory charter for the college.[56] Davies spent the late 1740s and early 1750s attempting to nurture Presbyterian churches in Virginia, thereby learning to cope with restrictions that colony placed on dissenters.[57] Finley, an itinerant follower of George Whitefield and Gilbert Tennent, ran afoul of Connecticut's restrictions on "foreign" ministers who preached without the consent of their local counterparts.[58] A fourth prominent Princeton leader, John Witherspoon (1768–1794), developed his political powers in Scotland during the factional infighting between the popular and moderate church parties.[59]

All these men became adept at politics during tense struggles of religious factionalism, but it was the Seven Years' War that awakened them to the wider significance of government and religion in British North America. For all of them, the war took on cosmic connotations, involving a struggle between the Godly forces of British Reformed Protestantism and the anti-Christian minions of French Catholicism and their heathen savage allies. Sharing convictions with Provost Smith, Francis Alison, and even Samuel Johnson,[60] these men believed the war had millennial overtones, with both civil and religious consequences. All this, these ministers tried to make clear to their parishioners and the wider public. On this base they built a political activism that would influence Princeton for two generations.

As leader of the Presbyterians who lived along the Virginia frontier, Samuel Davies recognized from the war's onset the military and political roles his followers could play. Early on he preached to dissenters using as a model of address the jeremiad, asserting that the war was a form of God's wrath directed at an immoral and irreligious people. The outcome of the war was, of course, in God's hands, but repentance and reform would probably restore God's favor. One method of reform would be to demonstrate courage and heroism in a Godly cause, and Davies certainly thought the war was that; moreover, it had significant civil implications as well. Davies argued that the war should be fought

to protect your Brethren from the most bloody Barbarities. . .to secure the inestimable Blessings of Liberty, *British Liberty*, from the chains of French Slavery. . .to guard such

a dear precious Religion. . . against Ignorance, Superstition, Idolatry, Tyranny over Conscience. . . and all the Mischiefs. . . with which Popery is pregnant.[61]

Davies continued to preach that the war was part of an apocalyptic clash
between Popery and Protestantism. Again and again, while in Virginia or even
after taking the presidency of Princeton, he hammered away at these themes,
urging his countrymen to demonstrate their religious and civic zeal by enlisting
to defend Protestantism from the forces of Antichrist. In the process, Davies'
view of his country widened from Virginia to include all the American colonies
and he repeatedly observed that the conflict would once and for all demonstrate
the viability of both British Protestantism and balanced government.[62]

Aaron Burr propounded many of these same themes. For him, too, the war
was a Godly retribution for the colonists' sins, and could result in success only
if the people repented of those sins. It involved the fate of both British Protestantism and civil liberty. And it had cosmic connotations. Like Davies, Burr
viewed the contest as taking place between the last bastion of Protestant Reformed
Christianity and the forces of Antichrist, and he expected it to have millennial
implications. For Burr, as for Davies, the war expanded horizons to the point
that he considered himself a British-American, not just a New Jerseyite. His
politicization awakened him to the character and needs of his country, not just
his province.[63]

Samuel Finley shared with Burr and Davies a developing attachment to the
colonies as a whole and clearly viewed the Seven Years' War from a political
as well as a religious perspective. He may not have imbued the war with the
same millennial significance as did Burr and Davies, but he did regard it as a
fundamental clash between Christian and Popish forces. He preached that the
war was being fought for both civil and religious liberty: "*Tyranny* is the *Genius*
of their *Government*, and *bloody Cruelty* of their *Religion*." A French victory
would leave Americans "robbed of their *Liberty, Property*, and *Religion* all at
once. . . . Shall we leave our *Children, Slavery* for *Liberty, arbitrary Government*
for *Law* and *Equity*, and *Popery*, for the pure *Christian Religion?*"[64]

In Scotland John Witherspoon proclaimed many of the same sentiments as
his American co-religionists. On the public fast day of 1758 Witherspoon delivered a jeremiad easily recognizable for its emphasis on national sin and the
need for repentence and reform before God would allow victory. Moreover,
Witherspoon conceived of the war as a cosmic struggle between the Protestant
powers and the forces of Antichrist. The sermon was indistinguishable from
hundreds delivered on the western side of the Atlantic.[65]

The political activities of Burr, Davies, and Finley took place almost entirely
in a period when their object was the preservation and strengthening of British
civil and religious liberty (although it would be revealing to know what Finley
thought of the Stamp Act). It was left to John Witherspoon to turn the thrust of
his political activism toward defending the American cause. During the years
after his 1768 arrival in America, Witherspoon familiarized himself with the

colonists' outlook on the dispute with Great Britain, especially their reaction to the Townshend Duties. He apparently imbibed their political convictions about the rights of Englishmen, the illegality of taxation without representation, and the powerlessness of Parliament over them.[66]

These convictions slowly made their way into Witherspoon's public discourse. His first pamphlet on the Anglo-American crisis appeared in 1772, contending that America had grown up differently from other countries because of the combination of her abundant resources and the British liberty the settlers had brought with them. This had redounded to the benefit of both Americans and Britons, but, not satisfied with naturally produced prosperity, the British had sought to exact more through taxation. This the liberty-loving colonists were bound to resist. Even the latest ploy, to lift the Townshend Duties while retaining the tax on tea, would not be successful, for the colonists were pledged to resist. By 1774, a militant Witherspoon saw no turning back in the crisis. He wrote arguing that the British king and Parliament would never understand or recognize the principles of liberty Americans contended for. He defended the Continental Congress and urged it to adopt resolutions which while professing loyalty to Great Britain nonetheless informed her that defense preparations were underway, that a trade embargo was in preparation, and that a plan of colonial union was contemplated.[67]

The worsening crisis after the enforcement of the Coercive Acts in Massachusetts in June 1774 saw Witherspoon turn from political commentator to participant. He became a member of the Somerset County Committee of Correspondence and later a delegate to the New Jersey Provincial Congress which passed a series of resolves quite similar to those he had urged in his pamphlet. When John Adams, passing through Princeton on his way to the Continental Congress, conferred with Witherspoon, he thought him "as high a son of liberty as any man in America." Once the Continental Congress assembled, Witherspoon journeyed to Philadelphia, consulted various delegates, and preached on several occasions.[68]

After Lexington and Concord, news of the war apparently made the Princeton president even more militant. By February 1776, he was, as chairman of the Committee of Correspondence, seeing to the arming of the militia. Within two months he was urging independence, first privately, and then in a strident May 17 fast day sermon. Again a delegate to the Provincial Congress in June 1776, he acted on his convictions, agreeing with the majority which accepted the Continental Congress's May 15 resolves suggesting the formation of independent republican governments and which also ordered the Loyalist governor's parole or arrest. That same June session elevated Witherspoon to national prominence by electing him to the Continental Congress.[69] Surely Witherspoon was the most politically active of all the pre-war college faculty members, but his was only the most extreme instance of a process that had been at work at these colleges for the preceding twenty years.

Although Witherspoon had learned the techniques of political discourse and activity at mid-century in Scotland, his first embrace of a secular politics came during the course of the American resistance movement. In this he typified what happened to faculty members at the other pre-Revolutionary colleges. These men came to politicization late and at some colleges the process made no significant headway before the Revolutionary War. Most faculty members did become politicized, however, gaining a reputation in their communities as advocates of the Patriot cause.

The Harvard faculty ended up demonstrating much the same pre-Revolutionary sentiments as Witherspoon displayed at Princeton. But there, while a tradition of political interest was long-lived, political activism came quite late. Edward Holyoke presided over Harvard from 1736 until 1769. Throughout his career he maintained at least a passing interest in political affairs. In 1735 he had delivered an election sermon to the General Court which dealt knowledgeably with political issues, asserting that since government originated with the people, they had the right to change its form if they wished. Throughout the 1750s and 1760s his diary entries show that he kept well-informed about the Seven Years' War and subsequent imperial policy. He rejoiced at Anglo-American wartime victories while lamenting such actions as the Stamp Act and the stationing of troops in Boston.[70] But he did not speak out publicly on these matters. Holyoke's contemporary, Edward Wigglesworth, the Hollis Professor of Divinity from 1722 to 1765, remained largely unaffected by politics. He preached a 1757 sermon in which he labelled the Church of Rome antichristian and warned of the threat that Protestant churches faced at the swords of their "Popish enemies," but this was his only public utterance that was even remotely political.[71]

It took the coming of a younger generation to infuse a spirit of political activism among the Harvard faculty. The men who served as president just before the Revolution, Samuel Locke (1770–1773) and Samuel Langdon (1774–1780), were known as ardent Patriots. Their sentiments enhanced their appeal to the Harvard Corporation which had itself become outspokenly political when Governors Bernard and Hutchinson instructed the Massachusetts General Court to meet at Harvard starting in June 1769.[72] Locke drew the support of John Adams and Andrew Eliot who thought him a "friend to liberty," but his patriotic reputation while at Harvard must rest on hearsay for no writings survive to indicate his stance on issues. After he retired from the presidency to Sherborn, Massachusetts, he was so outspoken for the American cause that his townsmen selected him head of the Committee of Correspondence and a member of the Committee of Safety.[73]

Samuel Langdon followed Locke to Harvard's helm at the behest of John Hancock, whom the college had elected treasurer in 1773 in a symbolic statement of its political sentiments. Langdon's record of political involvement went back some years. As early as 1760, preaching on the accession of George III and the victory at Quebec, Langdon described the war in cosmic terms as part of a Catholic plot to bring about the "extirpation of the protestant religion." That the British and Americans triumphed was due to God's favor, partly manifested

in the elevation of good kings to the throne. But good kings, Langdon emphasized, were those who protected both civil and religious liberty, who disclaimed
rule by divine right, and who did not promote passive obedience. Later, Langdon
reacted to news of the Quebec Act by preaching a sermon which linked the act
to his earlier themes, implicating British policies in the expansion of Catholic
influence in the world. The Harvard president capped his display of pre-Revolutionary patriotism by delivering the election sermon to the Provincial Congress
met at Watertown in May 1775. His message catalogued almost all the standard
Patriot themes. It was a jeremiad which bewailed colonial sin and promised
God's favor only if repentence and reformation were forthcoming. It attacked
British corruption as well, saying it undermined the constitution. Langdon described British policy as a deliberate plot to subvert colonial liberty, in part by
spreading Catholicism to lands claimed by the colonies. He complimented the
colonists' defense of their liberties, based as they were on natural law, government by compact, and consent of the governed. And he urged the colonists on
to victory.[74] The sermon confirmed official Harvard's patriotism in most striking
terms.

Other members of the Harvard faculty became ardent, if late blooming, Patriots. Most notable was John Winthrop, Professor of Natural Science and des-
cendant of the Massachusetts governor. He was relatively unversed in politics
until the General Court came to Cambridge. Then he met Massachusetts Patriots
and began to share their views. By the time he was elected to the Massachusetts
Council in 1773 he was adamant that British policy was an anti-colonial plot.
His sentiments brought dismissal from the Council, but his Cambridge followers
elected him to the Provincial Congress in 1774 and to the reconstituted Council
in 1775, where he rewarded them by advocating independence in the strongest
terms. Harvard's faculty, like Princeton's, helped lead the Revolutionary
movement.[75]

At Yale, too, patriotism came late although politicization long characterized
faculty leaders. Thomas Clap, the Congregational minister who presided over
Yale from 1739 until 1766, learned the ways of politics during the Great Awakening. His desire to preserve Connecticut and the college from the dangers of
enthusiasm and itineracy prompted him to oppose New Light preaching through
ecclesiastical pamphleteering, scrutiny of ministerial candidates, and by imposing
harsh reins on the revivalistic fervor of Yale students. But it also impelled him
to join with others of Connecticut's anti-revival ministers to put pressure on the
colonial legislature to have a number of statutes enacted to end itineracy and
make church schism more difficult.[76]

Clap strengthened his political ties and demonstrated real legal talent in his
negotiations with the Assembly over a new charter for Yale in 1745. Increased
powers awarded the Yale president under the charter tightened Clap's control
over the college and made him even more influential in Connecticut's religious
and political affairs.[77] Clap's prominence and power were put to the test after
1755 when his campaign to create a college church placed him in opposition to

Connecticut's Old Light Congregationalists. There followed nearly a decade of controversy, involving Clap in the religious split between Old Lights and New Lights, which paralleled the secular divisions in the colony over the Assembly's right to ''visit'' Yale and supervise its activities. During the furor Clap once again displayed his skill as a political pamphleteer and legal advocate.[78]

Yet, in all these years of political involvement, Clap never once seemed to realize that there was a larger political universe than the one formed by church, college, and Assembly. He remained totally oblivious to the imperial wars, both King George's and the Seven Years' War, thus differing markedly from his fellow clerical educators. He also cared nothing for the controversy enveloping Anglo-American relations. He was, for example, silent on the Stamp Act, the most serious incident to occur before he left Yale. If the issue was not religious and did not threaten his design for Yale, he was indifferent to it.

Not so his colleague Naphtali Daggett. His known activities indicate that he was Clap's opposite. Chosen Professor of Divinity in 1755 and chaplain of the college church in 1757, he also served as acting president from 1766 to 1778, all the while remaining aloof from the internecine squabbles of Connecticut's Congregationalists. Daggett was more interested in politics. He entered the Stamp Act controversy by writing a series of letters to Connecticut newspapers under the pseudonym ''Cato.'' They castigated Stamp distributor Jared Ingersoll, accusing him of corruption, tyranny, and disloyalty, and went on to question the alleged purpose of the act—paying royal troops to protect colonists from the Indians. Republication of the letters in New York papers fueled the controversy there as well as in Connecticut. Daggett also participated in the New England Congregationalists' efforts to prevent the appointment of an Anglican bishop. The Townshend Acts, too, drew his ire and it is reasonable to suppose that, like Francis Alison, Daggett perceived a connection between civil and ecclesiastical tyranny.[79] Yale's two presidents were no strangers to political activism during the two decades before the Revolution, but only Daggett embraced secular politics that centered on the pressing issues of the day.

The faculties of the other three colleges were also latecomers to political activism, but that was primarily due to the newness of their institutions. The College of Rhode Island was the first to begin operations, receiving its charter in 1764 and graduating its first class in 1769.[80] President James Manning and David Howell served as the faculty throughout the pre-war period. Manning, who attended Princeton under Davies and Finley, followed in their footsteps by becoming politicized in an attempt to end restrictions on dissenting religious minorities; in his case the cause was that of the Baptists in New England. The Baptists analogized their persecution to that of Americans by the British, and Manning joined Isaac Backus and other New England Baptist leaders to protest, even taking their plea to the First Continental Congress in 1774. Because of Baptist oppression, he was a firm supporter of the colonial stance against Parliament but advocated loyalty to the Crown until just before the war, hoping that the king might come to the rescue of New England dissenters. Once fighting began, however, he abandoned reconciliation, giving his total support to the Patriots even though he hated war.[81] Of Howell's pre-Revolutionary career not much is known. He practiced law from 1768 on and may have come to take an interest in politics through his profession. He was a Patriot, but his public activity in the colonial cause all took place after the start of the war.[82]

At Queen's College, much the same story unfolded. Chartered in 1766, the college commenced operations in 1771 with Frederick Frelinghuysen and John Taylor as tutors. Both were 1770 graduates of Witherspoon's Princeton and both became politically active in the pre-Revolutionary turmoil. Taylor, like Howell, became an attorney involved in city government. He joined the militia in 1775. Frelinghuysen, who apparently remained something of a protege of Witherspoon, was elected to the 1775–1776 session of the New Jersey Provincial Congress, where his votes showed him to be an early advocate of independence. He, too, joined the militia.[83]

Early Dartmouth was the province of the Reverend Eleazar Wheelock. He had resettled in New Hampshire a school for the education of Indian youth and in the process had turned it into a college, chartered in 1769 and graduating its first class in 1771. Wheelock, a 1733 graduate of Yale and New Light veteran of the Great Awakening, was more interested in religion than politics, and more interested in his college than either. Yet events forced him into political activity during the 1770s. His stance on the colonial defense of liberty was equivocal. He supported the non-importation agreement of 1770, but it irritated him for it cut off the flow of English contributions to his college. That English patronage greatly depended on the good will of New Hampshire governor John Wentworth, so Wheelock did everything he could to appease him, including sending college labor to Boston in 1774 at Wentworth's request, to help construct barracks for General Gage's troops (Boston carpenters had refused the job). Later that year, when asked if colonials holding royal commissions should resign because of the oppressive nature of the Coercive Acts, Wheelock gave a confused and ambig-uous answer urging loyalty both to the Continental Congress and the Crown.[84]

The climax of Wheelock's flirtation with Loyalism came in a sermon preached in 1775, justifying his refusal to observe a fast day set by the Continental Congress on the grounds he had already observed one shortly before. While Wheelock defended his actions by arguing that to hold another fast day would be to confuse the supremacy of the temporal and religious powers, he also made it quite clear that he resented the patriotic zeal that forced him to explain his actions. He professed loyalty to the Provincial and Continental Congresses, but observed that there was "seeming inconsistency, or want of sincerity in their directing us to pray for restoration of former union, or constitutional principles, when they have broken up our constitution, or suffered it to be done, and introduced something of their own instead."[85]

On the other hand, Wheelock argued to New Hampshire and Connecticut authorities that the college could be a bulwark to protect the colonies from Indian attack in the event of war, proposed sending an Indian missionary to Canada to spy for the Americans, and offered a mulatto student to Connecticut governor John Trumbull to be used to prevent slave rebellions. In 1774 the Hanover militia began training under Wheelock's supervision. A year later the committee of safety of Hanover and three nearby towns met to exonerate him of charges of Toryism. And he wholeheartedly backed his two sons who joined the Continental Army.[86] On the eve of independence, Wheelock's true political opinions remained a mystery, but whatever his beliefs he had been impelled to political activity.

The college faculties on the eve of the Revolution displayed predictable political loyalties. Those most closely connected with Anglicanism were either staunchly Loyalist or reconciliationist. Those belonging to dissenting faiths were Patriot, although the range of patriotism went from zealous to conservative (or suspected, in the case of Wheelock). But more significant than the immediate pre-Revolutionary political stances of the faculties was the fact that at most colleges political activism had become an accepted part of faculty behavior, and it had been practiced for some years. That activism could not be kept from college students. Just how the faculties transmitted their political attitudes to the students is the subject of the next chapter.

NOTES

1. Trustees' Minutes, College, Academy, and Charitable School of Philadelphia (UPA), February 4, 1758.

2. Accounts of Smith's libel trial and his subsequent activities may be found in Albert F. Gegenheimer, *William Smith, Educator and Churchman, 1727–1803* (Philadelphia: University of Pennsylvania Press, 1943), 139–48; Horace W. Smith, *The Life and Correspondence of the Reverend William Smith, D.D.* (2 vols., Philadelphia: Ferguson Bros. & Co., 1880), I, 167–87; Joseph E. Illick, *Colonial Pennsylvania: A History* (New York: Charles Scribner's Sons, 1976), 233–34; Benjamin C. Newcomb, *Franklin and Galloway: A Political Partnership* (New Haven: Yale University Press, 1972), 43–44. For the Moore memorial, see William Smith, ed., *The American Monthly Magazine for the British Colonies*, 5 (Feb. 1758).

3. Gegenheimer, *Smith, Educator and Churchman*, 3–6.

4. Ibid., 8–9; Smith, *Life of Smith*, I, 24–25; William Smith, *The Works of William Smith, D.D., Late Provost of the College and Academy of Philadelphia* (2 vols., Philadelphia: Hugh Maxwell and William Fry, 1803), I, 180–205.

5. Gegenheimer, *Smith, Educator and Churchman*, 30–41; Smith, *Life of Smith*, I, 26, 39, 45; B. Franklin to Samuel Johnson, August 9, 23, 1750, December 24, 1751, Samuel Johnson to B. Franklin, January ?, 1752, B. Franklin to William Smith, April 9, May 3, November 27, 1753, Leonard Labaree et al., eds., *The Papers of Benjamin Franklin* (25 vols. thus far, New Haven: Yale University Press, 1954–), IV, 37–38, 41, 222–23, 260–62, 467–70, 475–76, V, 120; Trustees' Minutes, College of Philadelphia, May 25, 1753.

6. Illick, *Colonial Pennsylvania*, 207–15; Newcomb, *Franklin and Galloway*, 24–27.

7. "An Earnest Exhortation to Religion, Brotherly Love, and Public Spirit, in the Present Dangerous State of Affairs...June 24, 1775," Smith, *Works*, I, 34–37, 41–42.

8. William Smith, *A Brief State of the Province of Pennsylvania* (orig. 1755; New York: J. Sabine, 1865), 11–15, 17.

9. Ibid., 19–20, 22–24.

10. Ibid., 28–30, 40–42.

11. "Letter on the Office and Duty of Protestant Ministers, and the Right of Exercizing their Pulpit Liberty; in the Handling and Treating of Civil, as well as Religious Affairs...and more especially in Times of Public Danger and Calamity (Aug. 21, 1755)," Smith, *Works*, II, 6, 9–10, 12.

12. "A Sermon Preached on the Public Fast, appointed by the Governor of Pennsylvania, May 21, 1756. Hardness of Heart and Neglect of God's Merciful Visitations, the Certain Forerunner of More Public Miseries; Applied to the Colonies, in a Parallel between their State and that of the Jews, in Many Remarkable Instances," Smith, *Works*, I, 100–102, 104, 110–11.

13. "The Christian Soldier's Duty, the Lawfullness and Dignity of His Office, and the Importance of the Protestant Cause in the British Colonies (April 5, 1757)," Smith, *Works*, II, 166, 174, 172.

14. Smith, *American Magazine*, 6 (July 1758).

15. Gegenheimer, *Smith, Educator and Churchman*, 143–44.

16. "A Sermon Concerning the Conversion of the Heathen Americans, and the Final Propagation of Christianity and the Sciences to the Ends of the Earth" (May ?, 1760), Smith, *Works*, II, 331–32; William Smith, *An Exercise Consisting of a Dialogue and an Ode, Sacred to the Memory of His Late Majesty George II* (Philadelphia, 1761); William Smith, *An Answer to Mr. Franklin's Remarks on a Late Protest* (Philadelphia, 1764); William Smith, *An Examination of the Connecticut Claims to Lands in Pennsylvania* (Philadelphia, 1774).

17. William Smith, *An Exercise Containing a Dialogue and Two Odes, Performed at the Public Commencement in the College of Philadelphia, May 20, 1766* (Philadelphia, 1766), 4–7; John Morgan et al., *Four Dissertations on the Reciprocal Advantages of a Perpetual Union Between Great Britain and Her American Colonies* (Philadelphia, 1766), 5, 10–12.

18. Gegenheimer, *Smith, Educator and Churchman*, 160–61.

19. "Sermon on the Present State of American Affairs; Preached in Christ Church, June 23, 1775; at the Request of the Officers of the Third Battalion of Volunteer Militia of the City of Philadelphia and District of Southwark," Smith, *Works*, II, 273–74, 279–81, 286; Gegenheimer, *Smith, Educator and Churchman*, 160–62.

20. "A Fast Sermon Preached at All-Saints Church, in the County of Philadelphia, July 20, 1775, Being the First American Fast Recommended by Congress," Gegenheimer, *Smith, Educator and Churchman*, 114, 123.

21. For the application of this term to the colonial dissenting clergy, see Douglass Adair and John A. Schutz, eds., *Peter Oliver's Origin & Progress of the American Rebellion* (paperback ed., Stanford, Calif.: Stanford University Press, 1967), 41–45.

22. Among others who played minor roles were Hugh Williamson and Jacob Duche. The first was an anti-royalist pamphleteer in the 1760s, the second a Patriot preacher in the 1770s. See *DAB*, s.v. "Jacob Duche" and "Hugh Williamson"; Hugh Williamson, *The Plain Dealer; or a Few Remarks Upon Quaker Politics, and their Attempt to change*

the Government of Pennsylvania (Philadelphia, 1764); Jacob Duche, *The Duty of Standing Fast in Our Spiritual and Temporal Liberties, A Sermon* (Philadelphia, 1775).

23. Elizabeth Ingersoll, "Francis Alison: American Philosophe, 1705–1779" (Ph.D. dissertation, University of Delaware, 1974), 108–11, 114–36.

24. Ibid., 160.

25. The argument that follows has been greatly influenced by the work of Nathan O. Hatch, who has presented a similar analysis treating New England clergy from the Seven Years' War through the Revolution in *The Sacred Cause of Liberty: Republican Thought and the Millennium in Revolutionary New England* (New Haven: Yale University Press, 1977), 21–54.

26. Ingersoll, "Francis Alison," 116–17, 138–39, 152, 154–55; James H. Hutson, *Pennsylvania Politics, 1740–1770* (Princeton: Princeton University Press, 1972), 153–55, 209; Francis Alison and John Ewing, *An Address of Thanks to the Wardens of Christ Church and St. Peter's . . .* (Philadelphia, 1764); Francis Alison to E. Stiles, April 15, 1764, *Stiles Papers M*.

27. Ingersoll, "Francis Alison," 139, 145–48; Francis Alison to E. Stiles, June 13, 1765, August 7, 20, 1766, March 29, 1768, *Stiles Papers M*.

28. Ingersoll, "Francis Alison," 160–66.

29. Ibid., 172; Francis Alison et al., *An Address of the Presbyterian Ministers of the City of Philadelphia to the Ministers and Presbyterian Congregations in the County of——in North Carolina* (Philadelphia, 1775), 4.

30. *DAB*, s.v. "John Morgan"; Morgan et al., *Four Dissertations*, 22–24, 9–19.

31. David F. Hawke, *Benjamin Rush: Revolutionary Gadfly* (Indianapolis: The Bobbs-Merrill Co., 1971); BR to Ebenezar Hazard, November 8, 1765, *Rush Letters*, I, 18–19.

32. Hawke, *Revolutionary Gadfly*, 54–55, 68–70, 74–75; George W. Corner, ed., *The Autobiography of Benjamin Rush* (Philadelphia: Princeton University Press for the American Philosophical Society, 1949), 46, 60–61; BR to Catherine Macaulay, January 18, 1769, BR to——, January 19, 1769, *Rush Letters*, I, 69–71.

33. Hawke, *Revolutionary Gadfly*, 104–5, 108–9, 110–11, 116–17, 128–30, 137–38; Corner, ed., *Rush Autobiography*, 109–12, 113–15; "To His Fellow Countrymen: On Patriotism," October 20, 1773, *Rush Letters*, I, 83–84.

34. Joseph J. Ellis, *The New England Mind in Transition: Samuel Johnson of Connecticut, 1696–1772* (New Haven: Yale University Press, 1973), 99–122; Peter N. Carroll, *The Other Samuel Johnson* (Rutherford, N.J.: Farleigh Dickinson University Press, 1978), 137, 147n; S. Johnson to the Archbishop of Canterbury, May 3, 1737, *Johnson Writings*, I, 88.

35. "Proposals Regarding the Government of this Colony (1749–51?)," *Johnson Writings*, I, 148–50; Carroll, *Other Samuel Johnson*, 165–66.

36. Ellis, *New England Mind in Transition*, 181–84, 245–46; David C. Humphrey, *From King's College to Columbia, 1746–1800* (New York: Columbia University Press, 1976), 29, 23–29; "Questions Relating to the Union and Government of the Plantations (1760)," *Johnson Writings*, I, 297–301.

37. Ellis, *New England Mind in Transition*, 256, 259–60, 262; S. Johnson to William Samuel Johnson, *Johnson Writings*, I, 439.

38. Clarence H. Vance, "Myles Cooper," *Columbia University Quarterly*, 22 (1930): 262–63; Humphrey, *King's College*, 127. For this reading of the campaign for Anglican bishops, see Bernard Bailyn, *The Ideological Origins of the American Revolution* (Cam-

bridge, Mass.: Belknap Press of Harvard University Press, 1967), 94–143, and Carl Bridenbaugh, *Mitre and Sceptre: Transatlantic Faiths, Ideas, Personalities, and Politics, 1689–1775* (New York: Oxford University Press, 1962), 207–340.

39. See, for example, Myles Cooper, *An Address from the Clergy of New York and New Jersey, to the Episcopalians in Virginia; Occasioned by Some Late Transactions in that Colony Relative to an American Episcopate* (New York, 1771).

40. Vance, "Myles Cooper," 274. For examples of such pamphlets, probably written by Thomas Bradbury Chandler, see *A Friendly Address to All Reasonable Americans on the Subject of Our Political Confusions: in which the necessary Consequences of Violently Opposing the King's Troops, and of a general non-importation, are fairly stated* (New York, 1774) and *The American Querist; or Some Questions Proposed Relative to the Present Disputes between Great Britain and Her American Colonies By a North American* (New York, 1774).

41. Myles Cooper, *National Humiliation and Repentence recommended, and the Cause of the Present Rebellion in America Assigned . . .* (Oxford, 1777), 12–15.

42. Humphrey, *King's College*, 140–41, quotations 141.

43. Ibid., 150–52; *DAB*, s.v. "John Vardill"; New York *Gazette and the Weekly Mercury*, December 7, 1772.

44. *DAB*, s.v. "Samuel Bard"; John McVickar, *A Domestic Narrative of the Life of Samuel Bard, M.D., LL.D. . . .* (New York: A. Paul, 1822), 95–98, 102, 106, 110–11.

45. *DAB*, s.v. "Robert Harpur" and "John Jones."

46. *DAB*, s.v. "William Stith."

47. William Stith, *The History of the First Discovery and Settlement of Virginia: Being an Essay toward a General History of the Colony . . .* (Williamsburg, 1747), 41, 76, vii, vi. For an analysis of the piece, see Alden Vaughan, "The Evolution of Virginia History: Early Historians of the First Colony," Alden Vaughan and George A. Billias, eds., *Perspectives on Early American History: Essays in Honor of Richard B. Morris* (New York: Columbia University Press, 1973). Vaughan argues that Stith had access only to the Virginia Company Records, so his perception of the actions of James I was distorted by the evidence (34–35), but considering Stith's background and subsequent activities, it seems more likely that Stith's historical judgment stemmed from his antipathy to British interference in Virginia's affairs.

48. John R. Alden, *Robert Dinwiddie: Servant of the Crown* (Williamsburg: Colonial Williamsburg Foundation, 1973), 23–25, 27–28, 30, quotation 24; *DAB*, "Stith"; Jack E. Morpurgo, *Their Majesties Royall Colledge: William and Mary in the Seventeenth and Eighteenth Centuries* (Williamsburg: College of William and Mary, 1976), 116–18.

49. Morpurgo, *Royall Colledge*, 119–21. For the petition, see "The Clergy of Virginia to the Bishop of London, 25 February 1756," William Stevens, ed., *Historical Collections Relating to the American Colonial Church* (5 vols., Hartford: n.p., 1870–78), I, 440–46.

50. Morpurgo, *Royall Colledge*, 122–24, 127; "Address of the Clergy of Virginia to the King, signed by John Camm" and "The Court at Kensington, 10 August 1759," William Manross, ed., *The Fulham Papers at Lambeth Palace Library* (Oxford: Oxford University Press, 1965), 13, 246–47, 268.

51. This dispute is best analyzed in Robert Polk Thomson, "The Reform of the College of William and Mary, 1763–1800," *Proceedings of the American Philosophical Society*, 115 (1971): 187–201.

52. Anne R. Shearer-Shineman, "The Trustees of William and Mary College, 1750–1800" (unpublished seminar paper, University of Wyoming, 1981), appendix B.

53. Morpurgo, *Royall Colledge*, 146; *NCAB*, s.v. "James Horrocks"; James Horrocks, *Upon the Peace, A Sermon* (Williamsburg, 1763), 14–15.

54. Morpurgo, *Royall Colledge*, 165–66; Bridenbaugh, *Mitre and Sceptre*, 171–206. For the pamphlet-newspaper war, see George W. Pilcher, "Virginia Newspapers and the Dispute over the Proposed Colonial Episcopate, 1771–1772," *The Historian: A Journal of History*, 23 (1960): 98–113, and "The Pamphlet War on the Proposed Virginia Episcopate, 1767–1775," *Historical Magazine of the Protestant Episcopal Church*, 30 (1961): 266–79; Ray Hiner, Jr., "Samuel Henley and Richard Gwatkin, Partners in Protest," ibid., 37 (1968): 39–50.

55. Thomson, "Reform of William and Mary," 200–201; Jane Carson, *James Innes and His Brothers of the F.H.C.* (Williamsburg: Colonial Williamsburg Foundation, 1965), 87–88; Morpurgo, *Royall Colledge*, 171–73.

56. See Alison B. Olson, "The Founding of Princeton University: Religion and Politics in Eighteenth Century New Jersey," and David C. Humphrey, "The Struggle for Sectarian Control of Princeton, 1745–1760," *New Jersey History*, 87 (1969): 133–50, and 91 (1973): 77–90.

57. George W. Pilcher, *Samuel Davies: Apostle of Dissent in Colonial Virginia* (Knoxville: University of Tennessee Press, 1971), 159–69; Samuel Davies, *The State of Religion among the Presbyterians in Virginia...* (Boston, 1751), 19, 41–42.

58. *DAB*, s.v. "Samuel Finley"; Edwin S. Gaustad, *The Great Awakening in New England* (New York: Harper & Row, 1957), 74–75, 123.

59. Varnum L. Collins, *President Witherspoon* (2 vols., Princeton: Princeton University Press, 1925), I, 27–30; Martha Lou Lemmon Stohlman, *John Witherspoon: Parson, Politician, Patriot* (Philadelphia: The Westminster Press, 1976), 36–38.

60. Stohlman, *John Witherspoon*, 218–19; "A Sermon on the Fast to Implore God's Blessing on the Expedition against Niagara and Crown Point, May 21, 1756" and "A Prayer to be Used Daily During the War," *Johnson Writings*, III, 548–56, 641.

61. Samuel Davies, *Religion and Patriotism* (Philadelphia, 1755), 18–19, 23, 7–8, 13.

62. See, for example, Samuel Davies, *The Crisis...* (London, 1757), 20–26; "An Ode...for the Annual Commencement of 1759," Richard B. Davis, ed., *The Collected Poems of Samuel Davies, 1723–1761* (Gainesville, Fla.: University Presses of Florida, 1968), 208–9; *The Curse of Cowardice* (London, 1759), 5, 9, 18; *Virginia's Danger and Remedy* (Williamsburg, 1761), 25, 36–38, 45; *Religion and Public Spirit* (New York, 1761), 4; *A Sermon Delivered at Nassau Hall...* (New York, 1761), 3, 9–11, 19–20. See also the analysis of Davies' wartime sermons in Alan Heimert, *Religion and the American Mind: From the Great Awakening to the Revolution* (Cambridge, Mass.: Harvard University Press, 1966), 327–31.

63. See Aaron Burr, *A Discourse Delivered at New Ark...* (New York, 1755), 5–16, 20–23, 27–30, 41; *A Sermon Preached before the Synod of New York...* (New York, 1756), 5–30, 42–43; *A Funeral Sermon...* (New York, 1757), 14, 20–22; William Livingston, *A Funeral Eulogium on Aaron Burr* (New York, 1757), 12–14. Heimert argues that the sermon at New Ark was a watershed in Calvinist doctrine, for it touched almost entirely on British and colonial government and policy, *Religion and the American Mind*, 14.

64. Samuel Finley, *The Curse of Meroz: or the Danger of Neutrality in the Cause of*

God and Our Country (Philadelphia, 1757), 9, 13–14, 27, 31–32. See also Heimert, *Religion and the American Mind*, 327, 332.

65. John Witherspoon, "Prayer for National Prosperity and for the Revival of Religion inseparably connected. A Sermon Preached on Thursday, Feb. 16, 1758, Being the Day appointed in Scotland for the late Public Fast," John Witherspoon, *Works* (9 vols., London, 1765–1815), I, 276–77.

66. Collins, *Witherspoon*, I, 118–19.

67. Ibid., 132–33; John Witherspoon, "Reflections on the Present State of Public Affairs, and on the duty and interest of America in this important crisis," (c. 1772) and "Thoughts on American Liberty (1774)," Witherspoon, *Works*, IX, 66–72, 73–77.

68. Collins, *Witherspoon*, I, 160–61, 166–67; Stohlman, *John Witherspoon*, 98, 102–3; Lyman H. Butterfield, ed., *The Diary and Autobiography of John Adams* (4 vols., Cambridge, Mass.: Belknap Press of Harvard University Press, 1962), II, 112–13.

69. Collins, *Witherspoon*, I, 170, 176–77, 184–90, 196–98, 205–9, 213; Stohlman, *John Witherspoon*, 103–7, 109–10, 115–17.

70. *DAB*, s.v. "Edward Holyoke"; "Edward Holyoke," *Sibley's*, V, 269–70; Edward Holyoke, *Integrity and Religion to be Principally Regarded by Such as Design Others to Stations of Publick Trust* (Boston, 1736), 12–13; George F. Dow, ed., *The Holyoke Diaries, 1709–1856* (Salem, Mass.: The Essex Institute, 1911), 14, 18, 19–23, 29–30.

71. "Edward Wigglesworth," *Sibley's*, V, 548–50, 553; Edward Wigglesworth, *Some Thoughts Upon the Spirit of Infallibility, Claimed by the Church of Rome* (Boston, 1757), 6–7, 31.

72. Josiah Quincy, *The History of Harvard University* (2 vols., Cambridge, Mass.: J. Owen, 1840), II, 149; Samuel Eliot Morison, *Three Centuries of Harvard, 1636–1936* (Cambridge, Mass.: Harvard University Press, 1936), 98–99. The Corporation formally complained about the interference with their routine in May of 1770; see Donald C. Lord and Robert M. Calhoon, "The Removal of the Massachusetts General Court from Boston, 1769–1772," *Journal of American History*, LV (1968–69): 739, 739n.

73. Quincy, *History of Harvard*, II, 151; "Samuel Locke," *Sibley's*, XIII, 622, 626.

74. Quincy, *History of Harvard*, II, 161–62; *DAB*, s.v. "Samuel Langdon"; Samuel Langdon, *Joy and Gratitude to God for the Long Life of a Good King and the Conquest of Quebec* (Portsmouth, N.H., 1760), 16–17, 24–25, 29–30, 8–9; Samuel Langdon, *Rational Explanations of St. John's Visions of the Two Beasts in the 13th Chapter of Revelation, Shewing that the Beginning...and Duration of Popery are Predicted in that Vision...* (Portsmouth, N.H., 1774); Samuel Langdon, *Government Corrupted by Vice and Recovered by Righteousness* (Watertown, Mass., 1775).

75. "John Winthrop," *Sibley's*, IX, 257–61; John Winthrop to John Adams, June 21, 1775, April ?, May 23, June 1, 1776, "Correspondence between John Adams and John Winthrop," MHS *Collections*, 44 (1878): 292–94, 296–98, 303–8. Of all the Harvard faculty, only Edward Wigglesworth, Jr., who succeeded to his father's divinity chair in 1765, was lukewarm toward independence, hoping until the last that reconciliation would come; "Edward Wigglesworth," *Sibley's*, XII, 512–13.

76. "Thomas Clap," *Sibley's*, VII, 37–41; Thomas Clap, *A Letter from the Reverend Mr. Thomas Clap, Rector of Yale College in New-Haven, to the Reverend Mr. Edwards in Northampton...* (Boston, 1745) and *A Letter from the Reverend Mr. Thomas Clap, Rector of Yale-College in New-Haven, to a Friend in Boston...* (Boston, 1745); Stephen Nissenbaum, ed., *The Great Awakening at Yale College* (Belmont, Calif.: Wadsworth

Publishing Co., 1972); Leonard Louis Tucker, *Puritan Protagonist: President Thomas Clap of Yale College* (Chapel Hill: University of North Carolina Press, 1962), 122–31.

77. Tucker, *Puritan Protagonist*, 73–74; *Yale Sketches*, I, 772, II, 1; *PRCC*, IX, 113–18.

78. Tucker, *Puritan Protagonist*, 175–230; Edmund S. Morgan, *The Gentle Puritan: A Life of Ezra Stiles* (New Haven: Yale University Press, 1962), 104–8. The pamphlet controversy was heated; see, for example, Benjamin Gale, *The Present State of the Colony of Connecticut Considered* (New London, 1755) and Thomas Clap, *The Answer of a Friend in the West, to a Letter from a Gentleman in the East, Entitled, The Present State of the Colony of Connecticut Considered* (New Haven, 1755).

79. "Naphtali Daggett," *AAP*, I, 479–82; Lawrence Henry Gipson, *American Loyalist: Jared Ingersoll* (New Haven: Yale University Press, 1971), 158–61, 167; Ralph Henry Gabriel, *Religion and Learning at Yale: The Church of Christ in Yale College, 1757–1957* (New Haven: Yale University Press, 1958), 34–35.

80. Walter C. Bronson, *The History of Brown University* (Providence: The University, 1914), 14, 40–43.

81. *DAB*, s.v. "James Manning"; Reuben Guild, *The Life, Times, and Correspondence of James Manning and the Early History of Brown University* (Boston: Gould and Lincoln, 1864), 27, 208; William G. McLoughlin, *Isaac Backus and the American Pietistic Tradition* (Boston: Little, Brown, and Co., 1967), 101–5, 129–31.

82. *DAB*, s.v. "David Howell."

83. William H.S. Demarest, *A History of Rutgers College, 1766–1924* (New Brunswick, N.J.: Rutgers University Press, 1924), 59, 82, 88–89; *DAB*, s.v. "Frederick Frelinghuysen."

84. Leon B. Richardson, *A History of Dartmouth College* (2 vols., Hanover, N.H.: Dartmouth College Publications, 1932), I, 78–84, 89, 110–11; *Yale Sketches*, I, 493–97; James D. McCallum, *Eleazar Wheelock: Founder of Dartmouth College* (orig. 1939; reprint, New York: Arno Press, 1969), 196–99.

85. McCallum, *Founder of Darmouth*, 200–201; Eleazar Wheelock, *Liberty of Conscience; or No King but Christ in His Church* (Hartford, 1776), iii–ix, 19–20, 23, 26, quotation 20.

86. McCallum, *Founder of Dartmouth*, 198–99, 202; Richardson, *History of Dartmouth*, 327; E. Wheelock to Gov. John Trumbull, March 16, 1775, E. Wheelock to the Provincial Congress at Exeter, June 28, 1775, E. Wheelock to Silas Deane, August 26, 1775, *The Microfilm Edition of the Papers of Eleazar Wheelock* (Hanover, N.H.: Dartmouth College Library, 1971).

3

Politicizing the Students

Between 1750 and 1775 the majority of the faculty at the colonial colleges became politically aware and active. By the beginning of the Revolutionary War no college community had resisted entanglement in the Anglo-American crisis. Whether Patriot, Tory, or torn between loyalties, the college faculties were involved. In the process of drawing on their own educations to become familiar with political literature and to use that literature in their public pronouncements, the collegiate instructors realized that education for civic purposes, for state service, had taken on added importance.

An increasing tendency on the part of the politically active public to equate civic education with the preservation of American liberties reinforced this conviction. John Adams early expressed the thoughts of his countrymen in his *Dissertation on the Canon and the Feudal Law* (1765). Adams urged all his fellow citizens to cherish "the means of knowledge," to "become attentive to the grounds and principles of government." He wanted them to know "the law of nature," "the spirit of the British constitution," "the histories of the ancient ages," "the great examples of Greece and Rome," and to know how their British forefathers had battled civil and ecclesiastical tyranny. He was especially concerned about higher education:

Let the colleges join their harmony in the same delightful concert. Let every declamation turn upon the beauty of liberty and virtue, and the deformity, turpitude, and malignancy of slavery and vice. Let the public disputations become researches into the grounds and nature and ends of government, and the means of preserving the good and demolishing the evil. Let the dialogues, and all the exercises, become the instruments of impressing on the tender mind, and of spreading and distributing far and wide, the ideas of right and the sensations of freedom.[1]

Others, less specific about the role of the college, were nonetheless sure of the necessity of education to preserve and extend American liberty. Samuel West explained at length to a 1776 session of the Massachusetts General Court the relationship among good laws, proper education, and a free society:

Our governors have a right to take every proper method to form the minds of their subjects so that they may become good members of society. The great difference that we observe among the several classes of mankind arises chiefly from their education and their laws: hence men become virtuous or vicious, good commonwealthmen or the contrary, generous, noble, and courageous, or base, mean spirited and cowardly, according to the impression that they have received from the governments they are under, together with their education and methods that have been practised by their leaders to form their minds in early life.[2]

Armed then by their own convictions, reinforced by popular opinion, college faculties sought to implement the second element of the political legacy of higher education left them by their English ancestors. The development of a curriculum designed for preparation for state service increasingly occupied educators. The elements involved, the ways in which faculty tried to communicate this heightened concern for political and governmental knowledge, and the success they had in politicizing the students, are the subjects of this chapter. Indications of how the process took place may be seen in a close examination of educational developments at Princeton in the two decades before independence.

I

The students at Princeton, in common with those elsewhere, arrived at an awareness of politics in four ways: they observed the actions of their instructors and others associated with the college in the larger community; they heard what their instructors and others said to them directly, either from the college pulpit or some other rostrum; they imbibed the teachings of the faculty through lectures, oratorical exercises, and assigned or suggested reading; and they participated in the extracurriculum, that is student organized activities such as debating societies and other formal or informal gatherings. In all these ways, highly impressionable youths generally between ages 16 and 20, often from rural backgrounds, gained exposure to the political beliefs shaping their elders' ideology and conduct.[3]

We have seen that the Princeton pre-Revolutionary faculty was quite active politically, and it was increasingly sympathetic to the American cause as the years passed. Not only the faculty, but others associated with the college, became Patriots. Many of the pre-Revolutionary trustees were staunch resistors to British policy. Several of the Presbyterian ministers on the board, most notably James Caldwell, Jacob Green, and Alexander MacWhorter, preached patriotism from their pulpits. Elias Boudinot and William Peartree Smith served on county and provincial committees of correspondence. William Livingston, a future New Jersey governor, went to the Continental Congress in 1774 and 1775, while Richard Stockton attended the 1776 session and signed the Declaration of Independence. Even the college steward, Jonathan Baldwin (class of 1770), served as post rider for the Princeton Committee of Correspondence.[4] If examples of patriotic activity influenced the students, there were many models to follow at Princeton.

A more direct inculcation of political principles occurred when the faculty addressed the students on important occasions such as public ceremonies and commencements. Before Witherspoon, few of the sermons and discourses were political. Finley and Burr never addressed their students on these occasions in an avowedly political vein, but privately Burr, at least, must have been free with his thoughts. At his funeral sermon, well attended by students, William Livingston referred to Burr as "reverend patriot." "Of our excellent constitution he entertained the justest idea; and glorified in the privileges of a Briton, as much as he lamented their prostitution and abuse." Indeed, Burr was extremely critical of British public corruption: "How did he lament, that Britain...should at length degenerate into the shameful seat of venality and corruption."[5]

Samuel Davies presided at Princeton just as the Seven Years' War drew to a close. In the euphoria of victory he lavished praise on George II, George III, and their royal representatives in the colonies. But George III stood above all. Davies knew the king was beloved "whatever clamors are raised against the ministry."[6] He applauded George not only for his military successes but also for keeping the royal prerogative in check, for observing the rights of Commons, and for promoting mixed government. But Davies' most important lesson for the students was not that they should praise good kings; rather it was that they should display public spirit, that they always combine their abilities with a dedication to the common good so that they would serve their fellow men. Such service, which should continue throughout life, would include a staunch patriotism: "The *Christian* cannot but be a *Patriot*. But he who loves all mankind...must certainly love his Country." Those properly educated had imbibed sentiments "in favor of our incomparable Constitution, and the success of the Hanover family; of Liberty, the Protestant Religion, and George IIId which are inseparably united." By living up to their principles the students would "give the World an honorable and just Specimen of the Morals and Politics inculcated at the COLLEGE OF NEW JERSEY."[7]

John Witherspoon agreed that the Christian should be a patriot and that the student's education was but the foundation of a lifetime of service to his countrymen, but he had, by 1775, formed other opinions about the House of Hanover. He urged Princetonians to be frugal, moderate and orderly, to be concerned with their own salvations, and to be active opposers of sin. This virtuous conduct was necessary because, with the outbreak of war, only repentence, reformation, and upright behavior would save the country from God's wrath. Their morals attended to, Witherspoon had some practical advice for his charges. First, hope of reconciliation with Great Britain was impossible; its claims were unjust, its abilities to manage the colonies proved non-existent. Secondly, since most of the students would either be going into the field or some other form of public service, their primary concerns should be to adhere to duty, to strive for union, and to avoid factional strife or jealousy.[8] Burr, Davies, and Witherspoon delivered messages that reflected the considerable oscillation in colonial sentiments toward Great Britain in the years before the Revolution, but the admonition to their students to be politically aware and involved remained constant.

Occasional addresses championing patriotism in the abstract and resistance to British oppression in particular were no doubt influential and inspiring, but the real political education of Princeton's students took place mainly in the classroom. The structure of the curriculum did not change dramatically in the twenty years before the Revolution. The only new courses introduced were those on history, chronology, and belles lettres, beginning probably with Finley in the early 1760s and continuing thereafter. Witherspoon did urge degree-holders to return to Princeton for a kind of independent study "and fit themselves for any of the higher Branches to which they will think proper chiefly to devote their future application, whether those called learned Professions, Divinity, Law and Physic, or such liberal Accomplishments in general as fit young Gentlemen for serving their Country in Public Stations."[9] Still, new ambitions for older courses were more the rule.

Most important for politics were studies that had traditionally carried a political message—classical languages, oratory, and moral philosophy. In these areas, the emphasis during the two pre-Revolutionary decades was ever more political and increasingly the principles expounded were those that supported American resistance to British policy. Oratory gained stature through an increase in the number of exercises that the students performed, the addition of forensic disputations to the exercises, and the inclusion of modern authors such as Milton, Shakespeare, and Joseph Addison as proper models for oratorical presentations. Witherspoon even encouraged the students' own compositions.[10]

The classics that had been read from Princeton's beginnings gained political value in the years when the college faculty became activist. Xenophon and Homer among the Greeks, Cicero, Virgil, Horace and Livy among the Romans, taught the students republican lessons. The Greek Xenophon (430–350 B.C.) was an historian who wrote clearly and possessed good judgment. Yet most college students in the colonial period did not read his history, except on their own. Rather, they read his *Cyropaedia, or the Education of Cyrus the Great*. This was a work of fiction not totally unlike More's *Utopia* or Erasmus' *Education of a Christian Prince*. Xenophon's purpose, like theirs, was didactic, for he sketched out his version of a just government and the duty and function of a prince philosophically educated. The Princeton presidents thought their students would find something congenial in both the educational philosophy and the benevolent monarchy that the fictional Cyrus employed to rule over Asia.[11]

Of the Romans most commonly read, virtually all lived in the first century before Christ, the period of the collapse of the Roman republic and the rise of imperial Rome. Their works are replete with commentary on these developments. No college student, at Princeton or elsewhere, could escape familiarity with Marcus Tullius Cicero. Translations of parts of his *Orations* were necessary for entrance, while *De Oratore* and *De Officiis* were widely read during the regular course. Cicero was born about 106 B.C. and attained manhood during the era of the Civil Wars. He had a long public career, highlighted by election as Consul in 64 B.C. He was continually caught up in Roman politics, moving in and out of power with Julius Caesar, for instance, and finally was executed in 43 B.C.[12]

Colonial students studied Cicero for his style, but it is hard to imagine that they could overlook the substance of his oratory. His most famous orations were against Cataline, delivered while he was Consul, and against Mark Antony, delivered in the interregnum after the assassination of Caesar. The former attacked Cataline for trying to use bribery to gain election as Consul in Cicero's stead, for then conceiving a plot to murder Cicero, and when that failed, for putting together a larger plot to attack the Senate and burn Rome. Cicero was anxious to point out the danger to the republic should such plots go unopposed and unpunished. He noted how the decline of virtue and the rise of luxury, vice, and corruption in contemporary Rome had made such conspiracies possible, and appealed repeatedly for virtuous Romans to be vigilant, to prevent their liberties from being taken away from them. The later orations against Mark Antony, called the Philippics, branded Antony as a danger to the republic in many of the same ways that Cataline had threatened it. Once more the themes of corruption and virtue dominated.[13]

Princetonians used Cicero's *De Oratore* as a manual of style, but he had some pointed comments on the role and responsibilities of orators as well as how they should deliver their speeches. Oratory was of prime importance to the society and the state; the orator was the public's conscience and as such his position was eminent, powerful, and gratifying. But it was also a grave responsibility, requiring that the orator be well-versed in political and moral science. The surest way to accomplish that was through training in history, law, and politics. Cicero's own career was witness to that.[14]

Cicero's contribution to moral philosophy, *De Officiis*, was an attempt to render Greek philosophy in terms comprehensible to his Roman contemporaries. Thus he often used Roman historical examples to illustrate his points. His political observations emphasized that virtue underlay the citizen's duty toward the state whether as private citizen or public official, but in the latter capacity there must be an extra measure of disinterestedness. The examples of the Civil Wars and Julius Caesar demonstrated what could go wrong.[15] The citizen's obligation is patriotism, including the acceptance of public office and the sacrifice of goods, honor, glory, and life if necessary. The failure of the citizenry to live up to its obligations was what brought about the collapse of the old republic.[16] Yet rulers should strive to keep the interests of the individual and the body politic identical. To take from individuals unless the welfare of the state demands it is wrong. To follow that path is to descend into plunder and despotism, and no one need obey a tyrant.[17]

Next to Cicero's, the most widely read Latin work was Virgil's *Aeneid*. The young scholars must have thrilled to Aeneas' adventures, wondered what to make of the repeated intervention of the gods, and perhaps they struggled to keep the characters straight, but once more, if they read carefully, they would have seen a political message tucked inside this mythical account of the origins of the Roman people. Virgil (70–19 B.C.) was born near Mantua and educated at Cremorna, Milan, and Rome. In 43 B.C., after Caesar's assassination, Virgil returned to Mantua. Soon he came to the attention of Octavian, the future Caesar Augustus. Virgil began to admire Octavian and his work subtley reflects that admiration.[18]

Several times in the *Aeneid* the narrative halts, interrupted by prophecy concerning the future of the race that Aeneas will found. In Book I Jove comments that Augustus will have unbounded empire, will stop civil wars, and will bring peace. Book VI presents Aeneas' father's shade, who praises Caesar Augustus as extending the empire, but also as ruling without war—a man who can crown peace with law. Finally, in Book VIII, Aeneas sees Rome's future in Vulcan's shield. Once more there is favorable commentary on important events in Roman history, especially those brought about by Caesar Augustus. No doubt there would have been more such adulation, but Virgil died in 19 B.C., before the end of Augustus' reign and before the *Aeneid* was finished to Virgil's satisfaction.[19]

Cicero came to oppose Octavian, Virgil admired him, and Horace retained an independent judgment. Still, Horace's comments on Roman affairs, either direct or philosophical, permeate the *Odes and Epodes*. Horace (65–8 B.C.) entered politics after Caesar's death, when Brutus took charge of his province and made him a military tribune. He came to Octavian's attention in 40 B.C. when, on the occasion of a threatened civil war involving Sextus Pompey, Mark Antony, and Octavian, he wrote a poem, "The Happy Isles," counselling against war. He took the bold step of refusing to enter Octavian's service but thereby preserved his independence and became an unofficial "poet laureate" of Rome. In that position he witnessed many events associated with the decline of the republic and the rise of the empire. He was often impressed by the actions and policies of Augustus. His poems praising those deeds and plans probably earned the ruler a substantial measure of public support. But the themes that infuse his poetry are love for Rome, great patriotism, and a desire for her success.[20]

Although read as poetry, the *Odes and Epodes* abound with allusions to Roman politics. Some of the more famous, besides "The Happy Isles," (Epode 16), were written to discourage Horace's republican friends from fomenting a civil war (*Odes*, Bk. I, 14), and to praise Augustus (*Odes*, Bk. I, 2, 7, 10). Perhaps the most important poems were those on social justice and peace in the second book of odes and the six odes that begin the third book. These last describe Horace's social and political philosophy, apparently addressed to Roman youth. They pair contrasting principles: justice against tyranny, courage against cowardice, righteousness against perfidy, education against ignorance, patriotism against treason, and modesty against immodesty. The moral of these odes is that the exercise of positive social virtues will enhance Rome's greatness; exercise of the vices will mean her ruin. That despite Horace's confidence in Augustus he was worried about Rome's fate appears in a poem describing her social practices, "The Luxury of the Age" (*Odes*, Bk. III, 10).[21] Independent political judgment, patriotism, and enduring moral values were all there as secondary messages for the student of Horace's poetic expression.

Livy (59 B.C.–17 A.D.) was Rome's most famous historian. He wrote a complete account of the Roman people "from the founding of the city" (his title) to his own times. Unfortunately, most of the history was lost during the Middle Ages and eighteenth-century readers were confined to accounts of the Punic, Social and Civil Wars of the first century B.C. But Livy's message to students was not the actual historical account, but rather the purpose of the discipline. He thought history should strive to impart ethical good. For him, the most inspirational facet of Rome's history was the basing of her power on morality and discipline. Rome was remarkable, he thought, because she had so long preserved righteousness and primitive simplicity, and had only recently fallen on evil days through moral decay. Moreover, there is perhaps a hint that under Augustus the golden age of Rome will return. Livy's introducton tells his readers what he wants them to learn from his history:

Here are the questions to which I would have every reader give his close attention—what life and morals were like; through what men and by what policies, in peace and in war, empire was established and enlarged; then let him note how, with the gradual relaxations of discipline, morals first gave way, as it were, then sank lower and lower, and finally began the downward plunge that brought us to the present time, when we can endure neither our vices nor their cure. What chiefly makes the study of history wholesome and profitable is this, that you behold the lessons of every kind of experience set forth as on a conspicuous monument; from these you may choose for yourself and for your own state what to imitate, from these mark for avoidance what is shameful in the conception and shameful in the result.[22]

At Princeton, these works became increasingly significant, for both Finley and Davies urged their students to seek in them models of virtue and selflessness, to emulate the authors' characteristics. Witherspoon told his classes in lectures on history and eloquence that the ancient poets perhaps conveyed a clearer idea of things than did the historians; one might gain more knowledge of Greece from Homer and of Rome from Horace than by consulting old histories.[23] Certainly, with the greater emphasis on oratory, more students studied these works more closely than ever before.

For the same reason, new classical works entered the curriculum, bearing familiar messages. Demosthenes, for instance, had direct lessons to teach the students. An orator who tried to rally Athenians and other Greeks to defend themselves against the imperial aims of Philip of Macedon in the mid-fourth century B.C., Demosthenes pointed out the dangers that foreign conquest would pose to domestic independence and autonomy. He contrasted monarchy with the peculiarly democratic character of Athenian politics. He urged the preservation of the city-state and the rejection of imperial unity. Pointing out the dangers of standing armies, he pleaded for Greek citizen armies, not mercenaries, to take the field. At last he was successful in pitting Greeks against Macedonians. In 338 B.C. the climactic battle took place, but the Greeks lost, forever ending the golden age of Greece. Yet Demosthenes' speeches survived to inspire others worried about the dangers of colonial existence.[24]

Classical studies and oratory contributed to a growing political component in the curricula, which moral philosophy made explicit. In the middle of the eighteenth century moral philosophy was moving through a developmental process, its focus shifting from the study of the divine to the secular bases of man's behavior—to shore up God's coercive power over human actions with mandates from reason and nature. In the process, moral philosophy assumed an ascendancy over the rest of the curriculum and became the capstone of the student's career. And, as courses at Princeton and elsewhere demonstrate, an increasingly important facet of moral philosophy was politics.[25]

Direct evidence of the political content of moral philosophy courses before 1768 is slight. The involvement of Burr, Davies, and Finley in politics suggests that the subject must have been part of the formal educational program, but only Finley's lectures survive to give a hint about its content. Quite clearly, he addressed political principles and based part of what he said on Locke, as indicated by observations such as "the power of monarchs is from the people originally," "all rights are equal by nature," and a government forfeits the "power committed to 'em if they invade the rights of the people."[26]

John Witherspoon brought to Princeton a moral philosophy course that has survived in several forms. It seems to have changed little over the twenty-five years that he taught it; consistently, half its content was political. The other half treated ethics (personal conduct) and it, too, possessed political relevance for the students. Witherspoon emphasized the complementary nature of reason and revelation as bases for man's conduct, the supremacy of the moral sense as a guide for action, and the combination of all three in the application of what he called common sense. The object of applied common sense was virtuous conduct, which he defined in lectures on man's duties to God, to his neighbors, and to himself. Among the politically significant precepts were a concept of public good that was more important than self-interest, a discussion of rights that described some of them as inalienable, and a definition of liberty that equated it with autonomy. Pulling it all together, Witherspoon noted that the success of society depended on the virtue of its citizens; the college had a responsibility to promote virtue by inculcating knowledge and admonishing students to put it to useful ends.[27]

Equipped with common sense, the properly virtuous student then contemplated the political relations among men and the administration of government. Here were discussions of several subjects of contemporary relevance. Witherspoon discoursed on the state of nature, natural rights, the compact as the basis of society, the sanctity of private property, and the right of rebellion. Among the intriguing observations in this context were that governments based on consent were typical of the colonies from their original planting, that because society was based on voluntary compact all men were originally and by nature free and equal, and that preservation of the public good was the real end of forming society.[28] The forms of government were subjects of a lecture in which Witherspoon defined three simple forms—monarchy, aristocracy, and democracy—pointed out the advantages and disadvantages of each, and asserted that no simple form could promote and protect liberty (using Sparta, Athens, and Rome as examples of their tendencies). Consequently, mixed forms must be the best governments, but they would only succeed if there was a separation of power which could serve as an "over poise," counteracting the effects of possible corruption of the governors. Witherspoon noted the necessity of a sovereign power somewhere in government, again discussed the conditions under which subjects might rebel, and condemned passive resistance.[29]

Another important discourse concerned the law of nature and nations, most especially the making of war and peace. Here were explanations of the causes of wars, the means of prosecuting them, the proper nature of peace treaties, and the rights of neutrals. Still other aspects of politics useful to future leaders were jurisprudence and contracts. Among Witherspoon's pertinent observations were that a constitution (which should exist as the basic law of a state) was excellent to the extent that it prevented offenses and made men good, as well as providing for their punishment when their deeds were evil, that luxury should be discouraged for it always tended to the ruin of a state, and that the objects of all civil law should be to give society's sanction to morality, to set out the regulations governing contracts, and to limit and direct persons in the exercise of their own rights while obliging them to respect the rights of others.[30]

The value of the moral philosophy course lay not just in what the students heard, but also in what they read to supplement it. Witherspoon's technique was to present both sides of the argument on controversial subjects, make his own stance known, and then suggest that students read authorities to help form their own conclusions. Presumably, the sources he suggested helped shape his own opinions. In the field of ethics Witherspoon recommended Samuel Clarke, *Demonstration of the Being and Attributes of God, more particularly in answer to Mr. Hobbs, Spinoza, and their Followers* (London, 1705); Samuel Pufendorf, *De Officio hominum & civium* (London, 1673); Cicero, *De Officiis*; Lord Shaftesbury's *Characteristicks of Men, Manners, Opinions, Times* (London, 1711); William Wollaston, *The Religion of Nature Delineated* (London, 1724); and Henry Home, Lord Kames, *Essay on the Principles of Morality and Natural Religion* (Edinburgh, 1751). On politics and government he suggested Hugo Grotius, *Of the Law of War and Peace* (London, 1654); Pufendorf's *De Jure Naturae et Gentium...* (1st Eng. trans., London, 1710); Richard Cumberland, *A Treatise on the Laws of Nature*, trans. John Maxwell (London, 1727); the legal scholar John Selden's *Works* (3 vols., London, 1726); Jean Jacques Burlamaqui, *The Principles of Natural and Political Law* (2 vols., London, 1748–52); James Harrington, *The Commonwealth of Oceana* (London, 1656); John

Locke, *Two Treatises of Civil Government* (London, 1690); Algernon Sidney, *Discourses on Civil Government* (London, 1698); Charles L. Secondat, Baron Montesquieu, *The Spirit of Laws* (Eng. trans., London, 1752); and Adam Ferguson, *An Enquiry on the History of Civil Society* (Edinburgh, 1767). Underlying all of Witherspoon's lectures was the work of Francis Hutcheson, *A Short Introduction to Moral Philosophy* (Edinburgh, 1747) and *A System of Moral Philosophy* (2 vols., Edinburgh, 1755).[31]

Students did not have to purchase these books, although some no doubt did. Most of them were in the college library. A liberal policy of admitting all classes except the freshman to the use of the library obtained from the earliest days of Davies and perhaps before. In the catalogue he drew up shortly after his arrival at Princeton, Davies urged the frequent use of the library:

It is one of the best Helps to enrich the Minds both of the Officers and Students with Knowledge.... If they have books always at Hand to consult upon every Subject that may occur to them, as demanding a more thoro' discussion, in their public Disputes, in the Course of their private Studies, in Conversation, or their own fortuitous Tho'ts; it will enable them to investigate TRUTH thro' her intricate Recesses; and to guard against the Strategems and Assaults of Error... and give at least such Hints, as their Invention may improve upon, when they appear in public Life.[32]

The library, some 800 titles in 1760, grew through gifts after Davies' administration and Witherspoon brought perhaps 400 works with him from Scotland. It contained not only almost all the titles suggested by Witherspoon but others as well that would have acquainted students with political thought and historical examples. A sampling includes Plutarch's *Lives*, Tacitus' *Germania*, Bishop Neal's and Thomas Prince's histories of the Puritans, Cato's *Letters*, the ancient history of Thucydides, the history of England by Paul de Rapin-Thoyras, the history of Charles V by Robertson, and the moral works of Doddridge, Watts, and Burgh.[33] There was much to be learned in Princeton's books if the students wanted to avail themselves of the knowledge.

Through example, through lecture and oratorical example, through assigned and suggested reading, through the acquisition of works for the library, Princeton's faculty sought to inculcate in the students precepts of virtue and principles of politics. Were they successful? Did students absorb the lessons their elders sought to impress upon them? Obviously, not all of them did, at Princeton or elsewhere. Some students were immature and derived little from college. Some were not bright and academic standards were not generally rigorous. Some were not interested in politics; some were more interested in play than study. And there is evidence, especially for William and Mary, that some students pursued higher education more for the status it conferred than for the knowledge it conveyed.[34] Even for attentive students, the degree of influence must be derived inferentially, for no student recorded then or later some great principle that affected his political choices or behavior and then attributed it directly to his college education. Nevertheless, a strong case for faculty influence exists. For many students, while in college or later, acted in ways that were sanctioned, even encouraged, by their teachers, and they justified those actions by invoking principles they had heard in the classroom, albeit they might have heard them elsewhere as well.

The collegiate behavior that demonstrates the effects of the educational experience on student beliefs I call the extracurriculum. One of its elements was student oratorical performance in class, at commencement, or in student debating societies. All these venues are included because the student selected the topic for his performance even if from a limited range and even if classroom and commencement orations necessitated supervision by the faculty.[35] Other expressions of student sentiment occurred in the formal and informal gatherings they held, which ranged from student pranks to formal protest meetings. Indirectly connected to these group experiences was student correspondence, often revealing to friends and family convictions hidden from classmates.

Very little evidence survives of the oratorical exercises that accompanied coursework. From the mid-1760s on, students declaimed or read weekly from Demosthenes, Livy, and Cicero, as well as various modern authors. Witherspoon increased the amount of oratorical practice, emphasized forensic disputation, and allowed students to pick their own subjects.[36] Just what subjects students addressed in class is not known, but one can assume that in-class oratory must have had some connection with public performances. There the sentiments came forth clearly and a pattern emerged during the years before the Revolution.

Before 1765, commencement orations were rarely political. The few that were expressed support for the British political system and its success in the Seven Years' War. But most of the exercises were ethical or theological. Politics had not yet become a prime concern.[37]

With the commencement of 1765 a new stress on politics appeared, and students were actively patriotic for the first time. The exercises, held in the context of the New Jersey Stamp Act protests, included a valedictory oration on "patriotism," and other orations on "Liberty," "Economy," "Frugality," and "Industry." The senior class, supporting the boycott movement, wore American homespun.[38] The student orations revealed an understanding of the values motivating colonial protest, and their actions showed they shared the outrage of their fellow colonists. That President Finley did not suppress this activity may tell us something about his own attitude toward the Stamp Act.

Subsequent commencements saw the student political commentary echoing the rising and falling tensions between the colonies and the mother country. Orators in 1766 again discussed "Liberty" and "Patriotism." The 1768 commencement, the first presided over by Witherspoon, took place in the midst of the agitation over the Townshend Duties. Students reflected the president's moral philosophy lectures as they debated the propositions "It is in the Interest of any nation, to have the Trade of its new Countries, as free from Embarrassments as possible," and "It is lawful for every Man, and in many Cases, his indispensable

Duty, to hazard his Life in defense of his Civil Liberty.''[39] James Madison, one of the 1769 graduates, heard his fellows address "The Present State of Political Affairs." He may also have learned something of the sharing of political convictions among faculty, trustees, and students, for he saw honorary degrees conferred on John Dickinson, author of *Letters from a Farmer in Pennsylvania*, on John Hancock, lately a victim of the Massachusetts Customs Commissioners, and on Joseph Galloway, Speaker of the Pennsylvania Assembly, not yet seen as the Loyalist he would later become.[40]

Early 1770s commencements followed the fate of the Townshend Duties. Before repeal was known, graduates wore homespun, while one student asserted that "the Non-Importation Agreement reflects a Glory on the American Merchants, and was a noble Exertion of Self-Denial and Public Spirit." James Witherspoon wove his father's teachings into a defense of the thesis that the law of nature obliged subjects to resist tyrannical kings, while others orated on the utility of American manufactures.[41] After the Townshend Duties were repealed, commencement exercises were less overtly political. Most orations were on traditional ethical lines. But before dismissing the traditional, consideration of the role of these topics in Witherspoon's philosophy is in order. For instance, there occurred a dispute on the proposition "Moral Qualities are confessedly more excellent than natural; yet the latter are much more envied in the possessor by the generality of mankind; a sure sign of the corrupt bias of human nature." In Witherspoon's lectures, discussion of the absence of moral commitment, of the corruption of human nature, served to introduce his idea of the need for "over poise" in government, and in a more general sense the conviction that society was tending toward corruption underlay the cosmic view of the course of events in the colonies. It made possible the jeremiads that Witherspoon preached to arouse the people.[42] Thus an exploration of fundamental values rather than current events did not mean the abandonment of politics. It signified political commentary on another level.

Several 1772 exercises explicated other aspects of Witherspoon's political creed. There was a disputation on the proposition "A mixed Monarchy is the best Form of Government," and orations on "Passive Obedience and Non-Resistance," "Independence of Spirit," "The Advantages of Political Liberty," and "Political Jealousy is a Laudable Passion." All these subjects appeared in the lectures.[43]

Witherspoon favored these student discussions. He wrote a broadly circulated appeal for funds in 1772 in which he praised "the spirit of liberty [which] breathed high and strong" among both students and faculty. But there were conservatives in New Jersey who thought such political commentary was unsuited to young minds and had no place in an academic setting.[44] This criticism made the trustees nervous. They responded by ordering that in future the topics and texts had to be cleared by the president four weeks before the commencement. Deviation from the submitted text would bring an end to the exercise.[45]

In this somewhat oppressive atmosphere, the 1773 and 1774 exercises were relatively tame, the former especially because New Jersey's royal governor, William Franklin, attended.[46] But by the time commencement took place in 1775, New Jersey had gone a long way toward independence, with both trustees and faculty in the vanguard. Once more the students could attend in homespun and the principal themes of the exercises, "The pernicious Effects of arbitrary Power" and "The Growth and Decline of Empires," while heard before, took on ominous new overtones when summing up a decade of protest.[47]

The private activities of the students paralleled their corporate, public demonstrations. The wearing of homespun at commencements was the extent of their activities until the late 1760s; then they formed the Whig Society in 1769 and the Cliosophic Society in 1770. The early society records fell victim to fire, but it is known that oratory was the focus of the meetings, featuring speeches, declamations, and disputes. Considering what they produced publicly, it is likely that similar subjects captured their interests privately. Another inference concerning the society exercises comes from the content of their libraries. Apparently, there were more contemporary political tracts belonging to the students' than to the college library, and by the eve of the Revolution *The Independent Reflector* of King's College controversy fame had become a model for student declamations.[48]

In the 1770s the students became more militant. When, in mid-1770, the non-importation agreement among American merchants came apart, the students registered their protest. As James Madison described it in a letter home, "We have no publick news but the base conduct of the merchants in New York in breaking through their spirited resolutions not to import. . . . Their letter to the merchants in Philadelphia requesting their concurrence was lately burnt by the Students of this place in the college Yard, all of them appearing in their black Gowns and the bell Tolling." A few days later the students once again resolved to wear homespun to commencement. They no doubt were pleased by the favorable response accorded their actions by New York and Philadelphia newspapers.[49]

As the early 1770s went by, patriotic students put pressure on their conservative peers to reform their political views. In 1774 their sense of outrage at British actions exploded. According to underclassman Charles Beatty, "we gathered all the Steward's winter Store of Tea, and all the students had in college, and having made a fire in the Campus, we there burnt near a dozen pound, tolled the bell and made many spirited resolves." They also burnt an effigy of Massachusetts Governor Thomas Hutchinson. This was at the end of January. In early February the students and college officers met in solemn ceremony to swear off tea drinking. Then the students sought to impose their will on the community, relieving a local tea drinker of his supply on February 7, and burning it in the streets of Princeton.[50] By June the students had formed a militia company. Enthusiasm flagged a bit at the end of the year, but after Lexington and Concord, student spirit picked up again. The college began to lose members to the New Jersey militia; those who stayed behind were also infused with martial spirit. Charles

Beatty wrote his sister what the campus was like: "You have heard of the skirmishes at Boston, and can you not sympathize with the distressed people there—you need not speak here without it is about Liberty—Every man handles his musket and hastens in his preparations for war—We have a company in college of about 50 officers and all among ourselves."[51]

The actions of the students, the sentiments they expressed, indicate that the faculty was successful in orienting the curriculum to inculcate virtue, to produce an interest in and knowledge of politics, and to instill patriotism. A profile of the matriculants during these years provides more proof. Of the 338 matriculants in the years before Witherspoon became president, 279 were still alive at the end of 1775. Only three percent were identifiably Loyalist, eighty-eight held some post of military responsibility during the war, and over one-third occupied public office of some sort. Out of Witherspoon's pre-Revolutionary classes, nearly half of the 178 matriculants fought in the war, only two were Loyalists, and forty-one held significant state or national offices.[52] Princeton was the premier Patriot college.

<h1 style="text-align:center">II</h1>

Princeton and the other Patriot colleges discussed below, for which it serves as a detailed illustration, taught not just a value system and a pro-American politics. Rather, they taught a particular value system and politics that have been established in recent years as the principal intellectual influence on the American Revolutionary elite. Through the work of Caroline Robbins, Bernard Bailyn, Gordon Wood, Trevor Colbourn, Lance Banning, J.G.A. Pocock and others, we have learned that the "Commonwealth" or "Country Whig" ideology permeated the thinking and writing of almost all the leading Revolutionaries.[53]

There were, to use Bailyn's term, several "sources and traditions" that contributed to the ideology. Revolutionaries had a passing acquaintance with the classics, but their greatest interest was in the political history surrounding the rise and fall of the Greek and Roman republics. For this they needed only to consult Plutarch, Livy, Cicero, Sallust and Tacitus. What they learned from these authors was that the republics at their height depended on virtuous people and once prosperity led to venality and corruption those republics collapsed. Ancient times thus served to illustrate what might happen again, and colonists marvelled at the similarities to modern history. Another contributor to Revolutionary ideology was Enlightenment rationalism. Colonists read John Locke on natural rights and on the social and governmental compacts. They read Montesquieu on British liberty and the forms of government best designed to preserve it. Voltaire taught them the evils of clerical oppression, Beccaria the necessity for reforming criminal laws. Grotius, Pufendorf, Burlamaqui, and Vattel held forth on the laws of nature and nations, and on the principles of civil government. Again the knowledge was superficial, but it contributed to the development of a Revolutionary world view. A third influence was that of the common law, a tradition of historical judgments concerning rights, equity, and the operation of government, available through the work of Coke, Blackstone, and Camden. New England Puritanism added yet another strand to the ideological fabric, asserting that what happened in America was part of God's plan, leading somehow to the millennium. Colonists who read Daniel Neal or Thomas Prince on the New England experience, or who got it secondhand from their ministers, knew that the evolution of American history was divinely ordered.[54]

Uniting all these disparate strands of thought, giving them shape and substance, were the works of those who sought to explain and justify the Commonwealth experiment of Oliver Cromwell and their followers of the country opposition in the late seventeenth and early eighteenth centuries. Bailyn points to John Milton in his political role, to James Harrington, Henry Neville, and Algernon Sidney among the Commonwealthmen. John Trenchard and Thomas Gordon, Robert Molesworth, Viscount Bolingbroke, Francis Hutcheson, Philip Doddridge, and Isaac Watts comprised the next generation of country political commentators. In the years before the Revolution a younger group, Richard Price, Joseph Priestley, John Cartwright, James Burgh, Catherine Macaulay, and Paul de Rapin-Thoyras, kept the tradition alive.[55]

The principal themes of the Commonwealth ideology centered on the existence of natural rights and of a contractual basis for society and government. The Commonwealthmen explained how these concepts underlay the English mixed constitution, making it uniquely able to preserve British liberty. In this the Commonwealthmen differed not at all from the mainstream English political writers of the eighteenth century. What set them apart was their belief that since the Revolution of 1688 British liberty was disappearing due to the people's loss of virtue and the government's corruption. If not stemmed, this progress would result in political slavery for the British. The Commonwealthmen urged vigilance and ultimately rebellion against the government if it continued to violate the people's rights. The bulk of the critique focused on the activities of the British ministry under Sir Robert Walpole during the 1720s and 1730s, but because of the way the colonists understood the operation of their own governments and societies, the critique seemed readily applicable to America. British imperial policy after 1763 seemed but British domestic policy and royal government in the colonies writ large. The pattern was familiar—and threatening.[56]

One reason this ideology so appealed to colonists was that it fit their concept of the way history worked. They believed history was cyclical; it behaved according to laws. One set of those laws governed the rise and fall of empires according to the prevalence of virtue or vice among their people. A subsidiary application of that set of laws viewed the English as originally pure and uncorrupt Saxons who were contaminated by Norman feudalism and who had struggled since the conquest to throw off Norman influence on their government and institutions. Various milestones had been reached in this process, the latest of which was the Revolution of 1688, but as was often the case, backsliding had occurred in the eighteenth century. The colonies, largely founded during the contest between Stuart absolutism and Parliamentary resistance, had escaped for a while from the cycles of history, but British imperial policy seemed to be pulling them inexorably back into the maelstrom. Again, it was cause for alarm.[57]

The Commonwealth Whig view of history thus provided another strain of thought to Revolutionary ideology. Many of its proponents have already been mentioned, but others merit notice. Colonists read popularizers of classical history who often editorialized on their subjects. Among the best known were Charles Rollin, Edward Montagu, Walter Moyle, and Oliver Goldsmith. Medieval history, too, had its Commonwealth interpreters—Thomas Gordon, Lord Kames, Obadiah Hulme. The later era of the Tudors, Stuarts, and Hanoverians received its most famous treatment from the aforementioned Rapin-Thoyras and Macaulay, but William Molyneaux and Sir William Temple also contributed to the colonists' understanding. A thorough reading of these historians went far to prepare American minds for revolution.[58]

Prevalent in virtually all of the component parts of the Commonwealth Whig ideology was an emphasis on the collective virtue of the people, called by many public virtue. This virtue consisted of the time-honored individual virtues of industry, frugality, and honesty, and added to them patriotism. The exercise of public virtue was crucial to the implementation of the republican form of government so dear to the Commonwealth Whigs. Colonists who absorbed the ideology reflected on the relative degree of virtue in England and America. Even if they gave the advantage to America, many wondered if their countrymen were virtuous enough to sustain a republic.[59]

In light of these popularly held beliefs, we need briefly to re-examine some facets of a Princeton pre-Revolutionary education. In the classroom students concentrated on many of the classical writers the Commonwealth Whigs recommended, especially Livy and Cicero. Witherspoon's lectures not only promoted many of the basic Commonwealth political ideas, such as government by compact, the superiority of mixed government, the right of revolution, and the necessity of virtue, but most of those ideas were based on the work of Francis Hutcheson whose moral philosophy was dear to the later Commonwealthmen. Moreover, among his suggested readings for students were many elements of the Commonwealth canon. The library had still more; students had access to almost thirty works important to the Commonwealth ideology by 1775 (see Table 3–1).

The exposure to Commonwealth Whig ideology in the classroom renders more significant the extracurricular activities of the students. Commencement exercises and debating society topics centering on themes such as natural rights, resistance to tyrannical governors, forms of government, virtues like industry, frugality, and patriotism, and even on the current state of American affairs, were more relevant and politically charged than they might at first seem.

Student participation in Patriot rituals such as non-importation demonstrations, tea parties, burnings in effigy, and militia companies also may have been more than adolescent imitations of their elders' behavior. The absorption of Com-

Table 3-1:
Pre-Revolutionary College Library Holdings

Category	Princeton	Harvard	Yale
Classics			
Plutarch	Library 1760	Library 1774	Library 1743
Livy	Library 1760	Library 1774	Library 1743
Sallust		Library 1773	Library 1743
Cicero	Library 1760	Library 1773	Library 1743
Tacitus	Library 1760	Library 1773	Library 1743
Enlightenment			
Locke	Library 1760	Library 1773	Library 1743
Montesquieu	JW sugg. 1768	Library 1773	
Voltaire		Library 1775	
Beccaria		Library 1773	
Grotius	Library 1760	Library 1773	Library 1743
Pufendorf	Library 1760	Library 1773	Library 1743
Burlamaqui	JW sugg. 1768	Library 1773	Library 1743
Vattel		Library 1774	
Common Law			
Coke		Library 1723	
Blackstone		Library 1723	
Camden		Library 1723	Library 1743
Spelman			
Brady			
Madox			
Petyt			
Puritans			
Neal	Library 1760	Library 1774	Library 1755
Prince	Library 1760		
Commonwealthmen			
Milton	Curric. 1764	Library 1773	
Harrington	JW sugg. 1768	Library 1723	
Sidney	Library 1760	Library 1773	
Neville		Library 1773	
Trenchard/Gordon	Library 1760	Library 1773	
Hoadly	Library 1760	Library 1773	Library 1755
Molesworth		Library 1773	
Bolingbroke			
Hutcheson	JW sugg. 1768	Library 1774	
Doddridge	Library 1760	Library 1773	
Watts	Library 1760	Library 1773	
Price		Library 1774	
Priestley		Library 1773	
Cartwright			
Macaulay		Library 1773	
Rapin-Thoyras	Library 1760	Library 1735	
Robertson	JW sugg. 1768	Library 1773	

Table 3-1:
Pre-Revolutionary College Library Holdings *(Continued)*

Category	Princeton	Harvard	Yale
Ferguson	Library 1768	Library 1774	
Burgh	Library 1760	Library 1773	
Historians			
Polybius		Library 1774	Library 1743
Virgil	Library 1760		Library 1743
Cicero*	Library 1760	Library 1773	Library 1743
Tacitus*	Library 1760	Library 1773	Library 1743
Thucydides	Library 1760	Library 1773	
Rollin		Library 1774	
Montagu	JW sugg. 1768	Library 1773	
Moyle			
Burgh*	Library 1760	Library 1773	
Goldsmith		Library 1774	
Addison's *Cato*			Library 1743
Gordon's *Tacitus*		Library 1773	
Rapin-Thoyras*	Library 1760	Library 1774	
Kames	JW sugg. 1768	Library 1773	
Hulme			
Coke*		Library 1773	
Sidney*	JW sugg. 1768	Library 1773	
Macaulay*		Library 1773	
Burnet	Library 1760	Library 1735	
Bolingbroke*			
Molyneaux		Library 1773	
Temple	Library 1760	Library 1773	Library 1755
Molesworth*		Library 1773	

Source: List of authors compiled from Bernard Bailyn, *The Ideological Origins of The American Revolution*. Cambridge, Mass.: Belknap Press, 1967, and Trevor Colbourn, *The Lamp of Experience: Whig History and the Intellectual Origins of the American Revolution*. Chapel Hill: University of North Carolina Press, 1965.
*Indicates author appears elsewhere in another category.

monwealth ideology with its conspiratorial view of British activities, its emphasis on public virtue, and its almost religious exhortation to resist tyranny must have infused the students with patriotic zeal, impelling them to become actors in the drama of resistance, both at college and later.[60]

III

The other colonial colleges politicized their students through the same process that prevailed at Princeton. The results, however, were not everywhere the same, for not all the college communities subscribed to the Commonwealth Whig ideology and of those that did, not all used it in the same way. Still, no college community totally escaped political involvement.

In addition to Princeton, Harvard, Yale, the College of Rhode Island, and Queen's College in New Jersey were clearly Patriot colleges. Dartmouth College and the College of Philadelphia are less easily categorized, Dartmouth because the prevailing atmosphere was less political than religious before the war, the College of Philadelphia because the political sentiments of the commuity were ambivalent. Both Patriot and Tory views found support among trustees, faculty, and students. William and Mary in Virginia and King's College in New York were homes of conservative, even Loyalist, teaching and yet even there the politicization of the students yielded varied results.

Other than Princeton, the College of Philadelphia was the only pre–Revolutionary school where a pattern of faculty address to students can be documented.[61] Two themes ran through the addresses of Provost Smith—an emphasis on education for state service and an ambivalence regarding the Anglo-American dispute. He advised students that they should "Let the world know that liberty is your unconquerable delight, and that you are sworn foes to every species of bondage, either of body or mind." Smith was sure that only a proper collegiate education could produce just guardians of the public weal: "The man best acquainted with the nature of civil government, the just bonds of authority and submission, and the universal principles of equity and virtue, will always be the ablest Politician and the Firmest Patriot."[62]

While Smith encouraged his students to prepare for state service, and while he recognized that his students took both Patriot and Tory views of developments after 1763, he was no more clear about his own political sentiments with them than he was with the public at large. With every movement toward or away from harmony, Smith was alternately elated or depressed. The Stamp Act angered him; its repeal renewed his belief in Britain's fairness. The deterioration in Anglo-American relations after 1773 left him virtually incapable of treating politics. Finally, in 1775 after the war had begun, Smith wrote a commencement ode that was a lamentation; "sacred freedom" mourned. It was a composition born of depression engendered by the inevitability of conflict.[63]

The few other surviving indications of faculty address to students played up the advantages of education and made veiled references to contemporary politics. For example, King's Samuel Johnson told his 1762 graduates that their future happiness depended upon the acquisition of knowledge and the exercise of virtue, "especially in the love of your country and zeal for the public welfare." Something of the same theme emerged in President Jacob Hardenbergh's address at the first Queen's College commencement in 1774. Extolling the necessity of education, he stressed the advantages to the state, noting that when societies based on compact made and sought to be governed by constitutions, they must be adorned by educated men well-versed in "the laws of nature and nations," and "the histories of the rise, glory, and fall of empires." That, of course, was the purpose of an institution such as Queen's. Hardenbergh then touched upon the politics of the time, although circumspectly, for his audience included New Jersey's royal governor, William Franklin. He asked God's protection and aid "to preserve and establish our dear bought liberties, handed down to us by our glorious Ancestors. O! may America never want Sons of consummate Wisdom, intrepid Resolution and true Piety to defend her civil and religious Liberties, and promote the public Weal of the present and rising generations!"[64]

While it is not certain just what contribution the faculty made to student politicization through direct address, there can be no doubt that the students were aware of the faculties' actions in the larger public arena (see Chapter 2). The same was true for the trustees. Because the collegiate communities were small, because trustees often participated in student examinations, because they were highly visible at commencement, and because they were usually the most prominent civic and religious leaders of the area, students were better acquainted with trustees in the eighteenth century than they are today. It was therefore to be expected that students would know of the activities of the college govenors.

Those activities and loyalties ran the gamut from total political indifference to leadership in the Anglo-American dispute and from staunch Patriot to adamant Tory. At most colleges, at least some of the trustees were then or now sufficiently obscure that it is difficult to calculate the political "leanings" of a college board. Yet some conclusions may be drawn. At Yale, all of the fellows of the corporation were ministers; many of them refused to participate in political affairs. But those who did were Patriots, delivering pro-American sermons, writing newspaper essays, or serving with the militia in 1775 as chaplains. Queen's College had as trustees ex officio the governor, the president of the council, the chief justice of the superior court, and the attorney general. Three of these four, as royal appointees, were Loyalists, but there was only one other Tory on the board. Most whose actions are known were uninvolved ministers or laymen who served the Patriot cause in the provincial assembly, committees of safety, the militia, or elsewhere. None was a famous Revolutionary. The trustees of the Colleges of William and Mary, Philadelphia, and Rhode Island, of Dartmouth and Harvard were less uniformly Patriot, although the majority embraced the American cause. With the exception of Dartmouth, each of these colleges included among its trustees prominent Patriots and Tories. Serving William and Mary were the Patriots Peyton Randolph, George Wythe, and Thomas Nelson, Jr., who worked alongside Tories Lord Dunmore, Robert Beverley, and William Byrd III. The College of Philadelphia had Loyalist governors such as John and William Allen, John and Richard Penn, and James Tilghman as well as Patriots Thomas Mifflin, Jacob Duche, Thomas Cadwallader, and Benjamin Franklin. Among the College of Rhode Island Patriot trustees were Isaac Backus, John and Nicholas Brown, and Stephen Hopkins; Tories included Governor Joseph Swanton. Harvard claimed the most famous trustees, Patriot and Tory. John and Samuel Adams, Charles Chauncy, James Bowdoin, and James Otis led the Patriots, while Governor Thomas Hutchinson, Reverend William Brattle, and Chief Justice Andrew Oliver were the most famous Tories. At these colleges students could have their choice of heroes.[65]

The only predominantly Loyalist board of trustees belonged to King's College.

In the early 1770s the King's governors were enthusiastic about turning the college into an American Oxford. Whatever the pedagogical ambitions, a primary goal was to use the college for "Cementing the Union between Great Britain and the Colonies," to "diffuse a spirit of Loyalty thro' his Majesty's American Dominions." This ambition embodied the political leanings of the original trustees. Twenty-one governors were regular contributors to college policy making in the early 1770s. Fifteen were Loyalists in the Revolution; nine left America permanently. Their attitudes seemed to rest on suspicion of the popular element of resistance and fears for the well-being of commerce on the part of the laymen, while the clergy wanted to advance the Anglican Church in the colonies.[66] Finding a Patriot model on the King's College board presented difficulties for the students. Trustee and faculty attitudes converged to make King's uniquely inhospitable to American patriotism in the years before the war. No other college presented a similar atmosphere.

At the other colleges, as at Princeton, the curriculum was an extremely important means of politicizing the students. Most of the pre-Revolutionary colleges followed a pattern of curricular evolution that the College of New Jersey exemplified: the rise of scientific instruction, a shift from divinity and God-centered learning toward the man-centered learning encompassed by moral philosophy, an increasing interest in belles lettres, and a movement in oratory from the syllogistic to the forensic disputation, signifying an embrace of inductive rather than deductive logic.[67] Individual colleges participated more in some of these developments than in others, but all drew on the classical languages, related oratorical exercises, occasional forays into history, and especially moral philosophy to bring political principles to their students. What differentiated the offerings of the period after 1750 from those of earlier years was the increased political content, the inclusion of much Commonwealth Whig material, and the relevance of the political commentary to contemporary affairs.

The classics in use at Princeton were the preferred choices of several colleges. Cicero was the most popular. His *Orations* were part of all the curricula, *De Oratore* appeared everywhere but at Harvard and possibly William and Mary, while Harvard, King's, Queen's, William and Mary, and the College of Philadelphia used *De Officiis*. In addition to these works, King's and the Philadelphia college used Circero's *Tusculan Disputations*. The Roman orator's republicanism thus reached all of America's collegians. Also favored were the mythological histories of Homer and Virgil. All the colleges used both the *Aeneid* and the *Iliad* with the possible exception of William and Mary. Horace, too, appeared almost everywhere.[68]

Beyond these widely used works, the colleges' selection of classics was more idiosyncratic (for a summary, see Table 3–2). Princeton's choices proved popular at some other schools: Demosthenes at Harvard, King's, and the College of Philadelphia; Xenophon's *Cyropaedia* at Harvard, King's, and the College of Rhode Island, his *Memorabilia* at the College of Philadelphia. Lucian's *Dialogues* found a following at King's and the Rhode Island college, and Livy was in use at the College of Philadelphia and William and Mary. From these works, too, the students drew lessons about the rise and fall of ancient republics.

Some other works in use before 1750 retained their value in a period of worsening Anglo-American relations. After 1763, Harvard and King's College used the work of Isocrates (436–338 B.C.). This Athenian orator lived in a troubled era for the Greek city-states, for they continually warred upon one another. Eventually, the disunited provinces fell under the control of Philip of Macedon. Isocrates tried to prevent this. He wrote a number of speeches and pamphlets the major theme of which was Pan-Hellenism. Not concealing an abiding love for Athens, Isocrates nonetheless urged a confederation of free states, an end to internal bickering, and unity against the Persians. When these efforts failed, he turned to Philip, asking that he take control. But here, too, Isocrates wanted a confederation, not imperial domination. Again he failed. A war between the disunited Greeks and the Persians led to defeat and Philip brought the Greeks together by force under a plan that his son Alexander the Great subsequently carried out.[69] Isocrates' work is full of commentary on the desirability of nationalist sentiment, on the dangers of internal strife, and on the consequences of being colonized. Its applicability to Anglo-American relations was obvious.

More food for thought was served to King's College students in the histories of Sallust (86–34 B.C.). Here was an active Roman politician who rose to become a quaestor and member of the senate, enjoyed a checkered military career in Africa, and survived charges of corruption back in Rome. This last occurence, coupled with Caesar's assassination, suggested to Sallust that a genteel retirement was in order, so he devoted himself to writing history.[70]

Sallust produced quite good history, of a new sort in Roman literature, for he produced historical monographs. His first work was a history of the Cataline conspiracy. In it he reviewed the rise of Rome, attributing its success to the cultivation of honor and virtue, to the expulsion of tyrannical kings in favor of annually elected consuls, and to the pursuit of glory. Unfortunately for Rome, success brought luxury, and with it came sloth, avarice, and a decline in public morals: "As soon as riches came to be held in honour, when glory, domination, and honour followed in their train, virtue began to lose its lustre." The loss of public virtue set the stage for Cataline, who corrupted those who could be bought and used his influence to persuade improperly educated young men to join him in a search for riches and power. Rome had become so corrupted that the populace divided. Many thought the government itself so driven by the individual self-interests of its members that it deserved rebellion. Others simply sought the main chance. In the end, the Romans who retained their virtue triumphed, but it was a near thing, and the Romans should have been warned about the consequences of their lifestyles and values.[71]

Sallust continued to explore the consequences of public corruption in his history of the war with Jugurtha. He began with a commentary on the relative effects of virtue and vice, this time on the individual intellect. Extending these observations into a warning about the current state of Roman morals, he explained that the climate of corruption was what had led to the rise of Jugurtha in Africa; he bribed the Roman Senate to overlook his crimes. This, said Sallust, was the key to Jugurtha's success and Rome's danger. It was not just that Jugurtha was an able warrior, but also that he had the wealth with which to take advantage of the cupidity of the Roman government. He bought senates, he bought armies, and he triumphed. That is, until he eventually went down to defeat at the hands of a military leader who rose to the Roman Consulship on the votes of the common people, who for once carried the day over the nobles. Explicit was the moral that neither they nor he could be corrupted. Only in the promotion of that spirit lay the salvation of Rome. The exercise of virtue and constant vigilance against corruption, these alone could save the Roman people.[72]

As is already apparent, Harvard, King's College, and the College of Philadelphia incorporated the greatest number of classics into their courses of study. In addition to the works already covered, Harvard students read Plutarch's *Lives*, while King's students read Tacitus' histories and Herodotus. All three schools used Plato's *Dialogues*, especially the *Laws*. Harvard and King's both required Caesar's *Commentaries*. The middle colony colleges read Thucydides.[73]

Most of these classical works touched on political matters in a way that emphasized republicanism, civic morality, or both. Prominent among the historians was Herodotus (c. 484–c. 424 B.C.), who was the first to weave a narrative out of the welter of confused facts available to chroniclers. He strove to relate the struggles between the Greeks and the Persians in the fifth century B.C. Herodotus was a moralist who analyzed the relative talents and wisdom of rulers through a series of finely drawn portraits. He showed the corrupting influence of power in the career of the Persian Cyrus, and portrayed Xerxes as the quintessential tyrant—weak, cruel, and licentious. By contrast, the Greeks Themistocles and Aristides emerged as patriots, clear of vision, interested in the public good, and talented, although the former was a lover of intrigue.[74]

Thucydides took the writing of Greek history one step further by applying the principles of philosophy to his subject. His history of the Peloponnesian War examined the workings of the Athenian democracy and Spartan oligarchy, contrasting the fall of the former with the rise of the latter. What also appeared was a moralistic examination of the motives and conduct of political systems, parties, and rulers. The history was a manual for statesmen, glorifying the democratic system under Pericles, but condemning the corruption that undermined Athens thereafter.[75]

The Roman history the students read centered on the empire. Julius Caesar's *Commentaries on the Gallic War* and *Commentaries on the Civil War* were self-serving pieces of political propaganda. The former, for example, explained the Gallic War as having been forced on him by the prospect of invasion. It was a patriotic gesture, not a means to gain more power. His account of the Civil Wars was similar.[76] The contrast with Cicero must have been quite marked. The legacy of the Civil Wars was the subject of the histories of Tacitus. Himself a public servant in the late first century A.D., Tacitus retired to comment unfavorably on the evolution of Rome during that hundred years. His *Annals* and *Histories* followed the reigns of the emperors from the accession of Tiberius in 14 A.D. to the death of Domition in 96 A.D. While admitting that public morals had been so abased during the republic that the empire was necessary to preserve order, Tacitus retained enough admiration for the republican form of government to condemn the operation of the empire and those who ruled it. The *Germania*, an account of the customs, commerce, agriculture, and government of the tribes to the north of Italy, contained a strong moralizing strain. Their society seemed to be utopian, and its depiction was an ill-disguised critique of Rome. This commentary served Tacitus' chief purpose: ''I regard as history's highest function, to let no worthy action be uncommemorated, and to hold out the reprobation of posterity as a terror to evil words and deeds.'' Students could not mistake this message.[77]

Asserting the moral, if not the historical, connections between the Greek and Roman leaders was Plutarch, Greek-born and educated, who spent his working life in Rome. His most famous work was the *Parallel Lives* which contained forty-six sketches of eminent Greeks and Romans often compared side by side. The edition most likely read by eighteenth-century collegians was that of Thomas North. It contained nineteen sketches, thirteen of which were figures associated with the end of the Roman republic and the rise of the empire. The selections show Plutarch's preoccupation with politics and reveal his own sympathies as well. For instance, his sketch of Lycurgus portrayed him as the ultimate lawmaker whose work helped form the perfect commonwealth, the admiration of the world for 500 years. His comments on Greece under Lycurgus demonstrate a preference for a natural aristocracy which would grant a strong senate constitutionally fixed powers, but which derived its authority from a populace with a broad suffrage. Other comments on the nature of power and its balance with toleration emerge in the sketches of Pericles and Phocion and in the comparison of Caesar and Alexander.[78] Altogether, these historical works complemented the republicanism of the other classics the students consulted.

Plato's *Dialogues*, especially the *Laws*, served as a classical bridge between history and moral philosophy. Two great influences on Plato's life were the Peloponnesian Wars and the execution of Socrates. Each of these events soured him on the workings of Athenian democracy. He cast about for alternatives, concluding that social reform would succeed only if it was grounded on philosophical principles and carried out by those who truly understood them. His great theoretical exercise along these lines was the *Republic*, but because he doubted true philosopher-kings would appear, he placed increasing importance on developing a code of conduct to guide rulers. This formed the message of the *Statesman*. Thereafter, Plato became more convinced of the necessity of guidance for rulers in the form of a detailed, immutable code of laws governing the entire conduct of society. The *Laws* established such a code for the utopia of Magnesia, governed by a system incorporating elements of democracy under

Table 3–2:
Curricular Offerings by Author at Pre-Revolutionary Colleges

Category	Harvard	Yale	William & Mary	Coll. of N.J.	King's	Coll. of Phil.	Coll. of R.I.	Queen's
Classics								
Xenophon	X			X	X	X	X	
Homer	X	X	?	X	X	X	X	X
Demosthenes	X			X	X	X		
Isocrates	X				X			
Thucydides					X	X		
Herodotus					X			
Plato	X				X	X		
Cicero's *Orations**	X	X	X	X	X	X	X	X
Virgil*	X	X	?	X	X	X	X	X
Horace			X	X		X		
Livy*			X	X		X		
Lucian			X	X		X		
Catullus			X	X				
Sallust*				X				
Plutarch*	X							
Tacitus*				X				
Caesar	X			X				
Oratory								
Cicero's *De Oratore**		X	?	X	X	X	X	X
Cicero's *Tusculan Disputations**					X	X		
Moral Philosophy								
Cicero's *De Officiis**	X		X	X	X	X		X
Clarke				x**				
Pufendorf*				x**	X			
Shaftesbury				x**				
Wollaston		X		x**				
Kames*				x**				
Grotius*				x**	X	X		
Cumberland				x**		x**		
Maxwell				x**				
Selden				x**				
Burlamaqui*	X			x**				
Harrington*				x**		x**		
Locke's *Essay**	X	X		x**				
Locke's *Two Treatises**						x**		

Table 3–2: *continued*

Category	Harvard	Yale	William & Mary	Coll. of N.J.	King's	Coll. of Phil.	Coll. of R.I.	Queen's
Sidney*				x**		x**		
Montesquieu*				x**				
Ferguson*				x**				
Hutcheson's *Moral Phil.**				x**	x	x		
Hutcheson's *Enquiry*	x							
Edwards' *Enquiry*		x						
Fordyce	x							

Source: See text, note 68. There was no information for Dartmouth.
  *Denotes Commonwealth canon
**Denotes recommended reading

the authority of an oligarchy.[79] This discussion served to mesh the modern concerns of classical language instruction, history, and philosophy, showing the necessity of ethical standards in government and society at large.

Pre-Revolutionary collegians derived a great deal of advice and comment on politics from their classical instruction. The other course that offered a consideration of politics was moral philosophy (for a summary of works used, see Table 3–2). This discipline was, however, still in transition and not all moral philosophy courses were alike. It should be noted at the outset that we know almost nothing of the moral philosophy courses at Dartmouth, Queen's, at the College of Rhode Island, or at William and Mary. President Wheelock taught the course at Dartmouth, but the contents remain obscure. The Dartmouth trustees refused to adopt a 1776 proposal that would have required instruction on "the Spirit of Laws, the nature of Liberty and Civil Government."[80] Perhaps that indicates the absence of political instruction from the moral philosophy course. For Queen's and the College of Rhode Island no records of the course survive. The instructors of moral philosophy at William and Mary have been identified. All but one were Oxford graduates, most from Queen's College.[81] This might suggest that their course greatly resembled the English offering. But the content of that course is hard to determine. Instruction in moral philosophy was left to tutors, there being no incumbent for the university chair. What Oxford students read on their own or at the direction of their tutors is unknown. The indications are that politics did not become an important part of the course until the last quarter of the century. At William and Mary, as at Oxford, most political knowledge came to students from outside the classroom.[82]

At Harvard and Yale, too, the emphasis was on the ethical side of moral philosophy. The contents of Holyoke's, Samuel Locke's, and Langdon's lectures do not survive in student notes. Most of the texts in use gave almost total attention to ethics: John Locke's *Essay*, Fordyce's *Elements of Moral Philosophy*, and Francis Hutcheson's *Enquiry into the Original of our Idea of Beauty and Virtue*. Only Jean Jacques Burlamaqui's *Principles of Natural and Politic Law* was much related to politics. It contained several observations useful to Commonwealthmen and to Revolutionaries, including the concepts that the purpose of government was the attainment of human happiness, that sovereignty originally resided in the people so their consent was necessary for the exercise of governmental powers, that power needed to be regulated because of its corrupting effect, and that the best way to do this was through the creation of a fundamental law delegating powers to the government.[83] Here was a modern complement to the classical treatises.

Yale students did no such reading. Their moral philosophy texts were William Wollaston's *The Religion of Nature Delineated* and Jonathan Edwards' *Enquiry into the Freedom of the Will*, supplemented just before the Revolution by Locke's *Essay*. These were all ethical treatises with no political component. So, too, were Thomas Clap's moral philosophy lectures, collected in 1765 as an *Essay on the Nature and Foundations of Moral Virtue*, and used by his successor Naphtali Daggett. The only politically relevant non-classical segments of a Yale education were Clap's occasional lectures on such subjects as British law and her system of courts, ancient history and chronology, and commerce. In conjunction with these lectures he recommended readings so that the students might pursue the subjects, but the content of the lectures and the readings are unknown.[84]

The broadest moral philosophy courses other than Princeton's existed at King's and the College of Philadelphia. Samuel Johnson, King's first president, was above all else a moralist. His course used a text he had written, *Elementa Philosophica*, which was a guide to the classification of knowledge. Its treatment of government was brief and morally charged. Proper government strove to promote the public good and the happiness of mankind. The citizens' duty toward government was to practice benevolence: "They should be led on to a sense of order and public virtue, and love of their country, and finally of the whole of mankind, and to look for their own weal in that of the whole community." They should read history to gather examples both of wise rule and of proper behavior by the ruled. Informed by these examples, citizens would be ready to live in a civil society founded on compact where certain rules and laws conforming to the common interest were enforced. Knowing how to behave, knowing the laws, supporting the common good, the citizenry would prosper.[86] Here was Whiggism, but not Commonwealth ideology, for this doctrine promoted passive obedience, not revolution by the oppressed.

Some of these observations, including the compact theory of government, the mutual obligations of rulers and ruled, and the moral limits placed on rulers derived from Samuel von Pufendorf's *De Officio Homines et Cive*, which Johnson had his sophomores read as preparation for the moral philosophy course. Here, too, the emphasis was more on the moral than the governmental facet of politics.[87]

This same stress on the moral pervaded the philosophical instruction of Johnson's successor, Myles Cooper. His collected lectures, *Ethices Compendium*, contains chapters on the will, the intellect, the internal and external norms of action, and the passions, but none on politics or government.[88] Cooper did ask his students to read Pufendorf and two other works with political observations, Grotius' *On War and Peace* and the moral philosophy of Francis Hutcheson. Grotius discussed more than international law. He was a proponent of the law of nature, putting his discussion of war and peace, as well as related observations on public law and government, in that context. His commentary on natural law and its application was not uniformly useful to the Commonwealthmen. On the one hand, he was one of the first to hint that there were subjective, intrinsic natural rights which one possessed simply by existing. He argued that rulers must govern in conformity to the natural law and he asserted that one basis of a just war was defense of self and property, all ideas held by American resistors to British policy. On the other hand, Grotius did not believe that sovereignty resided in the people and he did not sanction revolution against a governor who misruled. He deplored civil war.[89]

Hutcheson was more of a Commonwealthman. He associated with those British political thinkers who followed the civil war apologists, and his ideas were right in line with their thoughts. Hutcheson believed that an innate moral sense would harmonize the individual and the general good, and promote the greatest good for all through the exercise of virtue. His most notable contribution was to apply this view of human nature to particular political situations. For example, while advocating civic union and mutual obligation between rulers and ruled, Hutcheson stoutly defended the people's right of revolution against tyranny, and explicitly extended this principle to the relations between colonies and the mother country:

Large numbers of men cannot be bound to sacrifice their own and their posterity's liberty and happiness, to the ambitious views of their mother country, while it can enjoy all rational happiness without subjection to it.... There is something so unnatural in supposing a large society, sufficient for all the good purposes of an independent political union, remaining subject to the direction and government of a distant body of men who know not sufficiently the circumstances and exigencies of this society; or in supposing this society to be governed solely for the benefit of a distant country; that it is not easy to imagine there can be any justification for it in justice or equity.

He also advocated mixed government organized on classical lines as the best modern form, urged against a privileged ruling class, and endorsed frequent election by ballot. He favored citizen militias, easily understood laws, and discussed international law in terms similar to those of Grotius and Pufendorf.[90]

It is possible, but not probable, that these works were taught from a Commonwealth perspective. Johnson, for all his criticism of colonial governments, at least believed in the principle of government by compact, which implied consent of the governed. Cooper did not believe this, but his professor of natural law, John Vardill, hinted in the early 1770s that he upheld the right of revolution. Still, as noted previously, all three of these men as well as other King's instructors shared a commitment to hierarchical politics. It is hard to believe Hutcheson's conditions for colonial independence were viewed with much favor by Cooper, who asserted after July 4, 1776, that the "Health of a State requires a regular and due Subordination of its members to the governing Power....Let every Man then be contented with his Station, and faithfully discharge its attendant Duties," and who counselled Americans not to believe "that they may set up their pretended Natural Rights in opposition to the positive Laws of the State."[91] King's curriculum, despite its books, was probably Tory.

The College of Philadelphia's moral philosophy course was as broad as that of Princeton or King's. It was to contain "the Elements of Civil Law, the reading of History, and the Study of the Ends and Uses of Society, the different Forms of Government, etc." At various times before 1776, three different instructors taught the course: Provost William Smith, Vice Provost Alison, and Ebenezar Kinnersley. If they followed the curricular plan outlined in 1756, the students both heard lectures on a variety of topics and engaged in extensive reading.[92]

Provost Smith, despite his activity in Pennsylvania politics, apparently did not intrude his sentiments into his lectures. In 1756, the trustees investigated to find out the content of his course. Students reassured them that his teachings were based on Grotius, Pufendorf, Locke, and Hutcheson, "writers whose sentiments are equally opposite to the wild Notions of Liberty, that are inconsistent with all Government, and to those pernicious Schemes of Government, which are destructive of all Liberty."[93] Considering the Commonwealth possibilities of those authors, Smith must have offered a bland course indeed.

Smith's real loves were belles lettres and the sciences, so he early on turned over moral philosophy instruction to Francis Alison. Occasionally Ebenezer Kinnersley taught the course, but since he was Alison's student their lectures differed very little. The Alison-Kinnersley course resembled Witherspoon's, divided into sections on ethics, natural law, and economics and politics. And, like Witherspoon, Alison was a disciple of Francis Hutcheson, using his *Short Introduction* as a text. In the ethics section Alison did modify Hutchesonian philosophy, making his presentation much more God-centered, for he was less confident of the capacity of human reason than was Hutcheson. The natural law and politics sections were closer borrowings, but even here Alison did not have his students merely parrot the Scot. His technique was to draw up a list of controversial subjects and organize debates about them. He sent his students to a wide variety of texts on each side of the subject, let the debate proceed, and then tried to shape the outcome according to his own convictions.[94]

Regarding government, those convictions increasingly harmonized with the Commonwealth political ideology. Alison, suspicious of human nature, believed that human corruption necessitated government, which existed to further the mutual interests of all through promotion of the public good. To create a government, there must be a social compact among the people agreeing on a form, a decree of ordinance regulating that form, and a contract between rulers and ruled pledging faithful administration of government by the former and obedience by the latter. Alison went on to discuss the various forms of government in pure and complex arrangements, considering the advantages and disadvantages of each, and concluded that a mixed republic was best for an educated people. He was sure that no government could succeed that was not based on property and that did not allow a large measure of popular participation. He advocated such governmental limitations as a constitution, fixed terms for officers, rotation in office, and a code of civil laws based on the law of nature.[95]

Alison, like Smith, was reluctant to introduce contemporary political concerns into his course, so at first he left out Hutcheson's discussion of the rights of colonies to become independent. However, his conviction of the inevitability of an Anglo-American rupture at last induced him to sound like a Revolutionary: "After a great Empire is formed it becomes advisable for many small States to unite in a large one or to form some strongly united System that they may be able to resist the overgrown Empire." The defect of the empire centered in its using its power in a manner calculated to undermine the safety and happiness of the whole people. When liberty and safety were in danger it would be lawful and just to resist the government. The people must judge the situation, must not act hastily, but did have the right to rebel. Alison even considered the maintenance of order in the interim between an overthrown and a popularly reconstituted government.[96] In some ways he went beyond Hutcheson to apply general principles to the particular situation of the colonies in the late 1760s and 1770s.

A variety of readings supplemented these lectures; most have been mentioned in conjunction with other curricula. What distinguished the College of Philadelphia was its suggestion to read Locke on government, as well as Sidney and Harrington, who were direct advocates of the commonwealth form of government. Harrington's *Oceana* was an utopian commonwealth, actually a thinly-disguised interregnum England, for which he sought to describe the form of government and the political mechanisms best suited to accomplish the state's object of preserving liberty. Among Oceana's principles were government based on consent, operating through laws not men, the limitation of the influence of corruption through rotation in office, election by ballot, and a government balanced so that no one segment of the population could overpower any other. The most novel feature of Oceana was basing the government on property holders, these to be made as numerous as possible through limitations on individual ownership. In addition to reinforcing other Commonwealth literature, Harrington's doctrines were especially appealing to a predominantly rural culture.[97]

Sidney and Locke were both apologists for revolution. Sidney contributed to the Commonwealth canon by arguing that governments should be based on laws, not men, and that magistrates had an obligation to live up to their contract with the people to seek the common good. His particular emphasis was to proclaim tyranny worse than rebellion, thus justifying citizens in ridding the nation of an oppressive government. Locke reached many of the same conclusions as Sidney, but probably never read him. Drawing more from Hobbes than Harrington, he was not a defender of the commonwealth experiment, but rather a monarchist who even accepted royal prerogative. Yet there was in his work also the belief in the limiting force of natural law, the conviction that government was artificial, based on compact, and in need of the frequent consent of the people through election to continue operation. Above all, he asserted that a people faced with an oppressive government that would not respond to petition had the right to rebel to change the leadership or form of that government.[98]

The presence of these authors in a list of suggested readings combined with the classical studies and the tone of Alison's lectures to give the College of Philadelphia curriculum a surprisingly Commonwealth cast, considering the divided loyalties of the trustees and the quandry of allegiance affecting Provost Smith. At Philadelphia, as at Princeton, outside reading was important in politicizing the students. There is evidence that this was true at some other colleges as well.

Scant material has survived to indicate the contents of most pre-Revolutionary college libraries. Collections numbered no more than a few hundred volumes at Queen's College, the College of Rhode Island, and Dartmouth; the College of William and Mary, King's College, and the College of Philadelphia had larger collections but their content is not known. Only for Harvard and Yale do catalogs survive. In both libraries theology predominated, but there were many volumes of classics, ancient and modern history, and contemporary politics as well. The library holdings of Commonwealth and related authors appear in Table 3–1.

Harvard benefited from the contributions of the English Commonwealth Whig Thomas Hollis who, in the years following the disastrous 1764 library fire, sent many hundreds of books to the American Cambridge, including works on politics and contemporary American political tracts. Hollis donated most of the Commonwealthmen's works to Harvard in addition to other books that propounded his favorite political principles such as the right of resistance, government by compact, and popular sovereignty.[99]

The question, of course, is whether the Commonwealthmen and related works found student readers. The answer is yes, if Harvard students are typical of those at other colleges. The Harvard Hall fire of 1764 destroyed private libraries as well as the collegiate collection. Several students petitioned the General Court for restitution, specifying lost authors or titles. Among those listed were many in the Commonwealth canon, including twenty-two Virgils (presumably the *Aeneid*), seven Homers (the *Iliad*), seventeen Ciceros (the *Orations*?), and five Caesar's *Commentaries*, as well as Charles Rollin's *Ancient History* (2d ed., 10 vols., London, 1738–1740) and Adam Smith's *The Theory of Moral Sentiments*

(London, 1759). By 1774, students also often had in their possession Burla-maqui's *The Principles of Natural Law* and Adam Ferguson's *Essay on Civil Society*.[100]

The notebook of Harvard sophomore Benjamin Wadsworth for 1766–67 gives an insight into undergraduate reading. Among his notes history predominated, including William Douglass, *A Summary . . . of the British Settlements in North America* (Boston, 1755), Thomas Hutchinson's *A History of the Province of Massachusetts Bay* (2 vols., Boston, 1764, 1767), Daniel Neal's *History of the Puritans*, Charles Rollin's *Ancient History*, and David Hume's *History of England*. Wadsworth also commented on the moralists Philip Doddridge and James Burgh. This sampling indicates that Commonwealth works held a prominent place in the collegians' reading. A survey of the library charging lists from 1773 to 1776 confirms that indication. Harvard juniors and seniors, like those at most colonial colleges, could borrow books from the library. The classes of 1775 and 1776 made ample use of that privilege. Almost every student borrowed at least one book belonging to the Commonwealth canon and most read several. Well over one-third of the canon moved through the students' hands during these three years.[101]

The most popular works were William Robertson's *History of Charles V* and *History of Scotland*, the first a commentary on the decline of the Roman empire through the influence of sloth and corruption, the second an instructive narrative on how two sovereign and independent states might live successfully under the same king.[102] Closely following Robertson were Oliver Goldsmith's *Roman History* and *History of England*. These were popularizations based on the work of Vertot, Rollin, and others for the Roman history, and of Hume, Smollet, Rapin-Thoyras, and Voltaire for the history of England. Goldsmith was not an historian; the republicanism to be found in his work was probably unconscious distillation, but the books did serve to introduce students to the more profound sources from which he drew.[103] They read Hume's, Smollet's, and Thoyras' histories of England as well as Rollin's and Vertot's histories of Rome.[104] Other republican historians frequently read were Catherine Macaulay and Edward Montagu. The convictions regarding the fate of republics, the right of revolution, the effects of luxury upon virtue, and the evolution of English history gleaned from these works could have been reinforced by the political and philosophical arguments of other frequently consulted authors: Locke on government, Montesquieu, Pufendorf, Vattel, Sidney, *Cato's Letters*, Hutcheson's philosophy, and James Burgh. In short, the Harvard library proved a fundamental source for the dissemination of the Commonwealth canon to the college students. Unless Harvard men were strikingly different from those elsewhere, wherever Commonwealth literature existed it had avid readers.

What the pre-Revolutionary college students heard and read influenced what they said and did. Mirroring their mentors, at the Patriot colleges they became more overtly political as the imperial crisis deepened, and their politics progressively took on the arguments of the Commonwealth Whigs. Where confusion or Loyalism reigned, as at the College of Phildelphia or King's, student bodies reflected those political attitudes.

In New England the events of the 1760s aroused alarm and the collegians' exercises demonstrated the tension. At Harvard the Stamp Act prompted concern in 1765 and 1766: "Can the new Prohibitory Duties, which make it useless for the People to engage in Commerce, be evaded by them as faithful Subjects?", "Is it legal, under British government, to collect taxes by military force?" The audiences at the late 1760s celebrations heard more abstract, but still relevant disputes on "Does a promise that has been given bind the highest magistrate in a civil government?", "Is an inferior magistrate obliged to execute the orders of his superior, when they would plainly subvert the commonwealth?", and "Are the People the sole Judges of their Rights and Liberties?"[105]

During the 1770s Harvard exercises uniformly demonstrated student adherence to the Patriot cause. They delivered orations on "virtue" and "liberty," on "passive-obedience and non-resistance," on "the advantages of political liberty," and on "the disadvantages of unequal distribution of property in a state." They disputed whether political jealousy is a laudable passion and offered theses on questions such as "Is a government tyrannical in which the Rulers consult their own Interest more than that of their Subjects" and "Is a government despotic in which the People have no check on the Legislative Power?"[106] Harvard student sentiment may actually have run a little ahead of the faculty's politicization. Certainly, next to Princeton's, Harvard's commencements were the most overtly political and Patriot in the colonies.

The application of the tenets of Commonwealth Whig ideology to particular situations perceived in the Harvard exercises was true elsewhere as well. The College of Rhode Island held its first commencement in 1769. The exercises that year were highly political. Students debated the proposition "All power of maintaining laws and inflicting penalities is derived from the people; therefore, for a legislative body to impose taxes upon a peop'ᴇ who are not represented in that body is unjust." The valedictory address focused on republican orators. Charles Thompson demonstrated a thorough acquaintance with Greek and Roman history when describing the role of the orator in the republic. One can sense the real purpose of his speech when he asked his audience to imagine themselves in Greece and Rome, listening to Demosthenes and Cicero declaim against tyrants and portray the evils of colonial oppression.[107]

But the most startling exercise of the commencement was a disputation on the question "Whether British America can under Present Circumstances Consistent with Good Policy, Affect to Become an Independent State?" Nothing so bold had been advanced anywhere else at this time. The text survives, so we know that all the disputants agreed on a number of philosophical assertions that showed them familiar with Commonwealth Whig ideology: that public good should predominate over private interest in governmental policy; that taxation without representation violated the natural rights of the citizenry; that the right of resistance exists if every other means of redress fails. Indeed, what separated the participants were differences over whether the failure of petition had occured, whether commerce could be used as a weapon to influence British policy, and whether American society could survive a war. These were differences of judgment, not governmental theory. The advocate of independence dipped far into Commonwealth literature to argue that the Americans would triumph because theirs would be a citizen and not a standing army. He urged Americans to rally to the cause of liberty for it was virtually a crime to follow the course of Normandy, Saxony, Denmark, and Sweden, to fail to defend themselves and thus become slaves to another country.[108]

Every commencement of the 1770s saw Rhode Island students offer political commentary such as theses arguing "Standing Armies in Time of Peace are Detrimental to States" and "A Defensive War is permissable," orations on "The Discovery, progressive Settlement, present State, and Future Greatness, of the American Colonies" and "patriotism." The tone, however, was not universally in favor of resistance. Rhode Island moved reluctantly to independence and the hesitation appeared in considerations of the "Necessity of perpetuating the union betwixt Great Britain and her colonies" and "The Advantages of Peace."[109]

Yale and Dartmouth students reflected in their exercises the lateness of their faculties' politicization. At Yale, the only pre-Revolutionary political commencement topic was a 1774 dialogue treating the rights of Americans and the unconstitutionality of British measures. Only the 1774 exercises survive from Dartmouth, where a religious revival was then in progress. None of the topics was political.[110]

If Yale and Dartmouth students attested to the lack of politicization of their mentors, students at the College of Philadelphia reflected faculty ambivalence. During the 1760s, students and faculty were usually more concerned about the local contest between proprietary and anti-proprietary forces than about imperial questions. The exception was the Stamp Act crisis, which brought about the prize competition for the best essay on "The Reciprocal Advantages of the Perpetual Union between Great Britain and her American Colonies," a topic so sensitive that students alone could not be trusted with it. The winning essay came from a medical school faculty member. By 1768, things were calm again. In general, the political posture of the exercises was one of loyalty to the Crown, yet there was concern for the future of Anglo-American relations. Still, the students were as interested in science and belles lettres as they were in imperial politics.[111]

A reluctance to engage the imperial debate continued to characterize the college. Until 1775, the few Philadelphia exercises treating politics were still greatly outnumbered by those touching upon the arts, sciences, and abstract ethical questions. The 1775 commencement, however, took place after Lexington and Concord. With the Continental Congress in attendance, many students, if not their provost, decided no longer to ride the political fence. Several exercises treated political questions, probably the most pointed was Benjamin Chew's valedictory address on oratory. He noted that oratory was in decline in England because of faulty education, public corruption, and because the art was inimical to tyranny and slavery. Chew then went on to say what he had learned from ancient authors:

To have read them, merely as introducing us to the knowledge of a dead language, would have been to little purpose, if we had neglected the nobler lessons which they had to teach us—to mark the fate of kingdoms, and particularly the steps by which Rome, imperial Rome, rose to the summit of human glory, and fell again.

Vice, sin, and luxury were the banes of empires, leading eventually to "sloth, anarchy, slavery, and political death." So taught Lycurgus, *Cato's Letters*, Hampden, Sidney, and Locke, said Chew, and so taught the college, which aimed to "train up a succession of patriots, sages, and lawgivers, to support and dignify our great American cause."[112] At least, that is what some of the professors taught.

Even the ambivalence at Philadelphia stands in marked contrast to what took place at William and Mary or King's College. William and Mary's first commencement was in 1772. The sole known exercise was an oration in Latin, "Carthage Must be Destroyed," which showed an acquaintance with Roman history but had no political content. How the faculty may have affected the exercises is unknown. No other pre-war commencement records survive. In light of the political attitudes of the King's faculty and trustees, it is instructive, but not surprising, to note that the overwhelming majority of its commencement topics treated non-political subjects. The two most provocative political exercises came in the aftermath of the Stamp Act repeal: a Latin oration proclaiming "Salus Populi suprema Lex est" and a forensic disputation on the question "Whether a man ought to engage in war without being persuaded of the justness of his cause?" After that, no further political topics entered the commencement programs before the Revolution, probably because the students had to clear their subjects with the president.[113]

Students at King's who wanted to express themselves on politics had to do so outside the college. For some, this could be done through membership in the Literary Society, a debating club composed largely of King's College men, undergraduate, alumni, and faculty, who gathered weekly. Even there the topics were conservative. John Jay, for instance, noted in 1768 debates on "whether in an absolute monarchy it is better that the Crown should be elective than hereditary" and "whether the laws ought to compel a subject to accept public employment?" Another possible outlet for expression was publication, which Alexander Hamilton may have engaged in pseudonymously while a student in 1774, as he certainly did after leaving college. Hamilton, in *A Full Vindication of the Measures of the Congress* and *The Farmer Refuted*, espoused the Commonwealth Whig interpretation of the Anglo-American dispute. Having arrived too recently to have witnessed those events and too young to have remembered them anyway, Hamilton derived his views from Patriot friends who were imbued with the Commonwealth ideology, but he also profited from reading in the King's College library. His pamphlets demonstrated a knowledge of Grotius, Pufendorf, Burlamaqui, Locke, recent political pamphlets on the crisis, and Sir William Blackstone's *Commentaries*.[114] Hamilton, of course, did his writing without the approval of the faculty.

The intensity of the Anglo-American crisis in 1774–1775 prompted informal activity at several colleges that went beyond the ardor of the commencement exercises. Student militia companies formed at Yale, the College of Rhode Island, and at Dartmouth. College of Philadelphia students attended the debates of the Continental Congress. Once fighting began, Yale's Linonian Society cancelled its anniversary celebration, scheduled for April 20, and Rhode Island collegians petitioned to forego commencement, a request President Manning granted while commending the students for their patriotism: "though the Din of Arms, and the Horrors of Civil War, should invade our hitherto peaceful Habitations; yet even these are preferable to a mean and base submission to arbitrary Laws and lawless rapine."[115]

But it was at Harvard where student-inspired activity was of the greatest intensity and longest duration. As early as 1766 a rebellion against bad food had given students the opportunity to draw up a complaint couched in the terms of the colonial protests against British measures. Homespun clothes were the proper attire for college commencements during the late 1760s and again in the years just before fighting began. In the 1770s, the students refused to drink tea. They moved the publication of their commencement theses from the Tory Boston *News Letter* to the Patriot *Massachusetts Spy*. They formed a militia company in 1770 and a year later tried to get 100 stand of arms from the General Court, with no success. As early as 1768 Andrew Eliot of the Overseers wrote Thomas Hollis to boast "the young gentlemen are already taken up with politics. They have caught the spirit of the times. Their declamations and forensic disputations breathe the spirit of liberty." No doubt the residence of the Massachusetts General Court in Cambridge from 1770 to 1773 quickened the politicization of the students. It moved from Boston on order of Lieutenant Governor Thomas Hutchinson allegedly to escape smallpox and Patriots, but the heated rhetoric produced there simply inspired the students with higher notions of liberty. After the passage of the Coercive Acts in 1774, Harvard cancelled public commencements, partly to assuage student sentiment, partly to avoid incident should royal officials show up for the ceremonies.[116] And on the fateful day of April 19, 1775, six students rushed off to join the minutemen. When Lord Percy's columns returning to Boston asked directions of a Cambridge youth, Tutor Isaac Smith instructed them properly. It was his last Harvard instruction. He was shortly compelled to sail for England. Only one in six Harvard alumni alive in 1776 was even passively loyal to the Crown.[117]

At Princeton, Harvard, and the College of Rhode Island, it is certain that students during the 1760s and 1770s became politically conscious and overwhelmingly Patriot. The same process appears to have occurred at Yale and, despite a lack of evidence, we may surmise it to have taken place at Dartmouth and Queen's College. The other schools presented a different aspect. The College of Philadelphia politicized its students, but gave them contrasting political models; it could not be called a Patriot college. At William and Mary, student politicization, if it occurred, was self-generated, outside the curriculum, for the faculty was Tory and gave them no aid. King's College was the quintessential Tory institution. The faculty inhibited political expression and its atmosphere discouraged deviation from the conservative norm. Yet even there some students used the college's resources to become Patriots.

But at King's, the College of William and Mary, and the College of Philadelphia, the relative absence of patriotic fervor angered many Americans. Provincial and state governments were intolerant of Loyalism. Could not something be done about such a center of Toryism as King's? Many Virginians and Pennsylvanians asked the same question about their institutions. In the restructuring of the polity accompanying independence what was the proper relationship between government and higher education? The initial attempts to answer that question would take place in the midst of a revolutionary war, greatly affecting the resulting relationship for more than a generation. But first the war itself would have an impact on the colleges.

NOTES

1. John Adams, "Dissertation on the Canon and the Feudal Law," ed. Robert J. Taylor et al., *The Papers of John Adams* (4 vols. thus far; Cambridge, Mass.: Belknap Press of Harvard University Press, 1977–), I, 126–27.

2. Samuel West, "A Sermon Preached...May 29, 1776," ed. John W. Thornton, *The Pulpit of the American Revolution* (Boston: Gould and Lincoln, 1860), 297–98.

3. James McLachlan, ed., *Princetonians, 1748–1768: A Biographical Dictionary* (Princeton: Princeton University Press, 1976), xix-xx. Ministerial students tended to be older and more rural than others, an observation explained by Howard Miller, *The Revolutionary College: American Presbyterian Higher Education, 1707–1837* (New York: New York University Press, 1976), 100–102.

4. Sheldon S. Cohen and Larry R. Gerlach, "Princeton in the Coming of the American Revolution," *New Jersey History*, 92 (1974): 89–90. For a thorough biographical profile of the Princeton trustees from 1750 to 1776, see William L. Hewitt, "Trustees of the College of New Jersey, 1750–1800" (unpublished seminar paper, University of Wyoming, 1981).

5. William Livingston, *A Funeral Eulogium, on Aaron Burr* (New York, 1757), 12–14.

6. Samuel Davies, "An Ode...for the Annual Commencement of 1759" and "An Ode on the Prospect of Peace (1761)," ed. Richard B. Davis, *The Collected Poems of Samuel Davies* (Gainesville, Fla.: The University Presses of Florida, 1968), 208–9, 210–11; Samuel Davies, *A Sermon Delivered at Nassau Hall...* (New York, 1761), 3, 9–10, 12.

7. Samuel Davies, *Religion and Public Spirit*... (New York, 1761), 6, 7, 11, 16–17; Davies, *A Sermon...at Nassau Hall*, 20.

8. John Witherspoon, "An Address to the Senior Class on the Lord's Day Preceding Commencement, September 23, 1775" and "The Dominion of Providence over the Passions of Men, A Fast Day Sermon, May 17, 1776, at Princeton," John Witherspoon, *Works* (9 vols., London, 1765–1815), VI, 277, 283–84, 175, 181, 184–87, 190–91.

9. See David Freeman Hawke, *Benjamin Rush: Revolutionary Gadfly* (Indianapolis: The Bobbs-Merrill Co., Inc., 1971), 21, for the influence of Davies' *Religion and Public Spirit* on Rush. Francis L. Broderick, "Pulpit, Physics, and Politics: The Curriculum at the College of New Jersey, 1746–1794," *WMQ*, 6 (1949): 54; [Samuel Blair], *An Account of the College of New Jersey* (Woodbridge, N.J., 1764), 24–25; Cohen and Gerlach, "Princeton in the Coming of the Revolution," 84–85; "For the Information of the Public by Order of the Trustees of the College of New Jersey," *Documents Relating to the Colonial History of the State of New Jersey* (Paterson, N.J.: n.p., 1904); Varnum L. Collins, *President Witherspoon* (2 vols., Princeton: Princeton University Press, 1925), I, 112. Madison was one student who availed himself of the opportunity; James H. Smylie, "Madison and Witherspoon: Theological Roots of American Political Thought," *Princeton University Library Chronicle*, 22 (1961): 120.

10. Broderick, "Pulpit, Physics, and Politics," 54, 62; [Blair], *Account of the College of New Jersey*, 25–26; Collins, *President Witherspoon*, I, 107; Miller, *Revolutionary College*, 91–92.

11. James W. Thompson, *A History of Historical Writing* (2 vols., New York: The Macmillan Company, 1942), I, 34–35; Xenophon, *Cyropaedia*, trans. Walter Miller, (2 vols., New York: The Macmillan Company, 1914).

12. *Orations of Marcus Tullius Cicero*, trans. Charles D. Yonge (rev. ed., New York: The Colonial Press, 1900), iv–vi.

13. Ibid., 3–66, 323–40.

14. Cicero, *De Oratore*, trans. E.W. Sutton (Cambridge, Mass.: Harvard University Press, 1959), Bk. I, lines 30–34, 45–68, 148–59.

15. Cicero, *De Officiis*, trans. Walter Miller (Cambridge, Mass.: Harvard University Press, 1913), xiv–xvi, 17, 27, 85–87, 251–53.

16. Ibid., 59, 85, 127, 73, 75, 195–99.

17. Ibid., 293, 297, 303, 299.

18. *Virgil*, trans. H. Rushton Fairclough (2 vols., orig. 1913; reprint, Cambridge, Mass.: Harvard University Press, 1967), I, ix–x.

19. Ibid., 259–61, 567–69; II, 109–11.

20. Horace, *Odes, Epodes, and the Art of Poetry*, trans. John B. Quinn (St. Louis: Blackwell Wielandy Co., 1936), xvi–xxxii; cf. J.F. Dalton, *Horace and His Age: A Study in Historical Background* (London: Longman's, 1917), 1–33.

21. Horace, *Odes, Epodes*, passim.

22. *Livy*, B.O. Foster, trans. (14 vols., Cambridge, Mass.: Harvard University Press, 1919–59), I, xi–xxiii, quotation 76n; Thompson, *History of Historical Writing*, I, 73, 76–77.

23. Thompson, *History of Historical Writing*, 90–91; Ralph L. Ketchum, "James Madison at Princeton," *Princeton University Library Chronicle*, 28 (1966): 47.

24. Michael Rostovtzeff, *Greece* (paperback ed., New York: Oxford University Press, 1963), 224–25, 238; H.D.F. Kitto, *The Greeks* (paperback ed., Harmondsworth, Eng.: Penguin Books, 1957), 154–55, 159–60. For a thorough analysis of Demosthenes' po-

litical thought, see Werner Jaeger, *Demosthenes: The Origins and Growth of His Policy* (orig. 1938; reprint, New York: Octagon Books, 1963); for samples of his oratory, see *The Olynthiac and Other Public Orations of Demosthenes*, trans. Charles R. Kennedy (London: G. Bell & Sons, 1908).

25. Frederick Rudolph, *Curriculum: A History of the American Undergraduate Course of Study since 1636* (San Francisco: Josey-Bass, 1977), 39–42; G. Stanley Hall, "On the History of American College Textbooks and Teaching in Logic, Ethics, Psychology, and Allied Subjects," American Antiquarian Society, *Proceedings*, 9 (1894): 153–55; Broderick, "Pulpit, Physics, and Politics," 56–57.

26. Henry Parkinson, "Notes on College Reading" (Ms., PUA), 234–36.

27. John Witherspoon, *Lectures on Moral Philosophy*, ed. Varnum L. Collins (Princeton: Princeton University Press, 1912), 1–86 passim, esp. 4–5, 17–18, 30, 52, 56; Douglas Sloan, *The Scottish Enlightenment and the American College Ideal* (New York: Teachers College Press of Columbia University Press, 1971), 119–28, 144.

28. Witherspoon, *Lectures on Moral Philosophy*, 67–79.

29. Ibid., 87–89.

30. Ibid., 99–138.

31. Ibid., 4n–5n, 144.

32. [Samuel Davies], *A Catalogue of Books in the Library of the College of New Jersey* (Woodbridge, N.J., 1760), 111.

33. Ibid.; Collins, *Witherspoon*, I, 112; Ketchum, "Madison at Princeton," 48. Works referred to are: Plutarch, *The Lives of the Noble Graecians and Romans*, trans. Thomas North (8 vols., London, 1577); Tacitus, *Works* (including *Germania*) (2 vols., London, 1728–31); Daniel Neal, *The History of New England containing an impartial account of the civil and ecclesiastical affairs of the country to the year of our Lord, 1700* (2 vols., London, 1720); Daniel Neal, *The History of the Puritans* (4 vols., London, 1732–38); Thomas Prince, *A Chronological History of New England in the Form of Annals . . .* (2 vols., Boston, 1736, 1755); John Trenchard and Thomas Gordon, *Cato's Letters: or, Essays on liberty, civil and religious, and other important subjects* (4 vols., London, 1724); Thucydides, *The History of the Graecian War . . . Faithfully Translated from the Original by Thomas Hobbes* (London, 1676); Paul de Rapin-Thoyras, *The History of England, as well ecclesisticall as civil*, trans. N. Tindell (28 vols., London, 1726–47); William Robertson, *The History of the Reign of Emperor Charles V with a view of the progress of society in Europe, from the subversion of the Roman Empire, to the beginnings of the sixteenth century . . .* (2 vols., Dublin, 1762–71); Philip Doddridge, *A course of lectures on . . . pneumatology, ethics, and divinity . . .* (London, 1763); Isaac Watts, *Works* (6 vols., London, 1753); James Burgh, *The Dignity of Human Nature* (London, 1749).

34. For evidence of these student characteristics and behaviors at the pre-Revolutionary colleges, see Samuel Eliot Morison, *Three Centuries of Harvard, 1636–1936* (Cambridge, Mass.: Harvard University Press, 1936), 98, 110–20; Richard Warch, *School of the Prophets: Yale College, 1701–1740* (New Haven: Yale University Press, 1973), 259–65; Leonard Louis Tucker, *Puritan Protagonist: President Thomas Clap of Yale College* (Chapel Hill: University of North Carolina Press, 1962), 232–62; David C. Humphrey, *From King's College to Columbia, 1746–1800* (New York: Columbia University Press, 1976), 92–93, 194–95; Collins, *Witherspoon*, II, 107, 118, 145, 150, 206, 220; Jack E. Morpurgo, *Their Majesties' Royall Colledge: William and Mary in the Seventeenth and Eighteenth Centuries* (Williamsburg: The College of William and Mary,

1976), 131–55; Steven J. Novak, *The Rights of Youth: American Colleges and Student Revolts, 1798–1815* (Cambridge, Mass.: Harvard University Press, 1977), 1–15.

35. David Potter, *Debating in the Colonial Chartered Colleges* (New York: Teachers College Press of Columbia University Press, 1944), 13; Broderick, "Pulpit, Physics, and Politics," 46; Miller, *Revolutionary College*, 91–92.

36. [Blair], *Account of the College of New Jersey*, 25–26; Collins, *Witherspoon*, I, 107.

37. For political commentary, see New York *Mercury*, October 1, 1759; *Pennsylvania Gazette*, October 9, 1760, October 21, 1762. For other pre-1765 commencements, see New York *Gazette and Post Boy*, November 21, 1748; New York *Gazette*, October 2, 1749; New York *Mercury*, September 30, 1754, October 4, 1756, October 8, 1764; *Pennsylvania Gazette*, September 22, 1754.

38. On New Jersey's actions in the Stamp Act crisis, see Edmund S. and Helen Morgan, *The Stamp Act Crisis: Prologue to Revolution* (rev. paperback ed., New York: Collier Books, 1962), 139, 147, 198, 206–7, 224, 256, 259; *Pennsylvania Gazette*, October 10, 1765.

39. New York *Gazette*, October 2, 1766. The trustees took the opportunity of the commencement meeting to address George III, expressing opposition to the Stamp Act and thanking him for its repeal. "Minutes of the Proceedings of the Trustees of the College of New Jersey, Vol. I, 1748–96" (microfilm, PUA); New York *Journal*, October 6, 1768; Collins, *Witherspoon*, I, 119; Witherspoon, *Lectures on Moral Philosophy*, 56, 71, 89–90.

40. New York *Gazette*, October 9, 1769; Ketchum, "Madison at Princeton," 38. On Galloway's status, see Benjamin Newcomb, *Franklin and Galloway: A Political Partnership* (New Haven: Yale University Press, 1972), 200–202.

41. New York *Journal*, October 4, 1770; *Pennsylvania Gazette*, October 18, 1770; *New Jersey Archives*, 1st ser., XXVIII (1907), 275–79; Witherspoon, *Lectures on Moral Philosophy*, 71, 89–90.

42. *Pennsylvania Journal*, October 3, 1771; John Maclean, *The History of the College of New Jersey from Its Origins in 1746 to the Commencement of 1854* (orig. 1877; reprint, 2 vols. in 1, New York: Arno Press, 1969), I, 312–13; Witherspoon, *Lectures on Moral Philosophy*, 12–13, 94.

43. *Pennsylvania Chronicle*, October 31, 1772; Ketchum, "Madison at Princeton," 39; Witherspoon, *Lectures on Moral Philosophy*, 90–94, 96–97, 69, 56, 94–95.

44. John Witherspoon, "Address to the Inhabitants of Jamaica, and Other West Indian Islands, in Behalf of the College of New Jersey," *Works*, VIII, 309–10; *Pennsylvania Chronicle*, October 31, 1772; New York *Gazette*, December 7, 1772.

45. "Trustees' Minutes, College of New Jersey," October 2, 1772.

46. Cohen and Gerlach, "Princeton in the Coming of the Revolution," 79–80; New York *Gazette*, October 11, 1773; "Trustees' Minutes, College of New Jersey," September 30, 1773; Maclean, *History of the College of New Jersey*, I, 318; New York *Gazette*, October 24, 1774.

47. *Rivington's New York Gazetteer*, October 24, 1774.

48. Charles R. Williams, *The Cliosophic Society: Princeton University* (Princeton: Princeton University Press, 1916), 4, 5, 21, 29, 31; Potter, *Debating in the Colonial Chartered Colleges*, 36, 69, 79; William S. Dix, "Princeton University Library in the Eighteenth Century," *Princeton University Library Chronicle*, 40 (1978): 49; *Ind. Ref.*, 46.

49. James Madison to father, July 23, 1770, Robert Rutland et al., eds., *The Papers of James Madison* (14 vols. thus far, Chicago and Charlottesville, Va.: University of Chicago Press and University Presses of Virginia, 1962–), I, 50; New York *Gazeteer or Weekly Post Boy*, July 16, 1770; *Pennsylvania Gazette*, October 18, 1770.

50. Thomas J. Wertenbaker, *Princeton, 1746–1896* (Princeton: Princeton University Press, 1946), 55–57; Charles C. Beatty to Rev. Enoch Beatty, January 31, 1774 (Charles Clinton Beatty Papers, PUA); *Pennsylvania Journal*, February 16, 1774; Cohen and Gerlach, "Princeton in the Coming of the Revolution," 81.

51. Wertenbaker, *Princeton*, 57; Cohen and Gerlach, "Princeton in the Coming of the Revolution," 81–82; Charles Beatty to Betsy Beatty, May 28, 1775 (Beatty Papers, PUA).

52. McLachlan, *Princetonians, 1748–1768*, xxiii; Richard A. Harrison, *Princetonians, 1769–1776: A Biographical Dictionary* (Princeton: Princeton University Press, 1980), xxxi, 547–49.

53. See Caroline Robbins, *The Eighteenth-Century Commonwealthmen: Studies in the Transmission, Development and Circumstances of English Liberal Thought from the Restoration of Charles II until the War in the Thirteen Colonies* (Cambridge, Mass.: Harvard University Press, 1959); Bernard Bailyn, *The Ideological Origins of the American Revolution* (Cambridge, Mass.: Belknap Press of Harvard University Press, 1967); Gordon S. Wood, *The Creation of the American Republic, 1776–1787* (Chapel Hill: University of North Carolina Press, 1969); H. Trevor Colbourn, *The Lamp of Experience: Whig History and the Intellectual Origins of the American Revolution* (Chapel Hill: University of North Carolina Press, 1965); Lance Banning, *The Jeffersonian Persuasion: Evolution of a Party Ideology* (Ithaca: Cornell University Press, 1978); J.G.A. Pocock, *The Machiavellian Moment: Florentine Political Thought and the Atlantic Republican Tradition* (Princeton: Princeton University Press, 1975).

54. Bailyn, *Ideological Origins*, 25–33. Works not previously cited are: Francois Marie Voltaire, *A History of Charles XII, King of Sweden* (1st Eng. trans.; London, 1732); Beccaria, *On Crimes and Punishments* (Am. ed.; Philadelphia, 1763); Emerich de Vattel, *The Law of Nations* (2 vols., London, 1759–60); Sir Edward Coke, *The Second Part of the Institutes of the Laws of England . . .* (London, 1652) and *The Reports of Sir Edward Coke, Kt., in English. . .* (7 vols., London, 1738). Charles Pratt, Lord Camden, was the Whig Chief Justice of England in the mid-eighteenth century; colonists read his decisions, opposing general warrants, for example.

55. Bailyn, *Ideological Origins*, 41. Works not previously cited are: John Milton, *Eikonoklastes* (London, 1649), *The Tenure of Kings and Magistrates* (London, 1649), and *The History of Britain* (London, 1670); James Harrington, *The Commonwealth of Oceana* (London, 1656); Algernon Sidney, *Discourses on Government* (3 vols., London, 1698); Henry Neville, *Plato Redivivus; or, a Dialogue Concerning Government* (London, 1681); Benjamin Hoadly, *The Original and Institution of Civil Government Discuss'd* (London, 1710); Robert Molesworth, *An Account of Denmark in the Year 1692* (London, 1694); Henry St. John, Viscount Bolingbroke, *The Idea of a Patriot King* (London, 1743); Richard Price, *Observations on the Nature of Civil Liberty, the Principles of Government, and the justice and policy of war with America* (London, 1776); Joseph Priestley, *The Nature of Political, Civil and Religious Liberty* (London, 1769); John Cartwright, *American Independence the Interest and Glory of Great Britain* (London, 1774); James Burgh, *Britain's Remembrancer* (London, 1746) and *Political Disquisitions* (London, 1763);

Catherine Macaulay, *The History of England, from the Accession of James I, to that of the Brunswick Line* (8 vols., London, 1763–83).

56. Bailyn, *Ideological Origins*, 45–47; Wood, *Creation of the Republic*, 3–36. For the application of this theory to pre-Revolutionary American politics, see Bernard Bailyn, *The Origins of American Politics* (New York: Alfred A. Knopf, Inc., 1968).

57. R.N. Stromberg, "History in the Eighteenth Century," *Journal of the History of Ideas*, 12 (1951): 295–304; Colbourn, *Lamp of Experience*, 5, 8–9.

58. Colbourn, *Lamp of Experience*, 22–23, 26–31, 44–47, 51–54. Works not previously cited are: Charles Rollin, *The Ancient History*... (10 vols., London, 1730–1738); Edward W. Montagu, *Reflections on the Rise and Fall of Antient Republicks* (London, 1759); Walter Moyle, *The Whole Works*... (London, 1727); Oliver Goldsmith, *The Roman History*... (London, 1769); *The Works of Tacitus, with political discourses upon that author by Thomas Gordon* (2 vols., London, 1728, 1731); Henry Home, Lord Kames, *Essays upon Several Subjects concerning British Antiquities*... (3d ed., Edinburgh, 1763); Obadiah Hulme, *An Historical Essay on the English Constitution* (London, 1771); William Molyneaux, *The Cause of Ireland's Being Bound by Acts of Parliament in England, Stated* (Dublin, 1698); Joseph Swift, ed., *The Works of William Temple* (2 vols., London, 1750).

59. Bailyn, *Ideological Origins*, 83–93; Wood, *Creation of the Republic*, 53–70. For the relationship of virtue to the Puritan strain of thought, see Edmund S. Morgan, "The Puritan Ethic and the American Revolution," *WMQ*, 24 (1967): 1–43.

60. Wood, *Creation of the Republic*, 91–124; Perry Miller, "From the Covenant to the Revival," James W. Smith and A. Leland Jamieson, eds., *Religion in American Life: The Shaping of American Religion* (Princeton: Princeton University Press, 1961), 322–68.

61. The commencement address to the students seems to have been a widespread occurrence, but few records of them have survived.

62. William Smith, "A Charge Delivered May 17, 1757 on the first anniversary commencement of the College, Academy, and Charitable School of Philadelphia" (Ms., UPA); William Smith, "A Sermon First Preached Before the Trustees, Masters and Scholars of the College and Academy of Philadelphia, at the Anniversary Commencement, May 1761," Smith, *Works*, II, 348–49.

63. John Morgan et al., *Four Dissertations, on the Reciprocal Advantages of a Perpetual Union Between Great Britain and Her American Colonies* (Philadelphia, 1766), 6, 9 (Smith's introductory remarks); William Smith, *An Exercise, Containing a Dialogue and Two Odes Set to Music* (Philadelphia, 1775).

64. *Johnson Writings*, IV, 278–79; Rev. Jacob Hardenbergh, "Address at First Commencement, October 12, 1774" (Ms., RUA), 1–9, 15–16.

65. This analysis derives from: *Yale Sketches*, I–III; *A Catalog of the Officers and Alumni of Rutgers College (originally Queen's College) in New Brunswick, N.J., 1766 to 1916* (Trenton: Rutgers College, 1916); John E. Pomfret, *Colonial New Jersey: A History* (New York: Charles Scribner's Sons, 1973); Larry R. Gerlach, *Prologue to Independence: New Jersey in the Coming of the American Revolution* (New Brunswick: Rutgers University Press, 1977); Walter C. Bronson, *The History of Brown University* (Providence: The University, 1914), 34; David S. Lovejoy, *Rhode Island Politics and the American Revolution, 1760–1776* (Providence: Brown University Press, 1958); Sydney James, *Colonial Rhode Island: A History* (New York: Charles Scribner's Sons, 1975); Steven C. Schulte, "The Trustees of the College of Philadelphia and the University of

Pennsylvania, 1750–1800" (unpublished seminar paper, University of Wyoming, 1981); Anne Shearer-Shineman, "The Trustees of William and Mary College, 1750–1800" (unpublished seminar paper, University of Wyoming, 1981); *Sibley's*; Patrick McKnight, "The Trustees of Dartmouth College, 1769–1800" (unpublished seminar paper, University of Wyoming, 1981).

66. Humphrey, *King's College*, 141–44.

67. This evolutionary pattern is described in Rudolph, *Curriculum*, 25–53.

68. Unless otherwise indicated, information regarding materials used in specific fields such as classics, oratory, moral philosophy, and history derives from the following:

On King's College, see Joseph Ellis, *The New England Mind in Transition: Samuel Johnson of Connecticut, 1696–1772* (New Haven: Yale University Press, 1973), 224–26; Helen P. Roach, *History of Speech Education at Columbia College, 1754–1940* (New York: Teachers College Press of Columbia University Press, 1950), 5, 5n; *Johnson Writings*, IV, 56–57, 222; Humphrey, *King's College*, 163, 167, 172–73, 177–81; *Early Minutes of the Trustees of King's College, 1755–1770* (New York: Columbia University Press, 1932), September 1, 1763.

On Harvard, see Morison, *Three Centuries of Harvard*, 135–36; Louis F. Snow, *The College Curriculum in the United States* (New York: Teachers College Press of Columbia University Press, 1907), 48; "The Laws of Harvard College, 1767," *Harvard College Records*, CSM *Publications*, 31 (1935): 347.

On Yale, see Thomas Clap, *The Annals or History of Yale College* (New Haven, 1766), 81; Snow, *College Curriculum*, 90–91, 91n.

On the College of Philadelphia, see William Smith, *An Account of the College, Academy, and Charitable School of Philadelphia in Pennsylvania* (orig. 1756; reprint, Philadelphia: University of Pennsylvania Press, 1951); Edward P. Cheyney, *History of the University of Pennsylvania, 1740–1940* (Philadelphia: University of Pennsylvania Press, 1940), 71–87.

On Queen's College, see George P. Schmidt, *Princeton and Rutgers—The Two Colonial Colleges of New Jersey* (Princeton: Van Nostrand, 1964), 31–37; "Hardenbergh's Address at First Commencement."

On Dartmouth, see Clyde E. Dankert, "Hanover in 1776" (unpublished seminar paper, Dartmouth College, n.d.), 36.

On the College of Rhode Island, see Bronson, *History of Brown*, 101–3; Reuben A. Guild, *Early History of Brown University, including the Life, Times, and Correspondence of James Manning, 1756–1791* (Providence: Snow & Farnham, 1897), 31, 67.

69. *Isocrates*, trans. George Norlin and Larva Van Hook (3 vols., New York: G.P. Putnam's Sons, 1928–45), I, ix–xliv; see especially the *Panegyrics* where these themes all appear.

70. *Sallust*, trans. J. C. Rolfe (Cambridge, Mass.: Harvard University Press, 1921), ix–xii.

71. Ibid., passim, quotation 21.

72. Ibid., passim.

73. Works not previously cited are: Julius Caesar, *De bello Gallico et civil. . .* (London, 1742); *The History of Herodotus*, trans. Isaac Littlebury (2 vols., London, 1709); edition of Plato in use is not identifiable. Tacitus may also have been part of the William and Mary curriculum. William Stith, president from 1750 to 1752, wrote approvingly of him in *The History of the First Discovery and Settlement of Virginia; Being an Essay Toward a General History of the Colony. . .* (Williamsburg, 1747), vii.

74. *The Histories of Herodotus*, trans. George Rawlinson, (2 vols. New York: E.P. Dutton Co., 1964), xv–xvi, xviii, xix; Thompson, *History of Historical Writing*, I, 24–26; Rostovtzeff, *Greece*, 187–89.

75. *The Complete Writings of Thucydides*, introduction by John H. Finley, Jr. (New York: Modern Library, 1951), ix–x, xii–xiii; Thompson, *History of Historical Writing*, I, 30, 32; Rostovtzeff, *Greece*, 189–90.

76. Thompson, *History of Historical Writing*, I, 70–71.

77. Moses Hadas, ed., *The Complete Works of Tacitus*, trans. Alfred J. Church and William J. Broadribb (New York: Modern Library, 1942), xi–xviii, xix, quotation from *Annals*, Bk. 3, par. 65; Thompson, *History of Historical Writing*, I, 85, 87, 89–90; Rostovtzeff, *Greece*, 193, 204.

78. *The Lives of the Noble Graecians and Romans*, trans. Thomas North (5 vols., orig. 1579; reprint, New York: AMS Press, 1967), x–xi, xxv–xxvi, xxix–xxx; Thompson, *History of Historical Writing*, I, 107–8.

79. Plato, *The Laws*, trans. Trevor J. Saunders (New York: Modern Library, 1970), 18, 20–21, 23–32; Rostovtzeff, *Greece*, 234–35.

80. Leon B. Richardson, *A History of Dartmouth College* (2 vols., Hanover, N.H.: Dartmouth College Publications, 1932), I, 120.

81. Courtlandt Canby, "A Note on the Influence of Oxford University upon William and Mary College in the Eighteenth Century," *WMQ*, new series, 21 (1941): 244.

82. On the Oxford curriculum, see Charles E. Mallett, *A History of the University of Oxford* (3 vols., orig. 1927; reprint, New York: Barnes & Noble, 1968), III, 123–24, 130–39; Christopher Wordsworth, *Scholae Academicae: Some Account of the Studies at the English Universities in the Eighteenth Century* (orig. 1877; reprint, New York: A.M. Kelley, 1968), 120–21, 123–27, 151–53.

83. On Burlamaqui, see Ray F. Harvey, *Jean Jacques Burlamaqui: A Liberal Tradition in American Constitutionalism* (Chapel Hill: University of North Carolina Press, 1937). It is possible that Burlamaqui was read at William and Mary before the Revolution, but this is mere supposition on the part of the late librarian, Earl G. Swem; 98.

84. Thomas Clap, *An Essay on the Nature and Foundations of Moral Virtue* (New Haven, 1765); Clap, *Annals of Yale*, 84–85.

85. Samuel Johnson, *Elementa Philosophica: Containing Chiefly; Noetica, or Things Relating to Moral Behavior* (Philadelphia, 1752).

86. "Elementa Philosophica," *Johnson Writings*, II, 367, quotation 427, 429–30, 433.

87. Samuel von Pufendorf, *De Officio et juxta legem naturalem libri duo* (London, 1673). For an analysis of Pufendorf, see Leonard Krieger, *The Politics of Discretion: Pufendorf and the Acceptance of Natural Law* (Chicago: University of Chicago Press, 1965), 82–169.

88. Myles Cooper, *Ethices Compendium, in Usem Collegiorum Americanum* (New York, 1774).

89. Hugo Grotius, *De Jure Belli ac Pacis libri tres* (1st Eng. trans., London, 1654). On Grotius, see Richard Cox, "Hugo Grotius," Leo Strauss and Joseph Cropsey, eds., *The History of Political Philosophy* (Chicago: University of Chicago Press, 1963), 344–53.

90. Francis Hutcheson, *A Short Introduction to Moral Philosophy in Three Books, Containing the Elements of Ethics and the Law of Nature* (Glasgow, 1747) and *A System of Moral Philosophy, in Three Books* (2 vols., London, 1755), quotation II, Bk. III,

308–9. Cooper might have used either. On Hutcheson as Commonwealthman, see Robbins, *Eighteenth Century Commonwealthmen*, 185–95, and "When It Is that Colonies may Turn Independent: An Analysis of the Environment and Politics of Francis Hutcheson," *WMQ*, 11 (1954): 214–51.

91. Humphrey, *King's College*, 220–21; Poplicola, *Rivington's New York Gazeteer*, December 2, 1773; Myles Cooper, *National Humiliation and Repentence Recommended* (Oxford, 1777), 22–23.

92. Quotation from Thomas H. Montgomery, *A History of the University of Pennsylvania, 1749 to 1770* (Philadelphia: George W. Jacobs, 1900), 205.

93. Jacob Duche, Jr., et al. to Board of Trustees, June 21, 1756, quoted in Albert F. Gegenheimer, *William Smith, Educator and Churchman, 1727–1803* (Philadelphia: University of Pennsylvania Press, 1943), 51–52.

94. Elizabeth A. Ingersoll, "Francis Alison, American Philosophe, 1705–1779" (Ph.D. Diss., University of Delaware, 1974), 39–63, 82–85; Sloan, *The Scottish Enlightenment*, 89–91.

95. Francis Alison, " 'Moral Philosophy Lectures,' from the Notes of Andrew Allen, 1756" (Ms., UPA), 61–65; Ebenezer Kinnersley, "Lectures on Moral Philosophy [undated]" (Ms., UPA), 208, 210–11, 214–15.

96. Ingersoll, "Francis Alison," 157–58; Kinnersley, "Lectures on Moral Philosophy," 216, 219–21.

97. On Harrington, see Robbins, *Eighteenth Century Commonwealthmen*, 34–35, and J.G.A. Pocock's introductory material in *The Political Works of James Harrington* (Cambridge: Cambridge University Press, 1977), 15–76, 128–52.

98. On Sidney, see Robbins, *Eighteenth Century Commonwealthmen*, 41–47, and "Algernon Sidney's *Discourses on Government*: Textbook of Revolution," *WMQ*, 4 (1947): 267–96. On Locke, see Robbins, *Eighteenth Century Commonwealthmen*, 58–67, and John Locke, *Two Treatises of Government*, ed. Peter Laslett (2d ed., Cambridge: Cambridge University Press, 1967), 92–120.

99. Caroline Robbins, "Library of Liberty—Assembled for Harvard College, by Thomas Hollis of Lincoln's Inn," *Harvard Library Bulletin*, 5 (1951): 12–15, 8–9, 21–22, 183–87. For more on Hollis, see Robbins, "The Strenuous Whig—Thomas Hollis of Lincoln's Inn," *WMQ*, 7 (1950): 406–53.

100. Robert F. Seybolt, "Student Libraries at Harvard, 1763–1764," CSM *Publications*, 28 (1930–33): 449–60; Samuel E. Morison, "Note on Student Expenses at Harvard, 1772–1776," ibid., 301–5.

101. Benjamin Wadsworth, "Notebook, 1766–67" (Ms., HUA); "Library Charging List, 1773–1776" (Ms., HUA).

102. Work not previously cited: *The History of Scotland, during the Reigns of Queen Mary and King James VI till his Accession to the Crown of England* (2 vols., London, 1759).

103. Oliver Goldsmith, *The History of England, from the Earliest Times to the Death of George II* (4 vols., London, 1771). On Goldsmith, see Arthur L. Sells, *Oliver Goldsmith: His Life and Works* (New York: Barnes & Noble, 1974), 365–69.

104. Works not previously cited: Tobias Smollet, *The History of England from the Revolution of 1688, to the Death of George II* (5 vols., London, 1758–60); Rene Aubert, Abbe de Vertot, *The History of the Revolutions . . . of the Roman Republic* (2 vols., London, 1720).

105. Morison, *Three Centuries of Harvard*, 90–91; Edward J. Young, "Subjects for

Master's Degrees in Harvard College from 1665 to 1791," MHS *Proceedings*, 18 (1881): 126.

106. Howard H. Peckham, "Collegia Ante Bellum: Attitudes of College Professors and Students Toward the American Revolution," *Pennsylvania Magazine of History and Biography*, 95 (1971): 58; Morison, *Three Centuries of Harvard*, 90–91; Young, "Subjects for Master's Degrees," 127; *Virginia Gazette* (Purdie & Dixon), October 4, 1770, October 29, 1772; "Scrapbook of Newspaper Cuttings re Commencements, 1770, 1799 & 1800" (HUA).

107. Potter, *Debating in Colonial Chartered Colleges*, 23; Charles Thompson, "Valedictory Address, 1769" (BUA); Guild, *Early History of Brown*, 91–92.

108. Reuben A. Guild, "The First Commencement of Rhode Island College, and Especially the Discussion of American Independence, Which Constituted the Prominent Feature of the Commencement Exercises," *Collections* of the Rhode Island Historical Society, 7 (1885): 281–98.

109. Potter, *Debating in Colonial Chartered Colleges*, 23; Peckham, "Collegia Ante Bellum," 51–52; Bronson, *History of Brown*, 65–66; Guild, *Early History of Brown*, 189, 247, 260–61.

110. Peckham, "Collegia Ante Bellum," 51–52; Francis Brown, ed., *A Dartmouth Reader* (Hanover, N.H.: Dartmouth College Publications, 1969), 30–31.

111. See the *Pennsylvania Gazette*, May 28, 1761, May 27, 1762, June 6, 1765, March 20, May 15, 29, 1766, November 26, 1767, December 1, 1768, July 6, 1769.

112. Ibid., June 14, 1770, July 11, 1771, July 28, 1773, May 31, 1775; *Virginia Gazette* (Pinkney), June 29, 1775.

113. Roach, *Speech at Columbia*, 8–9; New York *Mercury*, May 26, 1766, June 1, 1767. The pre-Revolutionary commencements are reviewed in M. Halsey Thomas, "King's College Commencements in the Newspapers," *Columbia University Quarterly*, 22 (1930): 226–45. S.G. Tucker, "Carthage Must be Destroyed, student oration in Latin, May 21, 1772" (WMA).

114. "Minutes of the Literary Society, 1766–1772" (Ms., New York Historical Society); Richard B. Morris, ed., *John Jay, The Making of a Revolutionary: Unpublished Papers, 1745–1780* (New York: Harper & Row, 1975), 88–92; Broadus Mitchell, *Alexander Hamilton, Youth to Maturity, 1755–1788* (New York: The Macmillan Co., 1957), 54–59; Jacob E. Cooke, *Alexander Hamilton* (New York: Charles Scribner's Sons, 1982), 8; cf. *A Full Vindication of the Measures of Congress, from the Calumnies of their Enemies, In Answer to a Letter, Under the Signature of A.W. Farmer...* (New York, 1774) and *The Farmer Refuted...*, Harold C. Syrett, ed., *The Papers of Alexander Hamilton* (26 vols., New York: Columbia University Press, 1961–79), I, 45–78, 81–165.

115. Peckham, "Collegia Ante Bellum," 52, 59; "Linonian Society Records, 1768–86" (YUA); Richardson, *Dartmouth*, I, 327; Bronson, *History of Brown*, 65.

116. Morison, *Three Centuries of Harvard*, 117–18, 136–39, 141, 144, 145–46; William C. Lane, "The Rebellion of 1766 in Harvard College," CSM *Publications* (1905): 33–59; Peckham, "Collegia Ante Bellum," 54–56; "Records of the Speaking Club," I, 1773–1776 (HUA); Josiah Quincy, *History of Harvard University* (2 vols., Cambridge, Mass.: J. Owen, 1840), II, 163; *Virginia Gazette* (Purdie & Dixon), May 12, 1771, June 25, 1772.

117. Morison, *Three Centuries of Harvard*, 147, 147n.

4

The Colleges at War

The outbreak of the Revolutionary War intensified the tendency of many politically active Americans to embrace the Commonwealth Whig political ideology. It stimulated many clerics to persuade their congregations that the fighting was an example of God's wrath, and victory over the British would only come as the result of increased virtue and Godliness. In several ways these two lines of thought were complementary, producing an enhanced patriotism. Bringing about the same result was an incompletely understood sense of nationalism that infused many Americans, even some who could not articulate why they felt as they did. Whatever the cause, the overwhelming majority of Americans united to bring an end to British rule over her former colonies.[1]

The colleges took part in the crusade, and they continued to change because of it. One reason was that their physical plants proved tempting as refuges, either temporarily during battles or over longer terms as barracks, hospitals, or headquarters. Dislocation, dispossession, and damage afflicted many institutions at one time or another, and physical distress usually heightened politicization. The college communities were very active politically and, where necessary, they undertook academic reforms to bring their curricula into line with the prevailing political ethos. Abetting the change was a second major influence on wartime higher education, the greater concern of the public with the kind of education being offered by the colleges. An increasing number of Americans were convinced that the emerging nation needed republican citizens inculcated with public virtue and faithful to the state.

Acting privately and through agencies of government, members of the public sought to insure that colleges taught proper values. In doing so, the American people modified and intensified the third element of the English legacy to the colonial college—the activist state. To see these forces at work, we focus on wartime Virginia and the experiences of the College of William and Mary.

I

In military terms, war came late to Virginia. The British did not make the South the center of sustained activity until 1778, and it was December 1780 before a detachment of British troops arrived on the Virginia coast, attempting to take some pressure off Lord Cornwallis' forces in the Carolinas and to provide protection for local Loyalists. The campaign season of 1781 saw British raids on Richmond, the uniting of two units at Petersburg, an indecisive engagement at Green Spring, and Cornwallis' occupation and fortification of Yorktown. It was during the Yorktown campaign, culminating in British surrender on October 19, and the Franco-American occupation of the middle peninsula over the following winter that the College of William and Mary experienced war.[2] Her experience resembled what happened at most other institutions.

The college closed in June 1781 when Cornwallis' troops stopped briefly in Williamsburg on their way to Yorktown. With the Redcoats encamped only a few miles away, it did not seem safe to reopen. Soon the French troops who were helping to lay the siege commandeered the buildings as a hospital. The faculty enjoyed the companionship of the cultured French officers who stayed over the winter after the siege, but the occupation proved costly. One wing of the college burned down on November 23. The French offered a handsome sum for rebuilding, but that could not replace those parts of the president's library or scientific apparatus lost to the flames, nor would it speed up the process of rebuilding in labor-short, inflation-wracked Virginia. When the faculty officially reconvened in March 1782, it strove to hasten the French departure. A June farewell took place none too soon for the college.[3]

While the damage and disruption the war inflicted upon William and Mary were significant, the Revolution had already brought even more startling changes to the campus. The background lay in the long-lasting feud between the faculty and the Board of Visitors over the internal control of the college. It had continued into the 1770s, but new elements were added, including the quality of the faculty and its patriotism. These drew fire not just from the Visitors but from a general public which had become newly concerned about education due to the Revolutionary crisis.

The issues of proper education and patriotism were never far separated. As early as 1769 a spirited newspaper exchange occurred beginning with the assertion that Professor Camm was either unwilling or unable to translate a few lines of Virgil posed by a questioning citizen. That these lines had a patriotic meaning applicable to Virginia's quarrels with England implied that Camm was unpatriotic, incompetent, or both. Although Camm had his defenders, the exchange culminated in a charge that the faculty's views and competence were irrelevant since they did not teach; the facetious suggestion appeared that the college's financial affairs could be straightened out by charging faculty members ten shillings for each missed lecture.[4]

This combination of public and Visitorial criticism prompted some remedial action. In 1770 the faculty tightened academic regulations, instituted an examination process to insure the quality of those passing from the grammar school to the college, and filled in the professorships to the number specified in the charter. Still Virginians remained suspicious, for the professors soon became embroiled in the movement for an Anglican bishop and they showed a very friendly attitude toward the new royal governor, Lord Dunmore, pledging to render their students "religious without superstition or enthusiasm, true Sons of Liberty without licentiousness, and virtuous without ostentation." This was an equivocal message to send to Virginians who were increasingly dissenter, Patriot, and concerned about their virtue.[5]

In this atmosphere criticism reappeared. From late 1773 through 1774 Virginians urged reform of the college curriculum, both undergraduate and graduate. Suggestions included the establishment of a required curriculum for undergraduates incorporating work in history, chronology and geography, the addition of professorships in medicine and law so that the college might become a true university, and the elimination of the grammar school so that the education of men might cease to be hampered by the presence of boys. All these drawbacks loomed larger in light of the excellent collegiate education to be had at the North, elements of which were about to appear in Virginia through the maturing plans of Samuel Stanhope Smith, Princeton graduate and proposer of Hampden-Sydney Academy.[6]

To all this the faculty remained indifferent. Firmly attached to their thoroughly English educational ideal, they offered only classics, natural and moral philosophy, and divinity for aspiring ministers, all on the Oxford plan. Not content to rouse the ire of their fellow colonists with an inflexible educational program, the professors also refused to recognize the deepening political crisis. Generally, they ignored the Anglo-American debate, choosing rather to compete among themselves for possible ecclesiastical preferment. Occasionally they were outspokenly supportive of Virginia's royal government, a grave political error. For example, in December 1774 the faculty congratulated Lord Dunmore on the successful conclusion of an Indian campaign, but this same governor had recently prorogued the Burgesses in response to their protest against the Coercive Acts. "Optator" parodied the faculty address, congratulating them for repudiating the Burgesses and dissenting from the Continental Association. He fervently hoped that student sentiment was totally opposed to that of their preceptors. President Camm's 1775 commencement address did not meet with Patriot approval either. He argued for no more drastic change in the empire than dominion status, a position long deserted by many Virginians. It certainly had been abandoned by the collegians, for the faculty had just had to ban possession of arms by the students, and had tried to dismiss the Grammar Master for joining the militia (the Visitors intervened to save his position).[7]

The outbreak of war in New England, the loss of control over Virginia's government by Dunmore, and the Declaration of Independence combined to make the position of William and Mary's Tory faculty less tenable. Camm's insistence on upholding the forms of the royal charter was of no use. The faculty could not enforce discipline among the students, many of whom left to join the militia; it could not keep down criticism of the pedagogy and loyalty of its members; it could not ward off the Visitors. Some faculty left voluntarily, others met dismissal at the hands of the Visitors in mid-1777.[8]

The demise of the Tory faculty and the elevation of Patriot professor James Madison to the college presidency in 1777 were parts of a thorough reform planned for the college, involving not just the Visitors and the public critics of the institutions, but the state government as well. In early 1776 "Academicus" urged the Virginia Convention that, in its creation of a state government, it should not overlook education "for it is learning alone which can give any lasting stability to your structure." He stressed support for William and Mary: "If you do not reverence it as the parent of your virtue and knowledge, adopt it as your offspring, and make it the conveyance of these blessings to the latest posterity." Through the rest of the year "Academicus" refined his proposals, urging the appointment of new Masters and Visitors, none of the latter to live far from the college so that oversight could be constant. The Visitors should meet frequently and report yearly to the state legislature. The curriculum should be overhauled, a total of fourteen professors appointed, and new offerings should appear in moral philosophy, history and chronology, and law. This was the way to make William and Mary of "infinite utility to a community . . . especially a free one."[9] At least one Virginian wanted the college to be a state institution.

Another was James Madison, a 1772 graduate who was retained as Professor of Natural Philosophy, and who was virtually the only Patriot member of the faculty. Madison spent the winter of 1775–1776 in England, obtaining clerical orders. Considering his denunciation of English degeneracy and anti-Americanism, and his praise for the American quest for liberty, it is a wonder he was ordained, but his sojourn kept him away from the college struggles for a while and he was a natural candidate to try to accommodate the college to the new order. Madison wanted to seek a new charter, fully local funding, and to use the college to promote the American cause. The most recent historian of William and Mary thinks Madison wrote the "Academicus" letters. However that may be, there is no question that he wrote Provost William Smith of the College of Philadelphia in September of 1776 to ask for a copy of that school's educational plan, which he apparently thought excellent if backed by the proper politics. He anticipated that the next Virginia Assembly would reform the college: "They would fain have it beneficial to the Country, and I wish the Means to obtain so desirable an End, may be weighed with the attention which they deserve." Madison's acceptance of legislative control of the college was but one facet of a staunch patriotism that prompted him to captain the college militia company, become chaplain of the Virginia Legislature, and espouse consistently the most republican sentiments. While he saw no need for a connection between church and state, he did see the link between republican government and higher education.[10]

The other driving force behind the proposal for state control of William and Mary was Thomas Jefferson. For Jefferson, reform of the college went hand-in-hand with the creation of a state-wide educational system, under legislative control, designed to benefit a republican government. He made the purposes clear in the preamble to his "Bill for the More General Diffusion of Knowledge," proposed in late 1778. Fearing that even the best forms of government could, over time, degenerate into tyranny, Jefferson believed

that the most effectual means of preventing this would be, to illuminate, as far as practicable, the minds of the people at large, and more especially to give them the knowledge of those facts, which history exhibiteth, that, possessed thereby of the experience of other ages and countries, they may be enabled to know ambition under all its shapes, and prompt to exercise their natural powers to defeat its purposes.[11]

To prevent tyranny, to exercise natural rights, to inculcate virtue—for these reasons Jefferson proposed a system of universal education that would yield a natural aristocracy of talent while simultaneously allowing the wealthy to proceed in school as far as they wished. To ensure correct values of patriotism and pedagogy, there were provisions seeking to guarantee the fidelity of instructors to the commonwealth and giving to the Visitors of William and Mary the responsibility for designing the educational plan and soliciting the faculty for the schools.[12]

William and Mary would not only determine the content of the lower schools' offerings, but would also serve as the final destination for scholars whose abilities or purses carried them that far. Jefferson's purpose in seeking to amend its charter complemented his goals for the system as a whole. The college should become as publicly advantageous as it was publicly expensive,

and the late changes in the form of our government, as well as the contest of arms in which we are at present engaged, calling for extraordinary abilities in both council and field, it becomes the peculiar duty of the Legislature, at this time, to aid and improve that seminary, in which those who are to be the future guardians of the rights and liberties of their country may be endowed with science and virtue, to watch the sacred deposit.[13]

To effect these ends, Jefferson called for substantial reform in three areas: government, funding, and curriculum. The Board of Visitors would be reduced to five members, annually elected by joint ballot of the two legislative houses. They would be the legal successors of the original Visitors, enjoying all their powers, with some significant exceptions. The rights to remove faculty and to decide disputes involving the college statutes would rest with another body, the Chancellors. These would be selected by the Legislature out of the High Court of Chancery or the General Court and would continue in office as long as they remained on the bench.[14] The intent here was manifold—firmly to attach the college to the state and vice versa, considering the strained relations between the two bodies before the war; to render Visitorial government more intimate, thus more effective; to introduce legal scholars into the disputes over the respective powers of the faculty and Visitors and of the interpretation of the college laws, thus settling them once for all. Bonding the college to the state was also the purpose of the funding provision, which sought to replace all previous revenues foreign and domestic with a legislatively set export duty on tobacco.

Pedagogical reform aimed to produce Patriots, to bring the Enlightenment to the Virginia college, and to create a true university. Jefferson proposed eight professors, one to be president. The professorships would be: mathematics; anatomy and medicine; natural philosophy and natural history; ancient languages; modern languages; civil and ecclesiastical history; law and police; moral philosophy.[15] Professorships in law and medicine would make William and Mary resemble the universities of Europe in curriculum, if not organization. The modern languages, natural philosophy, and mathematics professors would bring the latest learning in these fields to the students and would introduce them to the intellectual world of contemporary Europe. A republican, state-service oriented education would be assured in the law, history, and moral philosophy classes. One last indicator of the public nature of the institution and its program was the absence of instruction in religion. Jefferson did not think that promulgating religion was the business of the state.

Jefferson's educational plans were ambitious, radically republican, and doomed to failure. Part of the problem with the state-wide school system was geography, for people lived too far apart to make the plan practicable. Another difficulty was the emptiness of Virginia's purse. There was not enough money to fund any substantial school system. But more important, according to Jefferson, was the very fear of Anglicanism that had inspired the reform. He maintained that despite the feelings of President Madison, the overhaul of the Visitors, the express prohibition of an Anglican allegiance, and the Legislature's control over the whole, Virginia's dissenters remained so wary of Anglican influence that they could not tolerate reform based on William and Mary. Perhaps so; the Presbyterian cleric who headed Hampden-Sydney Academy, Samuel Stanhope Smith, warned Jefferson of that very danger. Whatever the principal cause, the bill did not pass the lower house in 1779 and did little better under Governor James Madison's leadership in the mid-1780s.[16] Public education in Virginia had to wait.

The attempt to turn William and Mary into a state university failed, but educational reform did not. Patriotic, civic-oriented education became a reality at the college during the Revolution. When the Visitors at last dismissed Camm and the other Tory faculty in early 1777, making Madison president, they moved the college in a new direction. For one thing, they appointed Patriots to the faculty vacancies. Their choice for moral philosophy was Robert Andrews, a 1768 graduate of the College of Philadelphia and an Anglican priest, but a Revolutionary activist. Outspokenly patriotic, Andrews signed the House of Burgess' proposal to call a Virginia convention in 1775, then served on the York County Committee of Safety. He became chaplain to the Virginia militia in 1777, serving until 1780. After his selection to the college faculty in 1777, he gained prominence in Williamsburg, obtaining election to the city committee of safety in 1779 and soon thereafter becoming an alderman.[17]

Other appointments had to wait for reorganization of the college curriculum, a move spearheaded by Jefferson as Visitor after his bill for educational reform failed to pass the Legislature. Madison and Andrews stayed on. Three new professors joined the faculty: Carlo Bellini in the chair of modern languages, James McClurg in anatomy and medicine, and George Wythe in law and police. All were Patriots. Bellini had come to America from Italy in 1774, settling near Jefferson in Albemarle County. When war came he served in the Virginia militia until his health gave out. McClurg was a Virginian who had attended William and Mary, later obtaining a medical degree from the University of Edinburgh in 1770. Back in Virginia by 1773, he took no active role until fighting began but then became head of the Virginia militia's surgical and hospital staff, a post he held throughout the war. Wythe was the most distinguished of the three. The oldest, he had a long record of public service at the time of his appointment, including a brief tenure as colonial attorney general, several years as a Burgess, a term as mayor of Williamsburg, and six-years' clerkship of the Burgesses from 1769 to 1776. He had been radically American since the days of the Stamp Act, to which he responded by asserting that England and America were coordinate nations united only by a common sovereign; Parliamentary legislation therefore did not apply to the colonies. He took a leading role in the Burgess' Fast Day Resolution of 1774 which led to Lord Dunmore's dissolution of the Legislature and the movement for a continental congress. He was a delegate to that congress, an ardent supporter of independence who signed the Declaration. Back in Virginia he helped write the state constitution, was one of the revisors of the colony laws from 1776 to 1779, became Speaker of the House of Delegates in 1777 and one of the judges of the High Court of Chancery in 1778. His patriotic credentials were impeccable.[18]

This same emphasis on patriotism characterized the changing composition of the Visitors. Of those whose careers are known, only one Tory, Ralph Wormeley, served throughout the war. Another, William Byrd III, resigned in 1777. The other pre-Revolutionary Visitors who stayed on all served Virginia in civil or military offices. The group included Thomas Nelson, Jr., who became governor in 1781 and Carter Braxton, who signed the Declaration of Independence. Those Visitors added during the war were all Patriots, including Jefferson, James Madison the politician, and Benjamin Harrison IV, governor from 1781 to 1784.[19]

Did the installation of a Patriot faculty and administration produce a Patriot education, one which politicized students according to the Commonwealth Whig ideology? The answer is yes, but the evidence is indirect, for little is known about classroom activities. When the Visitors enacted their 1779 reforms they established a true elective system; students might choose to attend any two or three professors' lectures depending on the fees paid. This system, a reflection of Virginians' beliefs about the practical uses of education, produced varied attendance patterns. James McClurg had so few applicants for his medical lectures there is doubt he ever delivered them. Bellini offered no instruction in languages in 1780 and had few students thereafter. Andrews had considerable success with lectures on oratory, criticism and belles lettres, but what he did in moral philosophy is unknown. President Madison's natural philosophy lectures were popular and the biggest draw of the college was Wythe's law course. There he taught common law, equity, merchant, marine, and ecclesiastical law, adding some commentary on politics. The students enjoyed his classes in part because he followed the latest legal scholarship of Blackstone, in part because he instituted moot courts and mock legislatures to give them practice in their chosen fields, and in part because he was a superb teacher. Jefferson thought there was no better training ground for lawyers in America.[20]

Only Wythe's teaching directly suggests an orientation toward the Commonwealth Whigs. It was the extracurriculum that indicates the presence of a similar atmosphere across the campus. Surviving commencement exercises had a Commonwealth Whig focus. In 1777 there was an oration on that form of government which is most favorable to public virtue and the arts and sciences. The following year's topics included an address in praise of Washington, an oration on the advantages of classical learning, and a debate on whether arts or arms were most profitable to a state, which was a comparative analysis of the Roman and Carthaginian republics. The college awarded honorary degrees to Thomas Jefferson and the Marquis de Chastellux, a French army officer who was also a *philosophe*, in 1782. The award to the Frenchman was significant not just because of his nationality, but also because it produced a reply from him indicating some of the topics that had engaged the faculty over the winter of 1781–1782. Chastellux recollected discussions on the types of government of the several colonies and of the nation, on whether a broad franchise predicated on property holding would long be possible in a society with increasing extremes of wealth, on whether public virtue would continue to hold talented Americans in governmental office, and on the relationship of the arts and sciences to republican government, to luxury and leisure. All these questions derived from the Commonwealth canon. The similarity of Chastellux's reflections to commencement exercises suggests that discussion of these questions was ongoing, part of the curriculum and extracurriculum of the college.[21]

Other parts of the extracurriculum confirm the influence of the Commonwealth Whig ideology. The library assembled by the members of the F.H.C. in the early 1770s was heavily laced with Commonwealth works, and the historian of the college library thinks many of the volumes also were on its shelves. By 1781 the college collection may have numbered 3,000 volumes; it was opened to undergraduates as part of the 1779 reforms.[22] Even more revealing were the debate topics chosen by the undergraduate society Phi Beta Kappa. While many dealt with belles lettres or the personal concerns of youth in Virginia society, several treated politics. Some involved Commonwealth ideological issues: "Whether an agrarian law is consistent with a wise republic," "Whether anything is more dangerous to civil liberty in a free state than a standing army in time of peace," "Whether commonwealths or monarchies are most subject to sedition and commotions," and "Whether any form of government is more favorable to public virtue than a commonwealth." Others revealed a concern with the Whig view of history: "Whether the execution of Charles I was justified" and "Whether Brutus was justified in killing Caesar." Still others treated contemporary political issues: "Whether a general assessment for the support of a religious establishment is repugnant to the principles of a republican government," "Whether duelling ought to be tolerated in this or any other free state," and "Whether a state has any dearer interest than the education of youth."[23] Wartime reform brought the educational experience at William and Mary into line with that at other Patriot colleges.

The events at William and Mary demonstrated anew the overwhelming desire on the part of Americans to have their educational institutions acting in accordance with the values held dear by the society at large. The Revolution produced such a crisis that Virginians were unwilling to tolerate any discrepancy between the college's and their own views of political and intellectual values. As a result they called upon government to end the discontinuity. Sectarian religious jealousies prevented the state from performing that function. It fell to private hands to effect reform. But Virginians were not alone in their concern that higher education conform to community values. In several other states the citizens turned to government to bring order out of wartime chaos and to guarantee harmony between the republican values they professed and the teaching their sons received at the local colleges.

II

In order for any kind of reform to take place, the colleges had to survive the war. This they did, but at some cost depending upon their location. Armies, American, British, and French, marching or camping, devastated the colleges during the war. As in Virginia, college halls, often the largest buildings in the colonies, served as bivouacs, hospitals, and citadels. At best, occupying armies meant dislocation, at worst, destruction.

Harvard was the first to suffer. By early evening of April 19, 1775, after the skirmishes at Lexington and Concord, Massachusetts militia had rendered the Cantabrigians homeless. On May 1, the Committee of Public Safety made it official; Harvard was to be army headquarters for the siege of Boston. The Harvard Corporation would not brook permanent suspension, but had to use facilities in Concord to reassemble the students in September. Not until June 1776 did college activities return to Cambridge.[24] Luckily, little damage had been done, but enough that the Corporation sought reimbursement from the General Court.[25]

At the approach of British troops in 1776, most of New York's population evacuated. The defending American troops occupied King's College in May, using it as a hospital. When the British entered the city they appropriated the "hospital." Shortly thereafter fire gutted it. Not until Washington's re-entry into New York in 1783 did King's trustees recover their building.[26] Rhode Island College served first as a barracks for American militia when the British occupied Newport in December 1776. No sooner had the Americans left than the French, with Washington's blessing, turned it into a hospital. Consequently, the students had no hall until June 1782. When they got it back, they found severe damage.[27] This pattern of seizure and use for troops was repeated in New Brunswick, New Jersey, and Philadelphia. British troops occupied Queen's College in late November 1776 and slightly damaged it during their seven months' stay. The threat of disruption served to keep classes from resuming in New Brunswick until 1782.[28] The College of Philadelphia first served as a barracks to the Pennsylvania militia, then to the British. Altogether, the visitors stayed two years.[29]

At Yale and the College of New Jersey the wartime danger was battle. Yale's terror was real, although fleeting. On July 4, 1779, British ships appeared off West Haven. Their troops debarked and advanced on New Haven the following day. Yale president Ezra Stiles dismissed the students for the term and removed the library's books. Defenders rushed out to drive off the British but were unsuccessful. The British lingered less than a day, destroyed the wharfs but not the college, and left. New Haven was safe thereafter.[30]

The college at Princeton was devastated. In September 1776 the annual commencement took place without degrees or accompanying ceremony. The British Army was only fifty miles away. The students soon dispersed. On December 7 the British seized Princeton and the college, using them as a base of operations. Nassau Hall became a fortress as well as a barracks when, on January 3, the Americans briefly dislodged the Redcoats from Princeton, but lost it that same evening. American cannon fire had made the building uninhabitable and the British shortly withdrew, only to be replaced by the Americans (perhaps more used to primitive accommodations). Benjamin Rush observed that the fighting had turned the college and church into heaps of ruins. Whatever escaped damage in the battle, the Americans had plundered in their five-month occupation of Princeton. After that, until November 1778, the college served as a military hospital. College officials did not regain unrestricted use of their building until 1782. President Witherspoon ultimately received almost $20,000 from the United States in payment for the damage caused by the contending armies.[31]

Interrupted or lost studies and damage to the college buildings angered college students and administrators alike. If, as often happened, the Patriot armies caused the damage, the British drew the blame for forcing them into the field. It is quite possible that reaction against the British heightened the appeal of Commonwealth ideology on college campuses.

Despite destruction and dislocation, the colleges continued as best they could along paths previously trod. If possible, they broadened their educational fare, adding studies deemed necessary in an independent and maturing country. They continued to emphasize education for state service, increasing the importance of politics and allied pursuits while continuing to disseminate the Commonwealth Whig political principles. And those associated with the colleges—faculty, trustees, and students—ever more closely identified with the Revolutionary movement and American independence. In all these areas, public pressure, often exerted through state government, made itself felt at some colleges.

Most college faculties enthusiastically embraced the Revolution. Princeton, which had the most politically active pre-Revolutionary faculty, continued to lead the way. John Witherspoon spent most of the war years serving in the Continental Congress, journeying back and forth between Princeton and wherever the capital might be. He was very active, voting for the resolution proposing independence, signing the Declaration, and participating in debates and committee work on such issues as the Articles of Confederation, foreign alliances, the organization of executive departments, the western lands question, and the selection and instruction of the peace commission. He usually wrote Congress' fast day and thanksgiving proclamations. With respect to issues that caused divisions in the Congress, he was an advocate of the French alliance, but wanted the peace commissioners to retain some independence of action. He was a partisan of the small states, staunchly supporting the single vote per state provision of the Articles, and he wanted national administration of western lands.[32]

Outside Congress, Witherspoon served briefly in the New Jersey State Legislature and was active as a propagandist, justifying the Revolution to his fellow Scottish-Americans and decrying British atrocities during the war by measuring them against the criteria for the proper waging of war developed in his lectures.[33] He also preached often, asserting that America's fate rested in God's hands and that He would look after the newborn nation. The reason God supported America was that she desired liberty: "The knowledge of God and His truths have from the beginning of the world been chiefly, if not entirely, confined to those parts of the earth where some degree of liberty and political justice were to be seen."[34]

The Professor of Mathematics and Natural Philosophy, William C. Houston, was an equally ardent Patriot. He accompanied Witherspoon to the Continental Congress as deputy secretary in 1776. Leaving that post, he captained a New Jersey militia company until September 1777, when he had to resign to take over management of the college. Those duties did not keep him from two terms in the New Jersey Assembly. Then in 1779 he was elected to the Continental Congress, which he served intermittently until 1785, most often working on committees treating taxation and finance. Admitted to the bar in 1781, he also clerked for the New Jersey Superior Court. It was the press of all these duties that prompted his resignation from the college in 1783.[35]

The frequent absences of Witherspoon and Houston led to the engagement of Samuel Stanhope Smith in 1779 as Professor of Moral Philosophy. Smith was a Princeton graduate, former tutor, and son-in-law of Witherspoon. Before returning to New Jersey he had been a Presbyterian missionary to Virginia and had helped found Hampden-Sydney Academy. Once in Princeton, he was the least active Revolutionary, for his collegiate duties kept him close to campus.

Some indication of his political sentiments appeared in a sermon preached at the funeral of Richard Stockton, Patriot trustee, whom Smith commended as a public servant, judge, and New Jersey Representative to Congress. By implication, Smith agreed with Stockton's Revolutionary politics.[36]

The Queen's College faculty was similarly active. Temporary President Jacob Hardenbergh had been an early supporter of the Revolution. He repeatedly gained local public office in New Jersey, preached and wrote in favor of the American cause, and counselled George Washington, whose army camped within the bounds of his parish for two winters. The British despised Hardenbergh sufficiently to offer a reward for his capture.[37] The college tutors were also Patriots. John Taylor became a militia officer in 1776, eventually rising to the rank of colonel. He fought in New Jersey and New York, which left him time for occasional visits to the college, but military concerns and a dispute over his salary meant he was not regularly with the students during the war. Left in charge was John Bogart, a 1778 Queen's graduate. Since he was with the students, teaching when the movement of the armies allowed, he had no time to be an active soldier. But he followed the war vicariously through a large correspondence with former classmates, Taylor, and Hardenbergh. No doubt he passed on to his charges the details of battles he learned from a dozen or so participants.[38]

Some New England college faculties were also firm in their patriotism. At Yale, Naphtali Daggett, who had stayed on as Professor of Divinity after relinquishing the presidency, met the British 1779 raid on New Haven as part of the band of armed resistors. He was wounded, captured, then released. His exertions led to a decline in health and eventual death. Samuel Wales succeeded Daggett. He was not an active Patriot while on the faculty, but had served as a chaplain in the Continental Army in 1776.[39]

The Newport, Rhode Island minister Ezra Stiles, who assumed Yale's presidency in 1778, had been sympathetic to the Patriot cause for years. In many ways his politicization resembled those of the clerical educators active in the 1750s and 1760s. He possessed a religious version of the Commonwealth Whig view of history, believing that the human experience had been a long contest between liberty and tyranny, both civil and ecclesiastical. As an American he was gratified that the colonists, especially the Puritan element among them, had participated in two great victories for English liberty—the Civil War and the Glorious Revolution. Looking back on colonial history, Stiles concluded that the absence of an established artistocracy and of the doctrine of divine right in church and state gave the colonists even more liberty than their English counterparts.[40] Perhaps because he was so confident of the internal sources of American liberty, he was suspicious of threats from without. Stiles, like so many other colonial ministers imbued with incipient nationalism, regarded the Seven Years' War as a crisis—a Catholic conspiracy aimed at ending liberty in America, unwittingly aided in the beginning by a British society and government crippled by corruption. But William Pitt's ascendancy and the British victories in Canada had dispelled Stiles' fears. He became optimistic about the colonies' future, picturing a land blessed with a new code of laws, a government based on elections, a people whose interests would be served by a continent-wide congress, and a society devoid of aristocracy in which arts and sciences flourished. It was almost a utopia, existing under divine providence.[41]

British policy after 1763 ended Stiles' optimism and gave his vision a different orientation. From the time he learned of the peace treaty provisions he feared that both civil and religious tyranny were parts of the colonial future. The new customs service policies, the Sugar and Stamp Acts, coupled with Anglican activities designed to establish an American episcopate (and in the process revoke the Rhode Island Charter) convinced the Newporter that a conspiratorial design was afoot. He spoke out whenever possible to denounce British policy and the designs of the northern Anglicans, but he also was sure that the colonial troubles were God's punishment for falling away from the practice of piety and virtue. He counselled submission and reason, repentence and reformation, even though his anger at colonial exploitation increased.[42]

By the late 1760s he had decided to try to keep religion and politics separate, to look on colonial resistance as a spectator. He did not speak out publicly on issues, did not pen protests, did not participate in demonstrations. Nor did he reconcile himself to events. Stiles looked upon the Townshend Duties, the arrival of troops in Boston, the subsequent "massacre," the Regulator movement, the Rhode Island troubles culminating in the Gaspee affair, the Tea Act, the Tea Party, the Coercive Acts, all with mounting despair. This litany of oppression convinced him that religious and civil liberty were under such direct attack that recourse could no longer be had within the empire. He lost faith in the British king and constitution, began a correspondence with the English Commonwealth Whigs Catherine Macaulay and Richard Price, and looked upon the prospect of colonial union with favor. In short, he became a Revolutionary, if a quiet one.[43]

Once war broke out, Stiles devoured battlefield reports, visited army camps, and reflected on what he learned. He was probably better informed on the American military situation and its implications than anyone else outside government. From his reflections he developed the conviction that, granting the war was another punishment for Americans' sins, the people had the wherewithal, religious, virtuous, material, to regain God's favor and defeat the British. Not even his own exile from a Redcoat-occupied Newport could diminish his faith. Stiles brought his convictions and faith to Yale. He confided to his diary in April 1777, "I have an intense Confidence & Trust that the Great American Cause both as to Liberty & Protestantism will be carried through to eventual Success, Victory, & Triumph."[44]

While in charge of the college, Stiles kept to his decision not to mix religion and politics, at least publicly. His only discernibly political actions were to suspend lectures upon the receipt of news of important American victories.[45] When, however, the Connecticut Assembly asked him to deliver the 1783 election sermon, he revived his vision for America. It was an almost millennial vision. *The United States Elevated to Glory and Honor* pictured America once more as a city on a hill. He paralleled the American and ancient Hebrew experiences to show that God does reward or punish political communities according to their level of virtue or vice. A virtuous America, acting under divine providence, had conquered monarchy. Now she must serve the rest of the world as an example of the possibilities of a prosperous, democratic republic. In describing his model, Stiles revealed himself a Harringtonian republican. Following the Commonwealthman, he asserted that freehold tenure and equitable distribution of property were the keys to a successful republic. Americans held those keys, making possible a "well-ordered democratical aristocracy, standing upon the annual election of the people, and revocable at pleasure, [which] is the polity [that] combines the United States."[46]

The guarantee of the success of the polity, argued Stiles the college president, was an educated citizenry, especially at the highest level:

The cultivation of literature will greatly promote the public welfare....Travel, biographies, and history, the knowledge of the policies, Jurisprudence, and scientific improvement among all nations, ancient and modern, will form the civilian, the judge, the senator, the patrician, the man of useful eminence in society....It would be for the public emolument should there always be found a sufficient number of men in the community at large of vast and profound erudition, and perfect acquaintance with the whole system of public affairs, to illuminate the public councils, as well as fill the learned professions with dignity and honor.[47]

At wartime Yale Ezra Stiles was a quiet, highly philosophical Patriot.

Political loyalties at the other college campuses were not so certain in the late 1770s as at the New Jersey institutions and Yale.[48] The faculties became more patriotic as the war went on, but only because the schools made choice of new members at least partly out of a desire to conform to the surrounding communities' political values.

In April 1776, the Harvard Overseers required all the governors and instructors to assemble and give a statement of their political principles, this at the request of the General Court. The faculty performed satisfactorily, but some were grudging in their compliance. Divinity Professor Edward Wigglesworth never gave up hope of reconciliation between England and America; he was largely silent on Revolutionary affairs. Samuel Langdon presumably retained his pre-war patriotism, but he, too, said little publicly during the war. Perhaps he was concerned with his failure successfully to lead the college, which resulted in his ouster at the end of 1780. Language Professor Stephen Sewell and Natural Philosophy Professor John Winthrop were more active. The former became Cambridge representative to the General Court of 1777; the latter was an enthusiastic republican, an admirer of Paine's *Common Sense*, who served on the Massachusetts Council until 1777 when he resigned because of ill health.[49]

Those selected to the Harvard faculty during the war were all outspoken Patriots. Samuel Williams, a 1765 graduate and minister who had developed considerable expertise as an amateur astronomer, filled the professorship of natural philosophy after Winthrop's death. He had taken the American side early on in the taxation dispute. While on the faculty, he preached sermons linking the future of civil and religious liberty with the success of the Revolution. In them he warned about public corruption, noted the role of the Christian religion in preventing it, and argued that the additional element needed to secure liberty was a government of equal laws based on the consent of the governed.[50] Joseph Willard replaced Samuel Langdon in the Harvard presidency in December 1781. He, too, support the Revolution from the pulpit and had served his town of Beverley, Massachusetts, on various committees associated with the consideration of the Massachusetts Constitution of 1778 (his committees opposed it). Installed in Cambridge, Willard continued to preach in favor of the American cause. His sermons on public occasions displayed a Commonwealth Whig interpretation of English and American history, great admiration for George Washington, and an almost millennial vision of a divinely protected America characterized by public virtue and piety.[51]

When Harvard began medical instruction in 1782, both its teachers were Patriots. Benjamin Waterhouse spent almost all the war years in Europe, acquiring his education. His pro-American sentiments, although sincere, were necessarily confined to letters to John Adams and occasional outbursts before astonished companions at the University of Leyden. John Warren had been active in the Boston Tea Party, joined a volunteer militia company in 1774, and, after his brother was killed at Bunker Hill, moved into the Continental Army to hold various medical posts in New England and New York. Even while instructing at Harvard, he continued to supervise military hospitals in the Boston area. Called upon to deliver Boston's first Fourth of July oration in 1783, he responded with a discourse on political principles, emphasizing the need for virtue, patriotism, and frugality, and the desirability of open commerce and equality before the law. In those admonitions and in a Patriot rendering of the events after 1763, Warren repeatedly referred to classical and Commonwealth Whig historians and political commentators. The ideological slant of his message could not have been clearer.[52]

At Dartmouth, President Eleazar Wheelock had great difficulty dispelling the impression that his close associations with the royal governor and the S.P.G. had left him a Tory. As late as May 1777, a former student reported to him that the rumor was circulating in northern Massachusetts that Wheelock had written to British officers just before the war to advise them on strategy. Wheelock had not been an ardent Patriot, and once the war began he was more interested in preserving his college than in advancing the American cause. Still, he took some steps and acquiesced in others that suggest his sympathies lay with the rebels. There were his proposals to New Hampshire, Connecticut, and the Continental Congress that he use his Indian students to keep their tribes neutral. He sent Tutor Sylvanus Ripley with the American forces to Canada to unite Indians behind the colonies. The states rebuffed him, but Congress thought the effort worthwhile, reimbursing Wheelock over $900 in 1778 in what was the nation's first defense contract with a college.[53] Wheelock consented to two of his sons joining the Continental Army, and John served with distinction against Burgoyne before returning to Hanover in 1779 to take over the college when his father died.[54] Meanwhile, Tutor Ripley, who would become Professor of Divinity in 1782, kept both Eleazar and John informed of American military developments from his post with the army in Canada and after.[55] Dartmouth certainly leaned toward the Patriot cause.

The most drastic realignment of professors, involving the most direct interference by the state, took place at the College of Philadelphia.[56] The provocation was the Tory inclinations of some faculty and trustees. We have seen that instructors at the college had never been of one mind about resistance to Great Britain. Armed conflict and independence fragmented them even further. Most were Patriot. Francis Alison backed the war movement by urging Philadelphians to train sufficient militiamen to defend the city, by gathering supplies, and by preaching a sermon denouncing British battlefield tactics. The Redcoat occupation of Philadelphia forced him and his Patriot colleague Robert Davidson to flee to the countryside; shortly after their return Alison died. On the other issue that divided Pennsylvanians, the Constitution of 1776, Alison was among those who disapproved of its ultra-democratic character. He thought the drafters well-meaning, but ignorant of political theory.[57]

The medical school faculty, other than Adam Kuhn who seems to have been uninvolved, was pro-American. William Shippen, John Morgan, and Benjamin Rush all saw service in the Continental Army as physicians in charge of medical care in various theaters. Unfortunately, just who was in charge where, the competence of administration, and the quality of medical care became issues that embroiled the three in a lengthy dispute that damaged the reputations of all. They repaired the rift well enough to work together in the medical school, but their conduct was not a model of selfless patriotism for their students.[58]

Rush was concerned with more than army medicine, however. He and his colleague, Professor of Mathematics James Cannon, were leading figures in Pennsylvania's independence movement. Both were involved with the colony's efforts to enforce the Continental Association, and their work led to political collaboration and greater involvement. Cannon became secretary to the Philadelphia Committee of Privates, a radical group that sought broader participation by Pennsylvania citizens in the militia and democratization of the Pennsylvania Assembly through the addition of more backcountry and city delegates. Rush joined the campaign, but despite popular enthusiasm the May 1776 Assembly elections moved that organization no closer to broader membership nor independence.[59]

Rush and Cannon then switched from reforming the Assembly to abolishing it, mounting a public effort to persuade the Continental Congress to intervene in Pennsylvania. At least partly due to their polemics, the "independents" succeeded in discrediting the Assembly, in electing a provincial convention and

a constitutional convention, and in achieving formal separation from Great Britain.[60] At this point Rush and Cannon parted company on Pennsylvania politics.
Cannon, a true radical, believed in colonial virtue, British vice, and the evil
designs of the wealthy. He served in the constitutional convention, helping to
write the document that was the most popularly oriented constitution of the
Revolutionary era. It incorporated many of the reforms advocated by Commonwealth Whigs: broad suffrage, annual elections, rotation in office, and a weak
executive. Cannon, to promote the democratic tenor of the government, urged
his fellow citizens to elect plain people to man its offices.[61]

The constitutional convention deemed Dr. Rush a "plain person," electing
him to the Continental Congress. There Rush soon openly criticized the Pennsylvania Constitution, opposing the unicameral house, the absence of checks
and balances, executive weakness, and other features. Feeling betrayed, Pennsylvania's radicals did not re-elect him.[62]

Rush continued to support the Revolution as a private citizen and essayist.
He talked with generals and congressmen, wrote hundred of letters attempting
to influence policy, and addressed the general public on occasion to castigate
them for their faint-hearted patriotism, to urge a stronger navy, and to advocate
nationalist measures in the early 1780s. Cannon, probably because of the British
occupation, left Philadelphia for Charleston, South Carolina, in 1778.[63]

The accusations of disloyalty among the faculty centered on Provost William
Smith and Professor of Languages Jacob Duche. Smith continued to equivocate.
In February 1776, he addressed the Continental Congress, urging reconciliation
with Great Britain, yet showing himself more a friend to liberty than to the
British. Soon there followed *Plain Truth*, virtually a paragraph by paragraph
refutation of the arguments of *Common Sense*, in which Smith demonstrated
that knowledge of Montesquieu, Rousseau, Hume, and Burgh could be used to
justify continued union as well as rebellion. The "Cato" letters in the March
and April *Pennsylvania Gazette* revealed Smith's continuing frustration that
reconciliation seemed so utterly unlikely. As to state politics, Smith resisted the
"independents," helping to compose the May 1776 remonstrance designed to
ward off attacks on the Assembly. It all went for nought. Independence silenced
Smith, but suspicion of his loyalty lingered. When Howe's troops approached
Philadelphia, the government forced Smith to give bond not to speak or write
anything against the American colonies nor to give information to the British.
Even this chastening experience could not reconcile Smith to independence.
After Howe's evacuation, Smith preached a sermon praising George Washington
as a Cincinnatus, noting the Godly origin of government ruled by law and based
on popular assent, and arguing that those who contended for such a government
deserved praise. But it was an artful presentation that did not endorse independence nor the republican governments Americans were trying to establish,
certainly not the one in Pennsylvania.[64]

Exactly what produced a change in Jacob Duche is unknown. The preacher
deemed so patriotic he became chaplain of the Continental Congress exhibited

declining enthusiasm for the Revolution from the moment of independence. Although he still preached patriotic sermons and wrote encouraging letters to Washington, he pled ill-health in order to resign his chaplaincy. Perhaps the democratic nature of the Pennsylvania government offended the aristocratic Anglican. Perhaps it was his treatment by the British; when Howe arrived he clapped Duche in jail. Adversity did not strengthen his spirit. Within weeks he began to criticize the Congress. He then addressed an extraordinary public letter to Washington bemoaning the condition of the army, the lack of public support, and the sad state of Congress. He urged the general to repudiate independence, and surrender his army to Howe before it was annihilated and the country devastated. Not even the British general's protection could shield such duplicity. Duche fled the country in December 1777.[65]

Professors of such doubtful loyalty were intolerable to Pennsylvania Revolutionaries. The college reorganization of 1779[66] deprived Smith of his position. Duche had already resigned, Alison had died, and Cannon had left Philadelphia. The political tone of the reconstituted faculty altered significantly. Into the provostship moved John Ewing, a Presbyterian minister with a talent for astronomy. He had been a cohort of Alison's in the anti-Assembly politics of the 1760s, was an ardent supporter of the Revolution and a Constitutionalist (as those who defended the Constitution of 1776 were known).[67] Robert Patterson became Professor of Mathematics. He was a northern Irishman who had military experience prior to his 1768 arrival in Pennsylvania. At the outset of the Revolution, Patterson's military background enabled him to become first a militia instructor and then a brigade major. He ended his military stint when he joined the faculty.[68]

Probably the most distinguished appointee was David Rittenhouse, the famed astronomer and mathematician. Although a scientist, Rittenhouse was no stranger to politics. In the mid-1760s he had favored the Assembly in Pennsylvania's internal struggles, but British measures combined with Assembly vacillation on resistance to make him support both independence and an overhaul of local government by 1776. He became a Constitutionalist and held a variety of positions during the war, most prominently Assemblyman, delegate to the constitutional convention, and state treasurer. Rittenhouse was active both in education and state affairs. Only Samuel Magaw, the Anglican minister selected Vice-Provost in 1782, was politically inactive.[69] These men joined holdovers Rush, Shippen, Morgan, and Davidson, as well as the returning James Cannon, to form an unquestionably patriotic, if somewhat contentious, faculty.

The same general pattern of loyalty that held for the faculties was true of the trustees of these colleges. At the New Jersey schools, patriotism was the rule, both among trustees who continued to serve on the basis of pre-war appointments and those appointed during the conflict. Among Queen's College trustees, only Philip and Robert Livingston of New York could be considered even conservative Revolutionaries. While little is known of the Dutch Reformed ministers who served Queen's, many of Princeton's minister-trustees were chaplains in the Continental Army or state militias, and George Duffield was for a time chaplain of the Continental Congress. It was perhaps a recognition that the colleges served more than religious interests that induced both boards to include a higher proportion of laymen as the war progressed. Many of these men gained fame in the military or in state and national office.[70]

Yale continued its tradition of solely ministerial appointments to the Corporation. None of the pre-Revolutionary holdovers or the new appointees were Tories. Some were politically inactive while others were ardent Patriots, preaching Revolutionary election, fast day, or thanksgiving sermons. Moses Mather was even twice imprisoned by the British when they raided southeastern Connecticut.[71] Many College of Rhode Island trustees remain obscure. Only two pre-Revolutionary trustees continued to hold office after accusations of Toryism in 1776, but perhaps this resulted from the failure of the board to meet between 1776 and 1782; neither served beyond that point. Esek Hopkins, chosen to one of the vacancies, had gained considerable fame by 1782 as commander of the Rhode Island militia.[72]

Harvard's Overseers changed their makeup in much the same way that the faculty did. None of the holdovers, nor those who joined the board by the end of the war, were Loyalists. Only Robert Treat Paine was a conservative. Most prominent among the holdovers were Samuel Adams, the minister Samuel Cooper, James Bowdoin, and the military commander Artemus Ward. Among the newcomers were Francis Dana, Continental Congressman and Minister to Russia, John Hancock, Samuel Osgood, another Continental Congressman, and the minister Charles Turner, a friend of Sam Adams who served in the Massachusetts legislature between 1780 and 1788.[73]

At Dartmouth the loyalties of the trustees were as hard to discern as those of the faculty. Royal Governor John Wentworth remained on the board until 1784 even though he fled the province in 1775. Theodore Atkinson and John Jaffrey were both suspected of Loyalism but served into the 1780s. Eleazar Wheelock died in 1779 with his political sentiments still not fully understood. A number of other trustees, both clerical and lay, took no active part in the Revolution. Just five of the fifteen men who governed Dartmouth during the war were active Revolutionaries. Only John Wheelock, with his military career, and Samuel Phillips, who was in Massachusetts state office continuously over the last quarter of the eighteenth century, were conspicuous rebels.[74]

But the trustees of the College of Philadelphia were the most factionalized. Ten of the twenty-one carryover trustees were Loyalist to one degree or another, yet in the other group were Thomas Bond, who helped organize the Continental Army hospital system, Thomas Willing, a merchant who contributed thousands of dollars to the war effort, Continental Congressman Thomas Mifflin, and a Congressional chaplain, William White. New men appointed during the war were all Patriots, including Robert Morris, George Clymer, and James Wilson. What united many of these men despite their contrasting views on independence was their dislike of the Pennsylvania Constitution of 1776. Only one known Constitutionalist was an active trustee of the College of Philadelphia.[75]

The legislative reorganization of 1779 created the University of the State of Pennsylvania which took over the property and students of the College of Philadelphia even while its trustees were fighting the move. The trustees of this institution were not only all Patriot, but all were Constitutionalists. Included among them were George Bryan, David Rittenhouse, John Bayard Smith, Joseph Reed and others who were active in both state and national affairs.[76] It was quite clearly impermissable in the heightened political atmosphere of Philadelphia to be a public servant, even in the indirect capacity of college trustee, and not be a Patriot. It was the Tory cast of the College of Philadelphia trustees as well as the faculty that prompted legislative takeover. Yet even an all Patriot board and faculty would not have been sufficient by 1779, for politics operated on several levels in Pennsylvania and where one stood on the issue of the state constitution was as important as one's opinion of independence. All of this must have proved an intriguing spectacle for the students.

The other colleges did not face quite this degree of political scrutiny. But faculty and trustee appointments elsewhere (with the possible exception of Dartmouth) make clear that college governing boards were sensitive to public opinion. They did not wish to be at odds with community political values.

The desire to meet community needs had its effect on the college curriculum as well as personnel, at least where wartime damage did not prevent change. Independence brought with it a sense of nationalism that prompted cultural self-sufficiency, as well as a realization that the loss of British connections would force Americans to do some things on their own for which they had previously depended on the mother country. One result was a movement in the colleges toward greater "practical" instruction. More mathematics and science, more applied techniques such as surveying, entered the curriculum. The educational enterprise in Philadelphia strove to continue its medical school and in 1782 Harvard added one.[77] These were necessary developments for the success of the new nation, but they were essentially apolitical. Most colleges moved in some ways to strengthen the political component of their curricula as well.[78]

At Princeton, Harvard, and the College of Rhode Island, curricular development proceeded without off-campus pressures. Apparently, these schools offered instruction that pleased the larger communities and the students. Princeton continued to instruct much as in the past. There is no indication that the content of the classics or of moral philosophy changed. Some small additions to the curriculum took place, indicating heightened preparation for state service. In 1781, at the behest of Professors Houston and Smith, the trustees considered formalizing graduate instruction in theology and law. This would have provided earned degrees in fields where informal training had taken place for some time (and would continue), but the board decided the college could not afford it. It could afford to offer French, however, and so took part in a politically significant, increasingly popular trend which anticipated greater contact with America's wartime ally. Another development carrying political overtones was the act of Delaware's governor in endowing Princeton with £100 to fund a student essay contest on several topics, including "what are the most proper measures to be adopted by a government for promoting and establishing habits of piety and virtue among a people," and "no one or more of the United States can ever derive so much happiness from its dissolution as from its continuation."[79] These curricular changes were minor, but they show that Princeton continued to advance state-service education.

At Harvard, too, the changes were slight but were in the direction of more political material. Almost as soon as the scholars returned to Cambridge in 1776, the seniors petitioned the Corporation to be allowed more time in the study of both natural and moral philosophy. The board consented, but more time presumably meant more to study. Some support for this assumption emerges from the Corporation request that the General Court help supply a number of science books as well as Burlamaqui, Caesar's *Commentaries*, Sallust, Xenophon, and Homer's *Iliad*, all part of the politically oriented classics and moral philosophy courses. Instruction in French began as an elective in 1779; students were free to take the course as long as it did not interfere with their other studies. In 1782 there took place a movement to advance scholarship in several fields by rewarding top performers with prizes. Among the books tested in the classics were Livy's *History*, Demosthenes' *Orations*, and Xenophon; in moral philosophy the list included Burlamaqui on natural law, Price on morals, and Montesquieu on government, all parts of the Commonwealth canon.[80]

The College of Rhode Island held no classes between late 1776 and mid-1782. When courses resumed the trustees thought it best to strengthen the curriculum. They revised all fields, in the process increasing the Commonwealth content of the program. Classics now included Homer, Virgil, Cicero's *Orations*, Lucian, Xenophon, and Caesar's *Commentaries*. Hutcheson's *Moral Philosophy* and Doddridge's *Lectures* were new junior studies, while the seniors read Bolingbroke's *Lectures on History*.[81] The trustees also appealed to the King of France for help in replenishing the library, promising in return to implement the study of French, thus participating in another trend of the times.[82]

Overt public pressure influenced other colleges to reform their curricula. Connecticut citizens did not believe that Yale was responsive enough to their needs during the 1770s. The replacement of Thomas Clap with Naphtali Daggett had not greatly changed the curriculum. Many people thought the college concentrated too much on training ministers. Moreover, since many of the ministers produced embraced the New Divinity, a sort of second generation Edwardsianism incomprehensible to many laymen, even the religiously devout were upset at Yale. Both public and private criticism echoed throughout the decade after Clap's demise. For example, when tutors Timothy Dwight and John Trumbull introduced belles lettres to the students in 1777, college theatrical productions soon followed. These educational innovations were called frivolous, even dangerous, because they meant neglect of proper learning and they promoted vice. Repeated suggestions that the Assembly assert greater control over Yale reached their climax with the college's dispersion after the British invasion of 1777. With most instruction taking place in the Hartford area, some asked the Assembly to charter a second college there, leaving Yale to its own devices.[83]

Yale's very survival depended upon compromise. Yale and the state government conferred during 1777 to arrive at one. Its significance for college government appears below. For the curriculum, the most striking elements were the selection of Ezra Stiles as president and the suggestion that Yale expand its programs.[84] Stiles concluded that the future of the college rested largely with him. He felt considerable pressure to devise a system of education that was acceptable in the state.[85]

Stiles proposed a new curriculum even before accepting the presidency. It aimed to satisfy both the religious and political concerns of Connecticut's people. A president and three tutors would instruct in ethics, languages, the liberal arts and sciences. There would be a professor of mathematics and natural philosophy. This was traditional fare. A professorship of oratory and belles lettres was not, but under proper supervision the students could study even modern authors without being corrupted. Religious interests would be pleased with the professorships in divinity, ecclesiastical history, and Hebrew and oriental languages. Potential ministers would relish these courses, and a secular balance would be achieved by the presence of civil history in the program (its slant might be inferred from Stiles' desire to write Catherine Macaulay, asking her to endow a chair). Those wanting Yale to branch out would like the proposed graduate instruction in medicine and law; these chairs would turn the college into a true university. But Stiles favored legal instruction for everyday citizens as much as for lawyers, because they would be the public officials of the new country: "How happy a community abounding with Men well-instructed in the knowledge of their Rights and Liberties?" To produce such men Stiles wanted instruction in civil law ranging from the ancient Romans to the modern English, in common law so that Americans would understand their legal heritage, and in statutory law so that they could codify it. They should also know the legal codes of the thirteen states, the policies and forms of government of the nations of the world, and the international law that made intercourse among nations possible. Stiles imagined some sort of doctoral program for the mastery of all this, but it seems clear that undergraduates would have to face instruction in these fields as well.[86]

The plan was far-reaching both educationally and politically. It was also impossible to carry out in wartime Connecticut. But there is some evidence that Stiles went as far as he could personally to educate his students in accordance with his dreams. His classroom lectures might address almost any subject. He began formally to offer ecclesiastical history in August 1778, two months after taking office, but by that time he had also lectured on gravity, oriental learning, and chronology. The last became a fairly regular pursuit for he soon required reading in William Guthrie's *A New Geographical, Commercial, and Historical Grammar* (London, 1770). Later that year he discoursed on academic education and introduced lectures on "Cyclopedias of literature," which covered not only belles lettres, but also languages, geography, mathematics, natural philosophy, and astronomy. Stiles even allowed the acting out of plays, but they were serious, moralistic, and patriotic, witness the presentation of a dramatic representation of the invasion of the Susquehanna country by Tories and Indians. In June 1779 he began ethics instruction for the seniors; the first in a long time, he noted.[87]

With the exception of Guthrie, Stiles made few changes in the books students read, but the topicality of his lectures appeared in the questions his students debated during their oratorical recitations. Not all the debates were political, of course, but the seniors did discuss issues such as "Whether Learning is of Public Advantage to the State," "whether universal religious toleration is beneficial to the state," and "whether America would be more happy as part of the British Empire, than as an independent republic?" The question "Whether the lately proposed terms of pacification purporting to have been proposed by the court of Madrid (fictitious or not) as acknowledging American independence may be accepted consistent with the dignity and glory of the United States?" even had an answer recorded: yes, if the country gained fishing rights in Newfoundland, free passage on the Mississippi, and boundaries of 45° latitude on the north, the southern edge of Georgia on the south. Other questions on the conduct of the war and the governance of the new republic intrigued Stiles' students: "Whether agriculture or commerce needs the most encouragement in the United States at present," "whether representatives are to act their own minds or those of their constituents," "whether Long Island's trade with the British is justifiable in the present war," and "whether a standing army is dangerous to America?"[88]

Through these debates Stiles kept his students in close touch with philosophical and practical issues. Given his own Commonwealth sympathies, the analysis he applied to them is clear. His efforts here, in natural science, ecclesiastical history, and elsewhere, meant that Stiles was working hard to make the college acceptable to the public, the Corporation, and the students. The latter numbered 249 in early 1783, making Yale the country's largest college. With his pupils, at least, Stiles was a success.[89]

Curricular reform accompanied administrative reform in Philadelphia, all with an eye toward pleasing the people and their representatives, the Assembly. Noting that the trustees were much engaged in public business, that the university appeared to be the object of "immediate and great consequences to the state," a committee of the newly constituted faculty proposed in 1780 to broaden the curriculum. The objects were to render the institution more useful to a greater segment of the population while simultaneously creating an academic structure similar to European universities. These goals led the committee to propose professorships in law, divinity, history, chronology and geography, drawing and design, and in the traditional arts and sciences. It was an odd amalgam that would make the curriculum more professional and more practical at the same time. Another move in the latter direction, again no doubt responding to political pressure, was the creation of a German department in 1780. This never really evolved into more than a preparatory school for German-Americans wishing to continue their educations at the university where the instruction was in English, but it was an attempt to open up higher education to a politically significant group of Pennsylvania citizens.[90]

Putting these ambitious designs into effect proved too much for the new university. There was not enough money to fill the proposed professorships, nor were there enough students to fill the classes had they been taught. Within two years the trustees accepted a faculty plan for reorganizing the curriculum. There would be courses in natural philosophy, moral philosophy including logic and metaphysics, Latin and Greek, oriental and German languages, history, mathematics, English, and oratory. Apparently, students could choose from among these courses to pursue one of four parallel lines of study (content unknown) leading to the Bachelor of Arts. This did not work out quite as intended either. Yet for some years Robert Davidson did deliver what was one of the country's earliest courses devoted to history, and Samuel Magaw taught moral philosophy according to Francis Hutcheson's Common Sense approach and along lines quite similar to those of his mentor, Francis Alison.[91] It seems clear that the concern over curriculum at the Philadelphia institution was not what was taught, for that hardly changed; rather it was the character and politics of those who were teaching that mattered.

The University of the State of Pennsylvania and Yale, more than other institutions, responded to community pressures in refining their curricula, but within the limits imposed by the war, most colleges moved to emulate European universities and to embrace more closely the Commonwealth Whig ideology. Both were efforts dictated by American political conditions.

The disruption of collegiate life, however exciting it may have been for students not primarily interested in academics, must still have been disconcerting for those conscientiously pursuing their educations. Yet the threats and invasions by the British, the ever more patriotic faculties and trustees, and the growing Commonwealth influence on the curricula could not but intensify the importance of politics and patriotism on the nation's campuses. Student activities, formal and informal, show this to have been the case.

There were several college militia companies at the beginning of the war, but faculties and legislatures alike felt that students were more valuable to the country in class than in the ranks; most states passed laws exempting faculties and students from military service. William and Mary's company may have been the only one in action so late in the war. But students could act on their own. They helped fight British invaders in New Haven and outside Boston, and many left their colleges to join the armies for relatively long stretches. Two Princeton students even died in service in January 1777.[92]

Still, most collegians stayed on campus. Even then, they often had opportunities to come in contact with political bodies and patriotic figures. New Jersey's state government formed in Princeton in 1776. The town hosted the first legislative session and the inauguration of Governor William Livingston. The Assembly returned in 1778. Philadelphia college students had frequent chances not only to view the state government in action, but also the Continental Congress, which occasionally attended commencement. Princeton played host to the Congress in 1783, when the mutiny of the Pennsylvania Line made Philadelphia an unsatisfactory meeting place.[93]

Not all collegians could watch the nation's councils at work, but most administrations reminded their charges of the deeds of Patriots through the awarding of honorary degrees or other ceremonies. Dartmouth, Harvard, Yale, the University of the State of Pennsylvania, and Princeton honored such figures as Washington, John and Samuel Adams, and various French commanders and diplomats. All these ceremonies called forth patriotic displays of rhetoric, sometimes from recipients as well as presenters. Students always witnessed the celebration; sometimes they took part.[94]

As before, most student activities of a political nature took place at commencements (also in debating societies, but no records survive from the war years). The tenor of the pronouncements was a continuation of the intense political interest of the pre-war years, and the commitment to Commonwealth ideology increased. A few examples will illustrate student sentiment. Rhode Island College students, in their only wartime commencement in 1776, discussed the propositions "History sets forth the ideas and methods, the rise and fall, and the laws of very famous powers, as well as the character and virtue of their inhabitants" and "All men are born free, and it is glorious to meet death in securing their liberty by force of arms." Harvard's faculty introduced a separate category of political theses in 1778; there were at least a dozen presentations each year until the end of the war. Again, Commonwealth precepts influenced the topics: "If the highest civil magistrate assails the law of the people, it destroys the bonds of faith," "It is dangerous to enlarge the army in times of peace," "Two sovereignties are not able to exist naturally in the same federal republic," "Is the diffusion of knowledge among all the citizens necessary to the existence of the republic," and "Is public virtue the best security of republican liberty?" Toward the end of the war Princeton orators focused on "The Advantages of Civil Liberty to particular States," "The Powers of the People to Constitute their own Governments, to Alter and Reform them for their own Advantage," "The Advantages which the United States of America enjoy over other Republics which have arisen in the World for framing wise Systems of Civil Policy," and "In a confederation such as America whether large states or small are more favorable to union, population, and improvement in the arts."[95]

Two orations, one delivered at Yale in 1778, the other at Harvard in 1783, illustrate the depth of the penetration of the Commonwealth ideology. The Yale student, speaking on the progress of empire with respect to the arts and sciences, reviewed classical history according to a perspective that attributed Rome's rise to the exercise of virtue and her fall to the effects of luxury, vice, and slavery. Commenting on the great authors through the ages (which presumably he had read), he singled out Sophocles, Plato, Xenophon, and Thucydides among the Greeks, Virgil, Horace, and Livy in Rome, and Hume, Lord Kames, and Robertson among the Scottish authors. All, he said, were free to write when their countries enjoyed political, and thus artistic, freedom. America should enjoy a similar age when the war ended and peace settled on the community. The reason was in part because of American talents, but also because America's government "exercises neither the barbarous inhumanity of savage nations, nor the licentious cruelty of luxurious nations." Yet Americans should beware. Their golden age would be brief. Already the author could see a future wherein vice and luxury would arrive from the eastern shores through the medium of commerce. His countrymen were presently caught up in the spirit of gain from which nothing seemed able to dissuade them. Moral, governmental, and artistic decadence were on the horizon.[96] Here were many Commonwealth themes: the view of history, the progress of the arts, the relationship of cultural and political liberty, the superiority of republican forms, and especially the pervasive fear of commerce as the conduit of luxury and vice.

Harrison Gray Otis' Harvard oration of 1783 was more overtly political and contemporary. He set as his task the celebration of the glorious and happy Revolution, America's emancipation from thralldom, and her progress in freedom and empire. He described the immediate pre-war disputes with Great Britain as a deliberate plot to enslave the colonists. Americans resisted with rights and swords; Lexington was America's Thermopylae, giving her people confidence to act in defense of liberty. Sharing a view of America's past with other Commonwealth inspired Revolutionaries, Otis went on to apply strains of the ideology to her present and future. He praised Washington and other commanders, but warned of the dangers of military professionalism and a standing army. He noted that republics were founded upon good laws, that Americans were well-suited to make them, but he warned of lethargy, luxury, and vice, of the dangers of faction, and of the pernicious influence of the commercial interests and the landed gentry if allowed to reign unchecked by the people at large. Finally, he made the connection between higher education and good government: the ignorance of the masses leads to tyranny. "The greater part of the most distinguished Patriots, who early dared to unmask the illiberal Designs of Britain, imbibed their Love of Freedom in our public Academys."[97]

So, too, did later Patriots, who abounded at America's colleges. Student performances continued to demonstrate great concern for the political developments that affected their lives. They, with the aid of their teachers, strove to understand man's experience, his moral and physical qualities and abilities, in such a way as to make comprehensible their own destinies. Increasingly, they did this according to the political and philosophical guidelines set out by the Commonwealth Whigs of Great Britain and their American followers. For it would be in America, as Otis asserted, that there would be displayed a republican perfection which Plato, Harrington, and Hume had been unable to realize.[98]

The feeling that community values should be reflected in the choice of college administrators and teachers, in the courses taught, and in the political views those courses imparted, was but one manifestation of the growing conviction that in republican America colleges should serve the civil state. As we have seen, some boards of trustees and faculties sensed that conviction early and acted upon it even before the Revolution, thus creating a natural harmony between college and community, as at Princeton. In other cases, where institutions did not reflect community values or where there was fear they would not, the states sometimes took a hand. In this process Americans made new and extended use of the third part of the English higher educational legacy, the tradition of governmental supervision. Just how deeply involved the government became depended in part on its perception of the values inculcated by the college and in part on the college-state relationship that already existed.

At Princeton, Queen's College, and the College of Rhode Island, institutions with virtually no relationship to the state in the colonial period, the Revolution brought little change. Princeton's trustees asked the New Jersey Assembly to alter its charter to allow a smaller quorum, to exempt faculty and students from military service, and to make any other changes it felt comported with the Revolution. The Assembly granted Princeton's requests, endorsing the 1748 charter and requiring that college officers who were residents of New Jersey take an oath of allegiance to the state instead of the Crown. The New Jersey Assembly also helped Queen's, allowing an increase in the number of ministers on the board. It did ask the governor to preside over trustee meetings when convenient (it seldom was). The only action the Rhode Island Legislature took with respect to that state's college was to comply with its request to alter the oath of allegiance taken by corporation officers. With no tradition of state aid, and with political values that pleased the community, these colleges enjoyed very simple relations with their respective states.[99]

Elsewhere, the issues were more complicated. After working out a charter favorable to both college and province, Eleazar Wheelock no doubt expected Dartmouth to be the object of New Hampshire's largesse. He was disappointed. Despite the governor's urgings, the New Hampshire Assembly granted the college no money in 1770, only £60 in 1771. It gave the college ferry rights across the Connecticut, but that produced little revenue. In 1773 the Assembly granted Wheelock £500 for a new college building, but only after rejecting his request for a lottery which he expected would be more profitable.[100] The Dartmouth-New Hampshire connection was not to Wheelock's liking. Yet the college needed funds. It was probably this need that led to the unusual dealings between the college and the Continental Congress described earlier. But even more bizarre activities soon engaged the Wheelocks.

Eleazar Wheelock's seemingly Loyalist pre-war sympathies had created hostility toward the college in the New Hampshire Legislature. In turn, Hanover and the surrounding towns in western New Hampshire disliked the Assembly because under both the old government and the new they were underrepresented. To complicate matters, this irritant mingled with the concerns of the disaffected settlers on lands west of the Connecticut River, originally held by New Hampshire but also claimed by New York after 1764. The twists and turns of the political intrigue which took place between 1777 and 1784 are too lengthy to detail here.

For Dartmouth College, the maneuverings in which Professor Bezaleel Woodward and Eleazar and John Wheelock had leading parts, even visiting the Continental Congress to urge statehood for an independent Vermont (including Dartmouth), meant that at one time or another the college was part of an independent state known as Dresden, was subject to and gained support from two different Vermont governments, and at last returned to the fold in New Hampshire. These political escapades exacerbated New Hampshire's hostility and provoked a clause in the state's 1784 constitution specifically forbidding that any "president, professors, or instructors in any college should have a seat in either House of the Legislature or the Council.''[101] It is even possible that this incident started the train of events culminating in the Dartmouth College case.

While Dartmouth, to protect itself, tried to establish a government, elsewhere governments tried to take over colleges. Ever since the middle years of Thomas Clap's presidency, Yale College had operated under the suspicious gaze of the Connecticut Assembly. Legislators and others had for some time seen the college not as a religious seminary, but as a public institution designed to serve the whole people. Yale continued to receive appropriations from the Assembly, but it was required to submit its accounts for inspection. What with the Revolutionary conviction regarding the relationship of government and education, that inspection was not enough. There were even rumors about creating a state institution at Hartford. Finally, in May 1777, the college, which was in its tenth year of an interim presidency, and had its students undergoing tuition at three different locations in the state, became the subject of a legislative investigation. In July the Yale Corporation, probably to forestall any unilateral state action, asked for a joint conference to discuss college affairs. At the meeting the legislative committee offered monetary grants for facilities and professorships if the Assembly gained a voice in the selection of new faculty. The committee also proposed Ezra Stiles as the new college president. The Corporation agreed to an expanded faculty if the religious design of the college was preserved. It also concurred in the need for a new president.[102]

When Stiles learned of the July conference, he gained the impression that the Assembly was offering the Corporation an ultimatum: Stiles and money, or neither. Understandably loath to take charge of the college on those terms, Stiles consulted members of the Corporation, the Assembly, and the Connecticut clergy to determine the extent and type of support he commanded. He learned that while his own support was nearly unanimous, there was great division over the implementation of the plan for reform. He, for one, feared government takeover.[103]

Stiles' decision to accept the presidency led him to try to clarify the issues separating the Corporation and the Assembly. He drew up his "Plan for a University" at Corporation request to put a positive program of curricular expansion before both bodies. On it there was substantial agreement. Once more, the administration of faculty and funds proved the sticking point. The Corporation proposed to join with the state by adding or conjoining a board of civilians equal in size to the old board, chosen by them from a list nominated by the Assembly.

The whole board would then make all professorial appointments except divinity, but tutors would be chosen by the president. Old revenues would be administered by the old board, new state revenues by the new board. Other provisions were that the president should be a clergyman and should preside at all board meetings.[104]

The Assembly's proposal countered the Corporation's on major points. The committee asked for a combined board no larger than the current one, meaning that clergy would have to be replaced with laymen. The whole board would have appointment and removal power over all college officers except the divinity professor. In addition, it would administer all funds, regulate all salaries, determine courses of lectures, and hear appeals from all severely disciplined students. In exchange, the Assembly would endow chairs of physic and law, would establish a permanent fund to keep up the library and philosophical apparatus, and would supply the margin between college income and expenditures until the permanent income was established.[105]

The Corporation and the Assembly were on a collision course. The Assembly's proposals would have made possible governmental intrusion into the appointment of all future Corporation members and other officials. Further, the Assembly might interject itself into decisions of finance, salary, course content, and discipline. The proposal was, in short, a not very thinly disguised effort to turn Yale into a state university. The Corporation decided that to accept the Assembly proposal would be to abolish the college charter. That they refused to do. The reasonableness of Stiles and the persistence of the Assembly kept open the lines of communication throughout the war, but the issue was at stalemate.[106]

Some Massachusetts legislators shared their Connecticut counterparts' desire to make the state's college a public institution. Such direct control proved unacceptable to the General Court; instead it suggested careful attention be paid to Harvard in the new state constitution. Chapter five of the 1780 Constitution, "The University at Cambridge and the Encouragement of Literature," did just that, confirming the 1650 charter, its privileges and property. The constitution increased state influence over Harvard activities by making it the duty of the Legislature to cherish collegiate interests, and by altering the composition of the Overseers to include the governor, lieutenant governor, members of the council and senate, as well as the college president and the Congregational ministers of six towns in the Cambridge area. Finally, the General Court reserved the right to modify the "university" government "as shall be conducive to its advantage and the interest of the republic of letters." The rationale for these actions was that Harvard had always been a civic institution and it was only natural to provide for it under the constitution.[107]

While these provisions would seem to presage considerable public control over Harvard, they did not. The college section of the 1780 Constitution produced grumbling in the towns. The concern was that Harvard offered education to the elite while lower level education, desirable for all, fell by the wayside. Legislative protection and encouragement for Harvard demonstrated a poor perspective on the needs of the people. These criticisms, coupled with the fiscal demands of the Revolution, led the state government to back away from collegiate support. Salary grants, so free-flowing before the passage of the constitution, became intermittent afterward, and the General Court flatly refused Harvard's 1781 petition for a permanent and adequate presidential salary.[108] Perhaps because of the shrinking support, the state interfered very little in Harvard's affairs during the remainder of the century. In Cambridge, state supervision meant no supervision, and no aid.

The most dramatic instance of a new alliance between the state and higher education occurred in Philadelphia. There, for a few years, emerged the first state university, erected on the skeleton of the College of Philadelphia. When Pennsylvania's Constitutionalists gained control in mid-1776, they remodeled the state's government and institutions, although not without opposition. But resistance slowly faded, enabling the Constitutionalists to sweep the October 1778 elections. As a result, they were strong enough to tackle the College of Philadelphia, which they considered the last major stronghold of conservative, Loyalist spirit. While gathering its forces, the Assembly passed two acts in 1778, one suspending the trustees' powers during the British occupation and for three months afterward, the other requiring an oath of loyalty to the commonwealth from all college officers. By September, Pennsylvania President Joseph Reed could address the Assembly to criticize the college because it had not ''sought the aid of government for an establishment consistent with the Revolution, and conformable to the great changes in policy and government.''[109]

The real offensive began in 1779 when two Assembly committees investigated college affairs. Their report tolled the school's death knell. The case against Smith as a Loyalist was a foregone conclusion, but there was other evidence. The Charter of 1755 had prescribed an oath to the king. A trustee by-law of 1764 narrowed the foundation of the college by making it harder for non-Anglicans to become trustees. The Penn family had generously supported the college and they were Loyalists. Several trustees were Tories who had left with the British in 1778. The six trustees elected since 1776 were conservative Patriots. The college was inadequately funded. The most serious charge, though, was that the college showed ''an evident hostility to the present Government and Constitution of this State, and in diverse Particulars, Enmity to the Common Cause.''[110]

These charges were more than enough for the Assembly. Although some members defended the college, the majority voted in November to reorganize it. Ostensibly, they only altered the charter, but the University of the State of Pennsylvania was more than just a new name. The preamble of the bill explained the Assembly's purpose in acting:

[T]he education of youth has ever been found to be of the most essential consequence, as well to the good government of states, and the peace and welfare of society, as to the profit and ornament of individuals, insomuch, that, from the experience of all ages it appears that seminaries of learning, when properly conducted, have been public blessings to mankind, and that on the contrary, when in the hands of dangerous and disaffected men, they have troubled the peace of society, shaken the government, and often aroused tumult, sedition, and bloodshed.[111]

The "dangerous and disaffected men" were removed from office and replaced by a board composed of the President of the Supreme Executive Council of Pennsylvania, the Vice-President, the Speaker of the General Assembly, the Chief Justice of the Supreme Court of Pennsylvania, the Judge of the Admiralty, the Attorney General, and the senior ministers of the Episcopal, Presbyterian, Baptist, Lutheran, German Calvinist, and Roman Catholic denominations in Philadelphia. These were all members ex officio. In addition, several private citizens joined the board; as we have seen, they were Patriot and Constitutionalist. These were the proper governors of education. Lest they demonstrate some independence, they had to swear allegiance both to Pennsylvania and to the United States, to pass no laws repugnant to Pennsylvania, and to have their laws, accounts, and trustee nominations subject to Assembly review.[112]

The Pennsylvania move was the first actual takeover of a college by a state government. That it had political overtones cannot be doubted. The Constitutionalists had witnessed the effectiveness of the college as a political rostrum and desired one of their own. In keeping with eighteenth-century political practice they sought not to establish a rival institution, for that would have given legitimacy to Smith's faction.[113] Instead, they ousted Smith and his supporters, thereby appropriating the forum for themselves. It was this partisan motivation that prompted Assembly takeover. It was not curricular deficiency, for the studies actually suffered in the reorganization. Nor was it any serious possibility of "tumult, sedition, and bloodshed." As we have noted, Smith was not an advocate of armed suppression of the independence movement. His students, even his own son, were much more enthusiastic in their patriotism than was Smith. The Pennsylvania Assembly action was partisan politics, pure and simple.

The identification of liberty, virtue, knowledge, and education had then proceeded so far by the middle of the war that the Pennsylvania Assembly could seize and "repatriate" a college. That was the extreme case. But other colleges felt pressure to conform to popular opinion regarding higher education, for most Americans were firmly convinced of its relationship to good government and of the state's responsibility for promoting and regulating it. They would act on their convictions in various ways in the years to come.

The years of the American Revolution witnessed the continued, indeed heightened, desire of the country's colleges to educate for state service and to implement a curriculum designed for that end. They witnessed the further politicization of the campus and the increasing predominance of the Commonwealth Whig ideology as a way of viewing the world and the American republic's place in it. They witnessed a growing public concern with the direction higher education was to take, a concern often brought to bear on colleges through the medium of state governments. They witnessed, in short, the full application of the English higher educational legacy to the American colleges.

But the American victory meant that the country was no longer English. Its people had to find new governmental and cultural forms through which to express their emerging identity. The next two decades would be called the experimental period. What would it hold for the nation's colleges? What would be their role in the new republic?

NOTES

1. Gordon S. Wood, *The Creation of the American Republic, 1776–1787* (Chapel Hill: University of North Carolina Press, 1969); John Shy, "Hearts and Minds in the American Revolution: The Case of 'Long Bill' Scott and Peterborough, New Hampshire," John Shy, *A People Numerous and Armed: Reflections on the Military Struggle for American Independence* (New York: Oxford University Press, 1976), 163–80; Charles Royster, *A Revolutionary People at War: The Continental Army and American Character, 1775–1783* (Chapel Hill: University of North Carolina Press, 1979), 25–126; Robert Middlekauf, *The Glorious Cause: The American Revolution, 1763–1789* (New York: Oxford University Press, 1982).

2. A brief, reliable account of the Virginia involvement is Don Higginbotham, *The War of American Independence: Military Attitudes, Policies and Practices, 1763–1789* (New York: The Macmillan Co., 1971), 376–83.

3. Jack E. Morpurgo, *Their Majesties' Royall Colledge: William and Mary in the Seventeenth and Eighteenth Centuries* (Williamsburg: College of William and Mary, 1976), 202–6; Marquis de Chastellux, *Travels in North America in the Years 1780, 1781, and 1782*, trans. Howard C. Rice, (rev. ed., 1 vol. in 2; Chapel Hill: University of North Carolina Press, 1963), 374–75; Lyon G. Tyler, *Williamsburg, the Old Colonial Capital* (Richmond: Whittet & Shepperson, 1907), 167; "Journal of the Meetings of the President and Masters of William and Mary College," *WMCQ*, 15 (1906–1907): 266.

4. *Virginia Gazette* (Purdie & Dixon), November 9 supp., November 23, December 7, 14, 1769; *Virginia Gazette* (Rind), November 30, 1769.

5. *Virginia Gazette* (Purdie & Dixon), January 18, 1770, October 3, 1771; Robert Polk Thomson, "The Reform of the College of William and Mary, 1763–1800," *Proceedings* of the American Philosophical Society, 115 (1971): 197–99.

6. *Virginia Gazette* (Rind), December 30, 1773, May 19, 26, June 2, 9, 1774; Thomson, "Reform of William and Mary," 203–4.

7. "Journal of the President and Masters," May 2, 1770, *WMCQ*, 13 (1904–1905): 193; Morpurgo, *Royall Colledge*, 151–52, 161–62; *Virginia Gazette* (Purdie & Dixon), December 8, 1774; *Virginia Gazette* (Pinkney), December 22, 1774, June 19, 1775; "Journal of the President and Masters," May 12, August 4, September 14, 1775, *WMCQ*, 14 (1905–1906): 244, 15: 134–36.

8. "Journal of the President and Masters," November 29, 1776, *WMCQ*, 15: 141–42; *Virginia Gazette* (Dixon & Hunter), April 4, 1777; Jurgen Herbst, *From Crisis to Crisis: American College Government, 1636–1819* (Cambridge, Mass.: Harvard University Press, 1982), 149; Tyler, *Williamsburg*, 166.

9. *Virginia Gazette* (Dixon & Hunter), September 5, 1777; *Virginia Gazette* (Purdie), May 31, June 14, November 22, 1776.

10. Charles Crowe, "Bishop James Madison and the Republic of Virtue," *Journal of Southern History*, 30 (1964): 60; Morpurgo, *Royall Colledge*, 178–79; Horace W. Smith, *The Life and Correspondence of the Rev. William Smith, D.D. . . .* (2 vols., Philadelphia: Ferguson Bros. & Co., 1880), I, 507.

11. Julian Boyd and Charles Cullen, eds., *The Papers of Thomas Jefferson* (21 vols., thus far, Princeton: Princeton University Press, 1950–   ), II, 526–27.

12. Ibid., 526–33.

13. Ibid., 538–39.

14. Ibid., 539.

15. Ibid., 540–41.

16. Ibid., 247, 253–54, 543n, X, 574–77, XI, 152–55; Dumas Malone, *Jefferson the Virginian* (Boston: Little, Brown and Co., 1948), 283–85.

17. Wilford Kale, Jr., "Robert Andrews: 'A Forgotten Professor' " (unpublished seminar paper, College of William and Mary, 1966); Andrews to T. Jefferson, February 10, 1781, Boyd and Cullen, eds., *Jefferson Papers*, IV, 574.

18. "Carlo Bellini," Faculty/Alumni File (WMA); *DAB*, s.v. "James McClurg"; McClurg to T. Jefferson, April 6, 1776, Boyd and Cullen, eds., *Jefferson Papers*, I, 286–87; *DAB*, s.v. "George Wythe"; Julian P. Boyd, "The Murder of George Wythe," *WMQ*, 12 (1955): 513–18; William Latham to William Armistead Burwell, June 13, 1805, Boyd and Cullen, eds., *Jefferson Papers*, IV, 273–74.

19. Anne Shearer-Shineman, "The Trustees of William and Mary College, 1750–1800" (unpublished seminar paper, University of Wyoming, 1981).

20. "Journal of the President and Masters," December 29, 1779, *WMCQ*, 15: 169; Thomson, "Reform of William and Mary," 212, 212n; Morpurgo, *Royall Colledge*, 195; Lyon G. Tyler, "Some Early Courses and Professors at William and Mary College," *WMCQ*, 14: 77–78; T. Jefferson to James Madison, July 26, 1780, Boyd and Cullen, eds., *Jefferson Papers*, III, 507.

21. *Virginia Gazette* (Dixon & Hunter), August 22, 1777; *Virginia Gazette* (Purdie), August 21, 1778; "Journal of the President and Masters," March 1, December 31, 1782, *WMCQ*, 15: 264–65, 16: 73; Chastellux, *Travels in North America*, 533–36, 542–45.

22. John Jennings, *The Library of the College of William and Mary in Virginia, 1693–1793* (Charlottesville: University Press of Virginia, 1968), 61, 68–69; "Journal of the President and Masters," December 30, 1779, *WMCQ*, 15: 170.

23. "Phi Beta Kappa Minutes," *Doc. Hist. Educ.*, II, 248, 258–59; Lyon G. Tyler, "Original Records of the Phi Beta Kappa Society," *WMCQ*, 4 (1895–96): 236, 238, 239.

24. John H. Gardiner, *Harvard* (New York: Oxford University Press, 1914), 24; Josiah Quincy, *The History of Harvard University* (2 vols., Cambridge, Mass.: J. Owen, 1840), II, 165, 168–69; Samuel Eliot Morison, *Three Centuries of Harvard, 1636–1936* (Cambridge, Mass.: Harvard University Press, 1936), 147–48, 150; "Records of the President and Fellows of Harvard College" (Ms., HUA), September 6, 1775.

25. George B. Hill, *Harvard College by an Oxonian* (New York: The Macmillan Co., 1906), 33; Records of Harvard College, April 3, 1776.

26. J. H. Van Armringe, "Columbia University," Joshua L. Chamberlain, ed., *Universities and Their Sons* (5 vols., Boston: R. Herndon & Co., 1898–1900), I, 612; Howard Mumford Jones, *O Strange New World* (New York: The Viking Press, 1964), 320; "Literary Diary," *Stiles Papers M*, VII, 111; Edward P. Cheyney, *History of the University of Pennsylvania, 1740–1940* (Philadelphia: University of Pennsylvania Press,

1940), 116; "Columbia University Trustees [Minutes]," Book I, 1770–1781 (Ms., CUA), May 14, 1776.

27. Reuben A. Guild, *A History of Brown University with Illustrative Documents* (Providence: Providence Press Co., 1867), 66–67; Walter C. Bronson, *A History of Brown University, 1764–1914* (Providence: The University, 1914), 15; Howard B. Preston, "Rochambeau and French Troops in Providence in 1781–82–83," *Rhode Island Historical Collections*, 17 (1924): 2–5; "Minutes of the Corporation, College of Rhode Island, 1765–1810" (Ms., BUA), a note after the entry for September 3, 1777. The French abused their privileges during occupation. They converted one part of the hall into a stable, knocking out the walls at that end of the building. They also sold all the movable fixtures. Guild, *History of Brown*, 72–73.

28. William H. S. Demarest, *A History of Rutgers College, 1766–1924* (New Brunswick, N.J.: Rutgers College, 1924), 103, 106, 118–20, 126; Richard P. McCormick, *Rutgers: A Bicentennial History* (New Brunswick, N.J.: Rutgers University Press, 1966), 16, 18; "Transactions of the Athenian Society," November 20, 1776, ? 1778, May 30, 1781 (Ms., RUA), 19, 20, 87.

29. Edward P. Cheyney and E. P. Oberholtzer, "University of Pennsylvania," Chamberlain, ed., *Universities and Their Sons*, I, 79–80; Smith, *Life of William Smith*, II, 570–71; Samuel Hazard, ed., *Pennsylvania Archives* (1st ser., 12 vols., Philadelphia: J. Severn & Co., 1852–56), V, 198–99; "Application of the Faculty and Masters to the Committee on Public Safety, January 3, 1777" (Ms., UPA).

30. Edmund S. Morgan, *The Gentle Puritan: A Life of Ezra Stiles* (New Haven: Yale University Press, 1962), 332, 335; Henry P. Johnston, *Yale and Her Honor Role in the American Revolution* (New York: privately printed, 1888), 105–8; *Connecticut Journal*, August 11, September 15, 1779; "Literary Diary," *Stiles Papers M*, IX, 66, 69–72. Johnston maintains the college was saved from burning only through the intervention of Colonel Edmund Fanning (Yale 1755) who dissuaded his senior officer; 109.

31. "Minutes of the Proceedings of the Trustees of the College of New Jersey," Volume I, 1748–1796 (Ms., UPA), note after the minutes for meeting of September 25, 1776. The note obviously was appended at a later date, for it reads: "The incursions of the enemy into the state and the depradations by the armies prevented this meeting (scheduled for November 29) and indeed prevented all regular business in the college for two or three years." Thomas P. Wertenbaker, *Princeton, 1746–1896* (Princeton: Princeton University Press, 1946), 57–63; Varnum L. Collins, *Princeton* (New York: Oxford University Press, 1914), 78–80; Varnum L. Collins, *President Witherspoon* (2 vols., Princeton: Princeton University Press, 1925), II, 92–96; Howard C. Rice, Jr., *The Rittenhouse Orerey* (Princeton: Princeton University Press, 1954), 44–45.

32. Witherspoon's Congressional service is described in Collins, *Witherspoon*, II, 3–81; specific speeches on issues such as peace commissions during the war, voting procedures, and western lands are found in *The Miscellaneous Works of John Witherspoon* (Philadelphia: William W. Woodward, 1803), 218–25, 240–84.

33. Collins, *Witherspoon*, II, 110; "An Address to the Natives of Scotland, residing in America," John Witherspoon, *Works* (9 vols., London, 1765–1815), VI, 198–213; "The Druid" (1776), Witherspoon, *Miscellaneous Works*, 155–67.

34. Witherspoon, *Works*, V, 179, 198–99, 202–3.

35. Collins, *Princeton*, 78; *DAB*, s.v. "William C. Houston"; James McLachlan, ed., *Princetonians, 1748–1768: A Biographical Dictionary* (Princeton: Princeton University Press, 1976), 643–47.

36. *DAB*, s.v. "Samuel Stanhope Smith"; Richard A. Harrison, ed., *Princetonians, 1769–1776: A Biographical Dictionary* (Princeton: Princeton University Press, 1980), 42–51; Samuel Stanhope Smith, *A Funeral Sermon on the Death of Richard Stockton, Esq., March 2, 1781* (Trenton, 1781), 38–40.

37. "Jacob Hardenbergh," *NCAB*, III, 399; Peter Studdiford, *A Funeral Sermon on the Death of the Late Rev. Jacob Hardenbergh, D.D., President of Queen's College and Pastor of the Dutch Church in New Brunswick* (New Brunswick, N.J., 1791), 16; George P. Schmidt, *Princeton and Rutgers: The Two Colonial Colleges of New Jersey* (Princeton: Van Nostrand, 1964), 12.

38. "John Taylor," Harrison, ed., *Princetonians, 1769–1776*, 111–15; *The John Bogart Letters* (New Brunswick, N.J.: Rutgers College, 1914), 3–28; Demarest, *History of Rutgers*, 113; McCormick, *Rutgers*, 17.

39. "Naphtali Daggett," *Yale Sketches*, III, 257–61; *AAP*, I, 710–13.

40. Morgan, *Gentle Puritan*, 210–12.

41. Ibid., 212–14. For Stiles' version, see *A Discourse on the Christian Union...* (Boston, 1761).

42. Morgan, *Gentle Puritan*, 214–36.

43. Ibid., 255–74. For Stiles' notations of and reflections on colonial developments, see Franklin B. Dexter, ed., *The Literary Diary of Ezra Stiles* (3 vols., New York: C. Scribner's Sons, 1901), I, 40, 53–54, 107, 111–14, 136–37, 382–85, 427, 521.

44. Morgan, *Gentle Puritan*, 272–84; "Literary Diary," *Stiles Papers M*, VII, 201.

45. "Literary Diary," *Stiles Papers M*, X, 213, XI, 2.

46. Morgan, *Gentle Puritan*, 453–55; Ezra Stiles, "The United States Elevated to Glory and Honor (New Haven, 1783)," John W. Thornton, ed., *The Pulpit of the American Revolution* (Boston: Gould & Lincoln, 1860), 401, 404, quotation 419, 420.

47. Stiles, "The United States Elevated," 436–37.

48. The patriotic actions of President Manning and Professor David Howell of the College of Rhode Island have been described in Chapter 3, but both kept a low profile during the Revolution principally because the college closed from December 1776 to May 1782. Guild, *Early History of Brown*, 243, 259–60.

49. Quincy, *History of Harvard*, II, 168; *DAB*, s.v. "Edward Wigglesworth," "Samuel Langdon," and "Stephen Sewell"; "John Winthrop," *Sibley's*, IX, 261.

50. "Samuel Williams," *Sibley's*, XIV, 134–36; "Samuel Williams," *AAP*, I, 595–97; Samuel Williams, *The Influence of Christianity on Civil Society...* (Boston, 1780).

51. *DAB*, s.v. "Joseph Willard"; "Joseph Willard," *Sibley's*, XVI, 253–65; Joseph Willard, *The Duty of a Good and Faithful Soldier* (Boston, 1781), and *A Thanksgiving Sermon Delivered at Boston, Dec. 11, 1783* (Boston, 1784).

52. *DAB*, s.v. "Benjamin Waterhouse" and "John Warren"; "John Warren," *Sibley's*, XVII, 655–69; John Warren, *An Oration, Delivered July 4th, 1783...in Celebration...of American Independence* (Boston, 1783).

53. James D. McCallum, *Eleazar Wheelock: Founder of Dartmouth College* (orig. 1939; reprint, New York: Arno Press, 1969), 198–200, 202; David MacClure to EW, May 8, 1777, EW to Connecticut Assembly, May 31, 1776, Resolution of the Continental Congress, September 19, 1776, EW to Continental Congress, November 1, 1778, EW to Henry Laurens, November 4, 1778, EW to the Connecticut Delegates in Congress, November 5, 1778, EW to Continental Congress, April 2, 1779, *The Microfilm Edition of the Papers of Eleazar Wheelock* (Hanover, N.H.: Dartmouth College Publications, 1971).

54. McCallum, *Founder of Dartmouth*, 202.

55. "Sylvanus Ripley," *AAP*, I, 401; Sylvanus Ripley to John Wheelock, March 7, 1776, Sylvanus Ripley to EW, April 15, June 19, 1776, *Wheelock Papers*.

56. That most Tory of institutions, King's College, effectively ceased to exist during the Revolution. After Myles Cooper's departure, the Anglican minister Benjamin Moore became president ad interim. A few students earned degrees in 1776, but when the British occupied the college, instruction shifted to the home of trustee Leonard Lispenard, where it soon ceased. No trustee meetings took place after June 1777 and by 1784 only five of the twenty-one governors who ran the college in the 1770s remained in the city. The transformation of King's College to Columbia properly belongs to the next chapter. Early Minutes of the Trustees of King's College, August ?, October 31, 1776, June 1777; David C. Humphrey, *From King's College to Columbia, 1746–1800* (New York: Columbia University Press, 1976), 270.

57. Elizabeth A. Ingersoll, "Francis Alison: American Philosophe, 1705–1779" (Ph.D. Diss., University of Delaware, 1974), 173–75; *DAB*, s.v. "Robert Davidson."

58. *DAB*, s.v. "John Morgan" and "William Shippen"; Randolph S. Klein, *Portrait of an Early American Family: The Shippens of Pennsylvania Across Five Generations* (Philadelphia: University of Pennsylvania Press, 1975), 192–94; Betsey C. Corner, *William Shippen, Jr., Pioneer in Medical Education, A Biographical Essay* (Philadelphia: American Philosophical Society, 1951), 112–15; David F. Hawke, *Benjamin Rush: Revolutionary Gadfly* (Indianapolis: Bobbs-Merrill Co., 1971), 169–71, 174, 192, 208–13, 221–23, 236–38, 250–51.

59. Hawke, *Revolutionary Gadfly*, 142–45; Eric Foner, *Tom Paine and Revolutionary America* (New York: Oxford University Press, 1976), 115, 119, 125; Richard A. Ryerson, *The Revolution Is Now Begun: The Radical Committees of Philadelphia, 1765–1776* (Philadelphia: University of Pennsylvania Press, 1978), 113–15, 133–34, 162, 167–68.

60. Hawke, *Revolutionary Gadfly*, 146–49, 152–61; Foner, *Tom Paine*, 125; Ryerson, *The Revolution Is Now Begun*, 210–11.

61. Foner, *Tom Paine*, 129; Ryerson, *The Revolution Is Now Begun*, 239–41. On the character of the Pennsylvania constitution, see Wood, *Creation of the Republic*, 137–41, 226–27, 231–32, and Willi Paul Adams, *The First American Constitutions: Republican Ideology and the Making of the State Constitutions in the Revolutionary Era*, Rita and Robert Kimber, trans. (Chapel Hill: University of North Carolina Press, 1980), 236–55.

62. Hawke, *Revolutionary Gadfly*, 187, 196, 198–201; Wood, *Creation of the Republic*, 233, 441–42, 446.

63. Hawke, *Revolutionary Gadfly*, 189–90, 255–58; *Pennsylvania Packet*, March 18, 1777; *Pennsylvania Journal*, July 4, 1782; Foner, *Tom Paine*, 185.

64. Albert F. Gegenheimer, *William Smith, Educator and Churchman, 1727–1803* (Philadelphia: University of Pennsylvania Press, 1943), 176–78, 180; William Smith, *Plain Truth: Addressed to the Inhabitants of America* (Philadelphia, 1776); *Pennsylvania Gazette*, March 13, 1776; Smith, *Life of William Smith*, I, 572; Joseph E. Illick, *Colonial Pennsylvania: A History* (New York: Charles Scribner's Sons, 1976), 301; "A Sermon Preached...before...Free and Accepted Masons...December 28, 1778," William Smith, *The Works of William Smith, D.D., Late Provost of the College and Academy in Philadelphia* (2 vols., Philadelphia: Hugh Maxwell and William Fry, 1803), I, 61–72.

65. *DAB*, s.v. "Jacob Duche"; "Jacob Duche," *AAP*, V, 180–84; Jacob Duche, *A Copy of a Letter to George Washington* (Philadelphia, 1777).

66. The role of the state in this process is discussed in section III.

67. James H. Hutson, *Pennsylvania Politics, 1740–1770* (Princeton: Princeton University Press, 1972), 153, 161; Francis Alison and John Ewing, *An Address of Thanks to the Wardens of Christ Church and St. Peters...* (Philadelphia, 1764); *Rush Letters*, I, 297n; John Ewing, *To the Citizens of America, Who Are Creditors of the United States...* (Philadelphia, 1782).

68. *DAB*, s.v. "Robert Patterson."

69. *DAB*, s.v. "David Rittenhouse"; Brook Hindle, *David Rittenhouse* (Princeton: Princeton University Press, 1964), 119–240; "Samuel Magaw," *CAB*, IV, 173. In his acceptance address, Magaw indicated his belief that the university was "a training ground of senators and patriots." Samuel Magaw, "Address on Appointment as Vice-President, June 5, 1782," *The American Museum*, 4 (1788): 164.

70. This paragraph derives from analysis of William L. Hewitt, "Trustees of the College of New Jersey, 1750–1800" (Unpublished seminar paper, University of Wyoming, 1981); *Catalog of the Officers and Alumni of Rutgers College (originally Queen's College) in New Brunswick, N.J., 1766–1916* (Trenton: Rutgers College, 1916); Larry R. Gerlach, *Prologue to Independence: New Jersey in the Coming of the American Revolution* (New Brunswick, N.J.: Rutgers University Press, 1976); Richard P. McCormick, *Experiment in Independence: New Jersey in the Critical Period, 1781–1789* (New Brunswick, N.J.: Rutgers University Press, 1950); Carl E. Prince, *New Jersey's Jeffersonian Republicans: The Genesis of an Early Party Machine, 1789–1817* (Chapel Hill: University of North Carolina Press, 1964); Alfred F. Young, *The Democratic Republicans of New York: The Origins, 1763–1787* (Chapel Hill: University of North Carolina Press, 1967).

71. See *Yale Sketches* for college-educated trustees. Richard Salter (1771–1780 term) is profiled in *Sibley's*, X. 404–9.

72. For information on these men, see David Lovejoy, *Rhode Island Politics and the American Revolution, 1760–1776* (Providence: Brown University Press, 1958) and Irwin H. Polishook, *Rhode Island and the Union, 1774–1795* (Evanston, Ill.: Northwestern University Press, 1969).

73. These sketches are restricted to graduates of Harvard. See *Sibley's* for career details.

74. Patrick McKnight, "The Trustees of Dartmouth College, 1769–1800" (unpublished seminar paper, University of Wyoming, 1981).

75. Steven C. Schulte, "The Trustees of the College of Philadelphia and the University of Pennsylvania, 1750–1800" (unpublished seminar paper, University of Wyoming, 1981).

76. Ibid.

77. Brook Hindle, *The Pursuit of Science in Revolutionary America, 1735–1789* (Chapel Hill: University of North Carolina Press, 1956), 219–385; Frederick Rudolph, *The American College and University: A History* (New York: Vintage Books, 1962), 40–41; Frederick Rudolph, *Curriculum: A History of the Undergraduate Course of Study Since 1636* (San Francisco: Josey-Bass, 1977), 25–53.

78. The absence of formal curricular programs makes generalizations about Dartmouth in these years impossible. King's College did not instruct during the war.

79. "Minutes of the Trustees of the College of New Jersey," May 25, 1781, September 25, 1782; Ashbel Green to John Croes, May 21, 1782 (Ashbel Green Collection, PUA).

80. "Records of Harvard College," September 30, October 23, 1776, March 20, 1778, March 3, 1779, May 22, 1783.

81. Bronson, *History of Brown*, 103. Work not previously cited: Henry St. John, Viscount Bolingbroke, *Letters on the Study and Use of History* (London, 1752). Bolingbroke was not a Commonwealthman, but he perceived the same moral and political crisis overtaking England in the eighteenth century. His solution was a patriot king. Nonetheless, colonists could glean from him an appreciation of the uses of history; to him it was "philosophy teaching by examples." And they could find accounts of classical, Saxon, and modern English history that shared perspectives with the Commonwealthmen. On Bolingbroke, see Isaac Kramnick, *Bolingbroke and His Circle* (Cambridge, Mass.: Harvard University Press, 1968); on his influence in America, see H. Trevor Colbourn, *The Lamp of Experience: Whig History and the Intellectual Origins of the American Revolution* (Chapel Hill: University of North Carolina Press, 1965), quotation 5, 49–50, 84–85.

82. "Minutes of the Corporation, College of Rhode Island," September 3, 1783; Guild, *Early History of Brown*, 350–51.

83. Morgan, *Gentle Puritan*, 317–20; Herbst, *From Crisis to Crisis*, 152; John S. Whitehead, *The Separation of College and State: Columbia, Dartmouth, Harvard, and Yale, 1776–1876* (New Haven: Yale University Press, 1973), 36–37.

84. "Conference with the Committee of the Assembly, 1777" (Ms., Stiles Papers, YUA).

85. "Literary Diary," *Stiles Papers M*, VIII, 41–42, 57–60, 108, 109.

86. "Plan of a University," Ezra Stiles to Eliphalet Williams, December 3, 1777. Stiles submitted it to the Corporation February 4, 1778; "Literary Diary," *Stiles Papers M*, VIII, 233. Cf. Morgan, *Gentle Puritan*, 321–24.

87. "Literary Diary," *Stiles Papers M*, VIII, 312, 330, 394, 434, 438, IX, 17, 63; Morgan, *Gentle Puritan*, 376–403.

88. "Literary Diary," *Stiles Papers M*, IX, 120 for books used, IX, 169, 170, X, 22, 238, XI, 95, 98, 124, 164, 219 for debates.

89. Ibid., 230.

90. John Ewing, James Davidson, James Cannon, and Robert Davidson to Trustees, September 1, 1780 (Ms., UPA); Cheyney, *History of the University of Pennsylvania*, 132, 134; John Henry Dubbs, *History of Franklin and Marshall College* (Lancaster, Penn.: Franklin and Marshall College Alumni Association, 1903), 8–9.

91. Cheyney, *History of the University of Pennsylvania*, 134–35. A copy of Samuel Magaw's moral philosophy lectures for 1783 survives in the university archives. The discussions of ethics and natural law are highly Hutchesonian and Alisonian. Regrettably, the section that would be devoted to politics is missing.

92. Collins, *Witherspoon*, II, 91.

93. Ibid., 87, 100; Cheyney, *History of the University of Pennsylvania*, 137; Varnum L. Collins, *The Continental Congress at Princeton* (Princeton: The University Library, 1908).

94. "Trustees' Minutes, Dartmouth College" (Ms., DaCA), September 17, 1782; "Records of Harvard College," June 12, 1776, June 18, 1779, July 18, 1781, June 11, 1782; "Yale Corporation Records, 1701–1800" (Ms., YUA), April 27, 1779, April 24, 1781, September 10, 1783; Cheyney, *History of the University of Pennsylvania*, 140–41; Witherspoon, *Miscellaneous Works*, 285–86; "Minutes of the Trustees of the College of New Jersey," September 24, 1783.

95. "Commencement Theses, Rhode Island College, 1776, 1786–1799" (Ms., BUA); "Theses & Quaestiones, 1737–1810" (Ms., HUA); Edward J. Young, "Subjects for Masters Degrees in Harvard College from 1655 to 1791," MHS *Proceedings*, 18 (1881): 127; *New Jersey Gazette*, October 11, 1780, September 27, October 3, 1781, October 9, 1782, October 8, 1783.

96. "Compositions and Disputations." Declamation, July 18, 1778 (Ms., YUA).

97. Harrison Gray Otis, "An English Oration, 1783" (Ms. HUA).

98. Ibid.

99. "Minutes of the Trustees of the College of New Jersey," April 16, 1778; "Corporation Records, Rhode Island College," September 4, 1782; William Paterson, ed., *The Laws of the State of New Jersey* (New Brunswick, N.J.: Abraham Blauvelt, 1800), 384–85; Herbst, *From Crisis to Crisis*, 188.

100. Leon B. Richardson, *A History of Dartmouth College* (2 vols., Hanover, N.H.: Dartmouth College Publications, 1932), I, 112, 131.

101. Frederick Chase, *A History of Dartmouth College and the Town of Hanover, New Hampshire* (2 vols., Cambridge, Mass.: J. Wilson & Son, 1891–1913), I, 431, 434–507; Levi Frisbee to EW, March 9, 1775, EW to the State of Vermont, June 4, 1778, Vermont House of Representatives Resolution, June 15, 1778, *Wheelock Papers*.

102. *PRSC*, I, 424; "Literary Diary," *Stiles Papers M*, VIII, 57–60; Morgan, *Gentle Puritan*, 299–300; Stiles, "Conference with the Committee of the Assembly, 1777." Similar analyses of these events appear in Herbst, *From Crisis to Crisis*, 152–54, and Whitehead, *Separation of College and State*, 36–39.

103. "Literary Diary," *Stiles Papers M*, VIII, 60, 108, 109.

104. Ibid., 233–34.

105. Stiles, "Conference with the Committee of the Assembly, 1777."

106. "Yale Corp. Records," June 13, 1778; "Literary Diary," *Stiles Papers M*, X, 287, XI, 68–69, 203.

107. Quincy, *History of Harvard*, II, 174–76, 507–9; Herbst, *From Crisis to Crisis*, 185–86; Whitehead, *Separation of College and State*, 16–17; Oscar and Mary Handlin, eds., *The Popular Sources of Political Authority: Documents on the Massachusetts Constitution of 1780* (Cambridge, Mass.: Belknap Press of Harvard University Press, 1966), 465–67.

108. Handlins, eds., *Popular Sources*, 483, 699; "Records of Harvard College," January 31, 1781; Herbst, *From Crisis to Crisis*, 186–87; Whitehead, *Separation of College and State*, 17–18.

109. Robert L. Brunhouse, *The Counter-Revolution in Pennsylvania, 1776–1790* (Harrisburg: Pennsylvania Historical Commission, 1942), 77; James T. Mitchell and Henry Flanders, eds., *Statutes at Large of Pennsylvania* (16 vols., Harrisburg: C. M. Busch, 1896–1919), IX, 175–76; "Minutes of the General Assembly of Pennsylvania" (September 9, 1778), quoted in Herbst, *From Crisis to Crisis*, 177.

110. Brunhouse, *Counter-Revolution in Pennsylvania*, 78; "Trustees' Minutes, College, Academy, and Charitable School of Philadelphia" (Ms., UPA), October ?, 1779.

111. Alexander Dallas, ed., *The Laws of the Commonwealth of Pennsylvania* (4 vols., Philadelphia, 1797–1803), I, 815.

112. Ibid., 815–21.

113. On the legitimacy of opposition parties and their tactics, see Richard Hofstadter, *The Idea of a Party System* (Berkeley: University of California Press, 1970), chapter 1, and Bernard Bailyn, *The Origins of American Politics* (New York: Alfred A. Knopf, 1968), 106–61.

5

Old Colleges in the New Republic

The most pressing need in the early years of the republic was to insure its success, to change its nature from experimental to permanent. Much of the activity necessary to accomplish that goal would be governmental, both national and state. Viable forms of government had to be created for the individual states and the United States as quickly as possible. To abet these developments, America needed favorable foreign relations, both commercial and diplomatic. By the end of the century the great experiment seemed a success. Most of the states had effected Revolutionary settlements that had addressed the problems left over from the conflict, and the peaceful transfer of the national government from the group in power to an organized opposition suggested that its structure was secure, even if the policies of those controlling it might vary greatly.

These years formed an era that called for America's colleges to increase their efforts along paths now familiar—to emphasize state service and to provide a curriculum and extracurriculum for that goal. The older colleges did these things naturally, continuing well-established practices. But this was also an era of great political debate. Questions regarding the proper forms of government and the domestic and foreign policies of the states and nation seemed much more divisive than had been the question of loyalty to Great Britain or American patriotism during the imperial crisis. Now college communities, charged with the responsibility of producing leaders for the civil state, faced choices concerning the brand of politics they would adopt. The colleges had become too enmeshed in politics during the Revolution to back away from partisanship in its aftermath. They could not simply teach students the principles of government and leave it at that. Rather, the colleges embroiled themselves in the political struggles of the 1780s and 1790s. They took sides on the acceptability of the Constitution of 1787, on the Hamiltonian program, on the French Revolution, and other issues. In short, campuses developed a distinct aura, federalist or antifederalist in the late 1780s, Federalist or Republican by the mid-1790s. As an examination of the evolving political atmosphere at Yale College will show, the politicization of the old colleges became complete.

I

The continuing commitment to education for state service and the developing partisanship of Yale appeared in the changing nature of the faculty and in the tone of the curriculum and extracurriculum. Compared to most other pre-Revolutionary colleges, post-war Yale had a very small permanent faculty before 1800. A president, a professor of divinity, and a professor of mathematics and natural philosophy were the positions the Corporation authorized, but the professorships were not always filled. As a result, the men who most influenced Yale students during these years were four—Ezra Stiles, who presided until 1795, Professor of Divinity Samuel Wales (1782–1793), Professor of Mathematics and Natural Philosophy Josiah Meigs (1794–1801), and Stiles' successor Timothy Dwight.

After the war, Stiles generally continued his practice of remaining silent on political issues, although he was more forthcoming on issues that had religious implications. For example, he disapproved of deism, largely on the grounds that deists placed too much emphasis on man's capacity to reason and ignored matters that Stiles thought were plainly indicated by scripture, but had to be taken on faith: resurrection, the trinity, predestination, the last judgment. The increasing popularity of deism and infidelity, and a general decline in religiosity in America, including the shrinking number of young men who chose divinity as a career, caused Stiles to reverse his earlier support for the separation of church and state. He concluded that in trying times religion needed the helping hand of the state if it were to exercise a beneficent influence on the people.[1]

Stiles confined his comments on civic matters to his diary and private correspondence. There he felt free to adhere to his faith in democracy. Sure that the normal channels of government were sufficiently open to accommodate disagreements about public policy, he felt no sympathy for Shay's rebellion. But that same confidence enabled him to counsel others, including Washington, not to worry about the rebellion; it was an isolated incident. The Constitutional Convention that the rebellion helped bring about Stiles thought somewhat premature. Americans had not yet had enough time to accumulate the experience necessary to judge properly about forms of government. Stiles considered the document the convention produced to be good but not perfect. Much of it would last through the ages but some things required change. He was sure that the central government needed more power to succeed in treating national problems.[2] When the necessary majority of states had ratified the Constitution, Stiles was pleased, and he noted when the laggard states of North Carolina and his long-time home Rhode Island joined the Union.[3] He approved most measures of the new government, but did worry in February 1790 that the United States was contracting too many foreign debts.[4]

What finally induced Stiles to break his official silence on matters political was the fate of the American Revolutionary principles abroad and the domestic reaction to it. The French Revolution thrilled and delighted the Yale president.

He watched its progress affectionately, confident that its libertarianism would succeed in spite of the war launched against France by the European monarchs, confident, indeed, that the Revolution would spread beyond France. Even the execution of Louis XVI and the reign of terror did not diminish Stiles' enthusiasm. As he wrote in July 1794 to a Newport friend,

I have never entertained the least depending Doubt of the final and ultimate glorious Triumph of Liberty in France. But I believe there must be more use of the *guillotine* yet. As I believ[e] it has hitherto been exercised with *great Justice* in general, so there is much more hurtful and poisonous Weeds to be mown down in the Field of Liberty, before Right Liberty and Tranquillity can be established.[5]

Stiles' sentiments flew in the face of a general New England reaction against this stage of the French Revolution. His dismay at his contemporaries' revulsion stimulated him to an extraordinary literary production. Stiles had already been at work on a history of three of the judges who had taken part in the execution of Charles I during the English Revolution. To Stiles, their actions were a high point in the Puritan quest for religious liberty. As his work on what proved a tedious and somewhat ahistorical narrative approached its end, his countrymen's attacks on French activities prompted him to append to his justification of a single tyrannicide a broader defense of tyrannicide in general. In it he argued that democracy was the only true guarantor of liberty. Monarchy and aristocracy, whether foreign or domestic, were liberty's sworn enemies. Thus, contemporary criticism of tyrranicide, of French activities, and of France's American supporters was wrongheaded. The American government was a democracy and had no reason to fear popular societies. In fact, the men who would suppress them were the real enemies of liberty for they were curtailing the people's right to assemble, to express themselves freely, and to use the press. Meaningful criticism of American actions might even bring improvement in the government. In this treatise Stiles showed himself a true democrat, going beyond the majority of his fellow New Englanders. He was, in Edmund Morgan's phrase, a "Yale Jacobin."[6]

Stiles' cohort Samuel Wales unfortunately never performed well as professor of divinity. Soon after his appointment he was afflicted with what was evidently a form of epilepsy. His health steadily declined thereafter. Stiles recorded many instances of his incapacity and only Corporation good will allowed Wales to continue as long as he did. For most of his Yale career Wales had other things than politics on his mind, but when called upon to deliver the Connecticut election sermon in 1785, Wales preached a jeremiad that showed his appreciation of contemporary political issues. Among the nation's sins he listed injustice to the most deserving element of the population—those Patriots who had endangered their lives and property—because they were not being properly repaid (he especially urged prompt redemption of wartime securities). Also prevalent was a lack of true patriotism; factions disrupted the affairs of states and made them unwilling to support the central government. This he linked to a disregard of civil authority. The people would not obey their elected leaders who in turn relaxed the proper measures of government in order not to offend their constituents. This portended anarchy. The foundation of these problems was the national tendency toward luxury and extravagance, especially the insatiable desire for foreign manufactures. Virtue and republicanism would give way if this onslaught were not checked.[7] These views were not unusual in the New England of the 1780s,[8] but they did differ from the optimism of Stiles' vision for America. After the election sermon, however, no more was heard from Wales on political matters. Presumably, his illness prevented a political rift from forming in the Yale faculty.

A more congenial political ally than Wales was Josiah Meigs, selected by Stiles in his last year to teach mathematics and natural philosophy. Meigs had very briefly been a Stiles student and had tutored at Yale from 1781 to 1784. An able speaker, he had delivered New Haven's celebratory oration after Cornwallis' surrender. Its themes were right out of Stiles' reflections on politics and history as passed on in his lectures. America's founders had fled political and religious tyranny in England to settle in a land of freedom. The colonists had built a rising empire through the exercise of liberty and virtue, but Great Britain, herself increasingly corrupt, had plotted to deprive America of her freedom. There followed a Patriot rendition of the war, praise for American commanders and French allies, and a warning that since political prosperity was founded on virtue, it must be continually inculcated and exercised. Meigs ended by recommending support of education to guarantee the inculcation of virtue.[9]

Meigs' themes were commonplace by that stage of the war, but they were also highly popular. He rode them to public office after becoming an attorney, and then left Yale for the editorship of the New Haven *Gazette*, which he kept going with various partners until 1789. The paper vigorously supported the Constitution of 1787.[10]

During these years Meigs occasionally delivered philosophical lectures at Yale, but it was the mid-1790s before the school could afford a permanent professor. Through their four months together on the faculty, Meigs and Stiles might well have amicably discussed their political views, for Meigs was fast becoming a Republican. He had from the start supported the French Revolution and did not recoil at the reign of terror. By the time speculation started on the contents of the Jay Treaty, Meigs was critical of Federalist policy both domestic and foreign. He wrote his brother in late July 1795 that he was "displeased with many things in the administration of Government. They appear to me to have lost sight of the great leading traits of freedom."[11]

Meigs' pro-French, anti-Federalist stand was unpopular in New Haven. After Stiles' death, it was unpopular at Yale. The Corporation forced Meigs to make a declaration of his political beliefs in 1798 that recanted his earlier convictions. His public aboutface notwithstanding, Meigs continued to be harassed by President Dwight. Rather than endure, he resigned in 1800 to take a position at the new college in Georgia.[12]

Meigs' departure symbolized the reversal in political sentiments that overtook Yale on the inauguration of Timothy Dwight. While he and Meigs held similar views on American politics through the ratification of the Constitution, the events of the 1790s affected them differently. Dwight had graduated from Yale in 1769 and then had tutored at the college most of the time from 1771 to 1777. He had been staunchly Patriot, urging independence in 1775. He told his students that they should prepare themselves to become leaders of a new nation and in a 1776 valedictory revealed that he had absorbed some Commonwealth Whig themes: the quest for political as well as religious liberty by the first New England settlers, the rise of an empire of civil and religious liberty in America contrasted with the growing corruption of Britain, the danger posed by the penetration of luxury and licentiousness, and the need to combat these influences by educating future leaders who possessed both the virtue and the skills necessary to the proper administration of the civil state.[13]

Dwight left Yale to join the ministry, but his parish duties did not prevent him from participating actively in politics before coming back to Yale. He had become chaplain to the First Continental Brigade in October 1777 and saw considerable service in New England and New York before resigning in 1779 to assume control over family affairs in Northampton, Massachusetts. There he wrote patriotic hymns, preached patriotic sermons, and served in the state legislature in 1781 and 1782.[14] In 1783 he had taken the pastorate at Greenfield Hill, Connecticut (now part of Stamford) where he had served until called to Yale. These years saw him evermore concerned about the democratic consequences of the Revolution and about the penetration of deism and infidelity from Europe. He published attacks on infidelity, and praised the Constitution and Washington's administration. Reacting to the economic instability of the war years, he approved Hamiltonian finance. Dwight deplored the French Revolution; one of the objects of his epic poem "Greenfield Hill" was to contrast the peace, security, and progress of America with the political broils of Europe, especially France.[15]

In short, Dwight had become a Federalist, and as president of Yale he joined his convictions about public policy with his fear of infidelity to produce a highly charged politics opposed to the French and their American sympathizers (read Republicans). His constant themes over the first years of his presidency were the inculcation of piety and virtue, staunch resistance to infidelity and deism, dissociation from France, and grave predictions that Jefferson would lead America into an alliance with the French Jacobins.[16]

From the quiet Republicanism of Stiles to the vociferous Federalism of Dwight, Yale's continuing politicization was representative of the process affecting other colleges. In New Haven, or elsewhere, that political involvement gained support from partisan trustees. Connecticut Republicans claimed that Yale was the center of a Federalist machine, led by President Dwight. They may have been right. The essential elements were the trustees, both clerical and, after 1792, lay. By an agreement reached that year (its significance for college-state relations is treated in Chapter 7), the Governor, Lieutenant-Governor, and the six senior members of the Legislature's upper house joined the previous minister-fellows to constitute the Corporation. All the state officials who served were Federalists, for that party dominated Connecticut politics until after the War of 1812. The clerics, sharing Dwight's fears of infidelity and democratic disorder inspired by the French, were also Federalist. In fact, self-proclaimed Republican ministers in Connecticut were subject to religious and social harassment.[17] Political toleration did not typify the Yale administration nor the state at large.

The political beliefs of Yale's leaders greatly affected her educational activities. Ezra Stiles continued his informal, singlehanded implementation of a university curriculum by adding new courses, toughening the scholastic standards, and introducing new books to the students. By 1787, the college laws indicated that seniors were for the first time formally studying history and civil policy. Actually, that reform did not take place until 1789. In July Stiles had the seniors read Montesquieu's *Spirit of the Laws*, thus augmenting his own lectures and the reading of Clap's *Ethics*. The following year he assigned juniors to read Joseph Priestley's *Lectures on History*, a guide to both classical and modern works. Most importantly, it used historical examples to teach principles of moral and political philosophy, and, considering Priestley's position as a later Commonwealthman, those principles were highly republican.[18] In 1793 Stiles introduced Vattel's *Law of Nature and Nations*. This perhaps supplemented or even replaced a series of lectures he had given the previous year on that subject, the Roman law, English law, and American law. Vattel was another Commonwealth favorite. These new books and lectures greatly heightened the political component of the standard curriculum.[19]

A more difficult book choice to understand was William Paley's *Principles of Moral and Political Philosophy*, introduced in 1791. Clap's *Ethics* was a limited essay, so a new book with an expanded focus was needed, and several of Paley's ethical perspectives no doubt appealed to Stiles because he shared Paley's Lockeanism. But Paley put forth political propositions that Stiles could not have supported. He rejected the social compact theory of government, preferring to trace government to patriarchal origins, thus making its natural form a monarchy. He observed that the United States was embarked on an experiment in social compact government, but was not sanguine about its prospects. Due submission to government was important to Paley; he did not deny the right of resistance, but hedged it with so many restrictions that a "just" rebellion would be hard to imagine, much less foment. And, working from a British perspective, he employed a standard measuring the utility of an action by the amount of happiness produced for the whole body politic to question the appropriateness of the American Revolution. An extensive, largely favorable examination of the British constitution denied that there was ever a period of Saxon constitutional purity. It also justified "influence" (corruption in Commonwealth terms) as the principal spring of governmental action. Other sections of the *Principles* defended the maldistribution of property and the extensive Church establishment that existed in England.[20]

Religiously tolerant, Harringtonian Ezra Stiles must have found these arguments appalling. No Yale student notes show how Stiles treated this work, but the presence of Montesquieu and Vattel among student readings suggests two alternatives. Either Stiles did not require his charges to read Paley on politics, or he used him as a straw man, criticizing his arguments.

Whatever the sources of political theory Stiles had his students read, they continued to serve as underpinnings for classroom debates. In 1784 Stiles increased the number of student performances. The topics, as before, ran the gamut of philosophical theory, but many of them touched on politics. A sample of the 1784 debates conveys the flavor: "Is the literary or military art most beneficial to society," "Ought the powers of Congress to be augmented," "Is hereditary monarchy preferable to elective," "Is the passion for public education good for the state," "Is it in the interest of the Union to form commercial alliances," "Is it [politic] to continue the eastern and western states in one Congressional convention," and "Was the grant of half pay for life and the commutation of that half pay a politic measure in Congress?"[21] Both theoretical and practical issues occupied the students. It was important to Stiles that prospective civic leaders be able to apply their knowledge to contemporary affairs.

The general tenor of these exercises remained constant to the end of Stiles' presidency, but from time to time current events were the subject of lively debate. The proceedings of 1787 raised the issues of "whether deputies or representatives are subject to the instruction of their constituents" and "whether the state acted wisely in sending delegates to the constitutional convention now sitting in Philadelphia?" America's troubles with western Indians suggested a consideration of "whether our ancestors were justified in their manner of becoming possessed of Indian lands in New England." And so it went. Stiles did not impose his own views; rather, he encouraged students to read outside works and apply their knowledge. For instance, in 1791 Eli Whitney read not only the assigned material in Paley, but also Robertson's *Charles V*, Rollin's *Ancient History*, John Gillies' *The History of Ancient Greece* (2 vols., London, 1786), Voltaire's *Philosophy of History* (London, 1766), and Vertot's *Roman Revolutions* in order to grapple with debate topics.[22]

Still, interesting omissions occurred. Stiles left no diary record of debates on Federalist policy or the French Revolution. Perhaps he was reluctant to expose personal views so at variance with the prevailing political climate even to his undergraduates. As it was, his students flirted with the doctrines of French Revolutionary politics and infidelity. If the memory of the elderly Lyman Beecher can be trusted, during Stiles' last two years many students (but not Beecher) were religious skeptics, read Thomas Paine, and called one another Voltaire, D'Alembert, and other names suggesting acquaintance with the *philosophes* whose sentiments underlay the Revolution. While Stiles recognized that religious and perhaps political rebelliousness were common undergraduate phenomena (he had briefly embraced religious skepticism while a student), it was an inopportune time for such goings-on.[23] Word could leak out, perhaps hurting Yale's image in the eyes of the citizenry and the legislature. Stiles did not want that to happen.

Throughout his presidency, then, Stiles used education to produce leaders for the civil state as well as the church by increasing the political and historical components of the curriculum while gently shaping it to emphasize a republicanism that involved support for the new Constitution, but not necessarily for the measures of the group that first administered it. Timothy Dwight shared Stiles' devotion to education for state service, his belief in the republican form of government, and his support for the Constitution, but he espoused political Federalism in the classroom.

Dwight made very few structural changes in the curriculum before 1800. The most politically significant was to increase even more the teaching of history. Entering freshmen had to have some familiarity with Sallust. The first year brought Livy and Alexander Adam's *Roman Antiquities* (Edinburgh, 1742), while juniors studied Alexander Tytler's *Elements of General History* (orig. unknown; 2 vols., London, 1801).[24] Some of this was Commonwealth Whig fare, but other text choices show that Dwight was interested to present Federalism as well as republicanism. Both Noah Webster and Jedediah Morse were Yale graduates, so the decision to use the *Grammatical Institutes of the English Language* and *The American Geography* may in part have been old school loyalty. Yet the books were also Federalist, anti-Jeffersonian, and critical of the French Revolution although neither work claimed to treat politics.[25] The continued use of Paley's moral philosophy text made some sense as well, for by the late 1790s Dwight was concerned to control the effects of democracy run rampant (of which Paley warned), was sympathetic to the Englishman's upper class predilections, was interested in preserving an effective religious establishment (Congregational, of course), and was an admirer of the English government. Thus Dwight found Paley's politics more congenial than did Stiles.[26]

Like Stiles, Dwight kept his students alert and thinking through frequent classroom debates, but Dwight's techniques differed. Several students would engage topics previously selected or approved by the president, who would then reply, sometimes lecturing for days if he felt the topic worthwhile. No doubt Dwight revealed his personal, highly Federalist convictions on topics such as: "Ought religious tests to be required of civil officers," "Ought representatives to be bound by the will of their constituents," "Ought foreigners to be admitted to public office" and "Ought the President of the United States to turn out officers on account of their political principles (this after Jefferson's election)?"[27] Dwight, then, was much more partisan than Stiles, unafraid to inculcate Federalist political principles into his pupils.

The enlarged political component of education and the partisanship of the college leadership had their effects on the undergraduates. After an initial less-ening of interest in politics during the early post-war years, student enthusiasm picked up at the time of the Constitutional Convention. Political absorption continued thereafter; with the coming of Dwight it sought an outlet in partisan politics. The students, not surprisingly, reflected their elders' opinions. By 1800, Yale was a Federalist stronghold.

With the end of the Revolution, opportunities for students to parade, boycott, enlist, or demonstrate largely disappeared. But they did continue to talk. Commencements annually gave seniors a chance to show off their skills, but the literary society meetings acquired added significance during this period, for the societies were larger, better organized, and more active than ever before. Yale's Brothers in Unity held forensic disputations by war's end. Consistently, the majority of topics bore on their classroom studies. Until 1787, most were moral philosophy propositions. Students debated the honor of duelling, the benefit of the theater, and relations in a state of nature, in marriage, and with their God.[28] In 1787, after Shays' Rebellion and during the drafting of the Constitution, attention shifted to politics, and decisions based on majority vote showed student preferences: "Would it be good policy to lessen the number of representatives (yes)," "Whether a limited monarchy would be preferable to a republican government for these states (no)," and "Whether it is good policy that want of estate disqualify anyone from holding office (no)."[29]

During the rest of Stiles' presidency most topics touched on politics in one way or another, both with the Brothers and with the Linonian Society, which began disputations in 1788. Many focused on Constitutional issues: "Ought delegates to be bound by instructions which they receive from their constituents (no)," "Would it be just and politic to force the two dissenting states of Rhode Island and North Carolina to join the Union (no)," and "Ought representation and taxation to be proportionate to one another?"[30] Other questions treated current matters of public policy: "Is it right to press men to go into the army against their will," "Whether it is politic for the United States to incorporate manufactures," "Is it consistent with justice and good policy to emancipate the slaves (yes)," "Would it be politic to dispossess the British of our western posts (no)," and "Would it be politic for the United States to confederate with France in a war against Great Britain?"[31] Even local politics occasionally provoked debate, as when the Brothers in Unity considered the propriety of dividing Connecticut into districts for the purpose of electing United States representatives (the decision was negative).[32]

It may be a measure of Timothy Dwight's influence over Yale that, while political interest continued apace in student debaters and while their topics ranged all over the political landscape, certain of the president's biases made their way into these unsupervised presentations.[33] For example, each society on several occasions considered the value of foreign immigration and of admitting foreigners to public office, always deciding in the negative.[34] Dwight's support of the Alien and Sedition Acts may also have influenced the students to change their minds about the liberty of the press, defending it unconditionally until 1798 but not thereafter.[35] Both societies opposed the French Revolution, the Brothers ultimately deciding that war measures in 1799 were proper, while the Linonians denied the French the right to revolutionize their government.[36] Dwight was less successful in religion than in politics. While the societies generally upheld the Connecticut establishment, only once in the course of several debates on the subject did they vote to exclude infidels from public office and the Brothers denied that reading Paine's *Age of Reason* would produce bad effects.[37]

As their Paine debate suggests, the students did read outside the classroom. Book borrowing records do not survive, but the library had added by 1800 a number of works in the Commonwealth canon, including Montesquieu and De Lolme on the British constitution, Beccaria and Vattel on law, Milton's prose works, Doddridge, Watts, Price, Priestley, Robertson, and Ferguson among the Commonwealthmen and their followers, plus the historians Thucydides, Rollin, Goldsmith, and Catherine Macaulay.[38] Moreover, the Linonian Society library had about twenty Commonwealth works by 1796, mostly history, but including Montesquieu, Burlamaqui, and Hutcheson's *Moral Philosophy*.[39]

The political message of the curriculum, the debates, and student reading received additional support at commencement when Dwight addressed the baccalaureate ceremonies for each class. His 1798 address, for example, attempted to demonstrate that the seniors still had much to fear from infidel philosophy, mostly that of Hume, Hobbes, and Shaftesbury. He strove to dissuade them from it by showing the pernicious nature of the philosophy and also that it was attached to the horrible convulsions afflicting Europe.[40] Dwight's performance was of a piece with his other political and religious statements. His Federalism, made known in and out of class, upheld by the trustees and the larger political community, formed a pervasive atmosphere that helped account for the political conservatism of the well-educated in nineteenth-century New England.

II

While not all schools were subject to every element of the evolution Yale experienced, the predominant pattern for pre-Revolutionary colleges in the early republic was the same: increased attention to state-service education with more emphasis on the political component of the curriculum and a growing partisanship, keyed largely to national issues.

A major element of this pattern was the propensity of the college faculties to take sides in politics. The New England faculties usually supported the Constitution, then became Federalists in the 1790s. The views of Dartmouth's professors remain the most obscure. We do not know the faculty's attitude toward the Constitution, but Hanover supported it and the faculty had historically helped shape town opinion. Regarding the 1790s, we know only that the historian of New Hampshire Republicanism calls John Wheelock the leader of a Federalist clique in the early 1800s.[41] Had he been a Federalist for long?

Harvard's faculty had been, even more so than Yale's. President Joseph Willard believed, like Ezra Stiles, that politics should be separated from his public functions, so he made no official political comments. But he could not conceal his values. In the 1780s he was a social conservative who questioned the democratizing thrust of the Revolution and deplored the local jealousies that impeded the national government. His support of the Constitution was enthusiastic, and he approved of the Washington administration. He welcomed the French Revolution but soon came to revile its excesses and, by extension, its American sympathizers. He thus became a committed Federalist during the 1790s.[42] Medical professor John Warren shared Willard's politics, but not his reticence. He supported conservative James Bowdoin for governor of Massachusetts in 1784 and was so outraged by Shays' Rebellion he organized his own militia company to help quash it. He favored the Constitution, and backed the national administration from the first in both domestic and foreign policy. The French Revolution disgusted him; its American apologists were Jacobins.[43]

The evidence regarding other Harvard professors' beliefs is more circumstantial. Professors Eliphalet Pearson and Samuel Webber were socially so conservative that it is hard to imagine them not reacting adversely to the "democratization" of state politics in the 1780s and to opposition to the national administration in the 1790s. Pearson contributed to the Federalist newspaper *New England Palladium* in the late 1790s. In Webber's case there are hints of Federalist leanings. George Washington appointed him to a federal commission to survey the border between the United States and Canada in 1796, and a predominantly Federalist Board of Overseers selected him as Harvard president in 1804. Webber's religious views were more important than his political opinions as a qualification for the post, but the Board would not have chosen a Republican.[44]

Harvard's most vociferous Federalist was David Tappan, named professor of divinity in 1793. Tappan, whom historian of Massachusetts Federalism James Banner calls "a stout defender of the Federalist faith," used his pulpit and professorship to warn the public about the dangers of religious and secular disorder. In his first year at Harvard he cautioned about encroaching infidelity, preventable only through the cooperation of minister and magistrate such as had brought about the adoption of the Massachusetts and United States Constitutions and the suppression of Shays' Rebellion. Later, the advent of the more violent phase of the French Revolution was for Tappan an example of what could happen in the United States. By the end of the decade he was excoriating Jefferson and other infidels, warning of the consequences should they capture control of national politics.[45] Harvard matched Yale's staunch Federalism.

The College of Rhode Island shared the politics of its New England neighbors. At the end of the war President James Manning was interested in the fate of the debt certificates the college had purchased. His 1786 election to the Continental Congress provided the opportunity to investigate for himself. He reported to friends in Rhode Island that congressional problems in financial, commercial, and diplomatic affairs were compounded by state indifference. Rhode Island was particularly guilty of thwarting national policy. Manning worked energetically for ratification of the Constitution in his home state and even travelled to Massachusetts to lobby its ratification convention.[46]

James Manning died in 1791, before party divisions had taken shape. His colleagues and successors, however, were solidly Federalist. Jonathan Maxcy, a 1787 alumnus, moved from the chair of oratory and belles lettres to the presidency in 1792. In demand as a speaker, he preached to his audiences on the glories of republican government and the necessity of virtue to preserve it. He approved of the Washington administration's policies. Oddly, as late as 1795 Maxcy praised the French Revolution. The Terror did not disturb him but the penetration of infidelity into America did. By 1799 his Federalism became almost hysterical:

Never has our country been exposed to greater danger; never has our government been assaulted with greater violence, by foreign foes and domestic traitors; never have more insidious, persevering and malevolent attempts to corrupt public opinion, to undermine the foundations of religion, to cut asunder the sinews of moral obligation, and to cover this happy land with carnage, desolation, and ruin [been attempted].[47]

Other faculty members diagnosed the events of the 1790s in the same terms. Peres Fobes used his Massachusetts election sermon in 1795 to warn that subordination to authority is necessary to Government. He decried the licentiousness of the press, the failure to promote virtue and piety, the division of the magistracy and the Christian priesthood, the promotion of improper connections with despotic Governments, and the neglect of the country's own Government, especially defense, all of which he associated with the Republican opposition. Fobes' colleague Asa Messer, Professor of Learned Languages after 1796, was even less discreet. By 1798 he blamed France for all of America's troubles: threatening war, ruining commerce, causing political factionalism. France had "killed her kings, but not her tyrants." Fortunately, George Washington and John Adams had led the nation away from peril. But there was danger near: "The politics of the man who would constitutionally succeed to the presidency, in case of President Adams decease or inability, are such as might expose us to a more servile yoke than was ever threatened by the British Court."[48]

If the New England colleges solidly supported the Constitution and Federalist policies in the 1790s, while fighting against the infiltration of infidelity and other side effects of the French Revolution, the middle states' schools joined them in the struggle. At the end of the Revolution King's College backers tried to resurrect the institution. In somewhat altered form it did rise again, with the name Columbia proclaiming its national allegiance. But if Columbia was now a loyal American institution, its political atmosphere was just as elitist and conservative as before. Certainly such sentiments underlay the politics of the school's most influential figure, William Samuel Johnson, president from 1787 to 1800. Johnson, son of King's first president, had been more circumspect than his father, but he, too, was torn before the Revolution between American liberty and British loyalty. Although politically prominent in Connecticut before the war, he sat out the fighting, thankful not to be prosecuted. Yet such were Johnson's talents that his fellow citizens forgave his Loyalism and launched him into national politics in the Confederation Congress in 1785. There Johnson's stances were nationalist, favoring a stronger central Government, which he helped produce as an active delegate to the Constitutional Convention. Even after his selection as Columbia's president, Connecticut kept him in responsible positions in the state Assembly and the United States Senate, where his Federalism manifested itself in support of Hamiltonian measures and negotiations with the British to preserve Anglo-American trade. Although he resigned from public office in 1791, his interest in politics continued long enough for him to criticize the excesses of the French Revolution and to favor the Jay Treaty.[49]

Many of Johnson's colleagues shared his politics. Peter Wilson had been a Federalist member of New Jersey's Legislature before joining the faculty and commented on public affairs in that vein thereafter. John Kemp eschewed politics until the war scare of 1799, when he suddenly became an ardent Federalist. Medical faculty Ebenezer Crosby and Charles McKnight left the college before the intense partisanship of the 1790s began, but both backed the Constitution and were incipient Federalists through membership in the Society of the Cincinnati. Almost as prominent as Johnson was James Kent, professor of law from 1793 to 1798. Kent had favored the Constitution as a young attorney in Poughkeepsie, and was an ardent admirer of the *Federalist Papers* and their co-author Alexander Hamilton. Connections made during the ratification struggle prompted opposition to Governor George Clinton in New York politics and election as a Federalist to the New York Assembly in 1790. He gained enough respect within the party to be a nominee for the United States House in 1792. His defeat helped lead to his removal to New York City and the Columbia position, in which he continued to support Federalist measures, such as defense of the Jay Treaty. Jay reciprocated after his election to the governorship by naming Kent to judicial posts. These soon would lead to a great reputation as a conservative jurist.[50]

The only flies in the Federalist ointment were Samuel Latham Mitchell, professor of natural history after 1792, and Samuel Bard of the medical school. As national party politics made an impact on New York, they downplayed the differences between Federalists and Republicans, deprecated factionalism, and urged united action by Americans to tackle the country's problems. By the end of the decade, however, forced by the quasi-war with France to choose loyalties, Mitchell became a Republican. Indeed, he left the college in 1801 after winning a seat in Congress.[51]

The New Jersey college faculties likewise favored the Constitution and became Federalist partisans in the 1790s. Queen's College President Jacob Hardenbergh was a pro-Constitution delegate to the New Jersey ratifying convention. After Hardenbergh's death in 1790, William Linn served as president pro-tem while also ministering to a Dutch Reformed Church in New York City. He had supported the Constitution and liked the administration's early measures. Initial defense of the French Revolution had turned to opposition by 1794. He still thought the Revolution embodied an extension of American republicanism, but was concerned about its violence and the deism and atheism that accompanied it. Ira Condict succeeded Linn as president and sole instructor at Queen's. He was a religious Federalist. An admirer of Washington, he thought the administration pursued "wise and prudent" measures, and wished that Americans would follow its political creed. He later lamented Washington's death for it came at a crisis in American affairs. In fact, the death demonstrated God's displeasure; in true jeremiad style, Condict argued that only national repentence and reformation could rescue the nation from its affliction.[52]

Princeton's politically prominent faculty members were still John Witherspoon and Samuel Stanhope Smith, both of whom continued their earlier involvement. Witherspoon was a delegate to the New Jersey ratification convention, where he helped write the statement approving the Constitution. State jealousy and the national Government's poverty had influenced him to favor acceptance. He became an enthusiastic backer of the new administration, but after 1790 said little about politics for he was blind, enfeebled, and much less active, even in the college.[53]

When Samuel Stanhope Smith succeeded Witherspoon as president in 1795, he apparently conceived the role to include duties as a political spokesman. Two sermons during his first presidential year defined his position. One on the day of the public fast listed a number of reasons for contrition: the savage war on the western frontier, the wars in Europe, which might shortly involve America, a plague of insects, the recent epidemics of fever, and above all, the degeneracy of manners and the progress of infidelity, both sparked by Thomas Paine's *The Age of Reason*. All this produced domestic discord and sedition "lighted up by faction, discontent, or popular ambition playing on ignorance." Smith, no friend of the common man, deplored excessive democracy and gave thanks that the Whiskey Rebellion had been quelled by the prudent measures of the chief magistrate. A little later, Smith had the opportunity to give thanks for public blessings, foremost among which he listed the current government. He praised the federal system for its ability to operate in spite of human corruption and George Washington for his able administration. Yet there was danger in allowing national power to be eroded, for then America might be sucked into the European wars or might be exposed to continued domestic eruptions such as the late Whiskey Rebellion. Although proclaiming nonpartisanship, Smith took pains to condemn the penetration of French infidelity, to criticize the actions of the French Revolution's American supporters, and to suggest that somehow there was a connection between internal unrest and external subversion.[54]

Like other Federalists, Smith continued a zealous critic of French infidelity and Republican factionalism. In early 1799 he congratulated Massachusetts Congregational minister Jedediah Morse on a speech which revealed the work of the Bavarian Illuminati in fomenting the French Revolution, in sponsoring "Jacobin Clubs" in America, and in seeking to attack both America's clergy and government. The death of Washington elicited a sermon praising the late general to the highest, belittling as envious those who had criticized him, and praying to God for salvation from the factions that he had overawed.[55] There were few more committed Federalists in the country than Smith.

The internal political composition of the faculty at the Philadelphia institution was quite complex. The University of the State of Pennsylvania continued to operate during the post-war years, but never without challenge from Provost Smith and the surviving trustees of the College of Philadelphia. In 1789 that challenge at last proved somewhat successful. The College regained its charter, but not its property. For two years both college and university operated side by side, but such an arrangement proved financially disastrous to both. In 1791 the two schools merged by mutual consent and what we know as the University of Pennsylvania was born.[56]

These arrangements produced four different faculties: the University before and after the merger, the College, and the medical school. There was faculty overlap to some degree, but political views, especially with regard to Pennsylvania issues, were often directly a product of which faculty one belonged to. The University of the State of Pennsylvania had, of course, been staffed with Constitutionalists in 1779. Several of those men continued in office for some years, but most were silent on politics. The most politically active professor was David Rittenhouse. He continued to serve the Constitutionalists as treasurer of the state until 1789. An opponent of the United States Constitution, he lost bids for membership in the state ratifying convention and later as a presidential elector. He also lost races for the Pennsylvania Assembly in 1791 and 1792, after the Republican counter-revolution in the state. Even an appointment to head the United States Mint could not reconcile Rittenhouse to George Washington's policies. He was involved in the pro-French activities surrounding Citizen Genet, resigned from the Philadelphia Democratic Society just before violence erupted in 1794, then rejoined in 1796 and gained a spot as a Jeffersonian presidential elector that year. At that point he died, the most thoroughgoing Jeffersonian on the University faculty.[57]

The reconstituted College of Philadelphia was still led by Provost Smith, but he had mellowed since the Revolution. An unrelenting conservative, he was much less overt in revealing his opinions. His one public performance while in office was a July 4, 1790 sermon before the Philadelphia Society of the Cincinnati, which complimented the members on their efforts to perpetuate the patriotism of the Revolution but gave most of its attention to the indirect promotion of the college. Despite Smith's inoffensive rhetoric, he still carried the stigma of his Revolutionary indecisiveness. When the merger took place, Smith was left off the faculty. He spent the rest of his days in land speculation.[58]

Of the professors appointed to the combined institution, James Wilson had the most notable politics. Wilson, who taught law at the University for almost a decade, had been a conservative in state politics. He had defended the College against Constitutionalist takeover in 1779. He supported the Republican state constitution of 1790. But it was as a national figure that he gained greater fame. Along with James Madison, he was the principal architect of the Constitution of 1787 and defended it in debate and essay thereafter. Because he soon became a federal judge and Supreme Court Justice, he took little part in the national party battles of the 1790s, but he remained a conservative, favoring Federalist measures throughout the decade.[59]

Most of the medical school faculty remained aloof from politics after the Revolution. The exceptions were James Hutchinson, who had been an active Constitutionalist during the war and retained some prominence as a source of counsel for his party into the late 1780s, and Benjamin Rush. An early critic of the Pennsylvania constitution, Rush turned his attention to national measures before the war's end. He deplored the weakness of the Confederation government, citing it for too frequent elections, its unicameral house, and its inability to curb the actions of state legislatures. He praised the Philadelphia Convention and helped obtain ratification in Pennsylvania. He followed up by pushing John Adams for Vice-President and Philadelphia as the site for the capital. It seemed that Rush's political influence was at zenith, but then his fortunes turned sour. He sought but did not receive an appointment under the new government, then helped plan the movement for a new Pennsylvania constitution in 1790, but was not elected to the constitutional convention. Having lost his eminence, Rush largely ignored politics after 1790, at least publicly.[60] Considering all the faculties, the Philadelphia college was primarily conservative and Federalist, with David Rittenhouse the only major exception.

The one avowedly Republican campus in the 1790s was the College of William and Mary. That was largely due to the exertions of President James Madison. No sooner had the war ended than Madison began to worry about preserving America's newly won liberties. He formed the college faculty and others together as the Society for the Preservation of Liberty to guard against attacks. They were not long in coming. By the time of the Constitutional Convention, Madison had found fault with the "anti-republican" views of John Adams and his followers. He overcame his dislike of the aristocratic tendencies of the framers and their balanced government to support the Constitution, but by the early 1790s, he had formed an aversion to Hamiltonian policy. He also opposed the government's foreign policy, reviling the Jay Treaty, for he never lost his enthusiasm for the French Revolution.[61]

Madison reserved special condemnation for John Adams. In 1797 he called the local freeholders together to criticize the administration for "unconstitutional" acts and anti-French policies. The next year he used his bishopric to turn Adams' call for a day of prayer into one of "Solemn Humiliation, Fasting, and Prayer," during which Madison protested the desertion of Christian liberty he said was involved in war preparations against France. By 1800 he was livid at Adams' extension of federal legislative and judicial power, and at the raising of a standing army. He was sure an assault on republicanism was imminent.

Later that year Hamilton's attack on Adams and Jefferson's bid for the presidency pleased him greatly.[62]

Although Madison worried about the penetration of infidelity and venerated Washington's Revolutionary prowess, he continued to denounce Federalist administrations. Buoyed by the Virginia and Kentucky Resolves, he hoped that Representative Madison, Jefferson, and other Republicans could purge the Constitution of the "Filth which Ambition, Avarice, and Ignorance was heaping up around it...[the] violation of Common Law, continuous Extensions of Power in the Federal Legislature & Executive, [and] the mad Ambition of forming standing Armies & Navies."[63] There was no more rabid Republican on any college campus.

Abetting Madison at different points in his presidency were law professors George Wythe and St. George Tucker. Before leaving William and Mary for a career on the bench in 1790, Wythe served briefly as delegate to the Federal Convention and touted the Constitution at the Virginia ratifying convention. Wythe's politics after his resignation only indirectly affected the college, but his Federalism was subdued once the new government took office. His opposition to the Jay Treaty brought a formal transfer of allegiance, and he was a Jeffersonian elector in the contest of 1800.[64] St. George Tucker, who succeeded Wythe, had favored a stronger central government during the 1780s, was a Virginia delegate to the Annapolis Convention, and had supported the Constitution. Yet disenchantment had soon set in. By 1792 he was criticizing the government. He declared the Alien and Sedition Acts unconstitutional and in 1800 was among Virginia Republicans threatening disunion if Jefferson were not elected.[65]

Federalism dominated, then, among the faculties of the old colleges in the new republic, with William and Mary the only exception. Part of the reason was the solidly Federalist political convictions of boards of trustees, many of which were now permeated with public officials. These men helped establish the atmosphere in which the faculties worked; in some cases they were responsible for hiring and firing faculty members.

For New England there exists too little information to determine the loyalties of College of Rhode Island officials, but Dartmouth and Harvard trustees held political views similar to those at Yale. Fears of infidelity, revulsion at the excessive violence of the French Revolution, and dependence on British trade inclined laymen and clerics alike toward Federalism. Of those Dartmouth trustees whose political loyalites can be ascertained, only one was a Jeffersonian in the 1790s. The Harvard Overseers were not quite so united. Several antifederalists and, later, Jeffersonians were on the board; John Hancock, Samuel Adams, and Moses Gill were the most well known. But the board comprised sixty-five or more members, including as it did a variety of Massachusetts public officials and Boston area Congregational ministers. Backers of the Federal Constitution and Federalists were overwhelmingly in the majority before the election of 1800, the first to give Jeffersonians any significant strength in state politics. Thus the

Federalist persuasion of the college faculties received reinforcement from the trustees.[66]

In the middle states the political inclinations of the Queen's College trustees remain obscure, but not so those at Princeton. Well over half the Nassau trustees left some record of their views. Approval of the Constitution and Federalism predominated, with thirteen men known to have held these positions and another two may have. By contrast, there were only three known Jeffersonians and one who switched from backing the government to opposition because of the Jay Treaty.[67] Princeton's Federalism was almost as complete in the 1790s as at the New England schools.

The revival of New York's college involved a much more patriotic body of men than had governed King's, but they were still politically conservative. In 1784 nine men, claiming to have some association with King's College, petitioned the New York legislature for a renewal of its charter. All had been Revolutionaries. While the legislature acted favorably on the petition, it placed the governance of Columbia College under the Board of Regents of the University of the State of New York (to be discussed in Chapter 7). Not until 1787 did the college acquire its own board. Seven of its twenty-eight members left within a year, but the great majority of the other twenty-one favored the Constitution. Twenty of these men served through the era of party formation; thirteen have left evidence of affiliation. Ten were active Federalist politicians or clerical backers of Federalism. Three were Republicans. Fifteen men filled vacancies on the board before 1800. All served through the era of party formation and nine have left traces of their allegiances. Seven were Federalists, two Republicans. Columbia's board of trustees continued the political conservatism of its predecessor, but its politics were now definitely American.[68]

In Philadelphia, the existence of two colleges and their merger produced a complex thicket of trustee loyalties, more so than for the faculty. The majority of the trustees of the University of the State of Pennsylvania were Constitutionalists in state politics and, as such, opposed the Federal Constitution in 1787–1788. Yet as time went on and the Republican (anti-state constitution) faction grew in electoral favor, some of the ex officio slots fell to them. Moreover, some of the later board appointees were also Republican, perhaps because the board sensed which way the political wind was blowing. The trustees of the College of Philadelphia during its brief resurrection were more ideologically pure. Insofar as their politics are known, they were all Pennsylvania Republicans who favored adoption of the Federal Constitution. When the University of Pennsylvania formed, it drew board members from both predecessors. It thus acquired trustees about evenly divided in their politics regarding the state and federal constitutions. The subsequent careers of most reflected the social and political assumptions demonstrated in their stances during the 1780s. One or two Pennsylvania Republicans, such as George Clymer, switched allegiances to become Jeffersonian by the late 1790s, but they were offset by Pennsylvania Constitutionalists who became Federalists. The trustees elected after the union also came from each political camp. The Philadelphia trustees were the most balanced group in the country.[69]

The College of William and Mary, with its staunchly Republican faculty, had a surprisingly large Federalist contingent among the Overseers. Almost all who served in the late 1780s approved the Federal Constitution. But in Virginia, perhaps more than elsewhere, approval of the Constitution did not mean backing for the government that operated under it. Still, a substantial group of Overseers such as John Marshall, Henry Lee, and John Page, declared their Federalism early and stuck with it. Their influence was possibly countered by the emerging Republicanism of Madison, Jefferson, Wythe, and Tucker, but during the 1790s the political affiliations of the Overseers accurately mirrored party divisions in the state.[70]

The expression of political allegiances by faculty and trustees in sermons, pamphlets, electoral contests, or military service all bore witness to the continuing politicization of college leaders who were the inculcators of knowledge and role models for the young. The vast majority of these men supported the Constitution of 1787, thus imparting a nationalist tone to the college campuses during the years of debate over the proper form for an American government. When the question became one of what policies the new government should follow, all the campuses except that of William and Mary exhibited Federalist tendencies. These communities could not resist taking politicization to its farthest extreme— partisanship. As a result, we must ask what, if anything, differentiated a Federalist from a Republican education?

The structural evolution of the college curriculum continued in the post-Revolutionary era. The most dramatic changes took place in the sciences. Virtually every college made some effort to increase its offering. By the end of the century, there were medical schools at Dartmouth, Harvard, Columbia, and the University of Pennsylvania. All the colleges offered natural sciences and mathematics, while Columbia and Princeton taught chemistry. The study of English grammar, rhetoric, and belles lettres also gained stature. Perhaps the greatest strides took place at Columbia and the College of Rhode Island where the presidents taught the course in the 1790s, but almost everywhere students spent more time studying their native language. Much of this was the collegiate community's response to requests for more "practical" education, both desirable and necessary in a culturally independent nation.[71]

The augmentation of political studies also proceeded apace. Most colleges either formally or informally increased the amount of instruction in history, focusing not on ecclesiastical or ancient history, but on modern history, often that of England and the United States. Some colleges, such as Dartmouth, added moral philosophy to the curriculum; others, such as Columbia, enlarged the focus from ethics to other fields. The result was that the science of government or politics appeared in every curriculum by the end of the century. The University of Pennsylvania and Columbia joined the College of William and Mary in presenting full scale law courses in the 1790s, while other schools injected at least some lectures on law into moral philosophy, as we have seen at Yale. Even the classics enjoyed a reorientation at some schools so that more attention was devoted to classical historians and political commentators rather than poets, philosophers, and playwrights.

All the colleges participated in these curricular advances except Queen's which, for most of the post-Revolutionary years, was struggling to survive and had too few resources to improve the quality of its education.[72] So, it was not the structure of the curriculum that revealed its partisan character, for that was the same everywhere. Rather, it was the tone of the education, determined by the content of moral philosophy and law lectures, by text selection, and by the choice of topics for in-class debates, that enable characterization of the curricula as Federalist or Republican. Using these criteria, all the colleges except William and Mary offered Federalist instruction before 1800. The Virginia school was decidedly Republican.

The offerings in moral philosophy illustrated the political temper of the collegiate communities. Moral philosophy lectures survive from Columbia, Princeton, and the University of Pennsylvania, offered by John D. Gros, Samuel Stanhope Smith, and John Andrews respectively. All three courses followed the common practice of dividing the subject into ethics, the relationships between man and his God, his neighbors and his family, and the nature of government, which often included comments on the law. The ethical components of the sets of lectures had different sources. Gros drew from Paley's principles of utility, reason, and the desire for happiness; Smith and Andrews worked in the Scottish Common Sense school, with its emphasis on inherent moral sense. But whatever the philosophical underpinnings, the thrust of the commentary on government was the same, the glorification of the republican form coupled with admonitions toward behavioral restraint by the people who were the foundation of political power.

All the lecturers undertook a general discussion of the forms of government describing the pure forms of monarchy, aristocracy, and democracy, the advantages and disadvantages of each. All favored mixed forms because they heightened the advantages and limited the liabilities of the pure forms. Inevitably for teachers in the United States, they all praised the republican form, by which they meant one wherein sovereignty resided in a portion of the whole people (usually determined by propertyholding), but was exercised by their elected representatives, thus avoiding the practical and political difficulties inherent in pure democracies.[73]

These discussions did not differentiate the lectures from earlier moral philosophy courses treating politics, nor from their Republican contemporary. What was different was the extrapolation of the concern over democratic excesses inherent in republics and the conservative response to that concern. Andrews, despite his lukewarm Revolutionary patriotism and his condemnation of the social dislocations caused by the war, was the least cautionary of the three. He stressed man's depravity, and that government derived from the unwillingness of man to sacrifice his self-interest to the public good. The chief object of government, therefore, was the promotion of the common good. That required obedience by the people; in emergencies, their rights might have to be compromised. It meant that virtue and piety must be promoted, thus obligating the state to protect religion and rulers to promote virtue through examples of piety, sobriety, industry, justice, and fortitude. Along the same lines, Andrews noted the need for patriotism, the need for a spirit of moderation when individuals considered their own interests, and the desirability of censors to prevent excesses by the government or the people.[74] Somewhat offsetting this call for popular restraint were observations indicating that the power of rulers must be curbed by fundamental law, that assemblies should be large, that there should be rotations in office, limited terms of office, and a broad franchise. Although cautioning that it should not be resorted to for transient causes, Andrews acknowledged the right of rebellion and dismissed passive obedience. Finally, he discussed the United States government, noting its democratic character, its representational process, the separation of powers, and the system of checks and balances. It was, he said, similar but superior to the English constitution; a primary advantage was that its alterability through constitutional change eliminated the necessity of resistance to government in America.[75]

John Gros' lectures at Columbia posited a more restrained, less politically active American population. Rather than rights, Gros stressed duty; that of the citizen to obey the law, that of the governor to uphold the law and follow it in a just manner. The governor was crucial to the workings of the government. The ultimate source of political power was the people, but the right to direct the moral action of the people lay with the governor. The citizen should remain passive, preserve his own virtue, and obey the law. This type of conduct in a nation of laws was true liberty. Discussing contemporary politics, Gros accepted American republicanism but criticized its tendencies toward direct democracy. Again rulers were the key. The goal of any society was happiness, but in America that was surely the achievement of the proven benevolence of "public rulers." They, supported by the property holders in the population, had the best interests of the whole society at heart. Thus direct expressions of popular will, especially if they were extralegal or violent, were inappropriate. Indeed, Gros had great difficulty imagining a course of conduct for an oppressed people; for him, open rebellion was truly a last resort. Because he feared popular expression, he counselled students to avoid partisan politics. Rather, they should look for true merit and public virtue in candidates for governmental office.[76]

Samuel Stanhope Smith was even more concerned about the democratic thrust in American republicanism. He told his students that "the mass of the populace is necessarily ignorant...and their passions inflamed by...insidious acts, and violent harangues." In another context he warned "the passions of the people are dangerous engines of faction and ambition. Often you may rouse them to a destructive fury by a grimace of false patriotism, or a fanaticism of mistaken liberty. But you cannot mark the point beyond which they shall not rise."[77]

To warn of the dangers of mass rising was a principal object of Smith's lectures. The larger the republic, he wrote, the greater the need for representative democracy. There were dangers in unlimited suffrage; it was better to limit the vote through property qualifications and as the country grew they could be raised. Open votes (presumably public) in both legislative elections and legislative proceedings would make voters and representatives more responsible. Yet there would always be those who acted to injure others or the state. What caused the crime was public corruption. In a democracy the danger was especially great because equality of opportunity was confused with equality of result, so the natural inequality in society became the object of criticism while deference for governors disappeared. Ultimately, faction and rebellion resulted, ending in tyranny. This could best be prevented by changing the manners of the people through the proper direction of public education, preferably by the state. Some education should be made available to all, so that they might know and obey the laws and choose good rulers. Higher education should train governors and statesmen. If education did not change public behavior, or even while it was bringing about desired results, the proper recourse was the prompt punishment of offenses against society by an extensive, independent judiciary which publicized its actions.[78]

Smith's few direct observations on public affairs reflected his anxiety over the fate of democratic republics. The United States Constitution was designed to protect civil liberties, but it would do so most successfully through the dividing, checking, and balancing of power, because man was corruptible. American government had not protected the people's liberties after the Revolution because the Articles of Confederation were the product of the reaction to British tyranny and too much optimism about public virtue. The result was a government wherein the executive was too weak and the legislature too strong—too much democracy, not enough order. The state constitutions were still too popular; state governments were inferior in quality to the national. Smith urged his students to interpret the Federal Constitution in light of the *Federalist Papers*. And, in a fleeting observation he must have explicated in class, he was skeptical (as of 1794) that the French people had the national character to sustain the democratic republic they were trying to create.[79]

These lecturers' conservative political principles clearly lacked the Revolutionary zeal of Witherspoon or Alison. America had had its revolution. One was enough, especially when it produced social and political consequences so unsettling to the elite that had long controlled American public affairs. The maxims these moral philosophy instructors set forth were precisely those that Federalist politicians were striving to communicate to the public at large.[80] The evidence suggests that college teachers were more successful in their narrow universes than were politicians in the larger world.

Conservative politics also infused the reading that supplemented the moral philosophy course, or constituted it entirely at Dartmouth where, it was said, John Wheelock was capable of little except repeating the strictures of his texts.[81]

Dartmouth used Dugald Stewart's *Elements of the Philosophy of the Human Mind* (Edinburgh, 1792) and Burlamaqui, which was a staple at Harvard, but the most widely used work was Paley's *Principles of Moral and Political Philosophy*. Not only did Stiles and Dwight employ it at Yale, but so also did Dartmouth, Harvard and the College of Rhode Island (which dropped Hutcheson's work in its favor in the 1790s), while Gros' lectures at Columbia drew heavily upon it. Paley's advocacy of church and state authority, of civilian obedience to constituted rulers, and his antipathy to revolution appealed to those faculties more concerned with social disorder at home and abroad than with resistance to tyrannical rulers.[82]

Law lectures, where they were offered, were also conduits for Federalist politics. The University of Pennsylvania's James Wilson and Columbia's James Kent were active Federalist politicians. Their lectures distilled their beliefs. Wilson began his work in 1790. His course, which took more than a year, divided into three segments: the first treated the law of nature and nations, municipal law, man's obligations, a comparison of the United States and British constitutions, and common law; the second looked deeply into the United States and Pennsylvania constitutions, the court system, the rights of corporations, of citizens and aliens, and natural rights; the last examined criminal law. The subject matter overlapped that of the moral philosophy course and Wilson infused his lectures with an ethics based on a belief in God and adherence to Common Sense philosophy.[83]

Wilson, interested to create an uniquely American view of law, incorporated in it a Federalist view of politics. He glorified the new Federal and Pennsylvania constitutions, which to him embodied the principles of good government: to allow broad participation by the people in the affairs of government, to elect the wisest and best men to the offices of state, to limit the evil effect on government of man's corrupt nature and to magnify his better traits, and to erect such a system of checks and balances as requires even corrupt men to act in the public interest through use of a strong executive and an independent judiciary. This was Federalism 1790 style, when the object was to restrain the "legislative despotism" of states while energizing an impotent central government. It sought a government of laws, not men, for the realization had dawned on America's elite that most men were not as virtuous as they had seemed at the beginning of the Revolution.[84]

James Kent's Columbia lectures, commencing in 1794, showed the effects of foreign and domestic developments on the components of Federalism. Kent, too, strove to present an American interpretation of law. His purpose was to promote republicanism and prevent corruption from other codes. He liked neither the more aristocratic features of the British law nor the excessively democratic innovations of the French, but of the two, he regarded French "Jacobinical" ideas as the more dangerous. To protect the republican form of government, then, it was necessary that all should know the law. Private citizens had both rights to defend and the responsibility of electors to execute. Almost any citizen might become a public official; university alumni were likely to serve the state. Legal training was a virtual necessity. To know the law one should be highly virtuous, well read in all knowledge, fit for the administration of public affairs, patriotic, and capable of leading by example. In other words, he should be an ideal Federalist.[85]

The system of law the citizen should know greatly resembled Wilson's presentation, covering almost identical topics. Like Wilson, Kent praised the energetic new governments, state and national. And, like Wilson, he touted judicial review as an uniquely American device to protect the public weal. But here the partisan nature of politics in the 1790s intruded, for Kent thought the power of the judiciary should be used to balance the excesses of the legislatures where the passionate multitude often prevailed. By the mid-1790s the passionate multitude were those who disagreed with Federalist domestic and foreign policy, who still supported the French Revolution, and who joined Democratic-Republican Societies. It was these people against whom the law should safeguard constituted government. No wonder the emerging Republican Party questioned the Federalists' advocacy of judicial review.[86]

Students in Federalist colleges read and recited from works in other courses that reinforced the political tenor of the curriculum. The classical works of Sallust, Livy, and Xenophon's *Retreat of the Ten Thousand* were introduced at Harvard in the late 1780s in place of Virgil, Cicero's *Orations*, and Caesar's *Commentaries*. The College of Rhode Island continued to use these works, while Princeton used them all but Livy, substituting Xenophon's *Cyropaedia* for the *Retreat*, and adding Kennet's *Roman Antiquities*. Columbia students read Sallust, Virgil, Cicero, Xenophon's *Cyropaedia*, Livy (after 1794), Demosthenes, and Tacitus. The University of Pennsylvania's fare included Sallust, Livy, Virgil, Cicero's *Orations*, Caesar's *Commentaries*, Xenophon's *Cyropaedia*, and Tacitus, probably the most complete offering of all the colleges. The republican classics had not lost their influence on the curriculum. In fact, by the mid-1790s, the University of Pennsylvania, Columbia, and Harvard all taught ancient history in separate courses. Harvard even tried to bring history up to date through the use of Claude Millot's *Elements of General History*. This was good, wrote one student, because "for philosophically tracing causes and effects, & thence inferring judicious reflections, the moderns are far superior to the ancients." The "moderns," while not receiving a separate course, were suggested reading at the University of Pennsylvania, Princeton, Columbia, and the College of Rhode Island. For example, Rhode Island's Maxcy asked a student to read in Robertson's volumes on Charles V, America, and Scotland, Vertot on revolution in Sweden, Portugal, and Rome, Rollin's *Ancient History* and Roman history, Kame's *Sketches of the History of Man*, and Gibbon, all in the same year.[87]

The students' class exercises indicate the political tone of the commentary on history and government, for the faculty closely examined and criticized student efforts. Conservatism was pervasive. At Harvard in the late 1780s, John Quincy Adams addressed a number of topics treating government. One was a disputation

Table 5–1:
Curricular Offerings by Author at Original Colleges Post-1783

Category	Harvard	Yale	William & Mary	Coll. of N.J.	Columbia	Univ. of Pa.	Coll. of R.I.	Queen's	Dartmouth
Classics									
Xenophon	+			+	x	x	x	+	
Homer	x	x	?	x	x	x	x	x	
Demosthenes	x			x	x	x			
Isocrates	x				x				
Thucydides					x	x			
Herodotus					x				
Plato	x				x	x			
Cicero's *Orations**	−	x	x	x	x	x	x	x	
Virgil*	−	x	?	x	x	x	x	x	
Horace			x	x		x			
Livy*	+		x	x	+	x			
Lucian				x	x		x		
Catullus			x		x				
Sallust*	+				x	+			
Plutarch*	x								
Tacitus*					x	+			
Caesar	−				x	+		+	+
Adam		+							
Kennet				+				+	
Oratory									
Cicero's *De Oratore**		x	?	x	x	x	x	x	x
Cicero's *Tusculan Disputations**					x	x			
Webster	+								
Moral Philosophy									
Cicero's *De Officiis**	x		x	x	x	x		x	
Clarke				x**					
Pufendorf*				x**	x				
Shaftesbury				x**					
Wollaston		x		x**					
Kames*				x**					
Grotius*				x**	x	x			
Cumberland				x**		x**			
Maxwell				x**					
Selden				x**					
Burlamaqui*	x		+**	x**					
Harrington*				x**		x**			
Locke's *Essay**	x	x	+**	x**					
Locke's *Two Treatises**						x**			
Sidney*				x**		x**			

Table 5–1: *continued*

Category	Harvard	Yale	William & Mary	Coll. of N.J.	Columbia	Univ. of Pa.	Coll. of R.I.	Queen's	Dartmouth
Montesquieu*		+	+	x**					
Ferguson*				x**					
Hutcheson's *Moral Philosophy**				x**	x	x	−		
Hutcheson's *Enquiry*	x								
Edwards' *Inquiry*		x							
Fordyce	x								
Vattel*		+	+						
Paley	+	+	+						+
Stewart			+**						+
Smith, Adam			+						
Reid			+**						
Rousseau			+**						
Paine			+**						
Godwin			+**						
History									
Tytler		+							
Priestley		+							
Morse		+							
Millot	+								
Robertson*		+**					+**		
Vertot		+**					+**		
Rollin*		+**					+**		
Kames*							+**		
Gibbon							+**		
Gillies		+**							
Voltaire		+**							

*Denotes Commonwealth canon
**Denotes recommended reading
+Denotes work added after 1783
−Denotes work removed after 1783

on "Whether inequality among the citizens be necessary to the liberty of the whole?" Arguing the affirmative, Adams asserted that power corrupted government and that tyranny of the whole people was the worst form of corruption; it resulted from perfect democracy. "What protection," he asked, "can any Laws afford a Citizen in a State where every Individual thinks he has a right of altering and annulling them at his Pleasure, and where nothing is wanting, but the capricious whim of a Vile Rabble, to overturn all Laws and Government?" The solution was a balanced government, and that before it was too late. The current alarming situation of America served notice of the dangers of unchecked democracy.[88]

An emphasis on virtue and patriotism, a concern about the dangers of democracy were constant themes in Federalist colleges. The Columbia student Daniel Tompkins prepared a pair of themes on government in 1794, criticizing the monarchical form because a "dissolute and vicious king will make a corrupt and debauched nation." But the solution was not equality, not if that meant all were on a level. Virtue and balanced government were the keys. Another exercise, on knowledge, stressed obedience and the dangers of ignorance among the people. The objects of Tompkins' concern were the Whiskey Rebels. Uninformed citizens, he called them, who knew only that excise taxes were complained of before the Revolution and who paid no attention to the effects of government policy. A well-informed people would not have resorted to violence and resistance to authority.[89] Here was reflected Professor Gros' obedient citizen.

The late 1790s saw Harvard students wrestling with the same topics. William Buckminster faced the task of writing a theme on the subject "A competence is vital to content; much wealth is corpulence, if not disease." Buckminster chose to write a parable, telling the story of an English nobleman's son, raised in luxury, who took the grand tour of the continent. He stopped in Paris, lived in high style, and exhausted himself both mentally and physically. Then he began to suspect the pernicious effects of riches. To recover, he travelled in the country where he met a poor cottager whose simple, happy existence caught his attention and from whom the noble son learned the value of having just enough and no more. It was a classic tale of virtue, but indicative as well, for Buckminster added a prominent footnote, informing his professorial reader that this all took place in France before the Revolution.[90]

This Federalist world view was pervasive. Fears of infidelity, of excessive democracy, and of French Jacobin influence haunted orthodox ministers, socially conservative politicians at all levels, and the college communities which were taught and governed by both. But this view did not penetrate the College of William and Mary. There another spirit prevailed.

As we have seen, the curricular format at the Virginia college was the most unusual in America, in effect an elective system in which the student chose from a variety of optional courses. On balance this did not work very well, for most students followed a course of study less complete than did those at other colleges, perhaps because southerners were more interested in the social status conferred by college attendance than by the education it offered. However that may be, the Overseers acted in 1792 to tighten up the academic regimen by establishing two curricula. To proceed Bachelor of Arts, the student needed to take mathematics, natural philosophy, logic, belles lettres, rhetoric, natural law and the law of nations, the general principles of politics, geography, and languages, both ancient and modern. A bachelor's degree in law required all the foregoing plus civil history, both ancient and modern, and municipal law and police (a term denoting the principles of public policy). Of course, there were some concessions to the impatient sons of Virginia gentry. The courses could be taken in any order; students who demonstrated their qualifications on entrance could exempt courses; and students could take courses without belonging to a degree program.[91] Still, on paper the William and Mary curriculum had a larger political component than any other in the 1790s.

The tone of that political instruction underwent an evolutionary development (somewhat the reverse of that at Yale), depending as it did on the views and the text selection of President Madison and the two professors of law, Wythe and Tucker. Before 1790, the college leaders shared the nationalist outlook of their colleagues elsewhere. In his courses on natural law and politics Madison used Vattel, Montesquieu, and Adam Smith's *The Wealth of Nations*. The first two were standard fare, while Smith both reinforced traditional governmental ideas and provided new ones. On the one hand, he argued that in pre-Revolutionary commercial relationships between Great Britain and the colonies, the Americans suffered. He commended the republican form of government. He asserted that government was absolutely necessary to protect property, the foundation of a nation's prosperity, and republics did this best. All these positions could have been used to support the Constitution of 1787, which both Madison and Wythe approved.[92]

Yet the major themes of Smith's essay, directed against the survivals of Europe's feudal and mercantilistic economic constraints, could become a potent critique of an American government that chose to pursue the same paths. Smith argued that the best economic policy left the actions of the individual unhindered, and the best government governed as little as possible, staying out of the individual's life. Moreover, Smith voiced a concern for the economic "common man," and some hostility toward the corporation, the large-scale commercial entrepreneur, and the financier. This is perhaps most easily seen in Smith's assertion that labor is the most important component in ascertaining the value of any product. The implications of all this did not cohere with Federalist policy.[93]

As Bishop Madison became a harsher critic of the Federalist measures of the new government, and as he maintained his optimism about the ultimate value of the French Revolution, he apparently made more use of Smith's democratic passages. This is partly conjecture, but during the 1790s Madison broadened his reading to include other Scottish Common Sense writers, English moral philosophers such as Paley, who advocated utilitarianism, and those who emphasized democracy, popular sovereignty, and the general will, such as Priestley, Rousseau, Condorcet, Godwin, and the radical *philosophes*. Madison shared his thoughts on social equality, political liberty, the virtues of the small property holder, the function of the general will, and the urgency of the republican mission with such *philosophes* as Pierre Brissot, the Abbe Raynal, Gabriel Mably, and others. As the decade advanced, Madison became more and more the political liberal.[94]

Just what Madison said to his students about government, equality, economics, and politics is unknown, for no lecture notes survive. We do know, however, what he asked them to read. On the workings of the human mind, students consulted Common Sense philosophers Thomas Reid and Dugald Stewart; on moral philosophy the source was William Paley; on natural law and the law of nations, students read Burlamaqui and Vattel. These might have been read at any Federalist college. But in the realm of politics William and Mary differed sharply, for there students consulted not only Adam Smith, but also Locke's two essays on government, Montesquieu, Rousseau's *Social Contract*, Paine's *The Rights of Man*, and William Godwin's *Inquiry into Political Justice*. This was not just commentary on balanced government and the superiority of republics. Rather, it was revolutionary propaganda, praise for popular sovereignty, advocacy of equality, and an extremely optimistic view of man's virtue and his ability to govern himself in the absence of formal institutions. The students were to read what Madison read; his private enthusiasms may well have been his public principles.[95]

Madison's political liberalism and Republicanism were shared by St. George Tucker. His lectures do not survive, but the foci of his law course were the principles of the civil government of the United States and Virginia. His edition of *Blackstone's Commentaries*, presumably based on his lectures, contained notes on those parts of Blackstone that were applicable to the correlative powers delegated to the federal government and Virginia, and how they had been altered by American circumstance. But the study was not abstract, as a student writing about the course after Jefferson's election observed: "You may remember that a notion formerly prevailed here that a Student of Law should make the study of his profession subservient to that of politics."[96] Only after the election of a Republican president was it safe once more to discourse abstractly on law and government.

Students at all of the pre-Revolutionary colleges faced exposure to a partisan political education by the 1790s. Except at William and Mary, the principles of Federalism issued forth from professors and texts, forming an essential part of student recitations, debates, and readings. Consequently, the prevailing political sentiment expressed in the students' extra-curricular activities was Federalist.

Wherever faculty addressed students directly during the 1790s the message was the same: warnings about infidelity, the French Revolution and its American backers, and praise for Federalist administrations. At Harvard, David Tappan repeated these themes from 1794 through 1800. Usually, Tappan phrased his addresses as general critiques of the evils affecting the country, but in 1796 he was quite open about the college position on the issues he raised, saying that he had long witnessed and favored Harvard's policies with regard to the community at large: support for the Constitution, the actions of the national government, and a "pointed abhorrence of a certain unprincipled faction." He went on to urge the students to conform to the beliefs of their university fathers in this matter. Similarly, Columbia's William Samuel Johnson advised his graduates to "see whether true liberty does not consist in an exact obedience to law, a submission to the public will, a surrender of all individual, inferior, partial, subordinate interests, emoluments, and objects to general, public, and universal welfare." Rhode Island's Jonathan Maxcy and Asa Messer took a comparative approach. In urging his students to combat irreligion, Messer asked them to look at the infidels Hume and Paine, then at the Christians Locke and Newton. Surely there was no question whom to believe. Applying this technique to government, Maxcy suggested a critical examination of governmental instability in France, then a look at America's government, impartially administered, evocative of respect for authority. Which was better? Which deserved support and protection?[97]

Commencement exercises, still at least partially under the control of the faculty, revealed the political opinions of the college communities. The majority of the individual performances dwelt upon themes related to the recently ended war, the virtue necessary to sustain a republic, and contemporary political affairs.

In New England, Rhode Island College seniors were concerned about "The Present Appearance of Public Affairs in the United States of America," commenting on the advantages of republicanism, advising the adoption of the Constitution, recommending the encouragement of domestic manufactures and the disuse of foreign goods. In 1790, the students congratulated the state for joining the union. The theses these students offered in politics reinforced their platform oratory, arguing, for example, that "For Republics, luxury is a source of destruction, but for Monarchies indigence is," and "The more powerful officials are, the more their tenure of office ought to be shortened."[98] The interests of Harvard students mirrored those of their southerly neighbors. Platform exercises stressed virtue and the operations of government: "To attain the end of Civil Government is it not necessary as well to reward the virtuous as to punish the vicious," "Whether a republic is more secure of the continuance of its liberties, where the officers in the higher branches of government are elected for several years, than where they are elected annually," and "Whether it is possible for civil liberty long to subsist in a community, without three orders in the government, vested with such powers as to make them mutually checks upon, and balances to, each other."[99]

Middle states colleges differed little from their northern counterparts. At the University of the State of Pennsylvania, a student could contemplate "The Former, Present, and Future Prospects of America," arguing that republics naturally produced eloquence, philosophy, and all the sciences, while a Queen's student orated on "The Evils of America." In 1788, other Queen's graduates disputed "Whether the Federal Constitution, as formed and recommended by the General Convention, ought to be adopted by the United States, in preference to the Confederation.''[100] Princeton and Columbia students also examined issues of virtue and good government. The New Jersey students spoke of "The Evils of Commerce in a Young Country," "Domestic and Political Discord," "The Abuses of Independence," and "The Influence of the New Constitution." In New York, at commencements often attended by the Continental Congress and New York General Assembly, students discussed the "Usefulness and Necessity of a Knowledge of the Laws of our Country," "The Impolicy and Imprudence of a Republic's aiming at being a conquering Nation," and "Liberty, Government, Education, and Manners."[101] All these exercises demonstrated student interest in politics and their absorption in the typical political concerns of the 1780s: analyses of the Revolution, the state of public virtue in the aftermath of war, and the desirability of reforming the national government.

The agenda changed somewhat in the 1790s. Abstract questions regarding public virtue and the forms of government continued to be staples of debate, but other questions intruded to reveal the impact of partisan politics upon the learning process. The clearest way to trace this development is to examine commencements at Princeton. The French Revolution and its implications for America were constant themes. At first, the exercises were examinations of the incidents of the Revolution and the European war. Then came alarm at the religious influence of the Revolution: "Is not the belief of a revealed religion central to the order of existence of society?" By 1794 and 1795, the character of the Revolution had become a greater cause for anxiety, as had its American political ramifications: "Are liberty and equality calculated to promote the happiness and improvement of mankind," "Is the institution of voluntary popular societies to watch the motions of government in the present state of the country wise or useful?" In response to fears about France, students specifically approved the Jay Treaty.[102]

Sufficient alarm existed about the French Revolution, its American impact, and governmental policy, to produce an increasingly strident, negative tone to the exercises beginning in 1796. Students juxtaposed orations on "Despotism" and "The Excellency of the American Government," and wondered "Is privateering a justifiable mode of hostility?" As the danger of war grew, students contemplated "The danger of foreign influence," and urged "The Necessity of the United States establishing a Navy." The hysteria reached its zenith both in the nation and at Princeton from 1798 to 1800. With the undeclared naval war in full swing students spoke of "The necessity of a permanent naval force in the United States," "The relative situations of America and France," and debated "Are temporary wars beneficial to a nation?" These seniors noted "the change in manners and policy brought about in France by the Revolution," and, as a result, asked "Is religion necessary for the preservation of civil order" and "Would the total prohibition of the immigration of foreigners into the United States be consistent with justice and humanity?"[103] These questions and orations indicate that the growing partisan outlook of the Princeton faculty appealed to the students as well, at least in the structured environment of the commencement exercises.

What was true of Princeton applied elsewhere. The merest glimpse at the other colleges shows that Rhode Island students asking early in the 1790s "Is it for the interest of the United States to assist the French Revolution against its enemies in the present war" and orating later on "The Indignities offered America by France." The progress of events during the 1790s prompted Columbia students to consider the rise of parties in orations on "Political Toleration" and "Liberty of the Press," and to note the effects of the French Revolution in "The Present State of America as Influenced by Foreign and Domestic Policy" and "The Refined Principles of Religion favorable to Liberty." Perhaps the general tenor of the Harvard commencements best appears in Timothy Fuller's shocked indignation in 1800 when his fellow graduate James Richardson spoke an oration "teeming with the narrow politics of *The Centinel* [a Republican paper] and with reflexions on the conduct of Pres't Adams, altho in his presence. When he was done it was loudly clapped by some and loudly hissed by others."[104] That a Harvard commencement speaker would criticize the Federalist President of the United States was unexpected; that some seniors would applaud showed the degree of political intensity they possessed.

When students had the opportunity to structure their own politically related activities, they espoused nationalist, then Federalist politics. Debating societies became more popular in the post-war period. Harvard had its Hasty Pudding Club and its Graduate Debating Society. Harvard, Yale, Dartmouth, and William and Mary all had chapters of Phi Beta Kappa. Yale also had the Linonian Society and the Brothers in Unity. The Federal Adelphi and the Philandrian Society engaged Rhode Island undergraduates, while Princeton students chose either the Cliosophic Society or the American Whigs, and Dartmouth had its United Fraternity. Politics dominated these societies' debates and orations. Almost ninety percent of the debate topics dealt with politics, either theoretical or practical. Only one group, Harvard's Graduate Debating Society, differed substantially from this pattern. Its members, Master's degree candidates presumably preparing for the ministry, devoted only two-thirds of their exercises to politics, the other third treating religion.[105]

Debates held elsewhere mirrored those of Yale's societies. Abstract questions regarding virtue and its relation to politics, forms of government, and other philosophical issues were matters of debate throughout the post-war period. But there were topical questions on current affairs as well. Through 1789 these questions touched most often on the conditions of the new republic and the Constitution. For example, Dartmouth's United Fraternity debated "Whether it would be beneficial for the American states to adopt the Constitution passed by the Federal Convention," "Whether a poll tax is advantageous to a republican government," and "Ought the clergy to be excluded from a seat in government?" Harvard's Phi Beta Kappa chapter considered state as well as national matters, debating "Whether civil discord is advantageous to society," "Whether the present scarcity of money in this Commonwealth be advantageous to it,'' and ''Whether internal tranquility be a proof of prosperity in a republic,'' all at the time of Shays' Rebellion.[106]

The debating societies' contemporary political commentary in the 1790s centered on the administrations' domestic policies and the issues surrounding the progress and impact of the French Revolution. In this the societies' discussions paralleled the topical concerns of the commencement exercises, the college faculties, and the communities at large. Among domestic issues debated were whether Congress should discriminate between present and original owners of public securities, the advantages of a permanent national capital, the harm done to the state by the presence of political factions, the preferability of a militia or a standing army, the appropriateness and humanity of various Indian wars, whether commerce or industry was best for the country and should be encouraged by law, the desirability of a limit to the United States President's term, the role of democratic societies in America, the benefits of a large number of newspapers in America, whether the general government of the United States should suppress the various state governments (this in response to the Virginia and Kentucky Resolves of 1798), and whether the Alien and Sedition Acts were proper. No significant national issue escaped student attention.[107]

From the middle of 1792 the students expressed grave reservations about the French Revolution, wondering whether America should go to its aid in the European war, whether the war would harm America, and whether a republican government was suitable for France. Along with worries about the foreign situation came unease about its domestic repercussions. Were there dangers in foreign immigration? Ought deists to hold public office? The problems of neutrality intrigued students; at first the question was whether to declare war against Great Britain, then the advisability of the Jay Treaty. By the mid-1790s, some doubts had arisen about the feasibility of the French Republic and the desirability of the Revolution; the students thus asked whether America should be in league with France and whether she should prevail in the European wars. The turning point came in 1798 with questions about an American declaration of war against France, about arming American ships, and about a defensive league with Great Britain. Only after the Adams peace mission did student animosity toward France decline.[108]

Other, even less formal, student activities indicated that their political convictions were Federalist. Student reading seems to have focused on Commonwealth or republican authors. Individual students at Harvard, Dartmouth, Princeton, and the College of Rhode Island have left records of reading in such works as Montesquieu, Adam Smith's and Thomas Reid's moral philosophies, Burlamaqui, Ramsay's history of America, and Hume's history of England. These individuals' tastes were representative of their peers. A sampling of library checkout lists at Harvard in 1795 and at the College of Rhode Island in 1783, 1789, and 1796 reveals that the most popular works were Hume's, Goldsmith's, and Robertson's histories, Montesquieu, Burlamaqui, and Blackstone on government and law, Locke, Burgh, and Priestley on human nature, and Plutarch, Gibbon, and Rollin in ancient history. Significantly, there is no record of borrowing for Paine's *Age of Reason*, Rousseau's works, or anything else associated with the Jacobinical or deistical aspects of the French Revolution.[109]

As with the curriculum, this informal student behavior at the Federalist colleges contrasted sharply with the atmosphere at the College of William and Mary. No commencement programs or debating society records survive, but an abundance of student correspondence depicts the activities at the college in the late 1790s. Student reading included Ramsay's history of America, Gibbon, Dugald Stewart's moral philosophy, and the *Federalist Papers*, but more popular were Locke, Rousseau, Constantin Volney's *The Ruins: or a Survey of the Revolutions of Empires* (which celebrated the French Revolution), Paine, and Godwin. According to one student, Rousseau, Locke, and Paine were "the most celebrated, and, perhaps, the most excellent that have written upon the Science of Politics. I suppose it will be considered an act of treason against truth, to utter a syllable to the prejudice of Rousseau."[110]

Federalist political policies upset the students. In mid-1798 they sent an address on the prospect of war with France to the Virginia Congressional delegation, and then had it published in the Republican newspaper, the Philadelphia *Aurora*. The students wanted war preparations stopped, not because they favored France over Great Britain, but "on a conviction of the injuries which would result to our own country from a contrary conduct—We believe an increase of power and influence in the executive branch of our government to be an inevitable effect of war." That they abhorred. The Alien and Sedition Acts left them in despair, one student lamenting:

Oh America! How fast art thou retrograding! Too soon wilt thou reach the very pinnacle of Despotism! I think...that nothing but a change of our Constitution, or at least an Amelioration of it, can possibly preserve us from slavery. To change or Amend our Constitution, nothing can be effectual but a Re-inspiration of the Principles of Democracy.[111]

The principles of democracy were, of course, those of the French Revolution. The student infatuation with it was general. They called one another "citizen," used the Revolutionary calendar, and extolled Revolutionary heroes. Wrote one student, "There is not a man among us that would not enlist himself under the banner of a Paine or a Volney....They say that there are a few Rusty Cats [aristocrats] among the students. Of this I am not certain. But the political principles of the great part of the students are purely Democratic."

These democratic principles prompted great contrasts in conduct between William and Mary students and those elsewhere. While Federalist college students gave or listened to fulsome praise of the late father of their country, at William and Mary it took two full days of debate for President Madison to convince the pupils to wear black armbands in Washington's memory. Even then, not all complied. While Federalist colleges attacked the atheistical Jefferson and trembled at the anticipated consequences of his election, a William and Mary student attributed that triumph to "the number of innocent victims of the oppressive sedition law, the frequent and repeated violations of the Constitution, the want of that cabalistic term 'French Invasion,' and perhaps the operation of Congressional taxes." These things had finally "taught the people to reflect and avoid the dangerous abyss, on the brink of which they have tottered so long."[112]

The early national period was, as Marshall Smelser and John Howe have observed, an age of political passion.[113] That colleges, primed by a generation of political activity associated with the Revolution, could have resisted involvement was not possible. That they became as partisan as the rest of the country was inevitable. Faculties and governors continued their political activity, and to inculcate partisan principles into their students required only the adoption of a few new texts and the subtle alteration of lecture and recitation emphases. Students followed their mentors as they had done before. If anything, they outdid their elders in partisan ferocity. Thus the pre-Revolutionary colleges reached their zenith of political involvement during the years of the early republic.

But what of the new colleges? What of those without a Revolutionary tradition? What of those located on the frontier away from centers of high culture and political agitation? To what degree did colleges founded after the Revolution share the preoccupations of their elder sisters? Just how united in its mission to educate republicans was the American college community going to be?

NOTES

1. Edmund S. Morgan, *The Gentle Puritan: A Life of Ezra Stiles* (New Haven: Yale University Press, 1962), 445–46, 450–51.

2. Ibid., 455; "Literary Diary," *Stiles Papers M*, XIII, 102–3.

3. "Literary Diary," *Stiles Papers M*, XIII, 165, 284, 357.

4. Ibid., 312; Morgan, *Gentle Puritan*, 455.

5. Morgan, *Gentle Puritan*, 456–57; ES to Jacob Richardson, July 9, 1794, *Stiles Papers M*.

6. Ezra Stiles, *A History of Three of the Judges of King Charles I* (Hartford, 1794), 274–75, 282; Morgan, *Gentle Puritan*, 459–60.

7. "Samuel Wales," *Yale Sketches*, III, 257–61; "Samuel Wales," *AAP*, I, 710–13; Samuel Wales, *The Dangers of Our National Prosperity; and the Ways to Avoid Them* (Hartford, 1785).

8. Gordon S. Wood, *The Creation of the American Republic, 1776–1787* (Chapel Hill: University of North Carolina Press, 1969), 396–403, 416, 418, 421–23, 424; Lance Banning, *The Jeffersonian Persuasion: Evolution of a Party Ideology* (Ithaca: Cornell University Press, 1978), 89–90.

9. *DAB*, s.v. "Josiah Meigs"; "Josiah Meigs," *Yale Sketches*, IV, 43–47; William M. Meigs, *The Life of Josiah Meigs* (Philadelphia: J.P. Murphy, 1887), 16; Josiah Meigs, *An Oration Pronounced before a Public Assembly in New Haven on the 5th Day of November, 1781, at the Celebration of the Glorious Victory over Lieutenant-General Earl Cornwallis, at York-Town, in Virginia, on the 19th Day of October, 1781* (New Haven, 1782).

10. *DAB*, s.v. "Josiah Meigs"; "Josiah Meigs," *Yale Sketches*, IV, 43–47; Meigs, *Life of Meigs*, 20, 25, 26.

11. Meigs, *Life of Meigs*, 33–35, quotation 33.

12. *DAB*, s.v. "Josiah Meigs"; "Josiah Meigs," *Yale Sketches*, IV, 43–47; Meigs, *Life of Meigs*, 35, 38–39, 42; Charles Cuningham, *Timothy Dwight, 1752–1817: A Biography* (New York: The Macmillan Co., 1942), 199.

13. *DAB*, s.v. "Timothy Dwight"; Cuningham, *Dwight*, 53–55; Timothy Dwight, *A Valedictory Address to the Young Gentlemen, Who Commenced Bachelor of Arts, at Yale College, July 25th, 1776* (New Haven, 1776).

14. *DAB*, s.v. "Timothy Dwight"; Cuningham, *Dwight*, 59–61, 68, 74–77, 85. For examples of sermons, see Timothy Dwight, *A Sermon, Preached at Stamford, in Connecticut, Upon the General Thanksgiving, December 18th, 1777* (Hartford, 1778) and *A Sermon Preached at Northampton, on the Twenty-Eighth of November, 1781: Occasioned by the Capture of the British Army, Under the Command of the Earl Cornwallis* (Hartford, 1781).

15. *DAB*, s.v. "Timothy Dwight"; Cuningham, *Dwight*, 341; Timothy Dwight, *The Triumph of Infidelity: A Poem* (no place, 1788), *Virtuous Rulers a National Blessing. A Sermon Preached at the General Election, May 12, 1791* (Hartford, 1791), and *Greenfield Hill* (New York, 1794), especially section titled "The Vision, or Prospect of the Future Happiness of America."

16. *DAB*, s.v. "Timothy Dwight"; Cuningham, *Dwight*, 342, 345; Timothy Dwight, *The True Means of Establishing Public Happiness* (New Haven, 1795), *The Duty of Americans, at the Present Crisis. Illustrated in a Discourse, Preached on the 4th of July, 1798...* (New Haven, 1798), *An Oration Spoken at Hartford, July 4, 1798* (Hartford, 1798), *A Discourse Delivered at New Haven, February 22, 1800; on the Character of George Washington...* (New Haven, 1800). Cf. Richard J. Purcell, *Connecticut in Transition, 1775–1818* (orig. 1918; reprint, Middletown, Conn.: Wesleyan University Press, 1963), 14–16.

17. Purcell, *Connecticut in Transition*, 191, xiv, 265, 197–98.

18. "Yale College Memoranda" (Stiles Papers, YUA), July 18, 1789, June 11, 1790; "Laws of Yale College, 1787" (Yale College Pamphlets no. 55, YUA); "Literary Diary," *Stiles Papers M*, XIII, 231; Morgan, *Gentle Puritan*, 389. Work not previously cited: Joseph Priestley, *Lectures on History and General Policy* (Dublin, 1788).

19. "Literary Diary," *Stiles Papers M*, XIV, 187, XV, 14. The 1793–1794 list of classes in Stiles' Yale College Memoranda shows which readings were for each class.

20. "Yale College Memoranda," June 17, 1791; William Paley, *The Principles of Moral and Political Philosophy* (London, 1785; Am. ed., Philadelphia, 1794), 384–89, 399–400, 407, 411, 442–43, 447–71, 525–36. A modern analysis of Paley's thought and its place in the eighteenth-century context is D. L. Le Mahieu, *The Mind of William Paley: A Philosopher and His Age* (Lincoln: University of Nebraska Press, 1976).

21. "Literary Diary," *Stiles Papers M*, XII, 6; "Yale College Memoranda," November 6, 1784.

22. "Literary Diary," *Stiles Papers M*, XII, 230, XIII, 15, 39, 158; Morgan, *Gentle Puritan*, 389.

23. Barbara M. Cross, ed., *The Autobiography of Lyman Beecher* (2 vols., Cambridge, Mass.: Belknap Press of Harvard University Press, 1961), I, 27. On Beecher's trustworthiness and Stiles' reaction to student infidelity, see Edmund S. Morgan, "Ezra Stiles and Timothy Dwight," MHS *Proceedings*, 72 (1957–1960): 101–19.

24. "Laws of Yale College, 1795" (Ms., Goodrich Collection no. 17, YUA); Cuningham, *Dwight*, 238–39, 244.

25. Purcell, *Connecticut in Transition*, 192; Joseph J. Ellis, *After the Revolution: Profiles of Early American Culture* (New York: W.W. Norton, 1979), 179–82, 190–91, 193, 201–3. Works not previously cited: Noah Webster, *A Grammatical Institute of the English Language* (Hartford, 1783) and Jedediah Morse, *The American Geography* (Elizabeth, N.J., 1789).

26. David Daggett's 1808 notes on Dwight's lectures regarding Paley suggest that the students read the text and the president merely commented on points he wanted to emphasize. Daggett's notes may be incomplete, but there are no comments on politics. David Daggett, "Dr. Dwight's Observations on Paley's Moral and Political Philosophy" (YUA).

27. Cuningham, *Dwight*, 245–46; Franklin B. Dexter, "Student Life at Yale College under the First President Dwight (1795–1817)," American Antiquarian Society *Proceedings*, N.S., 27 (1917): 324–25.

28. "Yale Brothers in Unity, Records 1783–1833" (Ms., YUA), February 26, April 1, July 2, 31, 1784, July 21, November 18, 1785, December 20, 1786.

29. Ibid., April 19, July 19, August 16, 1787.

30. Ibid., November 13, 1788, July 16, 1789, June 19, 1794; "Linonian Society Records" (Ms., YUA), March 13, 1794.

31. "Linonian Records," June 13, 1788, June 21, 1792; "Brothers in Unity, Records", August 21, 1788, March 8, December 20, 1792, July 4, 1793.

32. "Brothers in Unity, Records", November 10, 1791; "Linonian Records", June 26, October 6, 1788, March 28, 1792.

33. If Matthew Minor's notebook for 1798–1801 is typical, then on some occasions the debating societies considered the very same topics as did Dwight's recitations. "Notebook of Matthew Minor, Jr., 1799–1800–1801" (Ms., YUA).

34. "Linonian Records", March 9, 30, November 28, 1797, February 14, December 19, 1798; "Brothers in Unity, Records", August 2, 1797, March 19, April 2, 1800.

35. "Linonian Records", December 13, 1796, April 4, November 21, 1798; "Brothers in Unity, Records", August 20, 1795, March 14, 1797, November 20, 1799, November 5, 1800.

36. "Brothers in Unity, Records", February 22, April 26, 1797, March 27, August 14, 1799; "Linonian Records", November 7, 1798.

37. "Linonian Records", August 16, 1795, April 20, June 30, July 6, September 7, November 9, 1796, August 30, November 21, 1797, March 7, 16, June 27, 1798, April 17, June 14, 26, November 19, 1799; "Brothers in Unity, Records", November 24, 1797, December 26, 1798, February 20, December 11, 1799, November 19, 1800.

38. *Catalogue of Books in the Library of Yale College, in New Haven* (New Haven, 1791); *Catalogue of Books in the Library of Yale College in New Haven* (New Haven: Oliver Steele Co., 1808). Because of the heightened political atmosphere of the time and the legislative grant of 1792, part of which was set aside for books, I make the possibly unwarranted assumption that those Commonwealth canon titles new to the 1808 catalogue were purchased by Stiles or Dwight before 1800.

39. "Linonian Society Catalogue of Books, 1794–96" (YUA).

40. Timothy Dwight, *The Nature and Danger of the Infidel Philosophy...Addressed to the Candidates for the Baccalaureate in Yale College* (New Haven, 1798).

41. Donald B. Cole, *Jacksonian Democracy in New Hampshire, 1800–1851* (Cambridge, Mass.: Harvard University Press, 1971), 17, 29, 33; *DAB*, s.v. "Lyman Spalding."

42. "Joseph Willard," *Sibley's*, XVI, 253–65; *DAB*, s.v. "Joseph Willard."

43. "John Warren," *Sibley's*, XVII, 655–69; *DAB*, s.v. "John Warren."

44. *DAB*, s.v. "Eliphalet Pearson"; "Eliphalet Pearson," *AAP*, II, 126–31; James M. Banner, *To the Hartford Convention: The Federalists and the Origins of Party Politics in Massachusetts, 1789–1815* (New York: Alfred A. Knopf, 1970), 135n; *CAB*, s.v. "Samuel Webber"; "Samuel Webber," *AAP*, II, 24; Seymour M. Lipset and David Reisman, *Education and Politics at Harvard* (New York: McGraw-Hill, 1975), 51–52, 54–55.

45. "David Tappan," *AAP*, II, 97–103; Banner, *To the Hartford Convention*, 26, 135n; David Tappan, *A Sermon Preached before His Excellency John Hancock, Esq. . . .May 30, 1792* (Boston, 1792) and *A Sermon. . .April 11, 1793, on the Occasion of the Annual Fast of the Commonwealth of Massachusetts* (Boston, 1793).

46. "James Manning," James McLachlan, ed., *Princetonians, 1748–1768: A Biographical Dictionary* (Princeton, N.J.: Princeton University Press, 1976), 389–93; *DAB*, s.v. "James Manning"; Reuben A. Guild, *The Life, Times, and Correspondence of James Manning and the Early History of Brown University* (Boston: Gould & Lincoln, 1864), 348, 378, 391, 398, 404–5; Irwin Polishook, *Rhode Island and the Union, 1774–1795* (Evanston, Ill.: Northwestern University Press, 1969), 181–82.

47. *DAB*, s.v. "Jonathan Maxcy"; Jonathan Maxcy, *An Oration. . .at the Celebration of the Nineteenth Anniversary of American Independence* (Providence, 1795); Jonathan Maxcy, "An Oration. . .on the Fourth of July, 1799," Romeo Elton, ed., *The Literary Remains of the Rev. Jonathan Maxcy, D.D.* (New York: A.V. Blake, 1844), 381–91, quotation 381.

48. Peres Fobes, *A Sermon Preached before His Excellency Samuel Adams, Esq. . . .May 27th, 1795; Being the Day of the General Election* (Boston, 1795), quotation 17; *DAB*, s.v. "Asa Messer"; "Asa Messer," *AAP*, VI, 326–34; Asa Messer, *A Discourse, Delivered on the Thanksgiving-Day, the 29th of November, 1798. . .* (Providence, 1798), quotation 7, 9; "David Howell," McLachlan, ed., *Princetonians, 1748–1768*, 562–67; David Hackett Fischer, *The Revolution in American Conservatism: The Federalist Party in the Era of Jeffersonian Democracy* (New York: Harper & Row, 1965), 279–80.

49. *DAB*, s.v. "William Samuel Johnson"; Elizabeth P. McCaughey, *From Loyalist to Founding Father: The Political Odyssey of William Samuel Johnson* (New York: Columbia University Press, 1980), 176–77, 192–94, 195–209, 213–17, 230–34, 266.

50. *DAB*, s.v. "John Kemp" and "Peter Wilson"; Ebenezer Crosby" *NCAB*, X, 60; "Charles McKnight," *NCAB*, IX, 352; "James Kent," *Yale Sketches*, IV, 189–94; John T. Horton, *James Kent: A Study in Conservatism, 1763–1847* (New York: Appleton-Century Co., 1939), 56–58, 63, 67, 73–74, 106–9.

51. *DAB*, s.v. "Samuel Latham Mitchell"; Samuel Latham Mitchell, *An Address before the Citizens of New York. . .to Celebrate the Twenty-Third Anniversary of American Independence. . .* (New York, 1800); Samuel Bard to William Bard, May 20, 1798, February 9, 1801, John McVickar, *A Domestic Narrative of the Life of Samuel Bard, M.D., LL.D. . . .* (New York: A. Paul, 1822), 175–76, 174.

52. "Jacob Hardenbergh," *NCAB*, III, 399; "John Taylor," Richard A. Harrison, ed., *Princetonians, 1769–1776: A Biographical Dictionary* (Princeton: Princeton University Press, 1980), 111–15; "William Linn," *NCAB*, III, 399–400; William Linn, *The*

Blessings of America (New York, 1791) and *Discourse on the Signs of the Times* (New York, 1794); "Ira Condict," *NCAB*, III, 400; Ira Condict, *A Funeral Discourse...on the 31st of December, 1799...Paying Solemn Honors to the Memory of General George Washington* (New Brunswick, N.J., 1800), quotation 18.

53. Varnum L. Collins, *President Witherspoon* (2 vols., Princeton: Princeton University Press, 1925), II, 165, 190–92; "A Few Reflections Humbly Submitted to the Consideration of the Public in General, and in particular to the Congress of the United States," *The Miscellaneous Works of John Witherspoon* (Philadelphia: William W. Woodard, 1803), 233–36.

54. "Samuel Stanhope Smith," Harrison, ed., *Princetonians, 1769–1776*, 42–51; Fischer, *Revolution in American Conservatism*, 326; Samuel Stanhope Smith, *A Discourse on the Nature and Reasonableness of Fasting, and on the Existing Causes that Call Us to that Duty* (Philadelphia, 1795), quotation 23–24, and *The Divine Goodness of the United States of America* (Philadelphia, 1795).

55. Samuel Stanhope Smith to Jedediah Morse, February 24, 1799 (Samuel Stanhope Smith Collection, PUA); Samuel Stanhope Smith, *An Oration Upon the Death of General George Washington...* (Trenton, 1800). For a brief account of Morse and the Illuminati, see Henry F. May, *The Enlightenment in America* (New York: Oxford University Press, 1976), 260–63.

56. Edward P. Cheyney, *History of the University of Pennsylvania, 1740–1940* (Philadelphia: University of Pennsylvania Press, 1940), 147–69. The significance of these actions for college-state relations appears in Chapter 7.

57. *DAB*, s.v. "David Rittenhouse"; Brook Hindle, *David Rittenhouse* (Princeton: Princeton University Press, 1964), 272–73, 294–95, 327, 341–43, 344–46, 361–62, 364.

58. *DAB*, s.v. "William Smith"; Albert F. Gegenheimer, *William Smith, Educator and Churchman, 1727–1803* (Philadelphia: University of Pennsylvania Press, 1943), 91–93, 181–82; "A Sermon on Temporal and Spiritual Salvation, Preached in Christ Church, July 4, 1790, Before the Pennsylvania Society of the Cincinnati," William Smith, *Works of William Smith, D.D., Late Provost of the College and Academy of Philadelphia* (2 vols., Philadelphia: Hugh Maxwell and William Fry, 1803), II, 293–94, 303, 305–6.

59. Robert G. McCloskey, ed., *The Works of James Wilson* (1 vol. in 2, Cambridge, Mass.: Belknap Press of Harvard University Press, 1967), I, 2, 20–21; Charles Page Smith, *James Wilson, Founding Father, 1742–1798* (Chapel Hill: University of North Carolina Press, 1956), 107–15, 179–86, 221–55, 269–89, 305.

60. *DAB*, s.v. "James Hutchinson"; Robert L. Brunhouse, *The Counter-Revolution in Pennsylvania, 1776–1790* (Harrisburg: Pennsylvania Historical Commission, 1942), 74–76, 89–90, 192; Nathan Goodman, *Benjamin Rush: Physician and Surgeon, 1746–1813* (Philadelphia: University of Pennsylvania Press, 1934), 72–81, 117; David F. Hawke, *Benjamin Rush: Revolutionary Gadfly* (Indianapolis: Bobbs-Merrill Co., 1971), 338–57, 383, 385–87, 391.

61. Charles Crowe, "Bishop James Madison and the Republic of Virtue," *Journal of Southern History*, 30 (1964): 60–61; Bp. James Madison to James Madison, June 11, 1787, February 9, 1788, March 1, August 15, 1789, July 25, 1795 (Bishop James Madison Papers, CWMA).

62. Crowe, "Bishop James Madison," 61; Bp. James Madison to James Madison, January 9, October 9, 1800 (Bp. James Madison Papers); Bp. James Madison to ————, November 1, 1800 (Faculty/Alumni File, CWMA).

63. Crowe, "Bishop James Madison," 61; quotation from Bp. James Madison to

182   Educating Republicans

James Madison, January 9, 1800 (Bp. James Madison Papers); Bp. James Madison, *Manifestations of the Benevolence of Divine Providence Toward America* (Richmond, 1795) and *A Discourse, on the Death of General Washington* (2d ed., corrected, Richmond, 1800) which makes no mention of Washington's public career after the Constitutional Convention.

64. *DAB*, s.v. "George Wythe"; Richard R. Beeman, *The Old Dominion in the New Nation, 1788–1801* (Lexington, Ky.: University of Kentucky Press, 1972), 127, 143, 221.

65. *DAB*, s.v. "St. George Tucker"; St. George Tucker, *Reflections on the Policy and Necessity of Encouraging the Commerce of the Citizens of the United States of America* (New York, 1785) and *A Letter to a Member of Congress Respecting the Alien and Sedition Laws* (n.p., 1799); St. George Tucker to John Page, January 15, 1792, January 12, 1794, February 7, 1801 (Tucker-Coleman Papers, CWMA).

66. Patrick McKnight, "The Trustees of Dartmouth College, 1769–1800" (unpublished seminar paper, University of Wyoming, 1981); Paul Goodman, *The Democratic Republicans of Massachusetts: Politics in a Young Republic* (Cambridge, Mass.: Harvard University Press, 1964), 47–73; Banner, *To the Hartford Convention*, 122–267.

67. William L. Hewitt, "The Trustees of the College of New Jersey, 1746–1800" (unpublished seminar paper, University of Wyoming, 1981).

68. David C. Humphrey, *From King's College to Columbia, 1746–1800* (New York: Columbia University Press, 1976), 271–74, 277–78; Deborah S. Welch, "Governors and Trustees: A Biographical Inquiry into the Governing Boards of King's and Columbia Colleges, 1754–1800" (unpublished seminar paper, University of Wyoming, 1981).

69. Steven C. Schulte, "The Trustees of the College of Philadelphia and the University of Pennsylvania, 1750–1800" (unpublished seminar paper, University of Wyoming, 1981).

70. Anne Shearer-Shineman, "The Trustees of the College of William and Mary, 1750–1800" (unpublished seminar paper, University of Wyoming, 1981).

71. This paragraph and the next are based on the curricular outlines provided in: Leon B. Richardson, *A History of Dartmouth College* (2 vols., Hanover, N.H.: Dartmouth College Publications, 1932), I, 248; "Trustees' Minutes, Dartmouth College" (DaCA), February 7, 9, 1796; Louis F. Snow, *The College Curriculum in the United States* (New York: Teachers College Press of Columbia University Press, 1907), 83–96; John Clarke, "Letters to a Student in the University at Cambridge, Massachusetts, 1796" (HUA); Samuel Miller, *A Brief Retrospect of the Eighteenth Century* (2 vols., New York: T. & J. Swords, 1803), II, 494, 498–99, 501, 504; "Laws of Rhode Island College, 1784" (BUA); "Statutes of Columbia College, 1785" (YUA); William Samuel Johnson, *The Present State of Learning in the College of New York* (New York, 1794); "College of New Jersey, College Laws, 1794" (PUA); "Memorandum" (1791?), "Curriculum for the Freshman and Junior Classes in College and the Latin School, 1795" (UPA); *The Statutes for the University of William and Mary* (Richmond, 1792).

72. Richard P. McCormick, *Rutgers: A Bicentennial History* (New Brunswick, N.J.: Rutgers University Press, 1966), 23; William H.S. Demarest, *A History of Rutgers College, 1766–1924* (New Brunswick, N.J.: Rutgers College Press, 1924), 173–78, 185; George P. Schmidt, *Princeton and Rutgers: New Jersey's Two Colonial Colleges* (Princeton: Van Nostrand, 1964), 17–18.

73. John Andrews, "Lectures on Logick, Metaphysick, and Moral Philosophy-Notes by John Yeates, 1790" (UPA), chapter 6, "Of the Various Plans of Government";

Samuel Stanhope Smith, *The Lectures Corrected and Improved...on the Subjects of Moral and Political Philosophy* (2 vols., Trenton: D. Fenton, 1812), Lecture XXVI, "Of Politics"; John D. Gros, *Natural Principles of Rectitude, for the Conduct of Man in all States and Situations of Life...* (New York, 1795), Pt. II, Sect. IV, "Comprehending Politics."

74. Andrews, "Lectures on...Moral Philosophy, by Yeates," 244–45, 248–49, 256, 289–91; John Andrews, "Compend of Moral Philosophy: Notes taken by John H. Hobart, 1790" (UPA), 178–79.

75. Andrews, "Lectures on...Moral Philosophy, by Yeates," 278–79, 276–77; Andrews, "Compend of Moral Philosophy, by Hobart," 151–54, 195–215, 156–57.

76. Gros, *Principles of Natural Rectitude*, xii, 38, 364–71, 386, 388. See the discussion of Gros' lectures in Wilson Smith, *Professors & Public Ethics: Studies of Northern Moral Philosophers before the Civil War* (Ithaca: Cornell University Press, 1956), 81–94, and Humphrey, *King's College*, 299–301.

77. Smith, *Lectures on Moral and Political Philosophy*, II, 295; Smith, *Divine Goodness of America*, 28.

78. Smith, *Lectures on Moral and Political Philosophy*, II, 294–99, 308–11, 227–28, 305–6, 230–45.

79. Ibid., 320–29.

80. For indications of the Federalist world view, including political principles, see Banner, *To the Hartford Convention*, chapters 1, 2, 5, and Linda Kerber, *Federalists in Dissent: Imagery and Ideology in Jeffersonian America* (Ithaca: Cornell University Press, 1970), chapters 1, 4–6.

81. Richardson, *History of Dartmouth*, I, 261.

82. Ibid., 248; Irving Bartlett, *Daniel Webster* (New York: W. W. Norton, 1978), 23; Snow, *College Curriculum*, 89; Clarke, "Letters to a Student," 39; "Laws of Rhode Island College, 1784"; "Laws of Rhode Island College, 1793." The College of Rhode Island trustees voted in 1788 to allow faculty to choose texts as they saw fit, "Corporation Minutes, College of Rhode Island" (BUA), September 3, 1788; Miller, *Brief Retrospect*, II, 494; Humphrey, *King's College*, 299. For a discussion of Paley's influence, see Smith, *Professors & Public Ethics*, 48–57.

83. McCloskey, ed., *Works of Wilson*, 29, 32, 37–39.

84. Ibid., 28, 289–90, 399–493; Wood, *Creation of the Republic*, 393–467.

85. James Kent, *An Introductory Lecture to a Course of Law Lectures, Delivered November 17, 1794* (New York, 1794), 4–6, 8, 14, 18; Horton, *James Kent*, 90–91.

86. Kent, *Introductory Lecture*, 18–21; James Kent, *Dissertations: Being the Preliminary Part of a Course of Law Lectures* (New York, 1795), 19–24, 40–48; Horton, *James Kent*, 92–93; Forrest McDonald, *A Constitutional History of the United States* (New York: Franklin Watts, 1982), 60.

87. Snow, *College Curriculum*, 93; "Laws of Rhode Island College, 1784"; "Laws of Rhode Island College, 1793"; "College of New Jersey, Laws 1794"; "Statutes of Columbia College, 1785"; Johnson, *Present State of Learning*; Miller, *Brief Retrospect*, II, 498–99; (University of Pennsylvania), "Memorandum" (1791?) and "Memorandum: Draft of 'By-Laws for Regulating the Latin & Greek Schools, etc.' Dec. 13, 1792" (UPA); D. A. White, "Student Themes, 1795–1797" (HUA); Walter C. Bronson, *History of Brown University, 1764–1914* (Providence: The University, 1914), 147. Even at Queen's, where the curriculum remains for the most part a mystery, the classical texts were named: Caesar's *Commentaries*, Virgil, Cicero, Xenophon's *Cyropaedia*, and Kennet's *Roman*

Antiquities all continued an earlier emphasis on classical republican history; McCormick, *Rutgers*, 20. Works not previously cited: Claude F. X. Millot, *Elements of General History* (5 vols., London, 1778–1779); Henry Home, Lord Kames, *Sketches of the History of Man* (Edinburgh, 1774); Edward Gibbon, *The Decline and Fall of the Roman Empire* (6 vols., London, 1776–1788).

88. Robert J. Taylor et al., eds., *Diary of John Quincy Adams, 1779–1788* (2 vols., Cambridge, Mass.: Belknap Press of Harvard University Press, 1981), II, 258–62, 93, 99–101.

89. Ray W. Irwin and Edna L. Jacobsen, eds., *A Columbia College Student in the Eighteenth Century: Essays by Daniel D. Tompkins* (orig. 1940; reprint, Port Washington, N. Y.: Kennikat Press, 1964), 32–36, 44–46.

90. William Buckminster, "Theme, 1799" (HUA).

91. *The Statutes of the University of William and Mary*, 1792; Lyon G. Tyler, *Williamsburg, the Old Colonial Capital* (Richmond: Whittet & Shepperson, 1907), 175.

92. Tyler, *Williamsburg*, 170; Adam Smith, *An Inquiry into the Nature and Causes of the Wealth of Nations* (orig. 1776; reprint, New York: The Modern Library, 1937), 557–606, 670–71, 857–58, 866–73.

93. Smith, *Wealth of Nations*, ix-x.

94. Crowe, "Bishop James Madison," 63–64. For a good, brief discussion of political liberalism and the men who espoused it, see Franklin L. Baumer, *Modern European Thought: Continuity and Change in Ideas, 1600–1950* (New York: The Macmillan Co., 1977), 218–36.

95. Miller, *Brief Retrospect*, II, 503, and Bp. James Madison to James Madison, October 24, 1801 (Faculty/Alumni File, CWMA) indicate the books used in the curriculum. Works not previously cited: Jean Jacques Rousseau, *The Social Contract* (London, 1764); William Godwin, *An Enquiry Concerning Political Justice and Its Influence on General Virtue and Happiness* (2 vols., London, 1793); Thomas Paine, *The Rights of Man, Part II* (London, 1792).

96. St. George Tucker, *A Letter to the Rev. Jedediah Morse...by a Citizen of Williamsburg* (Richmond, 1795); Joseph C. Cabell to David Watson, April 6, 1801, "Letters to David Watson," *Virginia Magazine of History and Biography*, 29 (1921): 278.

97. David Tappan, *A Discourse Delivered...June 17, 1794, at the Request of the Senior Class* (Boston, 1794), *A Discourse...September 16, 1794, Designed Chiefly for the Younger Members of the University* (Boston, 1794), *A Discourse Delivered to the Students of Harvard College, September 6, 1796* (Boston, 1796), quotation 12, *A Discourse Delivered...June 19, 1798. Occasioned by the Approaching Departure of the Senior Class from the University* (Boston, 1798); Joseph Willard, *An Address in Latin, by Joseph Willard...and a Discourse in English, by David Tappan...In Solemn Commemoration of General George Washington* (Cambridge, Mass., 1800); Johnson quoted in E. Edwards Beardsley, *Life and Times of William Samuel Johnson, LL.D., First Senator in Congress from Connecticut, and President of Columbia College, New York* (New York: Hurd & Houghton, 1876), 144; Jonathan Maxcy, *An Address, Delivered to the Graduates of Rhode Island College, at the Anniversary Commencement...September 5, AD 1798* (Providence, 1798); Asa Messer, *A Discourse...to the Senior Class, on the Sunday Preceding their Commencement, 1799* (Providence, 1799).

98. Bronson, *History of Brown*, 85, 88–89; Guild, *Early History of Brown*, 447; "Commencement Theses, Rhode Island College, 1776, 1786–1799" (BUA).

99. General Folder, "Commencement 1786, Commencement 1787" (HUA); Taylor et al., eds., *Diary of John Quincy Adams*, II, 222.

100. Joseph Miller, "Address, Commencement, May 27, 1784" (typescript, UPA); Demarest, *History of Rutgers*, 159.

101. *New Jersey Gazette*, October 4, 1784, October 11, 1786, October 10, 1787; New York *Journal and Weekly Register*, April 12, 1787, April 10, 1788; New York *Packet*, May 7, 1789.

102. *Dunlap's American Daily Advertiser*, October 4, 1791; *New Jersey Journal*, October 2, 1792; *Dunlap and Claypoole's American Daily Advertiser*, October 7, 1794, October 8, 1795.

103. *Greenleaf's New York Journal and Patriotic Advertiser*, October 7, 1796; *The State Gazette and New Jersey Advertiser*, October 17, 1797; *The Daily Advertiser of New York*, October 4, 1798; *New Jersey State Gazette*, October 1, 1799; *The Federalist and New Jersey State Gazette*, October 14, 1800.

104. Bronson, *History of Brown*, 138; New York *Journal and Patriotic Register*, May 4, 1793, May 6, 1796; New York *Daily Advertiser*, May 9, 1794; New York *Gazette*, August 8, 1799; General Folder, "Commencement 1800" (HUA). See also "Commencement Theses: Rhode Island College" and Harvard College "Theses & Quaestiones."

105. I make this assertion based on my own research into the subject. While I do not pretend that my inquiries have been exhaustive, I have listed approximately 1,050 debates held by these societies during the period 1783–1800. Only 130, or 10.5 percent were unrelated to politics. Of the thirty debates Harvard's Graduate Debating Society held in 1792–1793, ten were non-political. See "United Fraternity Records, 1786–1810" (DaCA); "Records of the Graduate Debating Society, 1792–93" (HUA); "Minutes of the Cliosophic Society, 1792–1800" (PUA); "Records of the Philandrian Society, 1799–1810" (BUA); "Linonian Records"; "Brothers in Unity, Records."

106. "United Fraternity Records", January 8, June 10, 24, 1788, May 26, 1799; Taylor et al., eds., *Diary of John Quincy Adams*, II, 60–62, 87, 95.

107. "Minutes of the Cliosophic Society", July 12, August 22, 1792, August 21, 1793, February 5, June 3, July 17, 1794, February 4, December 23, 1795, March 9, 1796, February 7, 1798, March 13, 1799; "United Fraternity Records", April 20, 1790, May 31, June 7, November 8, 1791, January 31, April 24, December 11, 1792, March 15, November 1, 1796, April 10, 1798; R. H. Phelps, "One Hundred and Fifty Years of Phi Beta Kappa at Harvard," *American Scholar*, 1 (1932): 60; "Records of the Philandrian Society", November 19, 1800.

108. "United Fraternity Records", July 3, 1792, November 12, 19, 1793, October 31, 1797, March 20, June 26, 1798, March 26, April 9, 1799; Phelps, "Phi Beta Kappa at Harvard," 60; "Records of the Graduate Debating Society," December 17, 1792, September 9, 1793; "Minutes of the Cliosophic Society," November 21, 1792, January 16, February 13, April 2, December 10, 1793, February 26, March 19, June 11, 1794, July 15, August 5, December 23, 1795, February 10, March 2, 1796, January 4, 12, May 31, June 28, July 6, 1797, January 10, 24, March 21, May 23, June 6, August 22, 1798, January 3, May 29, June 19, July 17, August 14, 1799, February 1, March 5, June 11, July 17, August 20, November 19, 1800.

109. Taylor et al., eds., *Diary of John Quincy Adams*, II, 109, 127; "Journal of Nassau Hall, 1786" (General Mss., PUA); John Bisco to Abayah Bisco, April 21, 1798 (DaCA); Edwin B. Pomfret, "Student Interests at Brown, 1789–90," *New England*

Quarterly, 5 (1932): 139; "Record of Books Borrowed, 1780–1795, 1795–1800" (BUA); "Library Charging List, 1795" (HUA).

110. Joseph Watson to David Watson, February 11, 1798, February 9, 1799, January 17, 1801, "Letters from William and Mary College, 1798–1801," *Virginia Magazine of History and Biography*, 29 (1921): 139, 146, 159–60; May, *Enlightenment in America*, 246. Work not previously cited: Constantin Volney, *The Ruins: or a Survey of the Revolutions of Empires* (1st Eng. ed., London, 1791).

111. Philadelphia *Aurora*, June 18, 1798; W. Brockenbrough to J. C. Cabell, November 1, 1798 (Cabell Papers, University of Virginia Library), quoted in May, *Enlightenment in America*, 390.

112. Joseph C. Cabell to David Watson, March 4, 1798 (Garrett Minor and David Watson Papers, Library of Congress), quoted in May, *Enlightenment in America*, 247; Joseph Watson to David Watson, December 24, 1799, "Letters from William and Mary," 152; Chapman Johnson to David Watson, May 18, 1800, "Letters to David Watson," *Virginia Magazine of History and Biography*, 29, (1921): 271.

113. Marshall Smelser, "The Federalist Period as an Age of Passion," *American Quarterly*, 10 (1958): 391–419; John R. Howe, "Republican Thought and the Political Violence of the 1790s," *American Quarterly*, 19 (1967): 147–65. Cf. Richard Buel, Jr., *Securing the Revolution: Ideology in American Politics, 1789–1815* (Ithaca: Cornell University Press, 1972).

6

New Colleges in the New Republic

Between the last days of the Revolutionary War and the end of the century, sixteen colleges opened that still exist today. This near tripling of the nation's colleges demonstrated a growing interest in higher education. It also gave evidence of the restless mobility of the American people, for, with the exceptions of the College of Charleston and St. John's College in the Chesapeake port of Annapolis, these institutions arose on the edge of settlement: in upstate New York, the District of Maine, northeastern Georgia, western Massachusetts, and even the Territory South of the Ohio, two years before it became the state of Tennessee.

Just as the pre-Revolutionary colleges had partaken of a heritage of English higher educational traditions during their development, so these new colleges inherited much from the old: personnel, curricular plans, books, customs, and attitudes about the kind of education necessary in a newly independent America. Consequently the new colleges were conversant with the imperatives of republican education, the tradition of state service, and the curriculum necessary to promote that service. But, for most of these colleges, implementing a republican education was not simply a matter of replicating older institutions. The frontier intruded into the process in a number of ways. The paucity of resources in a sparsely settled environment inhibited growth and development. A scarcity of qualified instructors did the same. Since these upstart colleges were often one of the very few cultural resources available to the surrounding communities, they felt called upon to provide education in areas either not attempted or not emphasized at older schools. Because college founding on the frontier was often related to religious missionizing or the consolidation of a dissenting church, there was a less secular aura to the imparting of knowledge. Finally, most subtly, the attitudes of frontier dwellers were not quite the same as those of people who continued to live in more developed areas; frontiersmen had chosen their locations deliberately, thereby rejecting the communities they had left behind. Their views of "civilization" affected the colleges as well. To see these forces in operation and the kind of institution they could produce, we first examine Dickinson College, begun in central Pennsylvania at the end of the Revolution.

I

Dickinson College was subject to the contrary influences of the developing American higher educational tradition and the demands of the frontier from its very inception. Like so many of the new colleges, Dickinson evolved from a grammar school and would-be academy, established as early as 1760 in a town that was in the midst of a decades-long boom due to its location along the main route to the frontier. Peopled mainly by Scots-Irish immigrants, Carlisle was a Presbyterian community and so was its academy. During the 1750s and 1760s the town and school had been centers of Old Side-New Side feuding, but by the end of the Revolution the intra-denominational bickering had stopped, while the school had prospered. In October 1781, the school's trustees petitioned Donegal Presbytery to raise its status to that of an academy. It never happened.[1]

Dickinson skipped the academy stage because Benjamin Rush thought the central Pennsylvania school had a grander destiny. Rush had envisioned a college for the Susquehanna Valley as early as 1773. By war's end, he had taken the lead in persuading Pennsylvanians, both east and west, that Carlisle's school should become that college. Rush's motives were complex and not all were shared by other prominent supporters of the college, such as Colonel John Montgomery of Carlisle and Governor John Dickinson. Yet Rush made clear several themes. A college would civilize the frontier by serving as a center for the low cost education of the youth of the rapidly growing western counties and by offering Pennsylvania Germans a place to acquire American culture away from Philadelphia's corrupting atmosphere. Rush later observed that the college would "humanize even the half-civilized inhabitants of the western counties of Pennsylvania."[2] It would also serve as a religious enclave for Presbyterians. Rush worried that the sect would soon lose its influence on the Philadelphia college. This was undesirable, for religion was necessary "to correct the effects of learning. Without religion, I believe learning does real mischief to the morals and principles of mankind." The college would have a totally Presbyterian board and faculty so as to be able to combat the denomination's enemies in the state.[3] A third related motive was political. By the 1780s Rush had lost some of the enthusiasm for democracy he had shown at the Revolution's outset, and he hoped that education would be a means of restoring true republican character (meaning public virtue). Rush was tinkering with the idea of a comprehensive state educational system; meanwhile, a new college would help diffuse proper values. At another level, Rush's political concern was partisan. He strongly opposed the Pennsylvania Constitutionalists, counting among his enemies all who differed from him, even co-religionists such as Provost John Ewing of the University of the State of Pennsylvania. So Rush asked fellow Presbyterians to withdraw from that institution, to support the restitution of the old College of Philadelphia and the establishment of the new college at Carlisle. To John Montgomery, Rush wrote, "Let us be active my friend, in rescuing the state from the hands of tyrants, fools & traitors."[4]

Which motives were most powerful for Rush and the other college backers are impossible to tell, but despite some opposition to the scheme from the friends of Princeton and the Pennsylvania University, the legislature chartered the new college on September 9, 1783, naming it after John Dickinson, the state's governor. The charter placed Dickinson squarely within the tradition of state service education:

Whereas the happiness and prosperity of every community (under the direction and government of divine providence) depends much on the right education of youth, who must succeed the aged in the important offices of society, and the most exalted nations have acquired their preeminence, by the virtuous principles and liberal knowledge instilled into the minds of the rising generation [the college is established].

Religious, political, and frontier influences combined in the founding of Dickinson. They would continue to affect its operations.[5]

A college designed to civilize the frontier and to inculcate republicanism needed faculty and governors who held the proper political and religious values. Rush suggested clerics as the obvious officeholders, men who had been active in the Revolution but moderate in their political and religious sentiments.[6] Neither group totally fulfilled Rush's hopes.

Five of the seven men who taught at Dickinson through 1800 remain politically obscure.[7] The two politically outspoken Dickinson faculty were Robert Davidson, professor of history, and Charles Nisbet, the first president. Davidson came to Carlisle from the University of the State of Pennsylvania, apparently a Rush recruit. In Philadelphia he had assisted John Ewing at the First Presbyterian Church and was an active Patriot. In Carlisle he took over the pastorate of the Presbyterian church and continued to speak out on politics. He was pro-Constitutional and later Federalist. In 1787, he delivered the Fourth of July oration, embodying a Commonwealth Whig version of the coming of the war and a patriotic rendering of its conclusion, with praise for Washington and the people's wartime virtue. But, according to Davidson, there was more to be done to protect the republic. The national debt must be honorably paid; piety, Christianity, and virtue must be promoted (through seminaries of learning); and "Our character and consequence, as a people, depend on the firm union of these states, now called United." To effect this last, Davidson recommended approval of the Federal Convention then meeting in Philadelphia and he prayed for its success.[8]

The Constitution and the operation of the new government pleased Davidson greatly. When the Whiskey Rebellion of 1794 seemed to threaten that government, Davidson preached encouragement to the Pennsylvania militia on its stop in Carlisle. His sermon noted the popular origins of American government, its protection of civil and religious liberties, and the mechanism for removing unsatisfactory rulers through election. He favorably contrasted American peace and prosperity with the state of revolutionary France. Then, praising the patriotism of the soldiers while shaming the insurrectionaries, Davidson told the militia that they were there to teach the incorrigible that "we ought all to be obedient to lawful authority; that we ought to respect the government which [we] ourselves have made, and whose protection we have enjoyed; that in a pure republic, the will of the majority must be submitted to, and no lawless attempts made to weaken the energy of the government." The sermon was orthodox Federalism. It pleased both Pennsylvania and national leaders. An eulogy for George Washington in which he urged his hearers to emulate the founding father's many virtues indicates that Davidson's Federalism was unflagging throughout the decade.[9]

Charles Nisbet became an acerbic critic of American affairs during the early national period, even though he had come to America in 1785 full of enthusiasm for his post at Dickinson. He had been educated at the University of Edinburgh and Divinity Hall, had enjoyed a successful pastorate in Scotland, and had shared with John Witherspoon, whom he knew, both support of the Moderate cause in Scottish Presbyterian affairs and the Common Sense moral philosophy. A "lesser Commonwealthman," he had sympathized with America during the Revolutionary era, at one point warning in a wartime sermon that an English empire founded on bloodshed and violence could not last. When he left Scotland he assured friends he was heading for a land of "Liberty & Plenty," one where men's minds were free "from the shackles of authority."[10]

The freedom from authority Nisbet anticipated soon proved greater than he could bear. Indeed, it alienated him from his surroundings and disillusioned him of his hopes. Nisbet scholar James Smylie has noted that three themes of political criticism run through the Scotsman's correspondence: the absence of public men and public spirit in America, the exaggeration of the sovereign people's power, and neglect of the religion so necessary to virtue and sound government. These concerns made him fear for the fate of the republic.[11]

Some samples of his political beliefs show Nisbet to have been more socially conservative and more authoritarian than most Federalists, although he did share with them approval of the Constitution and the first two presidents' administrations, as well as antipathy toward the French Revolution, infidelity, and Republicans. The Constitution, "tho' imperfect, defective, & in some Respects impious, was judged however to be the Form of Government that could be adopted by a People in our Situation, & is still thought to be so, by all who love Order, Justice & the Happiness of Society." Still, his greatest fear about the new government was "the Want of Men of Honour & Public Spirit to manage Public Concerns, & the little Probability that such will be chosen by the People." The people, who possessed little political knowledge and less judgment, were too enamored of their own interests and powers to elect good men. Nisbet suggested that even a people's Bible might begin: "In the Beginning the Sovereign People created Heaven & Earth: and the Sovereign People spake to Moses, saying, Speak unto the Children of Israel, Thou shalt have no other Sovereign People before me."[12]

The French Revolution horrified Nisbet, especially as during the 1790s he linked it with a contagious social disorder that brought about not only the French calamity, but also the black uprising in Santo Domingo, the Irish Rebellion, the Whiskey Rebellion in Pennsylvania, and even disruptions among his own students. The French upheaval, though, began it all, drawing Nisbet's special brand of sarcasm as penned to a Philadelphia friend:

The Death of the King of France is a new Triumph of Liberty & Equality, supported by Philosophy. It is a Pity that Congress are not sitting otherwise you might have had a most pompous Rejoicing on the Occasion, & the pictures of the King & Queen of France, that are or formerly were in the Senate Chamber, might have been executed publicly in the Prison Yard, & buried with the same Circumstances of Ignominy as the Originals.[13]

Nisbet, like Davidson, held no brief for the Whiskey Rebels. He, too, preached to the troops on their stay in Carlisle. With President Washington in attendance, he was not bold enough to communicate his private thoughts that the administration was taking the crisis too casually, but he did stigmatize the Pennsylvania populace with the "guilt of rebellion." Nisbet's support for the administration led him to despise the emerging Republican Party. He accused Thomas Jefferson and Pennsylvania's Albert Gallatin of being French agents in 1797 when privateering raids on American ships came up before Congress, and even thought Jefferson's presidential bid in 1800 was paid for by France. In an age of political passion, there were few more vitriolic commentators than Nisbet.[14]

Compared to Nisbet's, the trustees' political sentiments seemed to lack intensity. About half of the sixty-four men to serve as Dickinson board members through 1800 have left indications of political activity. Of the forty charter trustees, sixteen are known to have been Republicans while three were Constitutionalists in Pennsylvania's internal politics. Of those appointed later, four were Republicans, two were Constitutionalists. No Dickinson trustee is known to have opposed the Federal Constitution, while in the 1790s ten trustees were known Federalists, four were known Republicans, and one switched from Federalist to Republican after 1795.[15] While political interest was constant, the board became more secular as time passed. More than twenty ministers served the college as trustees, but Nisbet's critique of American religion so offended the other clerics that only two actually attended meetings after 1796. The board fell under control of its lay members.[16] Rush's anticipated ministerial dominance failed in the board, but it was a politically conservative group, which matched the faculty's views on the values to impart to the students.

It was well that there was political harmony between the board and the faculty,[17] for unlike most colleges, Dickinson's curriculum followed the dictates of the trustees. Here again, Rush influenced the board. He proposed four classes that would receive instruction in languages (Latin and Greek, Hebrew, French, and German), mathematics and natural philosophy, logic, metaphysics, moral philosophy (including government and the law of nature and nations), history and chronology (ancient and modern, civil and ecclesiastical), the antiquities of

Egypt, Greece, and Rome, philology (including rhetoric and belles lettres), and divinity.[18]

This was an ambitious plan, fully comparable to those of the original colleges. Despite employing as many as four professors at a time, Dickinson's faculty never carried out all its mandated instruction. Moreover, it could never form four separate classes of students; in fact, the students refused to take their courses in the proper order and before 1796 they were not classified at all.[19] But the greatest irregularity came in the late 1790s. Frontier students evidently wanted their "book learning" fast, so fast they would not accept the class regimen in place at other colleges. As Nisbet reported it,

The Visitors ought to know, that the College is in a State of Insurrection & Revolution since the beginning of November last [1798] and that the Trustees when applied to refused their Aid & deserted the Masters altogether, so that the Students declared themselves the Sovereign People by bullying the Masters into a Promise to finish their Courses in the Space of one Year & five of them, conceiving even this period to be too long, deserted the Seminary in a few months after.

Dickinson's one-year course, followed in 1799 and 1800, dealt its reputation a blow from which it did not recover for some years.[20]

Not only did Dickinson students take few classes, they read few books. The curriculum mandated only the classical authors Lucian, Xenophon, Homer, Cicero, and Juvenal. Some of these were standard republican authors, others commonly studied classics. The only other book known to have been used in the curriculum was Robert Davidson's *Geography Epitomiz'd*, an apolitical rhymed survey of the world's nations, rivers, and mountains, which the students hated. For other courses, the professors gave their lectures without textual help.[21]

The library did not fill the gap. It was large, over 2,700 volumes in 1786, but contained mostly what were even then rare books, donated by John Dickinson. Of the 1,750 volumes he gave, few were in English. Most were Latin or French treatises, specializing in scientific or medical subjects or religious controversies. True, there were editions of Commonwealth canon works such as Cicero, Plutarch, and Tacitus, but they did not have the English translations so necessary to young scholars. Moreover, the library was periodically closed to the students for want of someone to supervise its use. Reading, out of class or in, was not a principal occupation of Dickinson students.[22]

When in class, Dickinson scholars gained exposure to a great deal of mathematics and English usage, criticism, and literature, this no doubt to bring desired skills to the frontier.[23] They also wrote out (for Nisbet required his lectures to be copied verbatim until student protest deterred him in the late 1790s) many principles touching upon government and law. The moral philosophy lectures contained observations revealing Nisbet's conservative bent on many subjects. In a sketch of the history of philosophy from ancient to modern, he evaluated the worth of philosophers by their religious orthodoxy. A discussion of the traits distinguishing men from animals included sidebars on the role luxury played in bringing down Rome, and the moral problems inherent in slavery. A lecture on the institutional arrangements of societies prompted comment on standing armies: they were dangerous to liberty and required a virtuous people to supervise them, but no satisfactory substitute for them had been devised and the laws would be poorly enforced without them. In his discussion of law, Nisbet got around to the distinctions among society's members and the way those distinctions were recognized even by republics. This led to a condemnation of democracy, a theme he addressed later when examining equality. All men, he said, have an "equal right to natural liberty & the pursuit of happiness in consistence with the interests of Society." But this was as far as equality went. American society at the time of the Revolution employed this concept; it was not upon the "old notion of the equal right & fitness of all Men to be Kings & Rulers that the Patriots of this Country resisted and expelled the powers of Great Britain & attained their present independence."[24]

Other matters pertaining to the proper forms of government appeared in a sort of moral philosophy catechism that Nisbet had his students using by the early 1790s. Again his conservative critique of society was evident. His anxiety over the sovereignty of the people influenced adverse comments on democratic governments (founded on suspicion and jealousy, greatly liable to overthrow through party activity) and on republics (they ignore reality by supposing the whole people virtuous; they can become tyrannies if the people are suspicious of private merit and ignorant of the public good). His fears also prompted the assertions that representatives ought to act on their own judgment, for the public delegates power to them through election, and that the people are therefore bound to obey the laws the representatives make. Other propositions informed students that the absence of virtue and harmony, of revenue, strength, and defense, coupled with the venality and ignorance prevalent in the legislatures could bring down republics and that the positive attributes necessary for legislative membership, knowledge, virtue, and independence, were possessed by very few citizens.[25] If anything, these views were more conservative than Federalism, and the students received them in large doses.

Robert Davidson's history lectures were generally straightforward chronological accounts. He did, however, project some of his own biases into his expositions. He presented a Whiggish view of America from settlement through the Revolution and then commenced a discussion of republican government. Modern republics were better than ancient ones because the older governments had no principle of representation and total democracies were subject to demagoguery. Representative democracies could assemble the general will and make possible the minority's acceptance of governmental measures. Indeed, said the Federalist who was shortly to oppose the Whiskey Rebellion, nothing was so absurd as for the people to delegate power to a government and then to rise in rebellion against it, especially when the Constitution could be amended and laws repealed.[26]

Students could not escape these Federalist strictures concerning morality and government. Nisbet made a habit of addressing the students not only at commencement, but also when they returned from vacations. He consistently urged them to study diligently, to practice piety and virtue, and occasionally related their efforts to the current political scene. In October 1787, for example, commenting on the utility of knowledge as it leads to careers of honor, Nisbet noted that Pennsylvania's recent history "may excite the people to be more desirous of men of letters and knowledge in the offices of government." He went on to say that the new federal government then under consideration would offer even greater opportunities for accomplished men. On a later occasion Nisbet observed that some legal abuses would always persist, but still counselled obedience and order, for "if we were to [debate] the public Constitution till every individual were as well satisfied with it as if he himself had made it, we would never have any to the end of the world."[27]

This unrelenting attempt to inculcate Federalist beliefs into the college students was in most cases successful. Roger B. Taney, the future Supreme Court Justice, claimed that his class disagreed with Nisbet's anti-Republican views, expressed in his lectures on the law of nations: "I believe a majority of the class would not write down these positions of his lectures; and, if the opinions had been expressed by any other professor, the class would probably have openly rebelled." Yet Taney's Republicanism, if it existed at this time, must have remained incipient, for he, as did others, followed Nisbet's guidelines when delivering the 1795 commencement address on the utility of seminaries of learning.[28]

Nisbet's views permeated commencement rhetoric. They appeared throughout the exercises, but particularly in student consideration of issues relating to the French Revolution. Student debates, orations, and Nisbet's own remarks during the 1790s charted the course of an anti-French struggle. In mid-1793, by asking "Were the French justified in beheading Louis XVI," the students defined the battle. Then followed a flurry of questions bearing on the Revolution and its meaning for America: "Whether men who have been governed by laws are not more wicked when freed from their restraint than those who have never been restrained by them," "Whether it would be prudent for America under her present circumstances to declare war on Great Britain under hers," "Ought republican governments to encourage the manufacture of luxuries," "Is it consistent with the interest and dignity of a republic to admit foreigners to legislative and executive offices," "Civil and military appointments ought not to be united in the same person in a well-regulated republic." Implicit in these questions were the spectres of the French mob and the Whiskey Rebels, of the loss of American virtue, of the folly of war with Great Britain, and of the rise of Napoleon.[29]

The fear of infidelity and the necessity to counter French commercial depredations led later students to contemplate "the Necessity of Moral Virtue," "the Necessity of Religion for the support of the Civil Government," and if "it is just in some cases for one nation to declare war against another." All this indicated a Federalist sympathy, one documented by a laudatory address sent to President Adams in 1798, commending him for averting open warfare and congratulating him on "the measures that have been pursued to maintain a policy of neutrality and peace." With this, the anti-French, pro-Federalist campaign peaked. The students in the 1798 commencement simply reviewed "the Politics of the Times and the French Revolution," while the Belles Lettres Society left the issue by debating "whether or no it is right for Americans to rejoice at the downfall of France."[30]

Students thus duplicated Nisbet's anti-French, pro-Federalist views in both the structured commencement ceremonies and in their private exercises, conducted by the debating society. They must have acted from real conviction, for they did it in spite of a community atmosphere that did not agree with Nisbet at all. Central Pennsylvania, Carlisle in particular, was an antifederalist and later a Republican stronghold. The town also betrayed signs of the less civilized behavior of the backcountry. From 1777 to 1787, eleven men and two women died on the scaffold in Carlisle. Death through duelling was frequent. Proponents and opponents of the Constitution came to blows at a demonstration in late 1787 and the antifederalists hanged the governor in effigy. Nisbet was on the wrong side of every other public issue as well, for the local citizenry supported the French Revolution, the Whiskey Rebels, and Jefferson. Only the force of Nisbet's personality and his position of authority kept him from actual harm at the hands of townspeople angry about his social and political stances.[31]

There were, however, other issues taken up by the students that showed their sensitivity to the local environment. They knew they were frontiersmen, knew the backcountry's problems, and were aware of the anomalies of civilization in the wilderness. So they asked themselves "whether do men's moral characters become better in proportion as the society in which they live becomes more civilized," "whether the practice of winning or losing money or any other property by betting is justifiable by the principles of justice and morality," "would not the time generally employed acquiring classical education be better employed in other pursuits," "whether is the war now carried on against the Indians just or not," "The Congress ought to pass a law prohibiting any subject from holding more than 4,000 acres of land," and "whether mankind in the savage or the civilized state enjoy the most happiness."[32] Some of these questions were debated at older colleges, of course, but at Dickinson the issues were closer to hand, both philosophically and geographically.

The student debate topics, like the lack of texts in the curriculum, the trustees' capitulation to the students' desire for a speedy education, and the very motives expressed in the founding of the school, reveal the mixed character that typified the republic's new colleges. They tried to emulate the older institutions and to varying degrees they were successful in dedicating themselves to state service education and in putting into practice a curriculum to attain that goal. Often, indeed, these college communities became nearly as thoroughly politicized as their seaboard siblings. But always the frontier intruded, limiting physical development, affecting curricular programs, influencing the tone of collegiate life. With these new institutions, the course of higher education in America was veering off in a new direction.

II

When men in the early national period convened to consider founding a college, they faced the question of what the college should do for the students. Overwhelmingly, college founders duplicated the path taken by Dickinson's backers. The Revolution had influenced the colleges in the settled areas to aspire to produce virtuous citizens, fit members in and leaders of the new republic. The goals of the new colleges had to be the same. This was both a case of seeking common ground and equal respectability with the existing colleges and of sincere conviction on the part of the college founders. James Bowdoin, the patron of Bowdoin College in the District of Maine, was certain that education was responsible for "Constitutions, laws, religion, and morals, which pursued in all their ramifications determine the fate of a country; whether it shall be virtuous, prosperous, and happy, or vicious, unfortunate, and wretched." A supporter of Franklin, the ethnically oriented new college in Lancaster, Pennsylvania, asserted that "the Germans, on account of their peculiar virtues, have hitherto been very necessary members of the Republic; but they have not considered that a true Republican must also possess education, so as to take part in directing the rudder of government, and to give his children the opportunity of rising to the highest levels of republican utility." University of North Carolina advocates held that "nothing can be more conducive to the existence of liberty, than such a system of education as gives every citizen the opportunity of gaining knowledge and befitting him for places of trust." The idea of a virtuous education also appeared in support of Union College, the University of Vermont, and Washington and St. John's College in Maryland.[33]

The charters of Virginia's Washington College and Hampden-Sydney, the College of Charleston, and Blount College in Tennessee proclaimed the necessity of a proper education of youth to preserve happiness, tranquility, prosperity, and a "succession of able and honest men, for discharging the various offices and duties of the community." The argument was best phrased in the University of Georgia's charter:

As it is the distinguishing happiness of Free governments that civil order should be the result of choice and not necessity, and the common wishes of the people become the law of the land, their public prosperity and even existence much depends on suitably forming the minds and morals of the citizens....This is an influence beyond the stretch of laws and can be claimed only by religion and education.[34]

A recognition that collegiate education played a part in shaping the political attitudes of students and that it therefore must aspire to insure the viability of the republican form of government thus linked the founding motives of the new colleges to the educational purposes of the old.

This concern for promoting republicanism was not the only motive for college founding. Another important goal of the new colleges was "civilizing" the frontiersmen. Most of these new institutions were remote from the established centers of learning and culture. Their founders were anxious that the colleges bring the people they served up to the level prevailing in the established centers. This desire received support from two separate sources. First, college founders were often clergy or devout laymen educated at established colleges who looked to the frontier both as an opportunity and a challenge. It was an opportunity in that they could take the orthodox gospel into the unsettled areas to minister to hundreds of thousands of the unchurched; it was a challenge in that they had to use both that gospel and education to prevent the frontier from descending into barbarism through lack of culture and religion.[35] Secondly, frontiersmen themselves recognized their lack of culture and polish, a defect many earnestly desired to correct. To be sure, they did not wish to emulate completely the character of easterners. Many of them would not have left the settled areas had they felt comfortable there. Rather, they wanted a minimum of polish, enough to be considered Americans, not savages.

The civilizing themes, then, loomed large in the founders' minds. The Dutch Reformed Missionary Michael Schlatter, interested in Franklin College, had long felt that the Germans needed education, for if they did not have it, "will not the children who are not instructed in reading and writing, in two or at least three generations, become like the pagan aborigines?" The founders of Tusculum College in Tennessee, Kentucky's Transylvania University, and the University of Georgia wanted to avoid having their youth "degenerate into ignorance and barbarism." The desire of Maine's Bowdoin College and Union College in upstate New York to provide higher education for residents of their areas at lower cost than would be possible if they attended the established colleges was implicit recognition of the need for civilization.[36] And the desire to establish a uniform identity with the rest of the nation appeared in the attitudes of the legislatures of Vermont and North Carolina, each holding that the ratification of the Constitution required the establishment of a college in the state.[37]

When they had the opportunity, frontiersmen demanded education. After the Revolution, South Carolina's backcountrymen had acquired power and, just as they had succeeded in moving the capital from Charleston to Columbia, and in disestablishing the Anglican Church, so they influenced the legislature in 1785 to charter three colleges, one at Charleston and two in the backcountry. Perhaps the frontiersmen were precipitous, for only the Charleston school survived the eighteenth century.[38]

The foundation motives of these new colleges are significant. They demonstrate that the political character of higher education, attributable at the older institutions to the English heritage and changes embraced during the Revolutionary movement, was built in at the start in these new schools. Laymen, and even governments, joined with occasionally politicized sectarian ministers to use all the colleges to produce fit leaders in the state as well as the church. Yet the motives also reveal that if the political goals were the same, what was needed to achieve them was not. On the frontier civilizing the students was a prerequisite to politicizing them. College founders recognized this and campaigned against barbarism as well as for republicanism.

The political concerns of the faculty and trustees of the new colleges were also affected by their location. Overall, those who taught and governed at the new colleges were less involved with politics than were their counterparts at the older schools. More members of these college communities have remained politically obscure. At these schools a move toward clerical predominance is evident. And, at some of the colleges, the religious affiliations of the trustees were more important than the political, this because sparsely settled areas generally experienced ministerial rather than lay efforts to found colleges.

The new northeastern colleges most closely resembled the older schools in political involvement, but even here some of the concerns differed. Williams College, raised from an academy in 1793, was the oldest of these institutions. Many of its faculty and trusteees were Yale or Harvard educated, many were prominent in religious or political office, and the majority were Federalists. Most influential among the faculty was the Reverend Ebenezer Fitch (Yale 1777), who became president when the college opened. At the same time, the Reverend Stephen West (Yale 1755) became vice-president (whether he ever taught is not clear). Both Fitch and West were New Divinity in religion, Federalist in their politics. Fitch was partisan enough to campaign for local delegates to the Massachusetts legislature, to rejoice at the adoption of the Jay Treaty, and to be pleased when the college community supported the Adams administration during the quasi-war with France.[39]

Williams College's trustees more accurately reflected the politics of the local community than did the faculty. That community divided over both the Constitution and the partisan political issues of the 1790s. Sixteen men served Williams from 1793 to 1800. Of the thirteen whose stances on the Constitution are known, eight supported and five opposed it. By the mid-1790s, six trustees were Federalist, six Republican and the loyalties of the rest are unknown. Ten of the sixteen held public office at one point in their lives, so it was a politically active group of men. One may surmise that the Federalist contingent exercised more power at the college than the Republican, for the trustees in 1794 selected as professor of law and civil policy Theodore Sedgwick, one of the most thorough-going Federalists in New England. On Sedgwick's refusal, no one else was named to the post; perhaps partisan strife prevented board action.[40]

No such discord afflicted Union College before the turn of the century. Its promoters deliberately chose the name to indicate the participation of all ranks of men in the college founding and to emphasize its non-sectarian nature. The name also described the political climate among those who ran the college, for they did not squabble over issues. The faculty was only vaguely political. Neither

John Blair Smith, the Princeton-trained Presbyterian minister who first presided over the college, nor the other early faculty made any public comment on the political controversies of the 1790s.[41] Only Jonathan Edwards, Jr., who became Union's president in 1800, had been a partisan in the 1790s. In mid-decade he identified with the politics of Roger Sherman, a Connecticut parishioner who had been a force in the writing and adoption of the Constitution and who had favored many Hamiltonian measures while a member of the early Congresses. Edwards also flayed the spread of infidelity, stressed religion as the basis of public order, and urged the people to elect only those candidates who believed in God and would regard His laws. Those positions in the Connecticut of the 1790s were orthodox Federalism. But by the late 1790s, Edwards was more involved with religious than political issues. He was silent on the French crisis and Jefferson's election, while devoting himself to the planning of what would become the Congregational-Presbyterian agreement to divide responsibility for western missions. During his Union presidency, Edwards, too, was apolitical.[42]

Union's trustees were more active in politics than the faculty, but they were not seriously divided. Thirty-seven men were Union trustees through 1800. At the time the Constitution was adopted, thirteen favored and four opposed it. During the 1790s support for the new government intensified. By 1800 Federalists dominated the board; only two Jeffersonians were noted by the future Union president Eliphalet Nott when he joined the board that year. Union's harmony existed in large part because the frenzied politics of the larger New York community did not penetrate the college.[43]

The other two northeastern colleges, despite receiving charters during the first half of the 1790s, were still not fully operational in 1800. By virtue of its 1791 charter, the University of Vermont had among its trustees the governor and the speaker of the house of representatives. Governor Thomas Chittenden, who served until 1797, was non-partisan, but his successor, Isaac Tichenor, was a Federalist, as were all the speakers of the house after 1793. The Vermont legislature, in which Republicans made gains after 1796, was still comfortably Federalist in 1800. But perhaps because of the striking political geography of the state, by which the more populous east was predominantly Federalist and orthodox Congregational while the west was largely Republican and religiously liberal, the assembly selected non-governmental trustees representing virtually every denomination in the state. This group avowed non-sectarianism and for most of these trustees there is no indication of political preference. One possible suggestion of the political posture of the majority was the selection of the Unitarian-leaning Congregational minister Daniel Clarke Sanders as the university president. Sanders, a Harvard alumnus, took the helm in 1800. He delivered the Vermont election sermon in 1798 and an euology on George Washington, both of which were overlain with Federalist rhetoric.[44] While the university community may have been mildly politicized, it seems that avoidance of political and religious contention in a fragmented state was more important than partisan politics, at least in the formative years of the college.

The Massachusetts legislature incorporated Bowdoin College at Brunswick, in the District of Maine, in 1794. The charter established a dual governing body composed of a small number of trustees and a larger number of overseers, following the example of Harvard. As with Vermont's board, the Bowdoin governors labored several years before launching their college. During that period almost eighty men served on the two boards. The vast majority were either laymen who served in state or national political office or orthodox Congregational clergy. The boards were overwhelmingly Federalist. Maine was sufficiently incorporated into Massachusetts that it shared its desire for education and its politics.[45]

These northeastern colleges constituted a spectrum of politicization that ranged from intense interest and activity to near apathy. The most persuasive trait in determining the degree of politicization was the complexity of the political and religious atmosphere surrounding the college. Ambivalent communities compelled the colleges to mute disagreement and bring all factions together behind the college. Other communities, where religious and political alliances seemed clear, allowed the colleges the luxury of politicization. Many other new schools adhered to this pattern.

Religious and cultural imperatives seemed to predominate at Franklin College in Pennsylvania, Virginia's Hampden-Sydney, Tennessee's Greeneville College (now Tusculum), and at Kentucky's Transylvania University, though the degree of politicization varied. Franklin College was founded to "Americanize" Pennsylvania's Germans. To some that involved politicization as well as acculturation. The college trustees reflected those mixed motives. There were forty-five trustees, thirty of whom were to be either Lutheran or German Reformed parishioners; the rest might come from any Christian denomination. The trustees actually may be divided into three groups. One contained about ten prominent local Lancaster figures who were Lutheran or Reformed, although laymen. Some had been active Revolutionaries and they generally tended to support the Constitution, becoming Federalists in the 1790s. But for them politics was not a major consideration. They were more interested in the education of the German population in English and in the prestige a college brought to the town. Another group consisted of Philadelphians with state and national political interests and connections, men such as George Clymer, Robert Morris, and Benjamin Rush. Politics was their reason for backing Franklin, for they wanted to politicize the Germans. When they discovered the difficulty of using the college for the task, they ceased to be participating trustees. The largest group, which had the most to do with forming the internal atmosphere of the college, was the ministerial contingent, largely Lutheran or German Reformed. These ministers were almost apolitical. They promoted the cultural and religious mission of the college.[46] Lack of politicization characterized the faculty as well. Some of them are simply unknown, but even the most prominent, John Hendel, Friederich Melsheimer, and President Henry Muhlenburg, were Dutch Reformed or Lutheran ministers more interested in church affairs or science than in politics.[47] Franklin College saw its frontier mission as the spread of non-political culture.

Hampden-Sydney was the child of Virginia's Hanover Presbytery, both as academy and college. Its trustees and faculty did become somewhat involved in politics, but that involvement seemed related as much to religious as to governmental issues. Thirty-eight men served the college as trustees from 1783 to 1800. The vast majority, even though they carried well-known Virginia names, were politically obscure. Those whose politics have become known divided pretty evenly over the Constitution and the major issues of the 1790s. A James Madison was, for example, offset by a Patrick Henry. Not very many Hampden-Sydney trustees were ministers, but most were Presbyterian laymen, for whom carrying religion to the backcountry was as vital as politics.[48]

The high point of Hampden-Sydney political activity came in the 1780s, and religious issues were the key to part of it at least. College president John Blair Smith opposed the Virginia legislature's proposals to incorporate the Episcopal Church and to provide for a general assessment for religion, with the object of ensuring support for recognized denominations. In this he sided with Madison, but angered Patrick Henry and other trustees, as well as other members of the legislature who favored the measures. Perhaps the antagonism between Smith and Henry and the friendship between Smith and Madison combined with principle to make the college president a supporter of the Constitution in 1787–1788. Again he found himself on the wrong side of Henry and many other trustees. Smith soon decided he preferred the church pulpit to the college podium; he lessened contact with the college after 1788, resigning in 1791. The trustees immediately sought to hire William Graham, rector of Liberty Hall Academy, who had favored the religious assessment and had opposed the Constitution.[49] But this political tempest was an aberration. Graham did not come to Hampden-Sydney, and no other eighteenth-century instructor has left any hint of political involvement. The college's main concern was to spread culture west of the Blue Ridge and to do it in a Presbyterian context.

Greeneville College, chartered in 1794 by the legislature of the Territory South of the Ohio, was also part of the Presbyterian missionizing movement. At Greeneville, the faculty set the tone of campus life, for the trustees, despite the inclusion of prominent Republican officeholders, met so seldom they had little effect on the college. Dominating the faculty was Hezekiah Balch, an orthodox Presbyterian, Princeton-educated, Virginia-trained. Soon after taking charge of the college, he tried to introduce the New Divinity to the Tennessee frontier, precipitating a wrangle among local Presbyterians that lasted the whole decade. There was little time for and less interest in political issues at Greeneville College. Religious quarrels were much more important influences on the lives of its students.[50]

Both religion and politics were important in Kentucky during early efforts to bring higher education to that part of the frontier. Virginia awarded degree granting power to Transylvania Seminary in 1783. Its trustees included important civic and religious leaders such as Caleb Wallace, a member of the state supreme court, George Rogers Clarke, the Revolutionary hero, and his fellow military leader Isaac Shelby, who became Kentucky's first governor. Shelby's successor, James Garrard, was also a trustee. Probably the most well-known minister was David Rice, the leader of Kentucky Presbyterianism. Neither the political leanings of the laymen, generally antifederalist and later Republican, nor the religious inclinations of the ministers, conservative Presbyterian, mattered very much until the mid-1790s when religious and political issues intruded on campus life.[51]

Several developments combined to embroil the college in religious and political disputes. In late 1788 the college moved from a spot near Danville to Lexington, a rapidly growing town wherein religious liberalism and antifederalism flourished. Over the next few years, men holding these opinions, led by William Bradford, editor of the *Kentucky Gazette*, and John Breckinridge, father of the 1860 presidential candidate and himself a United States Senator, increased their clout among the trustees. In 1794 this liberal element unseated the Episcopal minister James Moore from his position as instructor and replaced him with Harry Toulmin, an English-bred Unitarian with close ties to Joseph Priestley and acquaintanceships with Madison and Jefferson. Toulmin's election prompted Presbyterian withdrawal from the board, the creation of a rival called the Kentucky Academy, and ultimately a legislative investigation which led to a declaration that the board had acted improperly in choosing Toulmin. Under this pressure, Toulmin resigned in 1796. The two schools then sought to merge, a move effectuated in 1799 with the chartering of Transylvania University as a non-sectarian college.[52]

Transylvania's trustees came from the ranks of the rivals. They were religiously tolerant and politically active. Almost all were Republican, including Garrard, Wallace, Bradford, and six others who had or would become governors of the state or United States Senators. During all the maneuvering to establish the character of the college, the faculty, too, was active. James Moore, the first president, was at least mildly sympathetic to the French Revolution, as a member of the Lexington Democratic Society. Harry Toulmin quickly became a favorite of Kentucky Republicans; when he resigned the presidency of Transylvania, he was made Kentucky's secretary of state. The merger created a substantial faculty with professorships in law and medicine as well as arts and sciences. Moore, now an enthusiastic Republican, resumed the presidency, but the most politically powerful faculty were George Nicholas and James Brown, the first two law professors. Nicholas had been a federalist delegate to the Virginia ratifying convention, but fell in with the antifederal group in his adopted home. He was the principal architect of the Kentucky constitution, became the state's first attorney-general, and developed a large law practice, one part of which involved apprenticing would-be attorneys. His selection to the law professorship was one manifestation of the Republicanism of the university trustees. Implicitly, they agreed with the anti-administration views that Nicholas held. He defended Kentucky's pro-French, Republican opinions in a lengthy pamphlet which castigated the administration's laws, saying some were blatantly unconstitutional. Here he anticipated the Kentucky Resolves, which he may have had a hand in formulating. He made many of the same arguments in a Congressional speech in 1799, touching on the Alien and Sedition Acts. Shortly after that he died, but James Brown took up his Republican mantle so thoroughly that Jefferson advised students to study at Transylvania to pick up the proper principles of politics.[53] Both religious and political issues affected the Transylvania campus, but religious divisions did not mean political rifts in Kentucky.

At the two southern state universities politics was never very far from the minds of the trustees and faculties. In North Carolina, the movement for a state university emanated from the same people who favored ratification of the Federal Constitution. The charter, enacted the same year the state ratified the Constitution, provided that the trustees should be self-perpetuating, but that they should be divided among the state's judicial districts. Over the years, the trustees were almost all active in politics. Their leanings coincided with the changing fortunes of the parties in the state. Among the early trustees, backers of the Constitution predominated. Among those holding office in the late 1790s, Republicans were in the majority, but both parties always had board representation.[54]

The faculty, too, was caught up in politics. They, too, were divided. The university opened in 1795 under the tutelage of David Ker, presiding professor, and Charles Harris, who taught mathematics. Both were religiously unorthodox, which distressed some trustees, but the real source of trouble at the school was Ker's avid Republicanism, which did not sit well in the community. Indeed, the resentment prompted Ker's resignation. Harris initially opposed the administration on the Jay Treaty and was a devotee of Mary Wollstonecraft, but soon became a Federalist whose interest in politics was so strong that he left his professorship for a career in law and public office. Their successor, who soon became president, was Joseph Caldwell, a Princeton-educated minister-scientist who combined Presbyterian orthodoxy with political Federalism in an effort to bring peace to a divided campus.[55]

The University of Georgia charter, granted in 1785, established a two-part board, known as the Senatus Academicus. One part consisted of thirteen self-perpetuating trustees; the others included the governor, the speaker of the house and the chief justice of the state, all ex officio. Before 1800 almost no meetings took place, but when steps were taken to produce a functioning Senatus Academicus, Georgia's political climate was such that most of the members were Republican. Their politics and the connections of a few board members with Yale appeared in their selection of Josiah Meigs, the Republican friend of Ezra Stiles, to be the first professor in the school.[56]

These new colleges, and others not described here in detail,[57] did not become politicized in the same ways or to the same degree as did their older counterparts. There was no pattern of politicization. Some communities of governors and faculty were quite caught up in the political developments of the time, but only

George Nicholas of Transylvania resembled a William Smith in pre-Revolutionary Philadelphia or a Timothy Dwight in early national New Haven. Nisbet was a commentator, but not an actor, and that posture describes most politically aware professors and trustees at the new colleges. Many administrators were either more concerned with taking religion to the frontier than with politics, like Jonathan Edwards, Jr., or the faculty at Franklin College in Pennsylvania, or they were so obscure that their interests and involvement do not survive. These differences between the older and newer colleges should not be exaggerated. They were not stark contrasts. Rather, they were subtle shadings, indicative of slightly altered emphases. Politics was an important element in the educational atmosphere of the new colleges. But it was not as important as it was at the older institutions.

The political legacy of the Revolution and the cultural demands of the frontier carried over into the curriculum of many of the new colleges. Most new institutions sought to emulate the old. Eleven of the thirteen whose pre-1800 curricula are known [58] borrowed from established American colleges. Their basic curricula were thus much the same: a foundation in the classics, studies in English and possibly modern languages, an expanding role for mathematics and natural science, and a revolution-inspired recognition of the worth of history and government in producing good citizens prepared for state service. Still, in several cases the frontier intervened to mitigate the effort to reproduce the established colleges' curricula. The limited initial assets of many colleges prevented total implementation of the desired curriculum; there was not enough money for instructors, books, or scientific apparatus. The one-man domination of several new colleges, usually by a clerical president who might or might not be sympathetic to all branches of learning, produced the same result. The curricular models these men chose were sometimes out of date, reflecting the narrower focus of their own college days. Finally, as we have seen in the case of Dickinson, the frontiersmen imposed their own conditions. Few students were as impatient as those who came to Carlisle, but there were other difficulties. Often they needed grammar school education to prepare them for college. Moreover, despite their cultural yearnings, they were frequently more interested in the practical, useful skills than in "civilized" trappings. Mathematics, construction arts, bookkeeping, and the rudiments of law and medicine were more alluring than the learned languages, metaphysics, or moral philosophy. In spite of these difficulties, the new colleges tried to replicate known patterns of higher education, including the political component. How well the new colleges were able to do this differentiated them from their older counterparts and from each other.

Two of the new schools did not use the existing colleges as curricular models. Franklin College began in 1787 with the intent of promoting an "accurate knowledge of the German and English languages, of mathematics, morals, and natural philosophy, divinity, and all such other branches of literature as will tend to make men good and useful citizens." This early experiment in bilingual education had no American precedent. It did not work, for the college quickly divided into

German and English departments. The German department taught the higher studies, but to only fourteen students by 1788. The English department became a coeducational grammar school with few aspirants to the higher studies. Frontier Germans apparently had little interest in higher education. Also, fundraising proved difficult, with the result that three of the four professors could not be paid. The college never held any commencements and folded within three years, not be resurrected before the nineteenth century; an academy kept the name alive.[59]

Coastal South Carolina was not a frontier area in the post-Revolutionary era, yet, despite efforts to found a college that had gone on since the 1750s, the American higher educational tradition was not well known in the low country. Most planters' sons or would-be clerics had gone to England for formal education or had been taught by private tutors. When the College of Charleston began operating in 1785, it did so in the British mold. The first principal and instructor was the Episcopal priest Robert Smith, English-born, Cambridge-educated. In 1790 the college obtained a revised charter and broadened its educational base so as to teach at least some material on a high level, notably science and classical languages, including some works associated with the Commonwealth Whig canon, such as Cicero, Sallust, Livy, and Xenophon. Some other politically charged books appeared, such as Morse's geography and Priestley's lectures on history. Still, for several reasons it is not possible to determine the political content or import of the curriculum. South Carolinans sent neither their sons nor their contributions to the college. A small student body and a tight budget resulted in haphazard instruction and a bewildering variety of professors who taught briefly, then left. Then, too, there is no evidence that moral philosophy, government, politics, or law appeared in the curriculum at all. Finally, although there were commencements from 1794 to 1797, they may actually have signalled only the completion of a grammar school course. After 1797 the institution remained an academy until the early nineteenth century.[60]

Franklin College and the College of Charleston were rather unsuccessful attempts to produce an educated citizenry. Their troubles illustrate the difficulties, financial and cultural, of introducing higher education into communities unprepared to receive it. Similar obstacles would affect other institutions, but these two had the additional handicap of being unconnected to the traditions of existing colleges. The other new schools, which were so connected, were more in the American mainstream. Despite many variations in their attempts to create curricula, a pattern emerges. The new college founded in an area that had previously sent its sons to an established institution usually stuck closely to the plan of studies followed at that college. When settlement was too recent to have allowed college attendance or when no local alliance with an established school had been forged, the new colleges were more inclined to experiment with their curricula.

In the North, Harvard, Yale, the College of Philadelphia, and Princeton were successful in attracting students from all over the region. Williams, Union, Dickinson, and Maryland's Washington and St. John's Colleges were all close enough to these established schools to be competitors for students. They followed quite closely their curricular examples.

The Connecticut River Valley in the eighteenth century was a Yale Congregationalist preserve; not surprisingly, many Williams College trustees were Yale-educated. The first college president was Ezra Stiles' long-time tutor Ebenezer Fitch. Fitch brought Stiles' curriculum to Williams. Its 1795 laws followed the 1787 Yale laws. In both colleges the freshmen worked primarily in the classical languages and English. Sophomores continued those studies and added logic, rhetoric, geography, and some branches of arithmetic and trigonometry. Juniors continued mathematics with subjects such as trigonometry and surveying, while also beginning natural philosophy and astronomy. Seniors studied metaphysics, ethics, history, and civil policy. Fitch, as had Stiles, encouraged English composition and frequent forensic disputation. The only major differences from New Haven practice were the hiring of a French instructor to supplement the Yale-educated tutors, the addition of chemistry to natural philosophy, and Fitch's theological slant, for he had New Divinity leanings and sometimes had his students read Samuel Hopkins' *System of Divinity*. Early Williams was an upriver outpost of Yale.[61]

The Hudson River Valley was fertile field for the Dutch Reformed and the Presbyterians. Union, led by Princetonians John Blair Smith and Jonathan Edwards, Jr., stuck closely to Nassau's example, which meant emphasis on the humanities, not science. The languages were important throughout the curriculum. Students read a wide variety of Latin authors, French could be substituted for Greek, and English introduced Blair's *Lectures*, Rollin, the *Tatler*, the *Guardian*, and the works of Milton and Addison. In history and moral philosophy Union shone. Reading was diverse and extensive, including Hume, Dugald Stewart's *Philosophy of the Mind*, Priestley, Paley, David Ramsay's *History of the American Revolution*, Robertson's history of Scotland, Gibbon, Ferguson, Jefferson's *Notes on the State of Virginia*, Burke, Vattel, Burlamaqui, Doddridge, Blackstone, and Hutcheson. The bulk of this material fell within the Commonwealth Whig canon, but some featured a counter-revolutionary conservatism. Union's curriculum, closely related to Princeton's, was dominated by old disciplines, yet employed modern scholarship, departing somewhat from Nassau's pre-Revolutionary zeal.[62]

The two Maryland colleges, Washington and St. John's, replicated the College of Philadelphia. William Smith, former provost of the Philadelphia school, became the first president of Washington College and simply reproduced the curriculum he had earlier constructed. His *Original Account of Washington College, in the State of Maryland* even reiterated the language of his earlier pamphlet describing the course of study at Philadelphia. Examination records for 1788 indicate that Smith successfully pursued the earlier plan.[63] St. John's received its Philadelphia influence both through Smith, who was a trustee, and through President John McDowell, who was a College of Philadelphia alumnus and long-time tutor. Both colleges thus provided students with extensive readings in the

republican classics, with modern Commonwealth commentary in moral philosophy, and with an introduction to the principles of politics. In some ways the
old Philadelphia college never died; it just changed venues.[64]

In the South the pattern of replication also prevailed, but here some colleges
arose in areas so newly settled or so remote from established institutions that
their use of the older colleges' curricula did not conform to a single pattern. An
institution such as Hampden-Sydney drew leadership from Princeton graduates
of the 1750s and 1760s, who perpetuated what they had learned to produce a
curriculum rather out of date by the Princeton standards of the 1790s. The
University of North Carolina used the Princeton model as a base on which to
build an innovative curriculum unlike anything at the established colleges by
1800. And the University of Georgia made use of many years of Yale tradition
to develop a curriculum largely New Haven based but with some new twists
appropriate to its frontier student body. The theme of basic continuity between
established and newer colleges, yet with some differences attributable to frontier
influence, emerges once more.

Hampden-Sydney was the first new southern college, founded in an area that
had sent its Presbyterian sons desiring higher education to Princeton. The college
began as an academy in 1776 under the direction of Samuel Stanhope Smith,
and five other Princetonians were among the trustees. When it received degree
granting authority in 1783, Samuel's brother John Blair led the college. He was
a member of John Witherspoon's first Princeton class, but he chose to keep in
place the curriculum Samuel had installed, that of Princeton in the early 1760s
reduced to three years, for Hampden-Sydney had no freshman class. Actually,
this produced little curricular alteration, for Princeton students had used the
senior year for review, undertaking no new studies. The classics dominated both
systems: Horace, Cicero's *Orations*, Xenophon, Lucian, and the Greek Testament were staples for all classes, providing an introduction to the republican
authors. The differences between the curricula were slight: Princeton gave some
consideration to natural philosophy while Hampden-Sydney did not, but the
Virginia school spent more time on history and chronology than did Princeton
(although what was read is unknown). The Hampden-Sydney students did read
John Witherspoon's moral philosophy lectures, which fostered republicanism,
religion, and virtue, and were the element of Witherspoon's Princeton most
necessary to a college competing with it among Virginia's dissenters. This program changed little when Archibald Alexander became the college's second
president, for although he had been educated at Virginia's Liberty Hall Academy,
his mentor, William Graham, was Princeton, class of 1773. Hampden-Sydney,
then, chose to emulate Nassau as closely as possible in an effort to compete for
students, but even by the mid-1780s its curriculum no longer matched its older
rival's, which had incorporated much mathematics and science, and more modern
authors in many subjects.[65]

The University of North Carolina did not slavishly follow Princeton's example,
even though it was in Carolina's backcountry, where Presbyterian influence had

made a Princeton education desirable. William Davie and Samuel McCorkle, both Nassau graduates, determined the original curriculum, which was recognizably Princetonian, with extra features, especially in the practical sciences, such as agriculture and commerce. Yet shortly after the college opened, Professor Charles Harris wrote that the curricular trend was toward the practical, that the dead languages were to be dropped. By the end of 1795 a new curriculum had placed much more emphasis on English, history, and natural science, while the traditional studies received ambitious upgrading. Moral and political philosophy and history would use Paley, Montesquieu, Vattel, Burlamaqui, Priestley, Millot, Hume, the Federal Constitution and those of modern Europe; all these were recommended reading at Princeton but were not part of the curriculum. They represented an earnest effort to acquaint students with Commonwealth Whig authors, yet some works reflected the political conservatism of the college founders. The most significant curricular innovations included professorships of medicine, chemistry, agriculture, and mechanical arts; these went beyond Princeton. Language instruction emphasized English, with the classics confined to the republican authors Virgil, Cicero, Horace, Lucian, and Xenophon. A separate degree program for those desiring to concentrate on English and the sciences enhanced the practical side of the curriculum. Its designer, trustee William Davie, explained the purpose of separate degrees: "The ruling. . .principle in our plan of education is that the student may apply himself to those branches of learning and science alone which are absolutely necessary to fit him for his destined profession or occupation in life." Too little money and too few professors prevented the full enactment of the plan in the eighteenth century, but plainly the University of North Carolina recognized the desirability of a practical education and was not afraid to experiment to attract students.[66]

Franklin College, eventually the University of Georgia, was modelled after Yale, probably because of the efforts of Yale alumni Governor Lyman Hall and Abraham Baldwin, who together convinced the state legislature in 1785 to authorize a university and to appropriate land to endow it. Both men corresponded with Ezra Stiles about the proposed college and when it finally opened in 1801, Baldwin hired as president Josiah Meigs, recently deposed professor of natural philosophy at Yale, who brought the curriculum of his teacher and friend Stiles with him.[67]

There were thus great similarities between the two colleges. At both, freshmen and sophomores concentrated on Latin, Greek, mathematics, and a smattering of English. Juniors and seniors turned to belles lettres, the law of nations, logic, moral and natural philosophy. Many of the readings were the same, such as Nicholas Pike's *New and Complete System of Arithmetic*, William Enfield's *Institutes of Natural Philosophy*, and Joseph Priestley's *Lectures on History*. At both schools forensic disputations were important for sharpening young minds.

But the intellectual fare at Franklin went somewhat beyond that at Yale. Meigs' talents lay in the sciences, and he was both politically and religiously more liberal than Stiles. These traits found expression in the curriculum. There was more mathematics at Franklin than at Yale, and more of it was applied, as in bookkeeping. Franklin science included experimental natural philosophy, chemistry, and Linnaean botany; none of these appeared at Yale for some years. Classics included not only the traditional Latin and Greek authors, but also Gibbon's *Decline and Fall of the Roman Empire*, Robertson's Roman history, Rollin's ancient history, Vertot's *Roman Revolution*, and Gordon's Tacitus. English brought reading in Pope, Swift, Addison, and the normal Blair's *Rhetoric*. Among the political readings were the Locke, Montesquieu, and Vattel used at Yale, as well as Hume's *History of England*, Ferguson's *History of Civil Society*, Temple, Burgh, Adam Smith, and Blackstone. The political slant was heavily toward the Commonwealth authors. Religious works ran the gamut from pietists to skeptics. Franklin College, with no competition for students, set out to bring all the trappings of civilized society to the frontier. To do it, Meigs based the curriculum on established practice and then innovated. He probably tried to do too much, as the subsequent history of the college shows, and he may not have taught as thoroughly as Yale's Stiles or Dwight, but the frontier bred ambition as well as emulation and Meigs personified its spirit.[68]

These examples illustrate the range of curricular replication and innovation that characterized the new colleges. No matter what direction the curriculum took, moral philosophy, politics, and government continued to be important elements and works associated with the Commonwealth canon continued to appear. But in the absence of direct evidence such as moral philosophy lectures, just what kind of politics was taught at these colleges is difficult to deduce. Inference plays a large role in determining how political views were inculcated at the new colleges.

For many colleges even inference is difficult. The records of Pennsylvania's Franklin College tell us virtually nothing and the two southernmost colleges likewise present only hints of the political cast of their instruction. The College of Charleston, existing in the midst of a pro-French, Republican community, inhabited by large numbers of French descendents, taught French for several years, even after the XYZ Affair brought many Charlestonians to support the administration. Georgia's Franklin College probably emphasized Republican tenets, but the only evidence is the politics of President Meigs and some pro-Jeffersonian commencement exercises from 1804.[69]

The Maryland colleges both taught politics, but the only clues to its partisan nature are inconclusive statements from the college presidents. William Smith was so fond of re-using old rhetoric that one wonders if he did not live in the past. His 1784 account of Washington College repeated his earlier claims for the College of Philadelphia that it would train up "a succession of patriots, lawgivers, sages, and divines." It also informed those interested in the college that commencing seniors in 1783 had discoursed on the state of learning in Maryland and on the rising glory of America. This statement indicates that Smith had reconciled himself to the Revolution and that politicization was still part of his educational program, but the record is silent on the partisan stance espoused at Washington College by Smith and his successors. St. John's president John McDowell was also inscrutable. In an undated commencement address from the 1790s, he urged students to be good citizens, "warm friends of true liberty," and to "honestly endeavor to understand the real interest of your country and promote it with firmness and integrity." Again the implication is that politicization was educationally desirable, but what politics the students should imbibe McDowell did not make clear.[70]

In seeking to understand the political orientation of these colleges we are hampered by a lack of evidence, but that itself is significant. Many post-Revolutionary colleges were not well enough developed to have left a documentary record of their activities, and may not have been well enough developed to have had many activities. Or it may have been that the direction of those activities was not toward politics. Certainly, the off-campus behavior of many faculty and governors was more religious than political. Despite lip-service to the goal of educating their charges in politics, there may have been very little action taken to accomplish it. Other concerns were more important.

For a few colleges more evidence survives to suggest the political content of the curriculum and its effect on students. Even for these colleges it is clear that the political emphasis was not as great as it was at the older institutions. Moreover, unlike the original schools, not all the new colleges chose sides in the partisan struggles of the 1790s. To a greater or lesser degree something was at work at these colleges not found at the established schools.

A few colleges were quite interested in politics and did develop a partisan cast in the 1790s. Even though Williams College was unable to induce Theodore Sedgwick to teach politics and law, the tone of instruction was Federalist. Both moral philosophy and political precepts bore the mark of William Paley, who was recited in his entirety along with Montesquieu and Vattel. President Fitch, who taught moral philosophy to the seniors, reinforced his classroom rhetoric with commencement orations urging students to use their learning to promote patriotism and good morals, to support good government and the prevailing social order. This was especially important, he said in 1799, at a time of "general and alarming danger, when every civil and religious institution is threatened with ruin; when a spirit of VANDALISM, hostile to rational liberty, and to everything dear to us as men and Christians, has already devastated the fairest parts of Europe, and menaces the civilized world with universal carnage, rapine, and desolation."[71]

Other evidence confirms the college's Federalism. The professor of French, William Mackay, gave satisfactory service to the college and even tutored his students well enough so that one could give an oration in the language in 1797 on the spirit of party. Yet in 1799 his post was abolished. Students who wanted to read had access to the library if they were upperclassmen. What they found there included a small collection of works belonging to the Commonwealth canon, and various classical authors, but they could not have found any material championing the French Revolution or deism. Senior Thomas Robbins kept a diary during 1796 (having come from Yale for that year), which attests to student interest in politics. He and his classmates noted the intense electioneering in the Massachusetts and Connecticut gubernatorial races, the support Washington received for his stance on the Jay Treaty, and the ominous tide of news from Europe where the French seemed certain to triumph in her war against the combined powers.[72]

That interest in politics spilled over into commencement exercises, largely of a Federalist bent. In the late 1790s, as the crisis with France built toward possible war, and as the Republicans mounted an effective critique of administration measures, the partisan tone of the campus emerged. Orations took place on "Political Union," "The most effective means of rendering the American government secure and permanent," "the motives, which actuate the infidels and Jacobins in this country, and the manner of their operation," and "the Influence of Religion on human conduct, and its necessity to the existence of the Civil State." The students disputed "the characters and opinions of the present age," "the temporal advantages and disadvantages of Christianity," and "Would it be good policy in the United States to build a navy?" Even the music at the 1799 commencement had the intriguing title "Adams and Liberty."[73]

The Federalist tone of campus life was not limited to these formal exercises. Perhaps the best indicator of the political sentiments of these students was a letter to President Adams, sent by them in June 1798, which showed that they had learned their moral philosophy lessons well:

When we behold, Sir, a great and powerful nation exerting all its energy to undermine the vast fabrics of Religion and Government, when we behold them inculcating a disbelief in the Deity, of future rewards and punishments; when we behold them discarding every moral principle and dissolving every tie which connects men together in society . . . we weep over the awful calamities of anarchy and atheism.

But when we behold this Nation, not contented with its vast European dominions, but endeavoring to extend its Colossian empire across the Atlantic, every passion is roused. . . . We will oppose them with all our youthful energy and risk our lives in defense of our country.

The committee that wrote the letter claimed to be speaking for all 130 students at the college.[74] If so, the letter testified to a uniform absorption of Federalist principles regarding domestic and foreign policy, as well as the connection between orthodox religion and the welfare of the civil state. It was truly a credit to the political aims of a Williams College education.

Union College, despite faculty nonpartisanship, nonetheless displayed a Federalist atmosphere quite similar to that of Williams. There is little direct evidence to show how the curriculum contributed. As elsewhere, the college president taught moral philosophy. At Union that included a section on politics and on the Federal and various state constitutions, but there is no record of the text used, if any. That John Blair Smith must have done something to teach his students about government is suggested by his inaugural address, in which he argued that education served the populace as a whole by nourishing freedom, resisting autocratic domination, and exploring the rights of man: "thus office-holders of the republic are trained for their very important duty, and our leaders, magistrates, and legislators merit greatly in their achievements." As at Williams, the library contained a fair collection of Commonwealth canon authors from the classics to the modern ethical, historical, and political works. Also, there were some colonial and state histories written by pro-Revolutionary or pro-Constitutional authors such as David Ramsay and Jeremy Belknap. There were no works extolling the French Revolution or infidelity. Of course, whether students read any of this is unknown.[75]

If direct evidence only hints at the curriculum's political tone, student comment about it and literary society debates confirm its Federalism. The Bancker brothers, George and Evert, attended Union from 1798 to 1800. Their letters home expressed the frustration of belonging to the political minority. During the undeclared naval war with France George wrote

There are some of the students here who talk of sending an address to the President of the United States approving of his conduct. Most part of the students are of that party so that our party will not be able to do anything with them here, as there are only four or five of the Democratic party. I expect that if they do send an address, they will please Dr. Smith very much, as he is a great friend of Adams.

A little later in the year George bemoaned the nature of classroom instruction: "We are at present studying the Constitution of the United States and of the several States, so that Dr. Smith has made the greater part of the class Federals. He lectures daily on Federalism and tries to prove that the Alien and Sedition Bills are constitutional. . . . Poor Demos cannot escape. They get it from every quarter, newspapers, presidents of college, and every hot-headed, or rather English, Federalist abuses them." For Evert Bancker, one of the highlights of 1800 was the election of Jefferson. The townspeople he thought indifferent; most of the rest of the students were disappointed. A few supported Aaron Burr, but most were Federalists.[76]

Many of the debates held by the Philomathean Society (the Calliopean before 1797) also suggest that they drew inspiration from Federalist principles voiced in class. In 1794 the talk was of the war between Great Britain and France and whether it would be advisable for America to support the French. The domestic side effects also excited debate on topics such as the suitability of ministers holding public office, "whether Democratic Societies are admissable," and the fate of the Jay Treaty. Doubt about the progress of the French Revolution first appeared in a consideration of the justice of beheading the French Royal couple. By 1798, the students contemplated the advisability of war with France, whether stamp duties were legitimate ways to raise revenues to support a war, whether the Alien Bill was justifiable, and whether the French or the English had done the most damage to America. They blamed the French. During the height of the

French war scare the society decided that privateering was justifiable, that morality could not exist in America without Christianity, and that the country's political divisions were not advantageous.[77]

This pattern of discussion closely reflects the evolution of debating society rhetoric at Dickinson, while the phraseology of the questions, as well as the decisions, denote Federalist bias. These two northeastern colleges, Williams and Union, developed into pro-Federalist institutions that resembled, but did not quite match, their older colleagues.

In the South, the University of North Carolina was the one clearly politicized college,[78] but partisan identity was ambiguous. Just what tone the faculty gave to political instruction from 1795 to 1800 is hard to determine. With Professor Ker a "furious Republican," with Professor Harris a suspected infidel and devotee of Wollstonecraft, one might expect a pro-French, anti-administration view to have predominated. This supposition gains some credence from student John Pettigrew's observation that Paine's *Age of Reason* was commonly read with great approbation by the students. But at the same time, the texts for moral philosophy included Paley, Burlamaqui, and Montesquieu, none of which lent themselves toward a favorable interpretation of the French Revolution or the democratization of the American government.[79]

The possibility that the assigned curriculum and the classroom views of the professors were diametrically opposed gains confirmation from the exercises of the student debating societies during 1795 and 1796. As we have seen elsewhere, debate topics tended to reflect classroom teachings and in those schools where a clear partisan tone existed, the questions indicated that as well. This was not the case with North Carolina's societies. Also, internal evidence suggests that society members usually voted their own convictions; deliberate note was made of debates decided "on the arguments." A real division of opinion marked both societies. The Dialectic Society condemned the Jay Treaty, criticized standing armies, and recommended against paying the British debt. But it also thought excise taxes consistent with liberty, commended American neutrality in the dispute between Great Britain and France, and denied the right of foreigners to hold American political offices.[80] This contradictory approval and condemnation of Federalist measures typified the Philanthropic Society as well. It decided that America ought not to declare war against Great Britain, but should go to the aid of France, that the French were justified in regicide, that America should break the Jay Treaty, but that foreigners ought not to be admitted to public offices.[81] Again, the contradictions suggest a badly divided membership.

Campus divisions continued after Joseph Caldwell arrived late in 1796. Caldwell left no doubt of his Federalism, in or out of the classroom. Although Montesquieu disappeared from the moral philosophy course, its replacement was John Adams' *Defense of the Constitutions of the United States*, buttressed by De Lolme in praise of the British constitution, and by Burlamaqui. On Washington's birthday in 1800, Caldwell delivered an euology to the students in which he praised the Patriot's virtues and conduct at all stages of his career, recommending that the students emulate him whenever possible. He took the occasion to condemn the French "through whose veins have run the foulest streams of corruption, and which has been vomiting promiscuous destruction upon innocence and guilt." On the other hand, Caldwell's fellow instructors did not share his views. James Gillaspie was religiously unorthodox and Samuel Holmes, according to Caldwell, denounced all governmental authority, denied the existence of virtue, and promoted self-interest as a guide to human conduct.[82]

The students continued to mirror the divisions among their teachers. The Dialectic and Philanthropic Societies debated ambiguously on the propriety of Federalist measures, although a slow trend toward approval of Federalism was evident through 1798. Still, argument within the societies must have been heated. It took the Philanthropics two meetings to decide "whether the French or British are most justifiable in capturing our vessels," and then the British were favored by a single vote.[83]

The Federalist drift in student sentiment reached its apex in mid-1798. In June the members of both debating societies, after public meetings and consultation with Caldwell, issued an address in support of President Adams. The address made clear the reasons for the students' Federalism and also its ephemeral nature. After noting concern at the French government's actions, and relief that America had preserved her neutrality, the students went on: "Although our people have been divided in sentiment on this subject as well as others yet when we are told that our differences are made a ground on which to form a plan for destroying our government or infringing our rights we cannot but revolt at the injurious thought and excoriate the men who could think of acting on so base a principle."[84]

The nation's crisis with the French passed and so did student political unity. From the end of 1798 through the first few months of 1799, the Dialectic Society decided that the Alien and Sedition Acts were constitutional and proper (by a 12–10 vote), that they should not have been passed, that the press should be limited, that Porcupine, the ultra-conservative critic of the Adams administration, should be banished, and that liberty of the press was essential to American freedom. The Philanthropic Society debates demonstrated the same schizophrenic character. They determined that President Adams' conduct had been such to justify fears of monarchy and that he should not be allowed to make appointments (this at the time of the commissioning of the officers for the army to defend America from France), but they agreed with Adams' position that immigration should be restricted. On foreign affairs, the members thought the French justified in the measures they took to conquer Egypt, by a majority of two decided that French conduct had hurt the United States more than British conduct since 1789, and then by a majority of two voted that the United States should declare war on Great Britain. The votes were close on all these issues. The decisions reached depended on how many members from each political faction attended the meetings.[85]

This political friction brought about one last episode in 1799, a two-week riot against the faculty. In part this was the result of a trustee attempt to interfere with faculty discipline, but there were political causes as well. One faction of the students beat James Gillaspie, reviled him for his religious apostasy and political anarchism, and asked Joseph Caldwell to take over the management of the college. Yet, a group of Republican students felt duty bound to annoy Caldwell, who was subject at the time to newspaper attacks for his extreme Federalism. In the wake of the protests the faculty resigned. The trustees asked Caldwell to resume his position and invited Federalist trustee Samuel McCorkle to join with him. He refused, citing political considerations. He disliked what he called the Jacobin system of education. The university would fail, he said, unless religion and morality returned, a Federalist religion and morality to be sure.[86]

The University of North Carolina, although divided in opinion, was the most strongly politicized new southern college. The two Virginia campuses, by comparison, seemed little influenced by politics. Liberty Hall's William Graham supplemented John Witherspoon's moral philosophy with his own "Lectures on Human Nature." Those treating government did not address contemporary issues. Rather, they defined the types of government, noted the advantages and disadvantages of each, and concluded that men should form governments through compact. The closest that Graham came to commenting on the Federalist administrations was to observe that three conditions should be met by government: its officers should have no distinct interests of their own; every citizen should have the right to examine its conduct and free liberty to use the press; and the free exercise of religion should be granted to all. These may have been critical references to Federalist measures, and they would have been in character with Graham's opposition to the suppression of the Whiskey Rebellion, but they were so carefully veiled that it is hard to attach a partisan meaning to them. There is no record of how the students responded. Indeed, the extracurricular life of Liberty Hall before 1800 remains largely a mystery.[87]

One other item suggests a lack of interest in contemporary political issues at Liberty Hall. Graham put together a library for the college, the bulk of which he had acquired in Philadelphia in 1776. Among the titles were only a few republican classics and a handful of other works from the Commonwealth canon. The college obtained virtually no political tracts thereafter. No histories of the Revolution or pamphlets coming out of the Constitutional debate, the French Revolution, or the domestic events of the 1790s found their way into the library. Like their lectures, the students' reading material came from an earlier era.[88]

For Hampden-Sydney there is no direct evidence of the political cast given the instruction. Student extracurricular activity suggests that the campus atmosphere was mildly Republican, but that political questions were not much agitated. The Hampden-Sydney debating club, the Union Society, addressed what could be called partisan political issues only four times between 1793 and 1796 when the records temporarily end. The decisions were anti-administration. Students disapproved of England's declaration of war against France in 1793, objected to the Jay Treaty in 1795, and the next year opposed paying off debts in accordance with the treaty. In domestic affairs, the society decided that the United States would be better off to abandon central government and proceed on their own. These stances were consistent with John Powell Cocke's 1799 commencement oration on the "Republican Government of France." While condemning the atrocities of the Revolution, he argued that the country was better off than before it took place. And, looking askance at American critics of the Revolution, he asked "who is that friend of equal rights of man but will acknowledge the condition of man is meliorating?"[89] For Liberty Hall and Hampden-Sydney, then, all we have are hints that the campuses were mildly involved with politics, probably of a Republican stamp. They certainly did not display the political intensity of their sister institution, William and Mary.

Compared to the older colleges, few of these new institutions demonstrated the same political enthusiasm. Partisan instruction occurred less often, student agitation was generally mild. Some schools, like Union, Williams, and the University of North Carolina, were clearly politicized and partisan, but most campuses were not. As we have seen, the reasons for this political indifference included incomplete collegiate development, faculty preoccupation with other matters (usually religion), and the exaltation of religious rather than secular values by some student communities. But yet another reason for the lack of politicization and partisan enthusiasm appeared in the records of the backcountry collegians: the search for an identity in which could be blended the desirable traits of frontier life with what these students perceived as mainstream Americanism.

Even some political issues of special significance to the backcountry disclosed the search. Questions arose concerning an act for the recovery of debts, the excise tax, internal improvements, whether total ownership of land should be limited to 1,000 acres, and ultimately "Whether would it be most consistent with the interest of the United States for it to continue with its present government or for each state to be governed by its own legislature?" Just what should constitute the relationship of the central government to the backcountry was a matter of concern. Moreover, the repeated debates on the justice and propriety of Negro slavery suggest that the issue was of special interest to the frontier. That the heightened sense of equality characteristic of the frontier was offended by slavery was confirmed by a North Carolina debate on "whether have not the Africans as good a right to enslave the Americans as the Americans have to enslave the Africans?" Another racial question haunting the frontier was that of the Indians. Frontiersmen resembled other Americans when they asked if "the Europeans were justified in driving out the native Americans and taking possession of the land for themselves?" Then came the local question, "Whether it is justifiable to drive off the Indians or not?" Deciding that it was, the debates then shifted to immediate policy and practice: "Whether is the war now carried on against the Indians just," "Is the treaty made with the Indians by General Wayne profitable to the United States," "Would it be politic in the government to give a premium for all Indian scalps," and "the land in the western territories ought to be taken from the Indians without giving them any restitution."[90]

Troubled by their relations with the Negro, the Indian, and the rest of the nation, the frontier college students may have sensed some irony in their constantly reiterated question, "Whether mankind in the savage or civilized state enjoys the most happiness?" Who was civilized, blacks, Indians, themselves? The question was symptomatic of the identity problems reflected in other debates. On the one hand, many students hastened to participate in the political concerns of the nation, and all indulged in common philosophical speculations with their peers at older colleges: "Whether all children who die in infancy before they know their right hand from their left, or distinguishing good from evil, will be saved or not," "is matter eternal," "whether is honor or interest the most likely motive to action," "whether is liberal education or riches the greatest recommendation," and "whether a man in public or private life enjoys the most happiness?"[91] These questions and others like them were asked at institutions old and new, north and south. They gave the students a chance to think about what they had learned from ethics, moral philosophy, and divinity. That they were asked in both the old and new colleges demonstrates the common bond of learning uniting them, and shows that both country and city people shared convictions on the desirability of such knowledge.

On the other hand, there were questions, some even asked at both frontier and lowcountry colleges, that showed a different concern and were less symptomatic of unity. When a frontier student asked "Which is more preferable, country or city life?" it probably did not reflect pastoral supremacy. So, too, the question "Whether solitude or society is best adapted to form a useful character"; it took on greater meaning on the sparsely settled frontier. The Hampden-Sydney student's query "whether is the contemplation of the works of nature or art most calculated to improve and please the mind?" combined with "Whether is the lowcountry or backcountry the most eligible seat?" to show deep reserve about his surroundings, where works of art outside nature were few. A debate on "whether is duelling consistent with the laws of honor and justice?" was significant in a society where the legal institutions were weak, where personal honor was important, and where most men were armed. Students in such a society might well ask also "Whether the trial by jury is best calculated to produce equity and justice in society?" or "Whether do men's moral characters become better in proportion as the society in which they live becomes more civilized?" because they wanted these questions answered.[92] The very act of attending college was a commitment to civilization as well as to learning, a statement that students wanted some of the trappings of society they or their parents had left behind. But they did not want them all and did not want them to the same degree. At some colleges, at least, it was enough to fend off barbarism. Politicization could wait.

The internal dynamics of these colleges, old and new, have revealed a continuing commitment to state service education and an effort to implement a suitable curriculum, although we can readily see that substantial differences existed between old and new colleges and even within each group in their attempts to live up to their political heritage. The overall trend at the frontier colleges indicated a lesser degree of politicization and more concern with the religious and cultural imperatives of the settlement experience. Thus the colleges in the years after the Revolution did not follow a unified path. Against that backdrop, the third element of the English legacy as it applied to post-Revolutionary higher education remains to be considered. Just how did government carry out its acknowledged responsibility to foster colleges that served the state in an era when not all college communities agreed on its necessity?

NOTES

1. Charles Coleman Sellers, *Dickinson College: A History* (Middletown, Conn.: Wesleyan University Press, 1973), 22–31, 43; James H. Morgan, *Dickinson College, 1783–1833* (Carlisle, Penn.: Dickinson College, 1933) 2, 6.

2. Sellers, *Dickinson College*, 48–49, 54; David F. Hawke, *Benjamin Rush: Revolutionary Gadfly* (Indianapolis: Bobbs-Merrill Co., 1971), 283, 386–87; BR to John Dickinson, May 5, 1787, *Rush Letters*, I, 416.

3. Hawke, *Revolutionary Gadfly*, 286–87; Morgan, *Dickinson, 1783–1833*, 10; BR to John Armstrong, March 19, 1783, *Rush Letters*, I, 294.

4. Hawke, *Revolutionary Gadfly*, 284–85; Whitfield J. Bell, "Bulwark of Liberty," *Bulwark of Liberty*, Vol. I of the Boyd Lee Spahr Lectures in Americana (4 vols. thus far, Carlisle, Pa.: Fleming H. Revell Co., 1950–   ), 32–34; BR to John Montgomery, November 5, 1782, *Rush Letters*, I, 292. Rush continued to look upon Dickinson's role as primarily political. He informed John Jay in 1785 that "This college is at present wholly in the hands of gentlemen of liberal minds—men who have been uniformly friendly to the Union of the States and the power of Congress, and opposed to those romantic ideas of government which are generally destructive of liberty & republicanism." BR to John Jay, January 16, 1785 (DCA).

5. Sellers, *Dickinson College*, 54; Morgan, *Dickinson, 1783–1833*, 12–14; BR to John King, April 2, 1783, *Rush Letters*, I, 298; Dickinson College, Trustees' Minutes (DCA), I, 35.

6. James A. Bonar, "The Forms of Dickinson College, 1782–83" (unpublished Ms., DCA).

7. The men were classics professors James Ross, Henry Lyon Davis, and William Thompson, along with Robert Johnston and James McCormick, who taught natural philosophy. Sellers, *Dickinson College*, 45, 92, 94–95; "Henry Lyon Davis," *NCAB*, I, 504.

8. *DAB*, s.v. "Robert Davidson"; Sellers, *Dickinson College*, 66, 72–73; Robert Davidson, *An Oration, on the Independence of the United States of America, Delivered on the 4th of July, 1787* (Carlisle, Pa., 1787), quotation 14.

9. *DAB*, s.v. "Robert Davidson"; "Robert Davidson," *AAP*, III, 322–26; Robert Davidson, *A Sermon, on the Freedom and Happiness of the United States of America, Presented in Carlisle, on the 5th October, 1794...* (Philadelphia, 1794), quotation 24–

25; Robert Davidson, "Funeral Oration on the Death of General George Washington," *The Washingtoniana* (Lancaster, Pa.: R. Hamilton, 1802), 280–86.

10. Samuel Miller, *Memoir of the Reverend Charles Nisbet, D.D.* (New York: Robert Carter, 1840), 15–19, 29–30, 74; James H. Smylie, "Charles Nisbet: Second Thoughts on a Revolutionary Generation," *Pennsylvania Magazine of History and Biography*, 98 (1974): 189–90; Caroline Robbins, *The Eighteenth-Century Commonwealthmen: Studies in the Transmission, Development and Circumstances of English Liberal Thought from the Restoration of Charles II until the War with the Thirteen Colonies* (Cambridge, Mass.: Harvard University Press, 1959), 179; Charles Nisbet to John Witherspoon, April 3, 1784 (Historical Society of Pennsylvania).

11. Smylie, "Second Thoughts," 191–92.

12. Charles Nisbet to the Earl of Buchan, September 16, 1788 (DCA); Charles Nisbet to William Marshall, October 2, 1800 (Presbyterian Historical Society).

13. Smylie, "Second Thoughts," 195–96; Charles Nisbet to William Young, March 22, 1793 (DCA).

14. Smylie, "Second Thoughts," 197–98; Miller, *Memoir of Nisbet*, 227–29; Charles Nisbet to William Young, April 5, 1797 (DCA).

15. This trustee profile derives from Robert L. Brunhouse, *The Counter-Revolution in Pennsylvania, 1776–1790* (Harrisburg: Pennsylvania Historical Commission, 1942); James McLachlan, ed., *Princetonians, 1748–1768: A Biographical Dictionary* (Princeton: Princeton University Press, 1976); Richard A. Harrison, ed., *Princetonians, 1769–1776: A Biographical Dictionary* (Princeton: Princeton University Press, 1980); David Hackett Fischer, *The Revolution in American Conservatism: The Federalist Party in the Era of Jeffersonian Democracy* (New York: Harper & Row, 1965); Jacob E. Cooke, *Tench Coxe and the Early Republic* (Chapel Hill: University of North Carolina Press, 1978).

16. Sellers, *Dickinson College*, 65, 115–32.

17. By 1787, Rush had become dismayed by Nisbet's caustic critique of Pennsylvania affairs. He wrote to John Montgomery, noting that there was little difference between "Democratic" and "Federalist" money, and urged him to tone Nisbet down. Other trustees disagreed with Nisbet over college policies, but no criticism of his politics has survived. Bell, "Bulwark of Liberty," 52–53.

18. "Plan of Education for Dickinson College" (DCA).

19. See "The Honble the Board of Trustees of Dickinson College, from their very H^ble Servt Robt Davidson (May 10, 1786)", "State of Dickinson College...5th June, 1789," "Present State of Dickinson College, June 19th, 1798" (DCA).

20. Charles Nisbet to the Board of Trustees, July 29, 1799 (DCA); Joseph B. Smith, "A Frontier Experiment in Higher Education," *Bulwark of Liberty*, 90–91.

21. "Dickinson College, Trustees' Minutes," April 26, 1796; Robert Davidson, *Geography Epitomiz'd, or a Tour Round the World* (Philadelphia, 1784); Sellers, *Dickinson College*, 100–101.

22. *Columbian Magazine*, February 1787, inside cover; Marie E. Korey, *The Books of Isaac Norris (1701–1766) at Dickinson College* (Carlisle, Pa.: Dickinson College, 1976), 9, 32, 45, 75, 87, 104, 156, 235, 278, 279, 283, 292, 301; Sellers, *Dickinson College*, 114.

23. Excerpt from a book owned by Robert Smith, Class of 1790, in "Curricular Information" (DCA).

24. "Moral Philosophy Notes on Nisbet Lectures by John Young, 1787 [Jan.–Mar.]" (DCA), 9–10, 36–38, 39, 45, 72–73; Moral Philosophy Lecture, March 5, 1789, Nisbet,

"Lectures on Moral Philosophy" (Speer Library, Princeton Theological Seminary), quoted in Smylie, "Second Thoughts," 194.

25. "Questions and Answers on Moral Philosophy, Alexander Boyd's Notes, 1793" (DCA), 27, 29–30, 32–33, 291–92, 309–10, 336–37.

26. "Robert Davidson, Lecture Notes of Caspar Willis Weaver on Chronology & History, 1792" (DCA), 247–73.

27. Charles Nisbet, "To the Students after Vacation, Oct. ____, 1787" (orig. in John Young Papers, Centre College, Kentucky; DCA), 3; Charles Nisbet, "To the Graduates at 3d Commencement June 2d. 1789" (orig. Young Papers, Centre Coll.; DCA), 22–23.

28. Morgan, *Dickinson, 1783–1833*, quotation 113; Carl B. Swisher, "The Education of Roger B. Taney," *Bulwark of Liberty*, 157.

29. "Belles Lettres Society Minutes" (DCA), August 31, December 14, 24, 1793, February 27, March 22, July 12, 1794.

30. Quoted in Smith, "Frontier Experiment," 94; *Kline's Weekly Carlisle Gazette*, October 7, 1795, October 4, 1797, October 3, 1798; "Belles Lettres Society Minutes", March 19, 1796, April 28, December 8, 1798; "The Address of the Students of Dickinson College to the President of the United States," *Universal Gazette* (Philadelphia), July 12, 1798.

31. Smith, "Frontier Experiment," 77–78, 80, 94; Morgan, *Dickinson, 1783–1833*, 152–53, 162; *Kline's Weekly Carlisle Gazette*, January 2, 1788.

32. "Belles Lettres Society Minutes," August 1, 1788, August 22, 1789, ? 1791, March 2, 1793, June 20, 1795, March 30, 1798.

33. Robert S. Volz, *Governor Bowdoin and His Family: A Guide to an Exhibition* (Brunswick, Me.: Bowdoin College, 1969), 31–32; "Franklin College Trustees' Circular of January 19, 1787," quoted in Frederick S. Klein, *The Spiritual and Educational Background of Franklin and Marshall College* (Lancaster, Pa.: Franklin & Marshall College, 1939), 34; *North Carolina Journal*, July 10, 1793, quoted in *Doc. Hist. UNC*, I, 226; "Minutes of the Albany-Schenectady Town Meeting, 1794" (UCA); Ira Allen, "Memorial to the Assembly of New York, January 27, 1792" (UVtA); William Smith, *An Account of Washington College* (Philadelphia, 1784), 4; William Kilty, ed., *The Laws of Maryland* (2 vols., Annapolis, 1799–1800), Chapter 8, 1782, Chapter 37, 1784.

34. *Va. Stat.*, XI, 271–74; *Doc. Hist. Educ.*, II, 495–500; George Roulstone, ed., *The Laws of the State of Tennessee* (Knoxville: n.p., 1803), 43–44; "Charter of the University of Georgia" (UGA).

35. Perry Miller, "From the Covenant to the Revival," James W. Smith and A. Leland Jamieson, eds., *Religion in American Life: The Shaping of American Religion* (Princeton: Princeton University Press, 1961), 352–53; Howard G. Miller, *The Revolutionary College: American Presbyterian Higher Education, 1707–1837* (New York: New York University Press, 1976), 103–89.

36. "Michael Schlatter's 'Appeal'," quoted in Klein, *Franklin and Marshall*, 13; "Kentucky Academy Papers" (Shane Collection, Presbyterian Historical Society), no. 8; Roulstone, ed., *Laws of Tennessee*, 44–45; E. Merton Coulter, *College Life in the Old South* (2d ed., Athens, Ga.: University of Georgia Press, 1951), 4–5; "Extracts from the Journal of the House of Representatives," Acts of the General Court of Massachusetts Concerning Bowdoin College (BCA), Feb. 7, 1788, June 3, 1791; Calvin Durfee, *A History of Williams College* (Boston: A. Williams & Co., 1860), 62; "Albany-Schenectady Town Meeting, 1794."

37. *Doc. Hist. UNC*, I, 22–23, 209; F. H. Dewart et al., eds., *The State Papers of Vermont* (8 vols., Montpelier: n.p., 1919–1939), IV, 127.

38. J.H. Easterby, *A History of the College of Charleston* (Charleston: n.p., 1935), 17.

39. Leverett W. Spring, *A History of Williams College* (Boston and New York: Houghton Mifflin Co., 1917), 45, 67–69; "Ebenezer Fitch," *AAP*, III, 511–15; Ebenezer Fitch to Peter Van Schaak, Aug. 18, 1795, and to Isaac Beers, July 20, 1798, quoted in Arthur L. Perry, *Williamstown and Williams College* (New York: C. Scribner's Sons, 1899), 234, 239; "Stephen West," *AAP*, I, 548–56; Stephen West, *A Sermon, Delivered on the Public Fast, April 9th, 1801* (Stockbridge, Mass., 1901).

40. Perry, *Williamstown and Williams College*, 230; William Bryans, "College Trustees in the New Republic: A Biographical Examination of the Boards of Trustees for Union and Williams Colleges, 1793–1800" (unpublished seminar paper, University of Wyoming, 1981); "Free School and College Records" (WCA), October 20, 1794; Richard E. Welch, Jr., *Theodore Sedgwick, Federalist: A Political Profile* (Middletown, Conn.: Wesleyan University Press, 1965).

41. *DAB*, s.v. "John Blair Smith"; "John Blair Smith," *AAP*, III, 397–404; "John Blair Smith," Harrison, ed., *Princetonians, 1769–1776*, 342–46; "John Taylor," ibid., 111–15; "Andrew Yeates," *AAP*, IX, 126–38; Dixon R. Fox, *Union College: An Unfinished History* (Schenectady: Union College, 1945), 12.

42. *DAB*, s.v. "Jonathan Edwards, Jr."; "Jonathan Edwards, Jr.," *AAP*, I, 653–60; "Jonathan Edwards, Jr.," McLachlan, ed., *Princetonians, 1748–1768*, 492–96; Robert L. Ferm, *Jonathan Edwards the Younger, 1745–1801* (Grand Rapids, Mich.: Eerdman's, 1976), 68–170; Jonathan Edwards, Jr., *A Sermon Delivered at the Funeral of the Honorable Roger Shermon* (sic) (New Haven, 1793) and *The Necessity of the Belief of Christianity By the Citizens of the State, in Order to Our Political Prosperity* (Hartford, 1791).

43. Bryans, "College Trustees in the New Republic"; Codman Hislop, *Eliphalet Nott* (Middletown, Conn: Wesleyan University Press, 1971), 47.

44. Julian I. Lindsay, *Tradition Looks Forward. The University of Vermont: A History* (Burlington: University of Vermont and State Agricultural College, 1954), 28–29; David M. Ludlum, *Social Ferment in Vermont, 1791–1850* (New York: Columbia University Press, 1939), 11–14, 23; William A. Robinson, *Jeffersonian Democracy in New England* (New Haven: Yale University Press, 1916), 9, 12–13, 16, 19, 21–23, 33; David M. Stameshkin, "The Town's College: Middlebury College, 1800–1915" (Ph.D. Diss., University of Michigan, 1978), 56; "Daniel Clarke Sanders," *AAP*, VIII, 226–29; Daniel Clarke Sanders, *A Sermon, Preached Before the . . . Council and House of Representatives of the State of Vermont, October 11, 1798 . . . on Occasion of the General Election* (Vergennes, Vt., 1798) and *A Discourse Pronounced at Burlington, Vermont, in Commemoration of General George Washington* (Burlington, 1801).

45. Louis C. Hatch, *The History of Bowdoin College* (Portland: Loring, Short, & Harmon, 1927), 5–6; *Biographical Record of Alumni and Officers of Bowdoin College, 1794–1950* (Brunswick, Maine: Bowdoin College, 1950), 5–12.

46. Joseph H. Dubbs, *History of Franklin & Marshall College* (Lancaster, Pa.: Franklin & Marshall College Alumni Association, 1903), 25–26; Klein, *Franklin and Marshall*, 41–53.

47. *DAB*, s.v. "John W. Hendel," "Friederich Melsheimer," and "Gotthilf Henry Muhlenburg"; "Gotthilf Henry Muhlenburg," *AAP*, IX, 59–66.

48. "General Catalogue of Hampden-Sydney College" (H-SCA), 13–16; Herbert C. Bradshaw, History of Hampden-Sydney College: Volume I, From the Beginnings to the Year 1856 (privately printed, 1976), 16–63. Additional information on the politics of the trustees appears in Lisle A. Rose, Prologue to Democracy: The Federalists in the South, 1789–1800 (Lexington, Ky.: University of Kentucky Press, 1968), Norman K. Risjord, Chesapeake Politics, 1781–1800 (New York: Columbia University Press, 1978), and Richard Beeman, The Old Dominion & the New Nation, 1788–1801 (Lexington, Ky.: University of Kentucky Press, 1972).

49. Bradshaw, History of Hampden-Sydney, 83–87; DAB, s.v. "John Blair Smith"; "John Blair Smith," Harrison, ed., Princetonians, 1769–1776, 342–46; John Blair Smith to James Madison, June 21, 1784, c. May 16, 1785, June 12, 1788, John Dawson to James Madison, September 25, 1787, Robert Rutland et al., eds., The Papers of James Madison (14 vols. thus far, Chicago and Charlottesville: University of Chicago Press and University Press of Virginia, 1956–), VIII, 80–82, 282, XI, 119–21, X, 173.

50. Allen E. Ragan, A History of Tusculum College, 1794–1944 (n.p., 1945), 2, 4, 8–9; Thomas P. Abernethey, From Frontier to Plantation in Tennessee: A Study in Frontier Democracy (orig. 1935; reprint, Tuscaloosa: University of Alabama Press, 1967); Robert E. Corlew, Tennessee: A Short History (2d ed., Knoxville: University of Tennessee Press, 1981); "Hezekiah Balch," McLachlan, ed., Princetonians, 1748–1768, 545–48; "Hezekiah Balch," AAP, III, 308–19.

51. John D. Wright, Jr., Transylvania: Tutor to the West (Lexington: University of Kentucky Press, 1975), 8–24; Neils H. Sonne, Liberal Kentucky, 1780–1828 (New York: Columbia University Press, 1939), 47–48; William H. Whitsitt, The Life and Times of Judge Caleb Wallace (Louisville: J.P. Morton & Co., 1888), 108, 115–16.

52. Wright, Transylvania, 24–32; Sonne, Liberal Kentucky, 48–66; Charles R. Staples, The History of Pioneer Lexington (Kentucky), 1779–1806 (Lexington, Ky.: Transylvania Press, 1939), 107–8, 147; Robert Davidson, A History of the Presbyterian Church in the State of Kentucky (New York: R. Carter, 1847), 289–91.

53. Sonne, Liberal Kentucky, 28, 67; DAB, s.v. "James Moore"; Patricia Watlington, The Partisan Spirit: Kentucky Politics, 1779–1792 (Chapel Hill: University of North Carolina Press, 1972), 188, 191, 201, 216–22; DAB, s.v. "Harry Toulmin" and "George Nicholas"; Charles Kerr, "Transylvania University's Law Department," Americana, 31 (1937): 9–11, 13–15; Thomas D. Clark, A History of Kentucky (Lexington, Ky.: University of Kentucky Press, 1954), 107–8; George Nicholas, A Letter from George Nicholas of Kentucky to a Friend in Virginia (Lexington, Ky., 1798) and The Proceedings of the House of Representatives of the United States (Philadelphia, 1799), 22–32; DAB, s.v. "James Brown"; Wright, Transylvania, 44.

54. Kemp P. Battle, History of the University of North Carolina (2 vols., orig. 1907; reprint, Spartanburg, S.C.: The Reprint Co., 1974), I, 6; Henry W. Wagstaff, "Federalism in North Carolina," James Sprunt Historical Publications, 9 (1910): 3–21, 25–26, 44.

55. Battle, History of University of North Carolina, I, 100–103; Henry W. Wagstaff, "The Harris Letters," James Sprunt Historical Publications, 14 (1914): 16n. 34n, 6–7, 9–10, 13–16, 22–23; DAB, s.v. "Joseph Caldwell."

56. "Charter of the University of Georgia" (UGA); Rose, Prologue to Democracy, 26, 45, 59–69, 91–98, 186–87; E. Merton Coulter, "The Birth of a University, a Town, and a County," Georgia Historical Quarterly, 46 (1962): 142–46; DAB, s.v. "Josiah Meigs"; William Meigs, The Life of Josiah Meigs (Philadelphia: J.P. Murphy, 1887), 44–45.

57. Not discussed here are the College of Charleston, where the political involvement of the trustees and faculty members resembles the Universities of North Carolina and Georgia, but with a Federalist dominance; Liberty Hall (later Washington College) in Virginia, where the pattern of political activity essentially duplicates that of Hampden-Sydney, except that William Graham reversed John Blair Smith's positions on the Virginia religious assessment bill and the Constitution; and the two Maryland colleges, St. John's and Washington, too few of whose trustees can be traced to enable meaningful generalization.

58. I can find no evidence of Greeneville College's pre–1800 curriculum. The University of Vermont and Bowdoin College, although planning, had developed no courses of study by 1800.

59. "Petition of Trustees of German College and Charity School in Lancaster to Pennsylvania General Assembly, December 11, 1786," quoted in Saul Sack, *History of Higher Education in Pennsylvania* (2 vols., Harrisburg: Pennsylvania Historical Commission, 1963), I, 114; Klein, *Franklin and Marshall*, 53–54, 60–61; Dubbs, *Franklin & Marshall*, 71–77, 81–86, 89.

60. Easterby, *College of Charleston*, 1–18, 27–47; Colyer Meriwether, *History of Higher Education in South Carolina* (Washington, D.C.: Government Printing Office, 1889), 56–57; "Account Book of Robert Smith" (CCA); Charleston *City Gazette and Daily Advertiser*, July 2, 1799, October 7, 1800; *DAB*, s.v. "Robert Smith"; "Robert Smith," *AAP*, V, 170–73.

61. Spring, *History of Williams*, 32–33, 39–40; "Free School and College Records," August 6, 1793, August 20, 1794, September 2, 1795; "Laws of Yale College, 1787" (YUA); "The Laws of Williams College, 1795" (WCA); Durfee, *History of Williams*, 69–72, 65, 84; Increase N. Tarbox, ed., *The Diary of Thomas Robbins, 1796–1854* (2 vols., Boston: T. Todd, 1886), I, 1, 6, 15, 16. The full title of Hopkins' work is *The System of Doctrine Contained in Divine Revelation, Explained and Defended Showing their Consistence and Connection with Each Other* (Boston, 1793).

62. "Laws and Regulations for the Government of Union College, 1795" (UCA); "Union College Trustees' Minutes" (UCA), January 20, April 30, September 3, 1799; Samuel B. Fortenbaugh, Jr., *In Order to Form a More Perfect Union: An Inquiry into the Origins of a College* (Schenectady: Union College Press, 1978), 104–5. The trustees had to ask Jonathan Edwards, Jr., to upgrade the English offering, apparently to no avail; cf. "The Laws of Union College, 1802" (UCA). Works not previously cited are: Hugh Blair, *Lectures on Rhetoric and Belles Lettres* (2 vols., orig. 1783; Philadelphia, 1784); Charles Rollin, *Method of Teaching and Studying the Belles Lettres* (3d ed., London, 1742); *The Poetical Works of John Milton* (orig. 1695; Philadelphia, 1791); *The Works of Joseph Addison* (4 vols., London, 1721); Thomas Jefferson, *Notes on the State of Virginia* (Philadelphia, 1788); *The Works of Edmund Burke* (8 vols., London, 1792–1827).

63. Albert F. Gegenheimer, *William Smith, Educator and Churchman, 1727–1803* (Philadelphia: University of Pennsylvania Press, 1943), 82–83; George H. Callcott, *A History of the University of Maryland* (Baltimore: Maryland Historical Society, 1966), 13; Smith, *Account of Washington College;* "Dedication of Washington College, 1788" (WaCA).

64. Callcott, *University of Maryland*, 14; "St. John's College Board of Visitors and Governors Minute Book, Vol. I" (St.JCA), July 5, 1792.

65. Herbert C. Bradshaw, *A History of Prince Edward County, Virginia, 1754–1954* (Richmond: Dietz Press, 1955), 141; Donald R. Come, "The Influence of Princeton on

Higher Education in the South before 1825," *WMQ*, 2 (1945): 371–74; William H. Foote, *Sketches of Virginia, Historical and Biographical* (2 vols., Philadelphia: W.S. Martin, 1850–1855), I, 397, 404; James W. Alexander, *The Life of Archibald Alexander* (New York: C. Scribner, 1854), 200; *Virginia Gazette* (Dixon & Hunter), October 7, 1775; "Hampden-Sydney Records" (H-SCA), June 23, 1784, September 2, 1785; Samuel Blair, *An Account of the College of New Jersey* (Woodbridge, N.J., 1764), 24–25; Francis L. Broderick, "Pulpit, Physics, and Politics: The Curriculum of the College of New Jersey, 1746–1794," *WMQ*, 6 (1949): 62–63; "College Laws, 1794" (PUA).

66. Come, "Influence of Princeton," 383; "Trustees' Minutes, February 6, 1795" and "Charles W. Harris to Dr. Charles Harris, April 18, 1795," *Doc. Hist. UNC*, I, 360–61, 387–89; Battle, *History of University of North Carolina*, I, 94–97, quotation 97; "College Laws, 1794" (PUA).

67. Thomas W. Reed, "History of the University of Georgia" (19 vols., unpublished Ms., UGA), I, 6; E. Merton Coulter, *Georgia: A Short History* (Chapel Hill: University of North Carolina Press, 1947), 188–89, 96, 107; Henry C. White, *Abraham Baldwin* (Athens, Ga.: University of Georgia Press, 1926), 154–71; "Literary Diary," *Stiles Papers M*, XII, 5, 137, XIII, 103–3; Meigs, *Life of Meigs*, 40–43.

68. O. Burton Adams, "Yale Influence on the Formation of the University of Georgia," *Georgia Historical Quarterly*, 51 (1967): 180–81; Coulter, *College Life in the Old South*, 15–16; "University of Georgia Trustees' Minutes" (UGA), June 1801; "Minutes of the Senatus Academicus" (UGA), November 27, 1800; Ezra Stiles, "Yale College Memoranda, 1793–1794" (YUA). Works not previously cited: Nicholas Pike, *A New and Complete System of Arithmetic* (Newburyport, Mass. 1788); *The Works of Alexander Pope* (2 vols., London, 1717–1735); *The Works of Jonathan Swift* (4 vols., Dublin, 1735).

69. Charles Fraser, *Reminiscences of Charleston* (Charleston: J. Russell, 1854), 43–47; Easterby, *College of Charleston*, 36–37, 45–46; Augustus Longstreet Hill, *A Historical Sketch of the University of Georgia* (Atlanta: The Foote & Davies Co., 1894), 18; Coulter, *College Life in the Old South*, 18–19.

70. Smith, *Account of Washington College*, 4, 18; John McDowell, "Commencement Address," n.d. (Ms., Maryland Hall of Records), 11.

71. Tarbox, ed., *Diary of Robbins*, I, 1, 6, 9, 16; Ebenezer Fitch, *Useful Knowledge and Religion, Recommended to the Pursuit and Improvement of the Young, in a Discourse, Addressed to the Candidates for the Baccalaureate in Williams College, September 1, 1799* (Pittsfield, 1799), 27–28.

72. Spring, *History of Williams*, 56, 67–68; *A Catalogue of Books in the Library of Williams College* (Bennington, Vt., 1794); Tarbox, ed., *Diary of Robbins*, I, 7, 8, 11, 13, 14, 15, 17, 18.

73. Spring, *History of Williams*, 49; *Commencement at Williams College, September 6, 1797. Order of Exercises* (Bennington, Vt., 1797); *Commencement at Williams College, September 4, 1799. Order of Exercises* (Pittsfield, 1799); *Commencement at Williams College, September 3, 1800. Order of Exercises* (Stockbridge, Mass. 1800) .

74. Quoted in Spring, *History of Williams*, 329–30.

75. "Laws and Regulations for the Government of Union College, 1795'"; "Curriculum of Union College, 1795" (Ms., UCA); John Blair Smith, "On the Education of Youth" (typescript trans. of inaugural address, 1796, UCA), 3–4; "Union College, Board of Trustees' Minutes" (UCA), June 1796.

76. George Bancker to Abraham Bancker, June 21, December 10, 1798 (Ms., UCA);

Arthur A. Richmond, III, "Jonathan Edwards, Jr., and Union College," Union College Symposium, 1968 (Ms., UCA).

77. "Minutes of the Philomathean Society" (Ms., UCA), March 27, June 26, September 4, December 11, 1794, April 23, July 23, 1795, February 25, 1796, March ?, 1797, April 12, June 28, September 13, November 8, 1798, April 4, June 27, November 21, 1799.

78. Lack of evidence prevents the forming of conclusions about Transylvania, although John Wright notes that in 1799 Professor James Welch was brought to a sort of internal collegiate tribunal, accused by students of interfering in their debating clubs and of ridiculing students who espoused Jeffersonian views. At first the trustees, mostly Republicans, defended Welch from student criticism, but they retreated when fifteen students threatened to leave the college. *Transylvania*, 42–43.

79. "John Pettigrew to Charles Pettigrew, April 12, 1796," *Doc. Hist. UNC*, II, 11–12; Charles W. Harris to Joseph Caldwell, July 24, 1796, Wagstaff, ed., "Harris Letters," 29–33.

80. "Dialectic Society Records" (Microfilm copy, UNCA), July 30, 1795, September 8, 15, October 5, 12, November 9, 1796.

81. "Philanthropic Society Records" (Microfilm copy, UNCA), March 22, May 10, September 20, 27, November 8, 1796.

82. "Student Records and Faculty Reports" (UNCA), November 11, 1799, March 27, 1800; Joseph Caldwell, *Eulogy on George Washington...on the Twenty-Second of February, 1800* (Raleigh, 1800), quotation 29; Battle, *History of University of North Carolina*, I, 155; "An Attack on Samuel Holmes, 1798," *Doc. Hist. UNC*, II, 383–84.

83. "Dialectic Society Records," February 7, April 21, 27, May 25, June 1, 22, August 18, 1797, March 2, 15, August 3, 30, September 13, 1798; "Philanthropic Society Records," February 2, March 30, April 4, 25, May 2, June 20, 1797, February 6, March 6, May 29, June 5, July 31, 1798.

84. "Philanthropic Society Records," June 12, 1798.

85. "Dialectic Society Records," September 13, 1798, January 25, 31, March 20, 27, April 18, 1799; "Philanthropic Society Records," January 29, February 19, May 14, July 30, August 27, October 22, 1799.

86. Battle, *History of University of North Carolina*, I, 155–59; Blackwell P. Robinson, *William R. Davie* (Chapel Hill: University of North Carolina Press, 1957), 265; Samuel McCorkle to John Haywood, December 9, 1799 (Ernest Haywood Collection, Southern Historical Collections, University of North Carolina).

87. William Graham, "Lectures on Human Nature. Notes taken by Joseph Glass, 1796" (Ms., WLUA), 137–59; Ollinger Crenshaw, *General Lee's College: The Rise and Growth of Washington and Lee University* (New York: Random House, 1969), 23.

88. "A List of Books and Apparatus belonging to the Academy of Liberty Hall, 1776" (Ms., WLUA); Betty Ruth Kondayan, "The Library of Liberty Hall Academy," *Virginia Magazine of History and Biography*, 86 (1978): 432–36.

89. "Union Society Minutes" (H-SCA), June 21, 1793, September 1, 1795, January 22, March 25, 1796; Bradshaw, *Hampden-Sydney*, 107.

90. *Doc. Hist. UNC*, I, 504, 491, II, 140, 270, 127, 250; "Belles Lettres Society Minutes," March 2, 1793, June 20, August 1, 1795, January 13, 1796; "Union Society Minutes," July 19, 1783, November 27, 1795, January 22, 1796. For an analysis of the problems of the west and their implication for western self-definition, see Edmund S. Morgan, "Conflict and Consensus in the American Revolution," Stephen G. Kurtz and

James H. Hutson, eds., *Essays on the American Revolution* (Chapel Hill: University of North Carolina Press, 1973), 297–306.

91. The question of civilization arose repeatedly. Cf. "Belles Lettres Society Minutes," March 30, 1798, January 19, November 23, 1799; *Doc. Hist. UNC*, I, 488, 489, 495, II, 150, for example. "Belles Lettres Society Minutes," January 6, March 9, 1797; "Union Society Minutes," March 3, 1792, January 26, 1793; *Doc. Hist. UNC*, I, 498.

92. "Records of the Calliopian Society," August 20, 1795, April 3, 1797; "Union Society Minutes," February 24, 1792, December 4, 1795; *Doc. Hist. UNC*, I, 487, II, 274; "Belles Lettres Society Minutes," August 1, 1788.

7

Government and Higher Education in the New Republic

After the Revolution, the contention that America's colleges had an obligation to educate for service to the state met no challenge, but we have seen that old and new colleges fulfilled that obligation in different ways, with the new placing less emphasis upon it. Because of the differences, the various American governments faced a challenge in implementing the third element of the English educational legacy, the responsibility to oversee higher education.

Certainly there was no end to public injunctions that proper education was necessary to the survival of the republic. It would produce public virtue, the essential underpinning of the republican form of government. Supporters of the Revolution all over the country would have agreed with the sentiments of the Massachusetts minister Philips Payson: "despotism and tyranny want nothing but wealth and force, but liberty and order are supported by knowledge and virtue." The general diffusion of knowledge was "the likeliest means to beget and improve that public virtue."[1]

Many Americans agreed that the proponent of this diffusion of knowledge should be the state. It was again in Massachusetts where the idea was stated most clearly. Simeon Howard told his audience at election day ceremonies in 1780 that it was "of great importance to their happiness...that virtue generally prevail among a people: and, in order to [accomplish] this, government should use its influence to promote it." It was fitting "that the government should take all proper measures for this purpose—making provision for the establishment and support of literary schools and colleges."[2]

Others agreed. Magistrates should "endeavor to suppress vice and immorality" by lending "all necessary assistance to our schools and colleges; it being a matter of high political importance that knowledge should be diffused through...all ranks of men" because "the propagation of literature is connected with the security of freedom." The universality of virtuous education was important. Many Americans joined with the anonymous essayist in *The American Museum* in believing that the fate of republics "depends on the knowledge or ignorance of the great body of the people," thus "while education is a bulwark against tyranny, it is the grand palladium of true liberty in a republican government." Knowledge, then, was "not only necessary in rulers to qualify them to fulfill public posts with dignity and reputation: but also in the people to make them good subjects.''[3] Education, including higher education, was inextricably linked in the public mind with the preservation of republicanism. It was the state's duty to forge those links into indissoluble bonds.

To these admonitions the states responded in different ways. Some created a new order in higher education by establishing state-wide educational systems capped by colleges; some founded more modest but clearly state-controlled institutions; some demanded governmental presence on the boards of existing colleges; and some were content merely to charter private institutions. This variety in the relations of governments and colleges reflected not only the differing ideas of various state legislatures, but also the different priorities of college communities and a lack of consensus among the people about the proper form of state-college links.

To many Americans the differing state-college relationships were unsettling. Those convinced that proper education underlay republicanism saw little room for debate about the links between governments and colleges. If the state governments could not or would not support republican higher education, then the national government should. The emphasis on state sovereignty that dominated the national government under the Articles of Confederation rendered a government-sponsored national university an unlikely creation.[4] But coincident with the campaign to strengthen the central government there arose a movement to produce a national university. The objectives drew support from many of the same people. For these promoters, strong centralized government and nationalized republican higher education were but complementary policies in their attempt to make America's future secure. They did not succeed in producing an institution, but the campaign quite clearly revealed tendencies that affected state government relations with colleges and analysis of its failure also indicates some of the difficulties besetting the states in their efforts to oversee higher education.

I

It was Benjamin Rush, already active in the affairs of the College of Philadelphia and Dickinson College, who began the political campaign to create a national collegiate institution. He was the educational thinker closest to the Patriot pulse in Philadelphia, where the Continental Congress met. There he heard the lamentations over the people's declining virtue, and himself despaired of their fate for a time, but Rush's confidence returned when men of ''education'' gained control of the Revolution, and he was cautiously optimistic at its end. Education was vital, thought Rush, to the success of the new republic: ''To conform the principles, morals, and manners of our citizens to our republican forms of government, it is absolutely necessary that knowledge of every kind should be disseminated through every part of the United States.'' His plan for this dissemination was twofold:

Let us have colleges in each of the states, and one federal university under the patronage of Congress, where the youth of all the states may be melted (as it were) together into one mass of citizens after they have first acquired the principles of knowledge in the colleges of their respective states. Let the law of nature and nations, the common law of our country, the differing systems of government, history, and everything else connected with the advance of republican knowledge and principles, be taught by able professors in this university.[5]

Rush promoted his ideas in "Thoughts Upon the Mode of Education Proper in a Republic." He argued that the first obligation of every American was to have a supreme regard for his country. To achieve it, education had to add the prop of prejudice to the citizen's patriotism. It must make him feel as if he were public property. It might allow him amusement, social life, and convenience, but it must impress upon him that study and business came first, that wealth amassed was to go to the state. Above all, the republican "must watch for the state as if its liberties depended upon his vigilance." He and his fellows must become republican "machines." Such an education could succeed only if grounded on the Christian religion, because Christianity developed virtue, the foundation of liberty. The student would learn that there was no enduring liberty but in a republic; that a republic, like the sciences, was progressive; and that it contained the means for promoting human happiness. A curriculum to instill these principles would consist of the learned languages, eloquence (the first accomplishment of a republic), history and chronology, economics, chemistry, the arts of war and practical legislation, the laws of the national government, and physical fitness through exercise.[6]

Having established this theoretical basis, Rush, in "An Address to the People of the United States," made his projection more concrete. Prompted by the imminent assembly of the Constitutional Convention, he criticized a number of governmental defects under the Articles of Confederation. Among the remedies he proposed was a restatement of republican education, this time embodied in a national university. It would teach everything connected with government: history, the law of nature and nations, civil and municipal law, the principles of commerce, the war arts (gunnery and fortification), and economics as it was taught in Europe, with the professor to have a travelling European correspondent to keep him advised of the latest developments. The institution would be post-graduate, thereby training only serious scholars. To further insure the university's success in determining the character of republican life in America, Rush proposed that after a certain time all the nation's honors and offices be confined to its graduates.[7]

To the Pennsylvanian, no better institutional achievement could come out of the convention than a university designed to train Americans in scientific skills and public virtue. However, Rush's plan lost something of its vision in the translation from the "Thoughts" of 1786 to the specific proposal aimed at the Convention. While Rush's plan would produce a university designed to inculcate public virtue and thus sustain the republic, the definition of public virtue he put forth was not one with which all could agree. At the same time he was designing his national school for statesmen, he was trying to overturn the Pennsylvania Constitution of 1776. He did not think that it had produced a true republic. It was too democratic; the wrong sort of people controlled the government. Of course, Rush's political opponents in Pennsylvania argued that they had produced a republic, one that quite successfully embodied the will of the people.[8]

Pennsylvania was not the only state in which Rush's definition of republicanism would have been questioned, and in one respect his critics were right. By the mid-1780s, Rush had become an elitist, at least with regard to manning the government. His proposal to confine the offices of government to graduates of his national university was the furthest step he took in the direction of elitism. It was a step that did not appeal to many of his countrymen.[9]

The Rush plan attracted the attention of some Federal Convention delegates, and may possibly have spurred their debate on the idea of a national university, but neither it nor any other specific plan was the focus of that debate. On August 18, 1787, James Madison twice proposed that the legislative branch of the government be empowered to establish a university. Nothing came of it. Later on in the deliberations, Madison and Charles Pinckney again suggested that the legislature establish a university ''in which no preference or distinction should be allowed on account of religion.'' After some debate the measure lost in a close vote. The reason is not known. It may have been, as Gouverneur Morris maintained, that the legislature's exclusive power over the seat of government eliminated the need for a provision to establish institutions there. It may have been, as Roger Sherman later recalled, that the delegates feared such a power infringed on state's rights. Or it may have been that the delegates did not have a specific plan in mind and so could not agree to an idea so nebulous.[10]

When the Constitutional Convention did not provide for a national university Rush turned again to the public to advocate his cause. In an October 1788 letter to the *Pennsylvania Gazette* he warned that the Constitution would not succeed ''unless the people are prepared for our new form of government by an education adapted to the new and peculiar situation of our country.'' Then came an elaboration on his plan for a national university, this time designed for a wider public, with a purpose larger than just the training of eminent governors, although that continued to loom large in his scheme. Still to be a post-graduate institution, it would offer the principles and the forms of government as set forth in the Constitution, together with the law of nature and nations; history, both ancient and modern, and chronology; agriculture; manufactures; the mathematics essential to property, to finance, and to war; those parts of natural philosophy and chemistry pertaining to agriculture, manufacturing, commerce, and war; natural history; philology, including rhetoric, criticism, and the structure and pronunciation of English; German and French; and athletics. A further extension of the previous plan called for travelling correspondents in both Europe and America reporting on daily advances in agriculture, manufacturing, commerce, the art of war, and the principles of good government. Again the honors and offices of the United States, after a period of thirty years, were to be restricted to the university's graduates.[11]

Rush's proposal was still remarkable for its specific elitism. All the honors and offices of the United States would be confined to those who possessed the intellectual prowess to complete a traditional college program and then survive several more years of training in a post-graduate specialty. As important as intellect would be the money necessary to support a student for as many as eight years of collegiate instruction, probably at a far remove from his home. If followed, Rush's scheme would produce government by an affluent intellectual aristocracy. And that, in less extreme form, was the essence of the Federalist stance with respect to social class and government. Viewed in this light, the Rush proposals by the late 1780s were aimed at producing not just republican happiness, but federalist republican happiness. Partisanship, in the pro-Constitutional sense, had entered the campaign for a national university. Rush's plan, with its narrow educational and political focus, could not succeed.[12]

Noah Webster argued for an alternative in a pair of essays which ran in his own publication, *The American Magazine*, in 1787 and 1788. Although he disagreed strongly with the notion of Rush and Montesquieu that virtue was the basis of a republic, he drew on the Frenchman for his basic assertion that the laws of education ought to be relative to the principles of government. Essential to a republican government was a system of education designed to give every citizen an opportunity for acquiring knowledge and fitting himself for places of trust. Such a system ought to train all men in ethics, law, commerce, money, government, English, and republicanism, the last illustrated not through the study of antiquity, but through the history of America. Webster's proposal emphasized a curriculum sufficient to prepare intelligent men for any endeavor, yet equip them all with republican ideas. Webster held that it was up to the legislature to create such a climate by establishing a system of public schools, for it was through good government that America would profit from the proper education of youth.[13]

Webster shared with Rush a desire to foster republicanism, a fairly broad, anti-classical curriculum, and a reliance on government as the promoter of education. The Webster proposal differed from Rush's in two important respects. First, Webster did not rely on public virtue to produce republicanism. He did not believe governments operated that way. Webster urged an acquaintance with the republican form and with the laws, relying on self-interest and the restraining force of law to dispose the people toward the government. Second, Webster wanted the educational process extended to all citizens, for any man might desire or seek public office, and he should be prepared for it. Where Rush was an elitist, Webster was an egalitarian.[14] These differences meant that common men now had a plan that embodied some of their ideas. The alternative visions put forth in the two plans rendered the institutionalization of republican education even more difficult than before.

Many of the ideas characteristic of both the Rush and Webster plans appeared in later proposals for a national university. After the adoption of the Constitution, however, the political context which produced the plans changed. The objects of the newer proposals changed with it.

The ratification of the Constitution and the inauguration of George Washington as the country's first president lent some stability to the nation's politics. While men still bitterly debated the merits and defects of the new government, they tentatively agreed to abide by its laws and to hope that it would endure.[15] The republic was no longer in danger of immediate collapse. Americans now felt that their most pressing need was not to preserve virtue, but rather the fragile unity the Constitution provided. Preservation soon became a complicated task. The furor over the adoption of the Constitution had no sooner subsided when a renewed recognition of self-interest as a fundamental political force and the governmental measures of the 1790s brought partisanship to the forefront in the combat between Federalists and Republicans. The advocates of republican educational reform, still largely Federalists, took this need for unity into account. The thrust of their proposals altered from an emphasis on virtue to the promotion of unity.

Thwarted at the Constitutional Convention, the proponents of a national university, both within the federal government and without, renewed their efforts. John Fenno, printer of *The Gazette of the United States*, the major Federalist organ, wrote in *The American Museum* in late 1789. Advancing the typical republican rationale for education, he argued that schools and colleges should be everywhere, topped by a federal university, centrally located, ably staffed, where the students, graduates of other colleges, would learn mostly politics. This would tend to remove the local prejudices and factional politics which suffused and hindered government. This plan was reminiscent of Rush's in its organization, but its object was unity, not virtue.[16]

First James Sullivan, then Nathaniel Chipman, echoed Fenno's themes during the 1790s. Both had attained prominence in New England politics. Ardent supporters of the Constitution, both were Federalists at the time of the educational writings, although Sullivan later became a powerful Republican force in Massachusetts.[17] Sullivan's *Observations upon the Government of the United States* (1791) deplored American adherence to European ways and urged the cementing of American unity through the development of a distinctive American character. The federal government should abet this by creating a system of national education "to form the morals of the people to the genius of the government." A side effect, important in Sullivan's framework, was that national control of higher education should bring about a better political economy.[18]

Nathaniel Chipman also considered education necessary to promote preparation for republican citizenship. He thought it the best way to develop both broad culture and genuine patriotism. But to do so it had to be national in scope so as to promote country-wide unity.[19] Neither of these pleas for national education advanced any specific plan. They remained exhortations, and did nothing to solve the practical problem of starting a national university.

The sentiments stressed in the public prints during these years were echoed in the halls of Congress, stimulated by President Washington. The ends which he expected a national university to serve and his philosophical basis for urging its establishment, he made clear in his first annual message to Congress, delivered on January 8, 1790:

To the security of a free Constitution it contributes in various ways: By convincing those who are intrusted with public administration, that every valuable end of Government is best answered by the enlightened confidence of the people; and by teaching the people themselves to know and value their own rights; to discern and to provide against invasions of them; to distinguish betwen oppression and lawful authority; between burthens proceeding from a disregard to their convenience and those resulting from the inevitable exigencies of Society; to discriminate the spirit of Liberty from that of licentiousness, cherishing the first, avoiding the last, and uniting a speedy, but temperate vigilance against encroachments, with an inviolable respect to the Laws.[20]

Washington's remarks suggest that he was more inclined to Webster's conceptions of education than to Rush's. He wanted the people to recognize that self-interest and national interest were one. Their joining would be guaranteed by having an enlightened populace, fully aware of their rights, the country's laws, and its forms of government. The educational process had to center not on virtue, but on knowledge. The people would have the wisdom to use it. Moreover, Washington wanted education for all the people. In no other way could unity be achieved.

Both houses of Congress initially responded to the address with vaguely worded messages affirming their concern for the arts and sciences and their desire to promote them. Later on in the session, Representative William Smith of South Carolina moved that the parts of the President's message focusing on the arts and sciences be referred to a committee for consideration. Connecticut's Roger Sherman then pointed out that the subject had been considered an infringement of state's rights at the Federal Convention. The House of Representatives adjourned without voting on the measure and did not take it up again. The debate was so short, so vague, that there is no indication whether the content or the subject of the education was discussed.[21] But the basis for more dissension appeared here, for the national university exchange occurred in the context of the state's rights versus federal powers debate.

After Washington's initial proposal, governmental interest in a national university waned until Thomas Jefferson learned of the breakup of the faculty of Switzerland's University of Geneva. He proposed to bring the whole faculty to America and establish it as the basis of a national institution. When Washington learned of the proposal in November 1794, he objected that such a professoriate would instill neither American nationalism nor republican ideology.[22] Washington countered by touting the advantages of the newly created Federal District as the site of a university, principal among which was the proximity to the national capital, where law and governmental policy were better understood than elsewhere. The president had taken steps to insure his design. On January 28 he had informed the Commissioners of the Federal District of his hopes for a national university there, with the object of bringing American students home from Europe so they would not imbibe principles contrary to republicanism. He proposed to give his fifty shares in the Potomac River Company to the endowment of the university, and urged the commissioners to incorporate such a university into their plans.[23]

The commissioners deliberated slowly. Before they made their proposals known, Adams had been elected president and Washington was preparing to leave office. In early December 1796, Washington appealed to Congress, specifically seeking the creation of a national university. Such an institution would educate youth in republican principles and the science of government. In its halls residents of all parts of the country would mingle, developing homogeneity and national unity.[24] No better effort could be made to strengthen the country. Almost immediately, Madison introduced into the House of Representatives a measure for chartering a corporation to receive donations for a university in the Federal District. Debate was scheduled for late December.

Meanwhile, the Commissioners of the Federal District at last addressed their memorial on a university to Congress. Their proposed institution would seek to develop republican virtues while avoiding the anti-republican corruption attached to a foreign education. In fact, they expected to draw foreign students and wealth to America. Most important would be the "removal, or at least the diminution, of those prejudices which at present exist in the several states, by the uniformity of education and the opportunity of free interchange among the youth of all the various parts of the Union." There should have been something in the ideals expressed in the message to please everyone. But, as had been the case for many years, there were no specifics to discuss or contemplate.[25]

Nonetheless, on December 26 and 27 the House debated the measure. It is tempting to try to analyze the debate in the context of developing party politics or of North-South sectionalism, but no such analysis is possible. For one thing, the debate was brief. The House was preoccupied with other things (chiefly taxes and trade). Only thirteen members spoke on the issue, indicating its relative unimportance. Of the thirteen speakers, seven were for the measure, six opposed. Four Republicans favored the corporation, four opposed it; three Federalists favored and two opposed the corporation. Sectionalism offers no better analytical tool. All of those favoring the measure came from the Chesapeake or the deep South, but of those opposed three were northerners, three southerners. Actually, the Chesapeake members dominated the debate, appropriately since the proposed university would exist in a ten-mile-square district carved out of the Maryland shore of the Potomac. Three Marylanders favored the corporation, five Virginians split, two in favor, three opposed.[26]

A better way to make sense of the actions of the House is to focus on individual speeches, to note the arguments for and against the proposed corporation. Those who favored the proposal, especially Virginia's James Madison, Maryland's Richard Sprigg, and South Carolina's Robert Goodloe Harper, reminded their colleagues that the bill proposed only authorized a corporation to receive donations for a university in the Federal District (inspired by Washington's gift). It did not commit the Congress to endow or support the university, it did not promote the immediate creation of a university, and it did not call for a national university. Maryland backers William Vans Murray and William Craik informed the House that the State of Maryland, despite its superintendence over the Federal District until the capital officially moved there in 1800, had no authority to pass legislation for the District that would retain effect beyond that time. It could not, therefore, charter the proposed corporation. Murray, Craik, Richard Brent of Virginia, and Abraham Baldwin of Georgia all clearly envisioned the university as a local project, destined to serve the residents of the Federal District and such students as chose to come from elsewhere. Baldwin observed that there were no other colleges close enough to the District to be injured by the proposed university; Craik said Maryland's two colleges were in good health and would not be hurt.[27]

The proposal's opponents rejected these arguments. As Edward Livingston of New York put it, there was more in the measure than met the eye. For one thing, the university was not intended solely for the District; what was contemplated was a national university. Virginia's John Nicholas and Speaker of the House William Dayton of New Jersey were sure of it. Both Nicholas and fellow Virginian Abraham Venable called all talk of a local institution mere subterfuge. Nicholas went on to criticize the very idea of a national university. He understood it was the president's intent "to establish a uniformity of principles and manners throughout the Union." This he thought an impossible goal for an institution. There was no "Federal quality" in knowledge (and the implication was that such a quality would be undesirable if it existed). Nicholas was certain that every district of the country was competent to provide for the education of its own citizens, and he could be no part of a national educational plan.[28]

Nicholas opposed national homogeneity (was he thinking of Rush's republican machine?). The corollary to this criticism was to advocate localism, a tack taken by Samuel Lyman of Massachusetts. He could not imagine that people from remote parts of the United States would send their children to such an institution. It would, in fact, be an irritant to them to pay taxes to support a university from which they derived no benefit. Moreover, the establishment of a national university would encourage people to neglect local colleges to support the central one (why this would be true if they refused to send their children there he did not say), so the overall quality of education would suffer. Lyman touched on another source of popular discontent, arguing for the continued role of small, local colleges and academies because "the large institutions are generally out of reach of people in general, and of the middling classes in particular."[29] The arguments of Nicholas and Lyman in opposition to uniformity and elitism, in favor of local control and diversity may have derived from some remembrance of the ideas of Rush, or some prescience about the ideals of Washington, but as will be explained below, there may have been more immediate and easily detectable sources of inspiration for these positions. For the moment, it should simply be noted that here were attacks on the principles of the national university, not just on the proposed corporation.

Others objected to the proposal to collect donations without objecting to the university itself. William Branch Giles of Virginia, a long-time critic of all things Hamiltonian, apparently linked the proposal to the schemes of the former Treasury Secretary by noting that he did not believe that the federal government had the power to charter any corporations. Perhaps more pertinent were the fiscal objections. Whether believing the proposed university local or national in scope, Nicholas, Dayton, Venable, Livingston, Lyman, and even two of its supporters, Brent and Murray, opposed Congressional aid for the institution. A House quite sensitive to taxation was wary of assessing the people for an institution of doubtful purpose, even if it was to be located in the nation's capital.[30]

After two days of intermittent debate, the question was put to cut off the exchange and vote on the proposal. The decision was to continue the debate at some future date. The vote was very close, 37 to 36, yet no roll call took place so it is impossible to tell who voted which way, let alone why they voted.[31] In an ignominious end to the whole affair, the House never took the matter up again. Whether that was a deliberate decision or an accident is not known. Whatever the motives for shelving the issue, the Congress never again addressed the proposal for a national university in the eighteenth century.

It was a strange fate to befall an idea enthusiastically supported by men such as Washington, Adams, Jefferson, Madison, Rush, Fenno, and Webster, especially when there was such an underlying acceptance of the connection between proper education and the public's ability to support and sustain republican government. Analysts who have focused on the House debate itself have attributed the outcome to localism and the corollary fear of a strong central government, to failure to understand the implications of a national university and its relationship to other educational enterprises, and perhaps to fiscal conservatism.[32] It is not my purpose to gainsay these conclusions, but an examination of the relationships between state governments and higher education provides a context which makes clearer the objections of House members to the national university and suggests that they understood quite well what it might mean for the country. One measure of the relevance of state-college relationships is that five of the thirteen speakers during the House debate on the proposed corporation were themselves college trustees.[33] House members knew what was occurring in the states. So should we.

II

Even though Americans everywhere recognized the connection between proper education and the preservation of republican government, and even though almost every state eventually developed some kind of relationship with its colleges, those relationships were seldom the result of long-standing or intense commitments. During the Revolution only the constitutions of Massachusetts, Pennsylvania, and North Carolina among the new states provided for higher education. After the war, despite several constitutional revisions, and the formation of three new states, only Georgia, Vermont, and New Hampshire wrote constitutions mentioning higher education, and only the last contained a clear-cut statement of the connection between learning and government and of the need to inculcate public virtue:

Knowledge, and learning, generally diffused through a community, being essential to the preservation of a free government; and spreading the opportunities and advantages through the various parts of the country, being highly conducive to promote this end; it shall be the duty of the legislators and magistrates, in all future periods of this government, to cherish the interest of literature and the sciences, and all seminaries and public schools...to countenance and inculcate the principles of humanity and general benevolence, public and private charity, industry, and economy, honesty and punctuality, sincerity, sobriety, and all social affections, and generous sentiments among the people.[34]

Despite inattention to higher education in their constitution-making, states soon entered into a variety of relationships with colleges both old and new. The most striking development of the post-Revolutionary period was the appearance of state university systems in Maryland, New York, and Georgia.

Maryland acted first. The act chartering Washington College in 1782 indicated that sentiment had long existed for a state university, but that geography had inhibited its creation. The solution to the problem was to establish colleges on the eastern and western shores, allow them to grow, and then combine them. Toward that goal, the state in 1784 granted £1,250 per annum to be raised from taxes and license fees for the purpose of paying salaries and otherwise promoting the college. Later that same year, the Assembly chartered St. John's College on the western shore, granted it £1,750 per annum, and made provision to combine the two colleges into the University of Maryland. They would share a common board of visitors to be comprised of the governor as chancellor and the two boards of trustees, plus two faculty members from each college. Governance would be by a common set of by-laws to insure uniform educational standards and administration.[35]

This arrangement lasted for a little more than twenty years, but never functioned as it was supposed to. Not only were Maryland's residents dispersed on opposite shores of Chesapeake Bay, they were jealous of each other and not anxious to cooperate. There were religious divisions as well. Catholics and Protestants had vied for state support of their private educational enterprises and neither wanted to work with the other. Finally, there were class problems. When the idea of a state university was still at an early stage, many Marylanders manifested resentment at legislative appropriations for higher education while at the same time failing to award Revolutionary veterans their back pay. Some questioned the value of higher education for the poor. Maryland debtors wanted to stop college aid and appropriate the money to poor relief. Failing that, they wanted the money to go for elementary, not collegiate, education.[36]

The Episcopal cleric William Smith, founder of Washington College and principal teacher of the state university, tried to overcome objections by emphasizing to the poor that collegiate education was tied to democracy and that it was practical. The poor were not hurt by the university: taxes for it were on luxury items and so did not affect empty pocketbooks; elementary schools existed at each college; scholarships enabled poor children to obtain a college education.[37] Smith might have mollified the lower classes, but just as St. John's College opened to students in 1789, he left Maryland to return to Philadelphia and his old college there. Certainly no one else possessed the skills to check lower class discontent.

The result was the slow death of the university. For a while the colleges beat back attempts to diminish their funds, but in 1796 the Assembly established grammar schools in each county and the attack began in earnest. Two years later, Washington College lost £500 from its annual appropriation. In 1806 the grants to both colleges ceased. That same act abolished the University of Maryland, allowing the two colleges to continue under their separate charters as private institutions.[38] In Maryland cultural and economic divisions put an end to the state system. Those same problems would spell trouble for higher education elsewhere as well.

The New York and Georgia state systems incorporated a recognition of the demand for lower level education from their beginnings, yet each strove to meet other educational needs stemming from their respective environments. In New York the problem was cultural heterogeneity, the same difficulty that had plagued King's College in the pre-Revolutionary period. Indeed, the impetus for the University of the State of New York came from a number of King's trustees, who petitioned the Legislature in 1784 to reinvigorate the moribund college. The original act restored King's privileges and property under the new name Columbia, and made the college the centerpiece of a state-wide educational corporation. The Regents, as they were (and are) known, consisted of state and city officials, laymen and clerics. They had the power to create, inspect, and supervise the colleges, to handle property, and to award degrees. The president, professors, and fellows of each college would act as Regents with respect to their colleges as long as there were no conflicts of interest.[39]

Some historians argue that the King's trustees hoped to achieve through the Regents not only the resurrection of the old college, but also control over the state's higher educational system.[40] If that was the plan, it did not work, for the Regents were so numerous and so dispersed that it proved virtually impossible to assemble a quorum, and the body suffered from social rifts. The King's College element was urban, affluent, and politically conservative, while the other Regents were largely rural, less wealthy, and relatively more democratic.

A first step toward overcoming the paralysis that prevented the Regents from working was to enlarge their number, with the addition of thirty-three new members, while at the same time reducing the size of a quorum. Since twenty of the new Regents were New York City residents who supported Columbia, they had no trouble dominating the board, but other elements of the Regents objected to this. To what extent these differences were political as well as social remains unclear, but their resolution came in 1787 in the context of the Clinton-Hamilton contest over government centralization in New York and the federalist-antifederalist split over the United States Constitution. The Legislature that year passed a new "act to institute a university within this State and for other purposes therein mentioned." Its first seven sections created a state university under twenty-four Regents including the governor and lieutenant-governor ex officio and twenty-two legislative appointees, none clerical. The Regents' functions were to visit and inspect all colleges, schools, and academies in the state, and to incorporate new ones with their own self-perpetuating boards of trustees. The Regents could also raise academies to colleges. The later sections of the act confirmed the King's College charter of 1754, renamed the college Columbia, and made charter modifications appropriate to the Revolution. It was a fresh start for both Columbia and the state university system.[41]

The new act resolved a number of conflicts. It solved the problem of New York's heterogeneity by providing for institutional autonomy within a framework of overall standards and accountability. With regard to Columbia, it allowed New Yorkers to continue as much of the old tradition as they wished without imposing their values on the rest of the state. Union College would shortly become an example of the diversity possible under the university system. If politics truly entered into this contest, then the new bill was a model of "federalism." Sovereignty over the university remained with the people acting through their legislators, who named the Regents. Supervisory powers were centralized, but day-to-day operations were the province of the respective campuses. Answering another concern, educational interests of all segments of the population received attention through Regent oversight of all levels of schooling. In fact, beginning in the 1790s, most of the fiscal resources managed by the Regents were allocated to common schools.[42] Finally, perhaps ironically, the university system embodied the secular elements sought by William Livingston in the *Independent Reflector* and the educational diversity envisioned by Myles Cooper in his university. In the end, the King's College controversy looked more toward the future than the past.

With the Regents' backing, both Columbia and Union made significant strides before the end of the century. The trustees of both colleges came to regard the Legislature as a source of bounty. In most cases the Legislature, often acting on the recommendation of the Regents, responded generously. Both colleges received land grants, building funds, and money for books, equipment, and salaries.[43] Close ties with the state proved extremely profitable for the two schools.

Georgia's university system resembled that of New York in many ways, but

the major difficulty in implementing it was the indifference toward higher education shown by a frontier people. The Legislature created the university in
1785 by establishing two boards which would work together to oversee all public
education in the state. The first board comprised the governor and his council
(the senate after 1798 when the council was abolished), the speaker of the house
of representatives, and the state's chief justice; the second was made up of
legislative appointees. Together they would make by-laws and appoint the president of the university, keep informed about the schools in the state and found
new ones, all subject to legislative oversight.[44]

The university proved a paper promise, producing no college until 1801.
Whatever might have been the cultural yearnings of the lowcountry elite, by the
1780s the majority of the population lived upcountry and they set priorities. One
object was to become the seat of institutions: the state capital migrated from
Savannah to Augusta to Louisville, which was not even a town when the Legislature first met there. The state's first college was also a prize. Debate in the
late eighteenth century centered on which upcountry locale would become its
home. The Senatus Academicus chose Athens (again not yet a town) but did
little else. It met only twice before 1797 and then the concern was common
school education, for in 1786 the Legislature had directed that academies be
founded in each county. Six had opened by 1794. They were the important
institutions in the public mind, and so the Senatus Academicus regarded them.
Seemingly, upcountry Georgians, once they had secured the college, disregarded
it. Higher education was not vital to them before the turn of the century.[45]

State university systems were the boldest, most innovative creations of those
interested in higher education in the new republic. Centralization and involvement
with government, uniformity, accountability, and secularization typified the
Maryland, New York, and Georgia systems. But each shared problems as well
as characteristics; political, cultural, and social divisions were hard to reconcile
in an overarching system. These features of the human landscape would affect
all governmental involvement with higher education, but for the university systems they proved particularly troublesome. By 1800, Maryland's was on the
road to failure and Georgia's had barely begun to function. Only the New York
system had given evidence of long-term success.

Many Americans were interested observers of the problems and possibilities
demonstrated by this level of governmental activity in higher education. Few
were in better positions to understand both than those trustee-Congressmen Richard Sprigg of Maryland, Edward Livingston of New York, and Abraham Baldwin
of Georgia.

If state systems of education were the most dramatic forms of governmental
association with colleges, they were far from the only forms. The relationships
were almost as varied as the colleges themselves. Two state universities, in North
Carolina and Vermont, were the creations of legislatures independent of any
system for lower schools. But in each state, political and social divisions would
greatly hinder the early development of higher education.

Some North Carolina legislators first tried to create an assembly-controlled state university in 1784. Another legislative faction, many of whose members would shortly be thought of as antifederalists, blocked the bill. This set the stage for renewed efforts in 1789 at the time of the ratification convention for the new Federal Constitution. Apparently inspired by their fight for that document, the federalist-dominated Legislature enacted a university bill. This one created a self-perpetuating board of forty trustees, gave them the usual powers held by such boards, and for support granted the university all debts owed to the state as well as all lands that had escheated or would escheat to the state.[46]

From the very beginning, the university and its operation became embroiled in political and class disputes. The general public incorrectly perceived the successful university charter to have created a corporation as closely allied to the state government as was that envisioned by the abortive 1784 bill. This misapprehension probably arose because twenty-eight of the forty trustees named had been delegates to the ratification convention and twenty-one were members of the Legislature (many successor trustees also came from its ranks). This legislative connection was most irritating to many North Carolinians because the Assembly and the trustees in the early 1790s were largely Federalist. Even knowledge that the trustees were self-perpetuating did not appease the discontented for they were sure that the university was an elitist, partisan project. The actions of the faculty, trustees, and students did little to dispel this impression once the school opened in 1795.[47]

University opponents worked throughout the 1790s to gain some control over collegiate affairs. Their efforts employed political, social, and economic critiques. The first move was an unsuccessful attempt in 1790 to prohibit members of the Legislature from sitting on the university board.[48] Then followed a spirited newspaper exchange which set the bounds of the social critique of the university. Responding to a hostile word-of-mouth campaign, the collegiate defenders emphasized the necessity of good education for the survival of republican government, its utility to fit men for the highest ranks of the professions, and the financial waste of sending North Carolinians elsewhere for collegiate education.[49] The critique, while conceding the connection between education and public happiness, argued that North Carolina's efforts were misdirected. The university was geographically remote and financially out of the reach of most citizens. Universities, moreover, corrupted morals. True happiness stemmed from proper religious education which university learning opposed: "System will be opposed to system, opinion to opinion, with all the rancour of disputation, and the animosity of party virulence. By these impolitic cavils the ignorant will be led to conclude, that religion is the offspring of fiction, and nothing but the dread of temporal punishment will restrain them from committing the most heinous offenses." Much better than a university, said its opponents, would be a county school system with adequately paid teachers under local supervision.[50]

Visible here were many of the elements at work in opposition to governmental support of higher education in Maryland, New York, and Georgia. Despite the criticism of the college, the Legislature in 1794 increased its funding by allowing it money from the sale of confiscated lands, an act that generated little money, but produced a great deal of hostility toward the university, for its agents promptly began litigation to dispossess those who in some cases had spent twenty years or more on Tory lands.[51] Financially injured people now joined the politically and socially alienated. By the end of the century they had enlisted under the banner of the Republican Party and controlled the Legislature.[52] While they could do nothing about the makeup of the trustees or the daily operations of the university, they could try to starve it to death. In 1800 the Assembly repealed the confiscated lands act. The escheat act also suffered repeal in 1800, but the university trustees took that issue to court. The ruling prevented any further erosion of the economic base of the institution. The North Carolina Supreme Court held first, that the university was constitutionally, not legislatively, created, so the Legislature could do nothing to abolish it or lead to that end, and secondly, that the Legislature could not control trustee property once it had been granted.[53] The ruling may have saved the university's income, but it could not insure further support. The institution limped along, out of public favor, for many years thereafter.

The actions that led to the chartering of a state university betrayed Vermont's peculiar sectionalism, which often pitted the Congregationalist, Federalist east against the Republican, religiously liberal west. Through self-promotion, chicanery, and perhaps fraud, one of the more well-known Republican religious liberals, Ira Allen, managed to land the university for his part of the state.[54] Yet the charter outlined a school all could live with, if it ever became a reality. It created a state university, with the governor and speaker of the house as ex officio trustees, and named ten others who comprised a board that was non-partisan and non-sectarian. The charter gave the trustees the usual powers over property and internal management of the university. What it did not do was give the university any financial support. Nor did any subsequent legislature, despite occasional trustee requests, and despite the fact that so many legislators were trustees that the two bodies met concurrently in the late 1790s.[55]

In North Carolina the seizure of initiative by one faction of the politically active populace had alienated the others, bringing eventual retribution. In Vermont the attempt to placate all religious and political groups resulted in paralysis and no movement toward the actual establishment of a university. It was not until 1800, when private efforts to found another college in Vermont at Middlebury seemed about to bear fruit, that the university trustees set out to defend their educational record and to begin operating their institution. Of course, they did even that without any financial help from the state.

The college-state relationship in Vermont was abnormal, stunted. The apparatus for control was there (remaining unused), but the support that generally accompanied control was not. Factionalism inhibited growth. Although the course of events differed, the same causes produced the same results in North Carolina. And, with the exception of New York, social, political, and cultural differences had prevented the successful operation of state university systems elsewhere.

Heterogeneity of interests within the states crippled their governments' efforts to administer higher education directly before 1800. That same heterogeneity translated to a higher level inhibited the creation of a national university as well.

Partial, indirect, or temporary control were other avenues that states could explore in their relationships with higher education. The actual state-college interactions were quite varied and so were their results.

The University of the State of Pennsylvania limped along after the Revolution, short-staffed, caught up in factional politics, and chronically short of money, because the promised revenue from confiscated estates never materialized, in spite of legislative action.[56] In addition, the state's political climate was changing, with important implications for the university, because William Smith's arguments that legislative seizure of the College of Philadelphia was unconstitutional slowly found a receptive audience. Finally, he prevailed. In March 1789 the Legislature acted, deciding that the seizure of the College had violated constitutional provisions. It restored the rights and property of the College to its trustees while retaining those of the University, which would also receive funds appropriated under the 1779 and 1785 acts.[57] Now Philadelphia had both a private college and a state university.

Two institutions were more than even the nation's largest city could bear. Neither was financially able to carry out its programs and there was much bickering between the two faculties, especially the medical departments. The schools began negotiations for a union within two years. In 1791 they prevailed upon the Legislature to join them together. While at that task, the Assembly virtually put itself out of the college business. Twelve trustees from each institution, together with the governor ex officio, formed the new board. The faculties were to be combined equally. The new institution, to be known as the University of Pennsylvania, would have normal powers. The estates of the earlier schools were to be combined and the new trustees were to account to the Legislature for the expenditure of its funds. This was much less state involvement than had previously existed. Despite trustee appeals to the Assembly in 1792 and 1793, no more funds were appropriated. As the most recent historian of the university puts it, from this point on "the expectation of a close connection between the state government and the university gradually faded away."[58]

The Pennsylvania Legislature apparently turned its back on the University of Pennsylvania because it was weary of the perpetual wrangles involved in close administration. Yet there is evidence in its treatment of Dickinson College that it was a continuing friend of higher education. Although a number of Dickinson's early trustees were politically prominent Pennsylvanians, none was an ex officio board member, and there was no direct legislative supervision of the college. Still, the Dickinson board looked to the state for succor, petitioning the Assembly early and often. The petitions were remarkably successful. While the school did not receive the permanent endowment it sought, on several occasions the Legislature proved quite generous, giving thousands of acres of land, money, lottery proceeds, and subsidies for scholarships.[59] The grants to Dickinson demonstrate that Pennsylvania's government felt the Revolution-inspired obligation to support higher education, but its conduct regarding the Philadelphia colleges shows that day-to-day administration was not to be included in that obligation.

In Massachusetts the state adopted a similar line of conduct. The 1780 Constitution had confirmed Harvard's rights and privileges, and had altered the composition of the overseers to include many state officials plus the president of the college and six Congregational ministers. Another important section of the constitution had stipulated that the General Court reserved the right to alter the university's government "as shall be conducive to its advantage and the interest of the republic of letters." The Legislature included similar language in the charters of Williams College and Bowdoin College, although in neither case were there state officials named to the governing boards ex officio.[60]

Having established a mechanism for thoroughgoing state control at Harvard and having reserved the right to intervene at the other two colleges, the state government exercised its power very sparingly. Perhaps conscious of the hostility developed in some towns at the privileges accorded Harvard in the past and of the growing sentiment favoring aid to common schools, the General Court slowly but surely weaned Harvard from its financial breast. The college was slow to accept the process. It looked to continue the old relationship, asking repeatedly for grants throughout the 1780s and 1790s so that it could supplement faculty salaries, hire new instructors, regulate faculty conduct, build buildings, and a variety of other things. The board tried to inspire the General Court's patriotism, noting that its education was necessary "to maintain religion and virtue, and supporting the rights of mankind and the dignity and energy of republican government." When this invocation of the specific relationship between collegiate education and republicanism did not work, the board tried to create legislative guilt by lending the faculty money in lieu of state grants and then going to the General Court for repayment.[61]

To all this, the Legislature responded less and less favorably. What were formerly annual grants for salary supplements became sporadic after 1781 and ceased altogether in 1786. Non-financial requests were honored occasionally, such as a corporation petition for the right to dismiss tutors for causes other than death or misbehavior. Since this had to do with the better government of the college, the General Court had no trouble amending the permanent tutor act to allow removal for insanity, incompetence, or other causes.[62] The Legislature's conduct demonstrates decreasing involvement in college affairs, especially in the financial realm. The General Court did not want to be accused of educational elitism.

Williams and Bowdoin fared little better at the hands of the Legislature before 1800. On its incorporation Williams received £1,200 to be distributed in four annual grants, and the 1796 Legislature gave the college two townships in Maine. Bowdoin's incorporation gift was five Maine townships, but no money.[63] By 1800, Massachusetts had developed what might be called quasi-public institutions. That is to say the state reserved the right to exert legislative supervision, but rarely if ever exercised it, while at the same time it disclaimed financial responsibility for the colleges but sometimes made gifts. It was with the knowledge of this kind of state-college relationship that Samuel Lyman, the Massachusetts Representative, approached the national university debate of 1796.

One other state dissociated itself from higher education toward the end of the century. When the College of Charleston had been founded in 1785, its board had included the governor and lieutenant-governor ex officio, thus forging a continuing link between the state and the college. But the new South Carolina Constitution of 1790 granted freedom of religion and abolished the requirement that state officials be Protestant. This separation of church from state made continued official representation on the board of what had been essentially a religiously affiliated institution seem inappropriate. A new charter issued in 1790 separated the College of Charleston from the other South Carolina colleges and ended state representation on the board. There was no official connection between the college and the state thereafter.[64]

The Connecticut state government was moving toward, not away from, involvement with college education in the post-Revolutionary period. Criticism of Yale, muted during the war by Ezra Stiles' success with the college and his willingness to talk with the Assembly, began again even before the peace was officially known. A series of letters appeared in the *Connecticut Courant* attacking the board on several fronts. Its treatment of Yale's tutors had forced their resignation in 1777; likewise, shabby treatment of Mathematics and Natural Philosophy Professor Nehemiah Strong had led to his resignation and the loss of his discipline. There were other matters, too, but they all went to show that an incompetent, religiously-biased board had worked to keep the focus of education narrow and not very useful. Also appearing was a pamphlet which suggested that the proper remedy for board failures was to make the college accountable to the state. Similar remedial action was the object of petitions to the Legislature addressed by students and concerned Connecticut citizens.[65]

With all this pressure, there was reason to expect the Assembly to act, but it postponed consideration of the petitions and the furor gradually subsided. The continuing health of the college was probably most influential in staving off legislative interference, but also playing some role were the indifference of the majority of Connecticut residents to an outburst among intellectuals over an issue that did not concern them and a reluctance to see Yale become an object of legislative attention if that meant more aid for the college at the expense of the common schools. By refusing to get involved, the Assembly signalled, perhaps unintentionally, that it was unwilling to sink more money into higher education. In fact, despite Stiles' pleas, the 1780s were lean years for state aid to Yale. No money was forthcoming, and the Legislature's only contribution to the college was to protect its rights in the face of the incorporation of other educational institutions.[66]

By the early 1790s, some aspiring Connecticut politicians, united by religious skepticism if not by a positive legislative program, took advantage of the continuing suspicions of Yale to force a showdown. In 1791 they prodded the Assembly into launching an investigation of Yale, one the Corporation could not avoid. Under Stiles' leadership the trustees cooperated with the legislative committee to produce results that must have distressed the college's enemies. The report concluded that Yale was well run and provided a good education, but more funds were needed to broaden and deepen the curriculum. The sympathetic report invited compromise and, despite Stiles' fears of legislative dominance, the entry of deism, and the deterioration of the college, what the Assembly proposed proved acceptable. It would grant to Yale tax arrears amounting to £8,000–12,000 in return for the appointment to the board of the governor, lieutenant-governor, and the six councillors with the longest service. This arrangement would leave the clerical trustees in the majority and the ex officio trustees would not vote on successors for the ministerial members. Thus Yale became a quasi-state institution, responsible to, if not governed by, the state Legislature.[67]

For the next decade Yale prospered under joint supervision. Timothy Dwight, Stiles' successor, was especially adept at working in harmony with the Legislature, perhaps because they shared political philosophies. The largest benefit accruing to the college from Dwight's skill was a 1796 act supplementing the 1792 appropriation in return for annual fiscal accounting to the Legislature. From the two acts Yale realized about $40,000, enough to embark on a substantial building program. Interestingly, the 1796 act brought complaints from those who disliked the generosity shown the college. These may have been the same forces that persuaded the Legislature in 1792 to grant Yale Revolutionary tax arrears instead of Western Reserve lands, which they wanted for the support of common schools.[68] In Connecticut, as elsewhere, there was considerable public skepticism about governmental support of such an elitist enterprise as higher education. While most citizens agreed that the government should foster republican education, the level of education that deserved support remained a matter of debate.

In Virginia, under circumstances wherein funding was not a problem, the state government emulated that of Connecticut by imposing upon a private college. When Liberty Hall Academy received its charter from the Virginia Legislature in 1782, that document left it free from government or church authority. So it remained for more than a decade. But in 1795 George Washington wrote to Virginia's governor indicating that he would leave the fifty shares of stock presented to him by the James River Company to whichever "seminary" the Legislature chose. Since those stock shares were reputedly worth a great deal, the Legislature, in selecting Liberty Hall as their recipient, felt that this would be an excellent opportunity to new-model the college and further the cause of higher education in Virginia. The Assembly's December 1796 actions resembled the wartime attempt on the College of William and Mary. It repealed the Liberty Hall charter, enacting a new one that renamed the institution Washington College, created a new board of trustees to include the governor ex officio, and revised the curriculum in a way reminiscent of Jefferson's plan for William and Mary. It did all this without even consulting the Liberty Hall trustees.[69]

But Liberty Hall's board fought back. Meeting at the end of January 1797, they called the Assembly action "an unjustifiable infringement of the Rights of Liberty Hall and an instance of tyrannical imposition in the Legislature." They went on to argue against the legality of the move, claiming that it violated private property rights and that it threatened the sanctity of all corporate charters in the state. These protests were effective. In January of 1798 the Virginia Assembly repealed its 1796 act and restored Liberty Hall to its former trustees, asking only that the name Washington College be retained.[70] The legislative attack on private education had failed. The trustees of all Virginia's colleges, including Representatives James Madison and Abraham Venable, who had been anxious observers of this episode from the beginning, could breathe sighs of relief.

The Liberty Hall incident resulted in a legislative retreat, but Virginia's overall experience was representative of the variety of relationships developed between colleges and states. No state had succeeded in assuming unquestioned direct control over an institution of higher education. Either there were concessions to private interests, as with New York's system or with Yale, or there was a retreat from governance, as with the University of Pennsylvania or Maryland's colleges, or there was popular opposition that prevented successful development, as in Georgia, North Carolina, or Vermont. Those who advocated closer ties between colleges and state could point to no working model of a state institution by the end of the eighteenth century. This ongoing failure no doubt influenced the Congressional critics of the national university proposal.

The simplest possible relationship between colleges and states was the chartering of a private institution, that is, one with no connection to the state, no legislative oversight or responsibility. Such complete independence was a new form, but it would dominate college founding in the nineteenth century. It is a testament to the power of republican ideology that so few of America's late eighteenth century colleges enjoyed such a relationship. Almost all that did were thoroughly identified with a religious denomination, were on the frontier, or both. Such circumstances encouraged colleges to avoid close connections with the state, perhaps so as not to compromise religious convictions and denominational fundraising, perhaps because suspicion of state centers of government had combined with a spirit of localism.[71]

The college-state relationship pattern that emerged as a result of these conditions was sometimes limited to the grant of a charter and possibly something for an endowment with no other contact ensuing. The Pennsylvania Legislature granted Franklin College, the Dutch Reformed institution, 10,000 acres of land and a Lancaster town lot at its founding and that was it. Another Dutch school, Queen's College of New Jersey, had no post-Revolutionary contacts with the Legislature, nor did Greeneville College, the Presbyterian school in east Tennessee.[72]

More often, however, the private colleges petitioned the state legislatures for help in specific circumstances. Hampden-Sydney, a Presbyterian college, successfully memorialized the Virginia Legislature in 1784 for land to supply firewood and for the right to rent a store it owned, and it received 1,200 acres of land as a gift in 1795. On the other hand, a 1789 petition for receipt of surveyors' fees for work below the Blue Ridge (formerly granted to William and Mary) and an 1800 petition to be allowed to set up a lottery were both unsuccessful.[73] The College of Rhode Island, essentially under the control of the Baptists, could not even get the state to make good on its debts. Before allowing a 1789 lottery, the Legislature had twice refused trustee petitions to redeem college-held wartime securities.[74]

Princeton fared little better than the College of Rhode Island and paid a price for doing so. After futile pleading with both New Jersey and the United States for money to repair the damage to Nassau Hall caused by the Revolutionary warfare, the college trustees in 1793 dropped their quest, only to take it up again in 1796. This time they argued that the college was an institution of national importance as could be seen by the number of prominent public figures it had produced. Such an institution could not be allowed to languish. The New Jersey Legislature accepted the argument, granting £600 per annum for three years, but imposed its own conditions for receipt which the trustees reluctantly accepted. The chief legislative concern was denominational control and the trustees responded by proclaiming that there was no need for it any longer in the post-Revolutionary religious atmosphere. They made good their pledge by selecting Episcopalians to fill the next two trusteeship vacancies, but by that time public opinion in New Jersey had labelled the grant a politically unpopular measure, so the Legislature provided no more funds in the eighteenth century. What is more, much to the surprise of the trustees, the Legislature twice directed that grant money remaining be used to support specifically designated students. This was a condition that made receipt of state funds unpalatable to the board. The relationship with New Jersey was an unhappy one.[75]

Post-Revolutionary Dartmouth continued to be a college looking for a state to support it, but succeeded only partially. Still enamored with the prospect of help from Vermont, Dartmouth president John Wheelock managed to persuade the Legislature to grant the college over 23,000 acres of land in 1785. Not satisfied with that, Wheelock went on to ask that Dartmouth be granted all the SPG lands in Vermont and that the new constitution being drafted contain provisions making his the favored college. In return he would offer Vermont students tuition free education. These proposals proved too much for Vermonters. Public opinion turned against Dartmouth. It received no more from the Legislature and only influenced the drafting of the constitution to the extent that there was no clause inserted requiring the state to establish a university. After the mid-1780s, Dartmouth could no longer look to Vermont for aid.[76]

President Wheelock and the other trustees had never given up hope of aid from New Hampshire, but the college's actions during the war had fostered a hostility on the part of the state government that did not diminish quickly. The college repeatedly petitioned the Legislature for financial aid and other assistance, but was rewarded only occasionally and never achieved quite the alliance with the state that it desired. Dartmouth's most notable successes were the approval of lotteries in 1784 and 1795, and land grants of 60,000 acres total in 1789 and 1792. The trustees courted the state by inviting the president to serve on the board beginning in 1787, but it was not until 1794 that John Taylor Gilman agreed. Something of a high water mark in the rapprochement occurred in 1795 when Gilman's second inaugural took place at the college and the Legislature met in Hanover. Still, there is reason to believe that the government's interest was as much in protecting itself as in aiding Dartmouth. The land grants, for example, were in exchange for trustee cession of pre-Revolutionary grants that had provoked endless title disputes between residents of New Hampshire and Vermont. In addition, the acts contained the stipulation that for purposes of administering the lands, the state president and council would sit with the college trustees. New Hampshire aided the college, but the suspicion and hostility that would ultimately be felt in the Dartmouth College Case were still present.[77]

The only denominational college to enjoy a successful and financially rewarding relationship with a legislature was Transylvania in Kentucky. The Virginia Legislature organized Transylvania Seminary in 1783 as a corporation for the promotion of education, but with no direct ties to the state and with no special privileges for any denomination. But the board was mostly Presbyterian and when religious liberals used a small attendance at a 1794 board meeting to bring in the Unitarian Harry Toulmin as president of the seminary, orthodox sensibilities were offended and legislative sympathies aroused. The Presbyterians obtained from the Kentucky Assembly a charter for a rival institution, Kentucky Academy, which allowed denominational control. At the same time they persuaded the Legislature to take punitive action against Transylvania Seminary. Its presidency became a contractual obligation limited to one-year terms, its trustees ceased to be able to hold or administer property, its meetings became subject to legislatively imposed rules, and the local district court began to supervise the school. Additionally, while the Transylvania trustees were enjoined from holding property, the Assembly endowed "each" seminary in Kentucky with $14,000 and 6,000 acres of land. Only Kentucky Academy could benefit. These actions helped bring about a decline in the fortunes of Transylvania Seminary, pleas for union, and the creation of Transylvania University in 1799, under Presbyterian influence if not control.[78]

Many of the same forces that affected state university systems or other close relationships between colleges and states also came to bear on the associations between private colleges and states. Even though these colleges had generally displayed at least some commitment to the state service ideal and republican education, they could not become closely allied to the states because of religious denominationalism or suspicions about the motives and operations of government or both. In a way, these were forms of the heterogeneity of public interests and of the suspicion of elitism that had plagued other college-state relationships. The backers of these institutions took totally opposite positions from those who supported state university systems or government related colleges; they had more in common with those who opposed such alliances.

The diversity of operational relationships between colleges and states and the diversity of public opinion that required it form the context in which to evaluate the movement for a national university and the debate of 1796 which was its ultimate expression in the eighteenth century. By the time of the debates, a great variety of relationships had been forged between colleges and states and most of them were strained because of adverse public opinion. The great difficulties in making any relationship work were in overcoming the conflicting interests of a heterogeneous population and the suspicion of elitism that governmental support of higher education brought out in a people that sent so few of its sons to college. Either or both of these strands of criticism had worked to render inoperable state educational systems outside of New York, to slow down efforts of Vermont and North Carolina to create state universities, to inspire public suspicion of government-aided higher education in Pennsylvania, Massachusetts, Connecticut, Virginia, and New Jersey, and to cause several colleges to have nothing to do with state government at all.

These college-state relationships were matters of public knowledge and debate in 1796, and the link between them and consideration of the national university proposal became tighter with the participation in the House discussion of several college trustees. While the minds of the discussants and others cannot be read, the fears of a national university that several expressed make sense in light of contemporary developments. Certainly there were grounds for suspicion about government motives and goals when it became involved with colleges; just look at Connecticut, Pennsylvania, Virginia, or New Jersey. Certainly the great variety of college organizations and the desire of several to have nothing to do with government lent plausability to the argument that local colleges should be protected in their individuality. And certainly the popular suspicion of government's role in higher education, indeed of higher education itself, or the popular prejudice in favor of a particular kind of higher education perhaps provided by specific religious denominations suggested that there was ample ground for the belief that there were no federal principles of education to be inculcated.

No doubt national governmental poverty, fear of too much centralization, and a failure to understand what a national university would do in the absence of concrete plans all contributed to the demise of the proposal to establish a corporation to raise money for a university in the federal district. But so, too, did the knowledge of the course of college-state relations in the early republic. On balance, those relations were moving away from, not closer to, stronger college-state ties. In the early republic, then, Americans were unwilling to implement fully the third part of the English higher educational tradition—government sponsorship of colleges. That part of the tradition had metamorphosed beyond recognition. Diversity, not uniformity, was the wave of the future. A national university was impossible.

CONCLUSION

Dramatic changes took place in American higher education between 1750 and 1800. Responding to the growing imperial crisis, American educators seized upon a long-standing tradition of education for state service themselves to absorb and then impart to their students the Commonwealth Whig political ideology. Faculty and students alike embraced the ideology to such an extent in their curricular and extracurricular activities that the colleges became agents of revolution: their mission was to educate republicans. This activity on the part of the colleges enjoyed the support of the American people, who were so convinced of the connection between "proper" education and the success of republicanism that they influenced governments to take action when the political sentiments of some college communities did not meet the Patriots' standards.

In a very striking way these developments paralleled occurrences in the larger American political culture. Increasingly during the generation before 1776, politically aware and active Americans, whether college-educated or not, embraced the Commonwealth Whig ideology. In the years immediately surrounding 1776, the vast majority of Americans seemingly without hesitation chose republicanism as the desirable form for their governments and persuaded their political leaders to create states adhering to that form. Those states were, in turn, expected to enact legislation to preserve the republican form from degeneration. The developments in the college, I suggest, were not just parallel to, but were an integral part of, this transformation of American political culture.

The same observation holds true for the post-Revolutionary years. One of the characteristics of political culture in those years was the continued enthusiasm for republicanism, but there arose disagreement over the best way to promote and preserve it. One strain of thought, fondly recalling the almost revivalistic spirit of the early years of the Revolution, expected to base republicanism on a continuing manifestation of public virtue, to be fostered by religion and education, perhaps with the sanction of the state. Another strain, noting in the people the prevalence of self-interest often attached to an emerging American market economy, despaired of the continuation of public virtue and its ability to sustain republicanism. Instead, this line of thought advocated the establishment of governmental institutions and legal restraints that would preserve republicanism irrespective of the degree of public virtue that existed among the people. These convictions about politics were not mutually exclusive and political developments in the latter part of the eighteenth century reflected both sets. Moreover, these strands of thought did not correspond to party divisions over the Constitution or the government's policies in the 1790s. Indeed, as we have seen, they were inextricably linked in the minds of such politically diverse people as

Benjamin Rush, James Madison, George Washington, and Alexander Hamilton, all of whom advocated both the acceptance of the Constitution and government-sponsored higher education despite their party differences by the mid-1790s.

Again, what happened in higher education during these years reflected the larger political culture. Certainly, there remained the desire that colleges inculcate the pro-republican political ideology, and to varying extents they all did. But there were different emphases. Several colleges became so involved with the political process that they took sides in the party divisions of the late 1780s and 1790s. Others, especially on the frontier, which was politically remote and concerned with more basic questions of civilization, were less committed to inculcating republicanism and certainly less caught up in party broils. They preferred to emphasize religious values, necessary in combatting frontier barbarism, which they thought would indirectly support republicanism through the cultivation of a virtuous citizenry. These frontier colleges were clearly not as interested as their urban counterparts in producing graduates directly serviceable to the state. Thus, with respect to what was necessary to promote and protect republicanism, the colleges divided in their approaches along lines that were familiar to the larger society.

Divisions among the body politic concerning republicanism and the best methods to promote it also affected the relationships between colleges and states. Some states moved to regulate and support colleges directly, others indirectly, while still others chose not to become involved with higher education at all. But in every state the relationship between the government and the colleges became a political issue, part of the larger discussion of how best to realize the benefits of revolution and to ensure the future of republican government. Even in Congress, these questions were at the core of the debate over a national university. The failure to establish one was mute testimony to the diversity of opinion concerning the links between higher education and republicanism.

Throughout the half-century, then, the crucial element affecting the course of American higher education was its connection with the larger political culture. Those years witnessed first an intensified popular and collegiate concern with politics, which led in turn to a generally uniform acceptance and promotion of a distinctive American politics. The years of greatest collegiate uniformity in inculcating the Commonwealth Whig political ideology were just those which saw the highest degree of public faith in the efficacy of higher education in promoting republicanism. With the end of the war and the fragmentation of Revolutionary political unity, the belief in the ability of collegiate education to promote republicanism also ceased to be universally held. As a result, colleges stopped moving along a uniform path, with some associating themselves less and less with the American political culture.

That dissociation marked the end of an era. Most historians of higher education have labelled the "old time college" of the early nineteenth century as a retrogression from the Revolutionary era college and have variously linked it with the westward movement, the rise of denominational competition, the booster spirit of local communities, or all of these.[79] Such interpretations are not inaccurate, but they are incomplete, for they do not tell us what had been lost in the transition from the Revolutionary to the "old time" college, and that was an active association with the American political culture.[80] That association had supplied energy to the Revolutionary college, had acquainted it with the latest intellectual currents, and had cemented it to a dynamic national movement. When that association diminished, when the Revolutionary zeal and faith in public virtue faded, it became possible for the centrifugal forces of the frontier, religious parochialism, and geographic localism to take over. A few institutions, of course, resisted these trends, but it was not until the post–Civil War era, when the forces of industrialization and urbanization would exert pressure toward a uniformity of culture once again, that higher education would regain the status it had held when its mission was to educate republicans.[81]

NOTES

1. Philips Payson, "A Sermon Preached before the Honorable Council and the Honorable House of Representatives of the State of Massachusetts Bay, in New England, at Boston, May 27, 1778," John W. Thornton, ed., *The Pulpit of the American Revolution* (Boston: Gould & Lincoln, 1860), 337, 339. For similar statements from the 1780s, see Thomas Reese, *An Essay on the Influence of Religion in Civil Society* (Charleston, 1788), 76; William Symmes, *A Sermon Preached before His Honor Thomas Cushing* (Boston, 1785), 15; John Murray, *Jerubbaal* (Newburyport, Mass., 1784), 22; Simeon Baldwin to James Kent, October 16/20, 1782 (Baldwin Family Papers, YUA); Boston *Independent Chronicle*, December 16, 1784.

2. Simeon Howard, "A Sermon Preached before the Honorable Council and the Honorable House of Representatives of the State of Massachusetts Bay in New England, May 31, 1780," Thornton, ed., *Pulpit of Revolution*, 367.

3. Samuel Stillman, "The Duty of Magistrates [Boston, May 26, 1779]," Frank Moore, ed., *The Patriot Preachers of the Revolution* (New York: n.p., 1860), 274; "On Republican Government," *The American Museum*, 6 (July–Dec., 1789): 385–86; Samuel McClintock, *A Sermon Preached before the Honorable the Council* (Portsmouth, N.H., 1784), 37.

4. There was a plan for a university, drawn up by the German naturalist and adventurer Johann Reinhold Forster, that might have been feasible under the Articles of Confederation, for it catered to state sovereignty, diversity, and pride through a confederated college system. But the plan, supposed to be transmitted to Benjamin Franklin and through him to the United States, never reached the Pennsylvanian and did not come to light in the eighteenth century. See David W. Robson, "Pennsylvania's 'Lost' National University: Johann Forster's Plan," *Pennsylvania Magazine of History and Biography*, 102 (1978): 364–74.

5. Benjamin Rush, "An Address to the People of the United States," *American Museum*, 1 (Jan.–June 1787), 11; BR to Richard Price, May 25, 1786, *Rush Letters*, I, 388.

6. Benjamin Rush, "A Plan for the Establishment of Public Schools and the Diffusion of Knowledge in Pennsylvania; to Which is Added, Thoughts Upon the Mode of

Education, Proper in a Republic,'' Frederick Rudolph, ed., *Essays on Education in the Early Republic* (Cambridge, Mass.: Belknap Press of Harvard University Press, 1965), 14, 9–22.

7. Rush, "An Address," 12.

8. Gordon S. Wood, *The Creation of the American Republic, 1776–1787* (Chapel Hill: University of North Carolina Press, 1969), 396, 430, 466, 498; David F. Hawke, *Benjamin Rush: Revolutionary Gadfly* (Indianapolis: Bobbs-Merrill Co., 1971), 196–202, 229–30.

9. See Jackson Turner Main, "Government by the People: The American Revolution and the Democratization of the Legislatures," *WMQ*, 23 (1966): 391–407, and *The Upper House in Revolutionary America, 1763–1788* (Madison: University of Wisconsin Press, 1967) for commentary on the democratization of politics.

10. Max Farrand, ed., *Records of the Federal Convention* (4 vols., New Haven: Yale University Press, 1911–37), I, 321, 325, 616; *The Debates and Proceedings in the Congress of the United States, 1789–1824* (42 vols., Washington, D.C.: Gales & Seaton, 1834–56), I, 1551 [Hereafter cited as *Annals of Cong.*].

11. Benjamin Rush, "Plan of a Federal University," *Pennsylvania Gazette*, October 29, 1788.

12. Rush's role in the backing of the federalists at the Philadelphia Convention, and in securing the adoption of the Constitution in Pennsylvania, is treated in Hawke, *Revolutionary Gadfly*, 340–53.

13. Noah Webster, "Education" and "The Importance of Accommodating the Mode of Education to the Form of Government," *The American Magazine*, 1 (Dec. 1787–Nov. 1788): 22–26, 80–82, 158–61, 210–16, 311–13, 212.

14. Noah Webster is usually depicted as a conservative, especially in politics. This is an accurate evaluation of his later views, but before 1789 he often blended together quite radical notions derived from reading European philosophies. Two of the conclusions he drew from his studies were that relatively democratic propertyholding and political participation already existed in America. To preserve them became the object of America's government and educational system. See Joseph J. Ellis, *After the Revolution: Profiles of Early American Culture* (New York: W. W. Norton, 1979), 161–212.

15. See Lance Banning, "Republican Ideology and the Triumph of the Constitution, 1789–1793," *WMQ*, 31 (1974): 167–88.

16. *DAB*, s.v. "John Fenno"; John Fenno, "The Importance of a Proper System of Education," *The American Museum*, VI (July–Dec. 1789): 290–91.

17. *DAB*, s.v. "Nathaniel Chipman" and "James Sullivan"; James M. Banner, *To the Hartford Convention: The Federalists and the Origins of Party Politics in Massachusetts, 1789–1815* (New York: Alfred A. Knopf, 1970), 6, 274–75, 298.

18. James Sullivan, *Observations upon the Government of the United States* (Boston, 1791), 27.

19. Nathaniel Chipman, *Sketches of the Principles of Government* (Rutland, Vt., 1793), 214.

20. John C. Fitzpatrick, ed., *The Writings of George Washington* (39 vols., Washington, D.C.: Government Printing Office, 1931–44), XXX, 493–94.

21. *Annals of Cong.*, I, 971–73, II, 1601–3.

22. GW to John Adams, November 22, 1794, GW to Thomas Jefferson, March 15, 1795, Fitzpatrick, ed., *Writings of Washington*, XXXIV, 23, 148.

23. GW to Thomas Jefferson, March 15, 1795, ibid., 147; GW to the Commissioners

of the Federal District, January 28, 1795, *Doc. Hist. Educ.*, II, 16–18. Washington's stock, never used, depreciated in value and reverted to his estate in the 1830s; Theta M. Harrison, "A History of the Movement for a National University in the United States" (Ph.D. Diss., Stanford University, 1931), 74.

24. George Washington, "Address to Congress, December 4, 1796," *Annals of Cong.*, VI, 1595.

25. Ibid., 1600–1601; "Federal District Commissioner's Memorial to Congress, Dec. 7, 1796," *Doc. Hist. Educ.*, II, 23–24.

26. *Annals of Cong.*, VI, 1697–1702, 1704–11. Party identifications derive from the following: Lisle A. Rose, *Prologue to Democracy: The Federalists in the South, 1789–1801* (Lexington, Ky.: University of Kentucky Press, 1968); Norman Risjord, *Chesapeake Politics, 1781–1800* (New York: Columbia University Press, 1978); Alfred F. Young, *The Democratic-Republicans of New York: The Origins, 1763–1797* (Chapel Hill: University of North Carolina Press, 1967); Carl E. Prince, *New Jersey's Jeffersonian Republicans: The Genesis of an Early Party Machine, 1789–1817* (Chapel Hill: University of North Carolina Press, 1964); *Biographical Dictionary of the American Congress, 1774–1949* (Washington, D.C.: Government Printing Office, 1950).

27. *Annals of Cong.*, VI, 1698, 1700–1702, 1704–8, 1710.

28. Ibid., 1700, 1710, 1711.

29. Ibid., 1699–1700.

30. Ibid., 1699, 1700, 1704–5, 1709–11.

31. Ibid., 1711.

32. John W. Hoyt, *Memorial in Regard to a National University* (Washington, D.C.: Government Printing Office, 1892), 15; Albert Castel, "The Founding Fathers and the Vision of a National University," *History of Education Quarterly*, 4 (1964): 287; David Madsen, *The National University: Enduring Dream of the USA* (Detroit: Wayne State University Press, 1966), 36–38.

33. Edward Livingston served on Columbia's board, Richard Spriggs on St. John's, Abraham Venable on Hampden-Sydney's, James Madison on both Hampden-Sydney's and William and Mary's, and Abraham Baldwin was president of the University of Georgia.

34. See Chapter 6, note 1.

35. William Kilty, ed., *The Laws of Maryland* (2 vols., Annapolis, 1799–1801), 1782 chapter 8, 1784, chapters 7, 37.

36. Jurgen Herbst, *From Crisis to Crisis: American College Government, 1636–1819* (Cambridge, Mass.: Harvard University Press, 1982), 183; George H. Callcott, *A History of the University of Maryland* (Baltimore: Maryland Historical Society, 1966), 6–8; Risjord, *Chesapeake Politics*, 214–15; *Maryland Gazette*, April 1, 1785.

37. Callcott, *University of Maryland*, 11–12.

38. Herbst, *From Crisis to Crisis*, 183–84; Callcott, *University of Maryland*, 14.

39. John B. Pine, "The Origins of the University of the State of New York," *Columbia University Quarterly*, 11 (1909): 155–56, 158–60; Franklin B. Hough, *Historical and Statistical Record of the University of the State of New York from 1784 to 1884* (Albany: Weed, Parsons, & Co., 1885), 5–6; Herbst, *From Crisis to Crisis*, 168.

40. Sidney Sherwood, *The University of the State of New York: History of Higher Education in the State of New York* (Washington, D.C.: Government Printing Office, 1892), 50–57; David C. Humphrey, *From King's College to Columbia, 1746–1800* (New York: Columbia University Press, 1976), 274–75; John S. Whitehead, *The Separation*

of College and State: Columbia, Dartmouth, Harvard, and Yale, 1776–1876 (New Haven: Yale University Press, 1973), 21–23. This and the following paragraph derive from these works.

41. Pine, "Origins of the University," 161–62; Hough, *Historical and Statistical Record*, 7.

42. Hough, *Historical and Statistical Record*, 83–85.

43. "Minutes of the Trustees of Columbia College, Vol. II, Pt. 1" (CUA), April 4, 1785, January 25, 1790, January 12, February 6, 1792, February 24, 1796; "Book of Minutes of the Trustees of Union College" (UCA), December 8, 1795, January 8, September 11, 1798, September 3, 1799; *A History of Columbia University, 1754–1904* (New York: Columbia University Press, 1904), 75; *Laws of the State of New York* (5 vols., Albany: Weed, Parsons, & Co., 1886–87), III, 162–63, 635, 715, IV, 92–93, 462.

44. Allen E. Candler, ed., *The Colonial Records of the State of Georgia* (26 vols., Atlanta: Franklin Printing and Publishing Co., 1904–16), XIX, pt. 2, 363–71.

45. E. Merton Coulter, *College Life in the Old South* (2d ed., Athens, Ga.: University of Georgia Press, 1951), 5–10; Kenneth Coleman, *The American Revolution in Georgia, 1763–1789* (Athens, Ga.: University of Georgia Press, 1958), 225–27; Herbst, *From Crisis to Crisis*, 170.

46. *Doc. Hist. Educ.*, III, 1–5; *Doc. Hist. UNC*, I, 22–28; James Iredell, ed., *Public Acts of the General Assembly of North Carolina* (2 vols., New Bern, N.C.: Martin & Ogden, 1804), I, 472–74.

47. Blackwell P. Robinson, *William R. Davie* (Chapel Hill: University of North Carolina Press, 1957), 227–28; Herbst, *From Crisis to Crisis*, 187; *Doc. Hist. UNC*, I, 87.

48. Herbst, *From Crisis to Crisis*, 188; *Doc. Hist. UNC*, I, 88; Kemp P. Battle, *A History of the University of North Carolina* (2 vols., orig. 1907–12; reprint, Spartanburg, S.C.: The Reprint Co., 1974), I, 17, 37.

49. *North Carolina Journal*, October 24, November 14, December 12, 1792, March 20, July 10, October 30, 1793.

50. Ibid., February 6, 20 (quotation), 1793.

51. Battle, *Hist. of University of North Carolina*, I, 136–37; Iredell, ed., *Public Acts of North Carolina*, II, 54.

52. There is some evidence that at least one North Carolina Assemblyman, Thomas Person, was defeated for re-election in 1796 primarily because he was a staunch supporter of the university, this irrespective of any shift toward Republicanism on the part of the electorate. *Doc. Hist. UNC*, II, 55–58.

53. Battle, *Hist. of University of North Carolina*, I, 138–39; Iredell, ed., *Public Acts of North Carolina*, II, 133, 150; Edgar W. Knight, "North Carolina's Dartmouth College Case," *Journal of Higher Education*, 19 (1948): 119–21.

54. Julian I. Lindsay, *Tradition Looks Forward. The University of Vermont: A History, 1791–1954* (Burlington: University of Vermont and State Agricultural College, 1954), 10; Herbst, *From Crisis to Crisis*, 171–73.

55. Lindsay, *Tradition Looks Forward*, 19–34; George W. Benedict, "History of the University of Vermont," *American Quarterly Register*, 13 (1841): 397–98; F. H. Dewart et al., eds., *The State Papers of Vermont* (8 vols., Montpelier, Vt.: n.p., 1918–39), IV, 136–38; "University of Vermont, Trustees' Minutes" (UVtA), June 13, 1792, January 31, 1794.

56. In 1785 the Pennsylvania Legislature passed an act which, among other things, enumerated the confiscated estates that were to produce revenue for the University and made it easier for trustees to fill board vacancies. Neither provision helped the University attain solvency. Alexander Dallas, ed., *Laws of the Commonwealth of Pennsylvania* (4 vols., Philadelphia, 1797–1801), II, 395–414.

57. Herbst, *From Crisis to Crisis*, 180–82; Robert L. Brunhouse, *The Counter-Revolution in Pennsylvania, 1776–1790* (Harrisburg: Pennsylvania Historical Commission, 1950), 154, 220; William Smith, *An Address to the General Assembly of Pennsylvania, in the Case of the Violated Charter of the College, etc., of Philadelphia* (Philadelphia, 1788); William Smith to Daniel Clymer, ca. 1789 (UPA); Dallas, ed., *Laws of Pa.*, II, 650–54.

58. Herbst, *From Crisis to Crisis*, 182–83; Edward P. Cheyney, *History of the University of Pennsylvania, 1740–1940* (Philadelphia: University of Pennsylvania Press, 1940), 149–50, quotation 184; Dallas, ed., *Laws of Pa.*, II, 158–63.

59. "Dickinson College, Trustees' Minutes" (DCA), April 6, 1784, June 15, May 1, 1792, September 25, 1798; Nathan G. Goodman, *Benjamin Rush: Physician and Citizen, 1746–1813* (Philadelphia: University of Pennsylvania Press, 1934), 327–28; Frank W. Blackmar, *The History of Federal and State Aid to Higher Education in the United States* (Washington, D.C.: Government Printing Office, 1890), 156.

60. Herbst, *From Crisis to Crisis*, 214–16.

61. "Records of the President and Fellows of Harvard College" (HUA), January 31, 1781, quotation from June 24, 1783, January 29, 1784, May 2, 1786, May 20, 1791, January 24, 1792, August 27, 1793, January 14, October 27, 1796, January 5, 1799, January 30, 1800.

62. Josiah Quincy, *The History of Harvard University* (2 vols., Cambridge, Mass.: J. Owen, 1840), I, 244–49; Whitehead, *Separation of College and State*, 17–18; "Harvard College Records," April 29, 1796, April 1, 1800; Herbst, *From Crisis to Crisis*, 186–87.

63. "Free School and College Records" (WCA), August 6, 1793; N. H. Egleston, *Williamstown and Williams College* (Williamstown, Mass.: n.p., 1884), 29; Blackmar, *History of Federal Aid*, 123.

64. J. H. Easterby, *A History of the College of Charleston* (Charleston: n.p., 1935), 18–19; Herbst, *From Crisis to Crisis*, 209.

65. [Parnassus], *Connecticut Courant*, February 4, 18, March 18, April 1, 8, 15, 1783; [Complures], *Connecticut Courant*, April 20, 27, June 1, 1784, and *Connecticut Journal*, April 14, 21, May 12, June 16, 1784; *Yale College Subject to the General Assembly* (New Haven, 1784), 13–16, 28; Edmund S. Morgan, *The Gentle Puritan: A Life of Ezra Stiles* (New Haven: Yale University Press, 1962), 353–54; Herbst, *From Crisis to Crisis*, 175.

66. Morgan, *Gentle Puritan*, 357–59, 407–10; "Yale Corporation, Memorial to the General Assembly...requesting funds, 1788" (YUA); "Yale Corporation, Memorial to the General Assembly...requesting Indian Lands at Scaticock, 1788" (YUA); *PRSC*, V, 267, 406.

67. Morgan, *Gentle Puritan*, 413–20; Whitehead, *Separation of College and State*, 40–41; Herbst, *From Crisis to Crisis*, 175–76; *PRSC*, VII, 392–93.

68. Charles E. Cuningham, *Timothy Dwight, 1752–1817: A Biography* (New York: The Macmillan Co., 1942), 181, 185; "Yale Corporation, Memorial to the General

Assembly (1800?)'' (YUA); *PRSC*, IX, 403–4; Whitehead, *Separation of College and State*, 42.

69. Herbst, *From Crisis to Crisis*, 192; *Va. Stat.*, XI, 164–66; Fitzpatrick, ed., *Writings of Washington*, XXIV, 150–51; Robert M. Hutcheson, "Virginia's 'Dartmouth College Case','' *Virginia Magazine of History and Biography*, 51 (1943): 134–35.

70. "Trustees' Papers, Liberty Hall Academy'' (WLUA), January 31, 1797; Hutcheson, "Virginia's 'Dartmouth College Case','' 136–37; Ollinger Crenshaw, *General Lee's College: The Rise and Growth of Washington and Lee University* (New York: Random House, 1969), 30–31; Herbst, *From Crisis to Crisis*, 220–21.

71. Herbst, *From Crisis to Crisis*, 189–90.

72. Blackmar, *History of Federal Aid*, 156.

73. *Va. Stat.*, XI, 392–93; "Hampden-Sydney Trustees' Records'' (H-SCA), July 21, 1789, January 9, 1790, January 7, 1795, May 31, 1797. Incidentally, William and Mary received no legislative support after a 1783 grant of one-sixth of the surveyors' fees for land awarded Revolutionary soldiers and a 1784 grant of some land in and around Williamsburg; *Va. Stat.*, XI, 310, 406.

74. "College of Rhode Island, Corporation Minutes'' (BUA), September 1, 1784, December 5, 1792, December 23, 1795; *The Columbian Centinel* (Boston), January 13, 1798.

75. "Minutes of the Proceedings of the Trustees of the College of New Jersey,'' Vols. I & II (Microfilm, PUA), April 9, 1793, January 13, 1796, September 26, 1797, September 24, 1799; Varnum L. Collins, *Princeton* (Princeton: Princeton University Press, 1914), 102–3; Thomas J. Wertenbaker, *Princeton, 1746–1896* (Princeton: Princeton University Press, 1946), 120.

76. Lindsay, *Tradition Looks Forward*, 6–11; Whitehead, *Separation of College and State*, 33–34; Dewart et al., eds., *State Papers of Vermont*, III, 127, 141; Patrick McKnight, "The Trustees of Dartmouth College, 1769–1800'' (M.A. Thesis, University of Wyoming, 1983), 95.

77. *New Hampshire Provincial and State Papers* (34 vols., Concord, N.H.: G. E. Jenks, 1867–1919), XX, 105, 126, 219, XXI, 129, 382, 395, 405–6, 449, 536, XXII, 481, 571, 694; Whitehead, *Separation of College and State*, 34–35; McKnight, "Trustees of Dartmouth,'' 97–101; H. Harrison Metcalf, ed., *The Laws of New Hampshire, including public and private acts and resolves and the royal instructions* (10 vols., Manchester, N.H.: The John B. Clarke Co., 1904–22), V, 396–97, VI, 96, 294–95.

78. John D. Wright, Jr., *Transylvania: Tutor to the West* (Lexington, Ky.: University of Kentucky Press, 1976), 28–30, 32; Neils H. Sonne, *Liberal Kentucky, 1780–1828* (New York: Columbia University Press, 1939), 54–57, 59–61; Robert Peter, *Transylvania University: Its Origin, Rise, Decline, and Fall* (Louisville: J. P. Morton & Co., 1896), 64; Herbst, *From Crisis to Crisis*, 193–94.

79. See, for example, Donald G. Tewksbury, *The Founding of American Colleges and Universities before the Civil War, with Particular Reference to the Religious Influences Bearing Upon the College Movement* (orig. 1932; reprint, New York: Arno Press, 1969); R. Freeman Butts, *The College Charts Its Course: Historical Conceptions and Current Proposals* (New York: McGraw-Hill, 1939), 77–155; Richard Hofstadter, *Academic Freedom in the Age of the College* (New York: Columbia University Press, 1955), 209–74; Frederick Rudolph, *The American College and University: A History* (New York: Vintage Books, 1962), 44–135, 201–220.

80. A few recent studies have hinted at, but have not fully developed, the beneficial

relationship that existed between the political culture of Revolutionary America and higher education. See Lawrence Cremin, *American Education: The Colonial Experience, 1607–1783* (New York: Harper & Row, 1970), 415–71; Howard G. Miller, *The Revolutionary College: American Presbyterian Higher Education, 1707–1837* (New York: New York University Press, 1976), 103–285; David C. Humphrey, *From King's College to Columbia, 1746–1800* (New York: Columbia University Press, 1976); Steven J. Novak, *The Rights of Youth: American Colleges and Student Revolt, 1789–1815* (Cambridge, Mass.: Harvard University Press, 1977), 95–165.

81. Rudolph, *American College*, 264–306, 328–54; Lawrence R. Veysey, *The Emergence of the American University* (Chicago: University of Chicago Press, 1965), 1–259.

A Note on the Sources

This is not a comprehensive bibliography. Full publication information for all works published after 1800 appears in the chapter notes and will enable those interested to check the accuracy of my reportage. Rather, what follows may serve as a guide to others who wish to undertake research in eighteenth-century American higher educational history, enabling them to bypass some of the wrong turnings and dead ends I encountered. Still, the student who seeks to understand American higher education and its place in pre-nineteenth century society faces a formidable task, for several reasons. First, he or she will get little help from most collegiate histories, either general or specific. With the exceptions noted below, these works give scant attention to the colonial and early national periods, oversimplifying what they do cover. Both types of history suffer from the same problems. Until recently, they have been written by alumni or educators uninterested in or ignorant of the questions historians would choose to ask. Often the histories have been written as promotional tracts. They therefore tend to stress the present at the expense of the past and to gloss over episodes thought to be unattractive. Moreover, the histories fail to place the colleges in the context of the surrounding society; they are simply institutional histories. Finally, no matter how serious the researcher, one cannot go farther than the sources will allow. For the period under consideration, those sources are often inadequate. College archives have suffered fires, thefts, losses, and plain carelessness resulting in huge gaps in the record, if there were any records to begin with. Despite these shortcomings, the patient researcher can construct answers to many fascinating questions regarding early American colleges.

The best introductions to colonial and early national collegiate education are Frederick A. Rudolph, *The American College and University: A History* (New York: Vintage Books, 1962) and Lawrence Cremin, *American Education: The Colonial Experience, 1607–1783* (New York: Harper & Row, 1970). Rudolph's bibliography is quite valuable, while Cremin's book, the first of a series, covers much more than collegiate history, and in so doing places the college in perspective.

An acquaintance with the pre–1800 careers of the individual colleges is not always easily come by. The archives of those colonial colleges which are now Ivy League universities—Harvard, Yale, Columbia, Brown, Dartmouth, Princeton, and the University of Pennsylvania—are generally ample, although weak on curricular information. I relied most heavily on trustees' minutes, debating society records, and college laws, which usually specified the curriculum. Other types of documents were useful: letters from students, faculty, and administrators; library catalogues; and internal memoranda are only a few. Archival material at the other two colonial colleges, Rutgers and William and

Mary, is relatively sparse. Early Rutgers was not tightly organized and William and Mary has suffered two disastrous fires. Fortunately, the "Journal of the Presidents and Masters" has been published in the early volumes of the *William and Mary College Quarterly*.

The archives of the post-Revolutionary colleges present an even greater diversity in both quantity and quality of holdings. Little survives of whatever records once existed at Franklin and Marshall, Washington and Lee, and at the University of Tennessee concerning Blount College. Slightly more useful are the collections at Transylvania, Tusculum, the College of Charleston, and St. John's (where the archives are housed in the Maryland State Archives on the college campus). More documentation exists at the University of Vermont, at Bowdoin, and at the University of Georgia (none of which had any pre-1800 students). The archival collections that permit the broadest range of study are at Dickinson, Union, and Williams Colleges. There it is possible to perceive not only the skeleton of the college program, but also the flesh and blood of students' activities in a variety of documents. Much of this depth exists in R.D.W. Connor's compilation, *A Documentary History of the University of North Carolina* (2 vols., Chapel Hill: University of North Carolina Press, 1953), which allows off-campus examination of the first functioning state university.

Aside from the archives themselves, several published works must constitute part of the documentary record. Among the most useful are: Richard Hofstadter and Wilson Smith, eds., *American Higher Education: A Documentary History* (2 vols., Chicago: University of Chicago Press, 1961); Edgar W. Knight, *A Documentary History of Education in the South before 1860* (4 vols., Chapel Hill: University of North Carolina Press, 1949–53); Franklin B. Dexter, ed., *A Documentary History of Yale University, 1701–1745* (New Haven: Yale University Press, 1916); Thomas Clap, *A Catalogue of the Library of Yale College in New Haven* (New London, 1743); Clap, *The Annals or History of Yale College* (New Haven, 1766); Herbert and Carol Schneider, eds., *Samuel Johnson, President of King's College: His Career and Writings* (4 vols., New York: Columbia University Press, 1929); William Smith, *A General Idea of the College of Mirania* (New York, 1753), *An Account of the College, Academy, and Charitable School of Philadelphia* (Philadelphia, 1756), *An Account of Washington College* (Philadelphia, 1784); [Samuel Blair], *Account of the College of New Jersey* (Woodbridge, N.J., 1764); John Witherspoon, *Lectures on Moral Philosophy*, Varnum L. Collins, ed., (Princeton: Princeton University Press, 1912); William V. Manross, *The Fulham Papers in the Lambeth Palace Library: American Colonial Section: Calendar and Indexes* (Oxford: Oxford University Press, 1965).

Of the college histories, the best general works are Howard G. Miller, *The Revolutionary College: American Presbyterian Higher Education, 1707–1837* (New York: New York University Press, 1976); Steven J. Novak, *The Rights of Youth: American Colleges and Student Revolts, 1789–1815* (Cambridge, Mass.: Harvard University Press, 1977); Jurgen Herbst, *From Crisis to Crisis: American College Government, 1636–1815* (Cambridge, Mass.: Harvard University Press, 1982). Each of these belongs to a "new college history" that is sensitive to the cultural context of higher education.

For many years, Samuel Eliot Morison's *Harvard College in the Seventeenth Century* (2 vols., Cambridge, Mass.: Harvard University Press, 1935) has been unsurpassed as collegiate history. As part of the "new college history," other specific studies have risen to that mark: Richard Warch, *School of the Prophets: Yale College, 1701–1740* (New Haven: Yale University Press, 1973) and David C. Humphrey, *From King's College to Columbia, 1746–1800* (New York: Columbia University Press, 1976). Below these excellent histories lies another group quite useful in their factual presentations: Josiah Quincy, *A History of Harvard University* (2 vols., Cambridge, Mass.: J. Owen, 1840); John Maclean, *The History of the College of New Jersey from Its Origins in 1746 to the Commencement of 1854* (orig. 1877; 2 vols. in one, New York: Arno Press, 1969); Thomas J. Wertenbaker, *Princeton, 1746–1896* (Princeton: Princeton University Press, 1946); Edward P. Cheyney, *History of the University of Pennsylvania, 1740–1940* (Philadelphia: University of Pennsylvania Press, 1940); *A History of Columbia University, 1754–1904* (New York: Columbia University Press, 1904); William H.S. Demarest, *A History of Rutgers College, 1766–1924* (New Brunswick, N.J.: Rutgers College Press, 1924); Walter C. Bronson, *The History of Brown University, 1764–1914* (Providence: The University, 1914); Reuben A. Guild, *Early History of Brown University, including the Life, Times, and Correspondence of James Manning, 1756–1791* (Providence: Snow & Farnham, 1897); Leon B. Richardson, *The History of Dartmouth College* (2 vols., Hanover, N.H.: Dartmouth College Publications, 1932); Jack E. Morpurgo, *Their Majesties' Royall Colledge: William and Mary in the Seventeenth and Eighteenth Centuries* (Williamsburg: College of William and Mary, 1976); Charles Coleman Sellers, *Dickinson College: A History* (Middletown, Conn.: Wesleyan University Press, 1973); Leverett Spring, *A History of Williams College* (Boston and New York: Houghton Mifflin Co., 1917); James H. Easterby, *A History of the College of Charleston, Founded 1770* (Charleston: n.p., 1935); Kemp. P. Battle, *The History of the University of North Carolina* (2 vols., orig. 1907–12; reprint, Spartanburg, S.C.: The Reprint Co., 1974); E. Merton Coulter, *College Life in the Old South* (2d ed., Athens, Ga.: University of Georgia Press, 1951).

Beyond this group is another echelon of histories which for one reason or another is less useful to the researcher. This group includes: Varnum L. Collins, *Princeton* (Princeton: Princeton University Press, 1914); George P. Schmidt, *Princeton and Rutgers: the Two Colonial Colleges of New Jersey* (Princeton: Van Nostrand, 1964); Richard P. McCormick, *Rutgers: A Bicentennial History* (New Brunswick, N.J.: Rutgers University Press, 1966); Calvin Durfee, *A History of Williams College* (Boston: A. Williams & Co., 1860); Joseph H. Dubbs, *A History of Franklin and Marshall College* (Lancaster, Pa.: Franklin & Marshall College Alumni Association, 1903); Philip S. Klein, *The Spiritual and Educational Background of Franklin and Marshall College* (Lancaster, Pa.: Franklin and Marshall College, 1939); Louis C. Hatch, *The History of Bowdoin College* (Portland: Loring, Short, & Harmon, 1927); Ollinger Crenshaw, *General Lee's College: The Rise and Growth of Washington and Lee University* (New York: Random House, 1969); George H. Callcott, *A History of the University of Maryland* (Baltimore: Maryland Historical Society, 1966); Allen E. Ragan, *A History of Tusculum College, 1794–1944* (n.p., 1945).

The study of the men prominent in eighteenth-century higher education is often as useful as examination of the colleges. Helpful here are: Edmund S. Morgan, *The Gentle Puritan: A Life of Ezra Stiles* (New Haven: Yale University Press, 1962); Harold E. Selesky, ed., *The Microfilm Edition of the Ezra Stiles Papers at Yale University* (New Haven: Yale University Press, 1976); Louis L. Tucker, *Puritan Protagonist: President Thomas Clap of Yale College* (Chapel Hill: University of North Carolina Press, 1962); Charles E. Cuningham, *Timothy Dwight, 1752–1817: A Biography* (New York: The Macmillan Co., 1942); Albert F. Gegenheimer, *William Smith, Educator and Churchman, 1727–1803* (Philadelphia: University of Pennsylvania Press, 1943); Horace W. Smith, *The Life and Correspondence of the Reverend William Smith, D.D.* (2 vols., Philadelphia: Ferguson Bros. & Co., 1880); William Smith, *The Works of William Smith, D.D., Late*

Provost of the College and Academy of Philadelphia (2 vols., Philadelphia: Hugh Maxwell and William Fry, 1803); Varnum L. Collins, *President Witherspoon* (2 vols., Princeton: Princeton University Press, 1925); John Witherspoon, *Works* (9 vols., London, 1765–1815); Joseph J. Ellis, *The New England Mind in Transition: Samuel Johnson of Connecticut, 1696–1772* (New Haven: Yale University Press, 1973); Elizabeth P. McCaughey, *From Loyalist to Founding Father: The Political Odyssey of William Samuel Johnson* (New York: Columbia University Press, 1980); James D. McCallum, *Eleazar Wheelock: Founder of Dartmouth College* (orig. 1939; reprint, New York: Arno Press, 1969); *The Microfilm Edition of the Papers of Eleazar Wheelock* (Hanover, N.H.: Dartmouth College Publications, 1971); Normal S. Fiering, "President Samuel Johnson and the Circle of Knowledge," *The William and Mary Quarterly*, 28 (1971): 199–236; Charles Crowe, "Bishop James Madison and the Republic of Virtue," *Journal of Southern History*, 30 (1964): 58–70.

Other helpful articles and monographs pertaining to the operation of the eighteenth-century college are: Francis L. Broderick, "Pulpit, Physics, and Politics: The Curriculum of the College of New Jersey, 1746–1794," *The William and Mary Quarterly*, 6 (1947): 42–68; Louis F. Snow, *The College Curriculum in the United States* (New York: Teachers College Press of Columbia University Press, 1907); Frederick A. Rudolph, *Curriculum: A History of the Undergraduate Course of Study Since 1636* (San Francisco: Josey-Bass, 1977); David Potter, *Debating in the Colonial Chartered Colleges* (New York: Teachers College Press of Columbia University Press, 1944); Edward J. Young, "Subjects for Master's Degrees in Harvard College, 1655–1791," *Massachusetts Historical Society Proceedings*, 18 (1880–1881): 119–51; Robert Polk Thomson, "The Reform of William and Mary, 1763–1800," *Proceedings* of the American Philosophical Society, 115 (1971): 187–213; Howard Peckham, "Collegia Ante Bellum: Attitudes of College Students and Professors toward the American Revolution," *Pennsylvania Magazine of History and Biography*, 95 (1971): 50–72; Caroline Robbins, "Library of Liberty—Assembled for Harvard College, by Thomas Hollis of Lincoln's Inn," *Harvard Library Bulletin*, 5 (1951): 5–23, 181–96; Franklin B. Dexter, ed., *Biographical Sketches of the Graduates of Yale College with Annals of the College History* (6 vols., New York: H. Holt & Co., 1885–1912); John L. Sibley et al., eds., *Biographical Sketches of Those Who Attended Harvard College* (17 vols. thus far, Boston: Massachusetts Historical Society, 1873–   ); James McLachlan, *Princetonians, 1748–1768: A Biographical Dictionary* (Princeton: Princeton University Press, 1976); Richard A. Harrison, *Princetonians, 1769–1776: A Biographical Dictionary* (Princeton: Princeton University Press, 1980).

Index

About the Author

DAVID W. ROBSON is Chairman of the Department of History at John Carroll University, Cleveland, Ohio. His articles have appeared in *American Quarterly*, *William and Mary Quarterly*, *History of Education Quarterly*, and *PMHB*.